D1198285

TIME REFIGURED

Myths, Foundation Texts
and Imagined Communities

Edited by
MARTIN PROCHÁZKA and ONDŘEJ PILNÝ

þ
Litteraria Pragensia
Prague 2005

Published 2005 by Litteraria Pragensia
Faculty of Philosophy, Charles University
Náměstí Jana Palacha 2, 116 38 Prague 1
Czech Republic

Education and Culture

Socrates

This book has been published with the support of the Socrates Erasmus programme for Thematic Network Projects of the European Commission through grant 104329-CP-3-2004-1-IT-ERASMUS-TN, and research grant MSM0021620824 "Foundations of the Modern World as Reflected in Literature and Philosophy" awarded to the Faculty of Philosophy, Charles University by the Ministry of Education of the Czech Republic.

Image on cover: Josef Mánes (1820-71), "Záboj v úvalu" (Záboj in a Ravine), ca. 1857. By kind permission of The Museum of Decorative Arts in Prague.

Cover design by lazarus.
Language editor Linda Jayne Turner.
Index compiled by Ondřej Zátka.

Printed in the Czech Republic by PB Tisk.

ISBN 80-7308-102-4

CONTENTS

Martin Procházka
Introduction: Anachronisms, Machines, or Singularities?   1

I. APPROACHES

Jean Bessière
Literary Reiteration of Myths and Foundation Texts: Theoretical
    Notes   15
Riccardo Campi
Continuity and Discontinuity in Tradition   29
Vita Fortunati
Memory, Desire and Utopia: A New Perspective on the Notion
    of Critical Utopia   39
Stephanie Wodianka
Closeness and Distance of Memory to Joan of Arc: A National
    Myth in Transnational Imagined Communities   51
Anna Brzozowska-Krajka
Slavonic Cosmogonic Myth as a Matrix for Encoding Meanings   66
Wojciech Kozak
Beyond the Rational: Joseph Conrad's Portrayal of the Sea   81
Wiesław Krajka
Just So Stories by Rudyard Kipling as a Mythological-Aesthetic
    Foundation Text for Children   93
Martin Procházka
Imagined Communities Revisited: Beyond Romantic and
    Technological Approaches to Cultural Identity and Diversity   106
Erik S. Roraback
Jean-Luc Nancy, Being-In-Common, and the Absent Semantics
    of Myth   121

II. IMAGINING EUROPE

Aleida Assmann
Imagining Europe – Myths, Visions, Identities, Memories   139
Michael C. Frank
The Discovery of Europe in the South Pacific: Travel Writing,
    "Boundary Work," and the Construction of European
    Identity   162

Klára Kolinská
"What Happened to the Naming in This Strange Place?"
Remapping the Space of Ontario in the (Con)texts of Native
Canadian Theatre 176
Shelley Hornstein
Curating Place: Maps, Starchitecture and Museums-Without-
Borders 190

III. FUNCTIONS AND TRANSFORMATIONS

Peter J. Schwartz
Germans Are to Greeks as French Are to Romans:
Metamorphoses of a Topos in German Literature, 1755-1819   207
Kirsten Mahlke
The Myth of the Gauls in Sixteenth-Century French
Historiography:Secret Knowledge and Circular Concepts   226
Ann Heilmann
The Myth of Medea and the Feminist Imagination in Victorian
and Edwardian Britain 238
Martin Hurcombe
In Search of the National Revolution: French Nationalist
Narratives of the Spanish Civil War 256
Brigid Haines
Representations of "Bohemia" in the Works of Libuše Moníková
(1945-1998) 268
Rainier Grutman
Quoting Europe: Mottomania in the Romantic Age 281
Mara Cambiaghi
"Moving Times – New Words:" The Sixties on Both Sides
of the Channel 296

IV. MEDIATION AND ORIGINALITY

Mariangela Tempera
Looking for Riccardo: Two Italian Versions of *Richard III*   315
Monica Matei-Chesnoiu
"The Globe:" Romanian Poetry and Shakespeare's Histories   327
Mícheál Mac Craith
Wrestling with his Form: The Genesis of Macpherson's *Fragments*   344

Notes on Contributors 366
Index of Names 375

INTRODUCTION: ANACHRONISMS, MACHINES, OR SINGULARITIES?

Martin Procházka

This volume contains a selection of papers from the conference on "Myths, Foundation Texts and Imagined Communities" which took place at Charles University, Prague in November 2004 within the framework of the international ACUME project studying European cultural memory. Sponsored by the SOCRATES programme, the research was coordinated by Professor Vita Fortunati of the University of Bologna.

Like the conference, this book aims to present results of Subproject 5 coordinated by Professor Jean Bessière of La Sorbonne Nouvelle, Paris, and Professor Martin Procházka of Charles University, Prague. Focused on myths (or mythologies) and foundation texts in European cultural history, most papers deal with the present and past *functions* of these texts rather than their supposedly 'original' or canonic forms. Particular attention has been paid to the role of myths and foundation texts in the process of imagining communities and to the possibility of imagining Europe as a community. One of the specific purposes was to reconsider, in the context of European integration, the functionalist approach of Benedict Anderson, according to whom "imagined communities [...] are to be distinguished, not by their falsity/genuineness, but by the style in which they are imagined."[1]

---

[1] Benedict Anderson, *Imagined Communities: Reflections on the Origin and Spread of Nationalism*, revised ed. (London and New York: Verso, 1991), 6.

The papers in this collection fall into several thematic groups. Those in the first group discuss – either exclusively or in the context of specific political, historical or cultural phenomena – theoretical and methodological questions, such as the 'anachronistic' functioning of myths and foundation texts (Jean Bessière), the continuity and discontinuity of tradition (Riccardo Campi) and problems connected with the interpretation of myths. Should myths be approached as homogeneous, closed structures consisting of binary oppositions (Anna Brzozowska-Krajka), whose paradigmatic – cognitive and normative – functions are modified in modern literature with respect to subjective, aesthetic perceptions, moral or didactic objectives (Wojciech Kozak and Wiesław Krajka), or conservative, political and ideological purposes? Should they be understood as heterogeneous assemblages, "fuzzy aggregates,"[2] merging and transposing disparate elements of discourses (Martin Procházka)? Or should they be charged with generalizing and totalizing violence and discussed in their "*absence*" or in the state of "*interruption*"[3] (Erik Roraback)?

The common denominator of all these approaches is the problem of the *discontinuity of time* in relation to tradition, cultural and individual memory, historical and literary narratives. For Jean Bessière, the relation between continuity and discontinuity of time is manifested in the paradoxical relationship between the references of individual literary works to myths and foundation texts, and their self-referentiality, *autopoiēsis*, due to which

> time becomes the locus of its own reflexivity: it is self-temporalized. It undergoes endless reiteration within itself, and needs a semantics which sets valid accents for specific moments. This definition of the memory process is implied by Paul Ricœur's notion of refiguration of the past, which he identifies with the function of any narrative. It explains why

---

2 Gilles Deleuze and Félix Guattari, *A Thousand Plateaus: Capitalism and Schizophrenia*, trans. Brian Massumi (Minneapolis: University of Minnesota Press, 1987), 343-47.

3 Jean-Luc Nancy, *The Inoperative Community. Theory and History of Literature, Volume 76*, ed. Peter Connor, trans. Peter Connor, Lisa Garbus, Michael Holland and Simona Sawhney (Minneapolis: University of Minnesota Press, 1991), 47. Nancy refers to Georges Bataille's description of the abuse of myth in modern society which, in the status of community, results in "the sacred stripped of the sacred" (*The Inoperative Community*, 35). In contrast to Bataille, however, he emphasizes the transitory nature of this period by using the word "interruption" instead of "absence."

narratives at once mime the memory process and set up
semantics of time.

(18)

The unifying power capable of overcoming this discontinuity is symbolic
rather than mimetic: the work of art "symbolizes the community through
the fiction of individuals" and

paradoxically [...] establishes the dimensions of meaning
characterizing the community and the culture to which it
refers. This makes the reiterating work a cognitive
representation of the social institution of reality. The
reiterating work shows that this institution is always arbitrary
and that the order of meaning it founds in time and history is
always improbable.

(27-28)

While Riccardo Campi emphasizes – using the contrasting examples
of Gadamer and Benjamin – the importance of a critical approach to
tradition based on the radical understanding of its discontinuity, Vita
Fortunati, inspired by the latter thinker, argues for "critical nostalgia,"
whose "backdrop [...] is the idea of history as non-linear and
fragmented," a result of the modern loss of "the certainties of continuity,
identity and connection in the processes of recollection." (44) This
nostalgia "has a strong heuristic value because comparison between the
past and the present stimulates the subject to find in the past
potentialities and models in order to develop the future." It may be said
to function "as a kind of hinge, a bridge between personal and collective
memory" (45), presupposing "spatial or temporal displacement," which
not only links it to strategies of survival and "[u]topian projects [...] born
from the desire for a better world" (47), but also "can help us explain [...]
the traumatic past full of conflicts, the past which concerns all Europe
and with which we must come to terms." (50) Here, the discontinuity of
time is seen as a powerful incentive encouraging a critical approach to
the past and engendering affective energy necessary for changing the
present.

Unlike the above approaches, which attempt to overcome different
forms of temporal discontinuity through the logic of paradox or radical
dialectic, Stephanie Wodianka points out (using the conclusions of Jan

Assmann[4] and Astrid Erll) that the problem consists, rather than in the temporal discontinuity itself, in "the kind of memory produced, the collective ideas about the meaning of the remembered events and about its location within temporal processes" and in "a specific awareness of time (a culturally and historically variable phenomenon of collective mentalities)." (59-60)[5] This thesis underlies her interpretation of past and present forms of the Joan of Arc myth, where she uses a model of "'hybrid' forms of memory" (60) in order to demonstrate that

> [t]he hybridity of the myth's re-narrations between myth and history, between cultural and communicative memory, and between temporal, identificatory and modal closeness and distance of memory is not merely a gratuitous postmodern play but is inscribed into the myth [...].
>
> (65)

Wodianka's reading makes us reconsider some of its basic methodological assumptions, such as that of the difference between "the subjective awareness of time that characterizes mythic memory" and "the objective measurable distance to the historical event" allegedly typical of "historiographical memory." (62) As Hayden White shows,

> [h]istory does not [...] stand against myth as its cognitive antithesis. [...] Every history has its myth; and if there are different fictional modes based on different archetypes, so too there are different historiographical modes [...T]hese mythic modes are more easily identifiable in historiographical than they are in literary texts.[6]

It can be argued that the impossibility of making a reliable distinction between the "subjective" awareness of time in myth and the "objective" approach to time characteristic of historical consciousness results not only – as White has pointed out – from the fictional nature of historical discourse, but is caused by the heterogeneous nature of our

---

[4] Jan Assmann, *Das kulturelle Gedächtnis. Schrift, Erinnerung und politische Identität in frühen Hochkulturen* (Munich: Beck, 1992).
[5] Wodianka quotes Astrid Erll's study *Gedächtnisromane. Literatur über den Ersten Weltkrieg als Medium englischer und deutscher Erinnerungskulturen in den 1920er Jahren* (Trier: ELCH 2003), 49.
[6] Hayden White, *Tropics of Discourse: Essays in Cultural Criticism* (Baltimore and London: The Johns Hopkins University Press, 1978), 127.

field of research, characterized according to Homi Bhabha by "the separation of language and reality – in the *process* of signification [...]." Due to this separation, "there is no epistemological equivalence of subject and object, no possibility of the mimesis of meaning."[7] My discussion of myths and imagined communities approaches the question of temporal discontinuity as a specific aspect of the general problem of the heterogeneity of dynamic systems where time is "infinitely subdivisible," where "various times [...] start others that will in turn branch out and bifurcate in other times," and where any cohesion in terms of "resemblance, identity, analogy and opposition can no longer be considered anything but effects."[8] Contrary to Anderson, who assumes that the time in which communities are imagined is "empty" (being articulated by modern reproduction technologies which prompt our imaginings), I attempt to approach the heterogeneity of systems in a *positive* way demonstrated by Deleuze in his analysis of Marcel Proust's novel *À la recherche du temps perdu*. Not only modern works of art but also modern myths (or mythologies) gather

> fragments that can no longer be restored, pieces that do not fit into the same puzzle, that do not belong to a preceding totality, that do not emanate from the same lost unity. Perhaps that is what time is: the ultimate existence of parts of different size and shape, which cannot be adapted, which do not develop in the same rhythm [...].[9]

The only thinkable unity of this heterogeneous assemblage, which Deleuze calls "Antilogos," or, specifically, "literary machine," is that of "style," whose stream, however, "does not sweep [the fragments] along at the same speed."[10] In comparison to Anderson's unifying "style" of imagining communities, my essay traces different forms of imagination within the temporal heterogeneity of memory, history and myth. While my approach restricts itself to the works of art, the aesthetics of the picturesque, which emerged in another period of profound social

7 Homi Bhabha, *The Location of Culture* (London and New York: Routledge, 1994), 158.

8 Gilles Deleuze, *Difference and Repetition*, trans. Paul Patton (New York: Columbia University Press, 1994), 116-17. The first two quotations come from Jorge Luis Borges's story "The Garden of Forking Paths," in *Ficciones* (1956; New York: The Grove Press, 1962), 98.

9 Gilles Deleuze, *Proust and Signs*, trans. Richard Howard (Minneapolis: University of Minnesota Press, 2000), 113.

10 Deleuze, *Proust and Signs*, 113.

changes and cataclysms, offers a possibility of combining "volatile effects of art with domestic habits and local (not necessarily agricultural) economies as well as with rich references to European cultural heritage." (120)

Despite the productivity of myths, their traditional philosophical use tends, as Deleuze has pointed out, to establish a compact, "circular" structure, where "division" might exist only in order "to surmount the duality of myth and dialectic, and to reunite in itself dialectical and mythic power." This "myth" that "interrupts nothing" is "the story of foundation," permitting "the construction of a model according to which "the different pretenders" to power "can be judged."[11] Present-day resistance to this magisterial notion of myth as well as to its ideological and political abuse, may be exemplified, as Erik Roraback shows, in the work of Jean-Luc Nancy. Roraback argues that the attachment of the myth to generality typical of philosophical discourses "causes it to quite barbarically brutalize singular forms, movements, and structures. For myth authoritatively naturalizes, discriminates, normalizes, and thus sets up strictures for what it means to be a human being." (130) This conclusion of Roraback's supports Nancy's claim that myth can no longer become a means of transcendence, returning us to the "mythic humanity of the primal scene," nor even to what was considered human in the pre-Holocaust world. Since, as Nancy points out, "all that remains of myth is its fulfillment or its will, [w]e no longer live in mythic life [...]."[12] However, this does not mean that myth is completely absent from our social existence, as Georges Bataille used to maintain. Since "myth communicates the common, the *being-common*," in our current period, it can be regarded as "interrupted."[13] According to Nancy, this "absent semantics of myth" paves the way for a future community whose foundation is not "transcendence [...] which no longer has any 'sacred' meaning, signifying precisely a resistance to immanence," but the exposition of finite existence to death.[14] As Antonio Negri and Michael Hardt demonstrate, such a community cannot be founded on individuals, but on "singularities," which are neither individual nor personal: "Whereas the individual dissolves in the unity of the

---

[11] Gilles Deleuze, "The Simulacrum and Ancient Philosophy," in *The Logic of Sense*, ed. Constantin V. Boundas, trans. Mark Lester with Charles Stivale (New York: Columbia University Press, 1990), 255.

[12] Nancy, *The Inoperative Community*, 52.

[13] *The Inoperative Community*, 50, 47.

[14] ibid., 35 and xxxix.

community, singularities are not diminished but express themselves freely in the common."[15]

Most contributions in the second group deal with the possibilities of imagining Europe as a community and defining it as a cultural *and* political space. According to Aleida Assmann,

> in the European archive of [foundational] myths [...]stories of displacement and migration are much more conspicuous than stories of origin. The stories of flight, wandering and forced migration, however, have a clear telos and topographical center, that is, the building of a new nation and the foundation of a new empire. These two myths have lent themselves to illuminate and legitimate historically very different, and even opposite experiences and political claims as the liberation of an oppressed minority and the foundation of new empires. Moses and Aeneas are obviously very different kinds of heroes; they represent a duality and tension that is built into the foundational myths of Europe which incorporate a repertoire of diametrically opposed voices and perspectives.
>
> (142)

While the latter type of myths described by Assmann had been dominant until World War I and was revived in the bipolar world of the Cold War, its power seems to wane after the collapse of the Soviet Empire. In the 1990s, Central and Eastern Europe was shattered by "the upsurge of [the] explosive political energy of [...] the new (or rather old) national myths and memories that had been frozen in the bipolar constellation [...]." (151) The way out of this predicament is to implement "an identity model of dual membership: each nation defining itself both in terms of its unique and distinctive features and in terms of a common European reference." (156) This dialectics as well as specific institutional or informal civic activities discovering and promoting "shared memories" of the past full of conflicts and violence may gradually help the Europeans to form "a common cultural framework" excluding "national myths, obsessions and resentments that defy integration" and, at the

---

[15] Antonio Negri and Michael Hardt, *Multitude: War and Democracy in the Age of Empire* (New York: Penguin, 2004), 204. On neither individual nor personal "singularities" replacing "the Essences and divine Being of the old metaphysics," see, e.g., Deleuze, *The Logic of Sense*, 100-108.

same time, enable them to "learn to face their own memories and listen to each other with empathy." (160)

In contrast to Assmann, exploring the intrinsic aspects of the formation of European identity from diverse and often conflicting "myths," "visions," "identities" and "memories," Michael Frank deals with a different process, in the course of which "a substantial identity that relies on essence" is supplanted by "the relational definition of Europe on the grounds of – varying and unstable – conceptions of the Other." (173) According to his conclusions, drawn, among others, from a description of James Cook's second voyage around the world by German naturalist Georg Forster or Edward Said's *Orientalism*, Europe has always defined itself in relation to "non-European societies," which "are omnipresent in Europe's cultural memory. So much so, in fact, that 'Europe' itself seems to be located somewhere else, beyond the boundaries of Europe, where a (negative) mirror-image is sought." (175)

Another, and much more radical, form of dislocation is discussed by Shelley Hornstein, who shows how with the arrival of postmodern architecture and modern technologies of reproducing and disseminating images, a "new map of cultural tourism" is being made that is "no longer limited to geographic sites." (191) Drawing a distinction between traditional museums, functioning as "keepers of other cultures" for the local culture or "keepers of cultures no longer present to educate the local community," and "contemporary museums," which "have framed the direction of international art as unbound to nations, and [...] contribute to putting the tourist into the role of keeper of a new sort of passport to international travel and memory," Hornstein contends that rather than products of a specific "travel experience," these places are "anchored in memory through photography." (193) Buildings like the new Guggenheim Museum in Bilbao are no mere sights, they have become "landmarks," inducing tourists to make new "cognitive maps [...] assembled from guidebooks, films, photographs, or postcards of a place." (198, 204) Present-day tourists move like Deleuzean "nomads"[16] from one landmark to another. Their "reterritorialization" of landmarks in the form of a "mental map [...] calls into play the critical concepts such as national memory, national identity and borders" (204), thus working against attempts to delimit Europe as a cultural space with a distinct memory and identity.

While for Hornstein transformations of map-making are mainly caused by the development of tourism and modern technologies of mass

---

[16] Deleuze and Guattari, *A Thousand Plateaus*, 381-84 and passim.

production and dissemination, Klára Kolinská points out their more serious aspects connected with the impact of Europe on the life and culture of North American Indians. Arguing along with William F. Ganong that "[p]lace names," as "fossils exposed in the cross-section of [...] history," mark "its successive periods" and "form a permanent register or index of the course and events [...]" (180), she traces what Benedict Anderson has called "the alignment of map and power,"[17] in Canadian history and culture. Whereas in Europe

> place names are generally a product of long-term historical developments, and embody certain values or cultural significances, in the North American context place names often express the ambition to overcome the Old World's powers, with a telling trace of melancholy after what has been inevitably lost, after the high price that has been paid for national and political independence.
>
> (181-82)

As Kolinská demonstrates, the post-colonial approach to place names in Canada may effect some changes by "applying Aboriginal languages [...] to describe, define, and demarcate Canadian spatial, and thus also social realities." Recent attempts to rewrite cultural memories imprinted in Canadian place names, "can – hopefully – be read as a sign of intention to not only acknowledge the validity of [native American] cultures, but also create a freer and balanced geo-political space in general" (189), no longer shaped by colonial power and European history.

Contributions in the third group focus on the specific functions and transformations of individual myths and foundation texts articulating national, social and European identities. Peter Schwartz illustrates how the emphasis on the "*originality*" of ancient Greek culture was typical of eighteenth-century German middle class, as a "strategy [...] to challenge" the aristocratic "legitimation by origins in the past with legitimation by originality conceived as immanent, as potentially present in every present, and thus available, in principle, to individual members of any class." (216) However, this basically democratic ideology also germinated a Romantic nationalist myth contrasting German "originality" with the derivative, imitative nature of the French and emphasizing the

---

[17] Anderson, *Imagined Communities*, 173.

importance of the cultural *and* political mission of the Germans as "the new Greeks of a changing Europe." (225)

A different use of myths of origin is explored by Kirsten Mahlke in her study of the genesis of the myth of the Gauls in the Renaissance Kabbalist writings of Guillaume Postel and Guy Lefèvre de la Boderie, where the alleged link between Noah and the Druids gave rise both to the "insistence on French supremacy" and to a different, more global than national tendency, the utopian effort "to restore the final harmony of the world." (237)

The transformative function of myths in modern culture is studied by Ann Heilmann who focuses on the specific changes and functions of a single myth – that of Medea – "at a particular moment in time and in a particular location: Victorian and Edwardian Britain." (239-40) Tracing "the female and feminist dimensions of the cultural 'memory' of Medea," Heilmann demonstrates its functioning in the process of "a momentous social transformation in gender relations" (240), and its assimilation into contemporary discourses of eugenics, madness, transgression, and women emancipation. Thus, the Greek myth evidently loses its identity and enters a new, creative existence in the form of "singularities."

An ideological transformation of the myth of the Cid in a conservative representation of the Spanish Civil War is analyzed by Martin Hurcombe, who demonstrates how through the use of a "binary system" of signs transforming – as Roland Barthes has shown in his *Mythologies* – the accounts of historical events into the "metalanguage" of myth, "the war becomes [...] a battle between abstract values" – barbarism and civilization – "that, allegedly, transcend politics." (263)

In contrast to the approaches dealing with diverse uses of traditional myths, Mara Cambiaghi traces the transformations of a relatively recent myth of the year 1968 in the works of British, Italian and German novelists. Presenting three different ways in which "the archaeological discourse of knowledge" is transmuted "into the language of fiction" (304), she also points out vital imaginative links of the fictional works to "the contemporary discourse of memory" in psychology, history and cultural studies. (309)

Relationships between mythical, political and historical thought in the work of Czech expatriate writer Libuše Moníková are discussed by Brigid Haines, who demonstrates how the "imaginary cartography" (270) placing Bohemia (or the Czech lands) by the sea becomes a gesture of resistance to the contemporary distribution of power in Europe, as a result of which the Czech lands have lost their "share in what is most essentially European – its coast." (280) This geographical as well as mythical displacement[18] establishes a major tendency in Moníková's work – "to counter official histories by allowing space within her literary text for memory, subjective experience and the most diverse material." (273) There is a productive tension between this tendency and Moníková's creative use of the traditional "store of [Czech] myths, facts and stories:" both enable her "to reinvent a sense of Czechness." (280) The function of foundation texts, or rather quotations from them used in epigraphs, is studied by Rainier Grutman. Having drawn a "literary map of Europe" (285) based on his analysis of "Romantic mottomania," he finds instances of "overlapping between the international and national dimensions of literary systems in the Romantic age." While individual Romantic literatures function as national "institutions,"[19] their "intertextual repertoire" becomes "increasingly cosmopolitan." (291-92)

The last essay mentioned points to another thematic group of papers discussing the mediating role of specific foundation texts. Two of them study the function of Shakespeare's histories in European cultures. Analyzing two Italian versions of *Richard III* – a sophisticated poetic translation by Patrizia Valduga using the language of Renaissance Italian literature and an experimental, theatrically effective adaptation by Carmelo Bene, "subtracting" from the text a number of genealogical and historical details, while "superimposing" on it literary and theatrical reminiscences from Italian and other cultures – Mariangela Tempera shows how in the twentieth century, "Shakespeare became the inevitable mediator between the episodes from English history he has treated in his work and European culture." (325) Interpreting "The Globe" by Romanian poet Ion Stratan, an absurdist text composed largely from the names of the characters in Shakespeare's histories, Monica Matei-Chesnoiu argues that the poem should be understood in relation to Jan Kott's "Grand Mechanism" of history. She demonstrates how it succeeds in integrating "both the interpretative expectations related to Shakespeare's histories as assimilated by Romanian culture at a particular moment in time (i.e., the notion of history as a great mechanism versus

---

[18] The importance of the displacement of myth in history and fiction was discussed by Northrop Frye, "New Directions from Old," in *Fables of Identity* (New York: Harcourt, Brace and World, 1963), 52-66. His argument was critically revised by Hayden White (*Tropics of Discourse*, 61-62, 78n, and passim).

[19] See Harry Levin, *Gates of Horn: A Study of Five French Realists* (New York: Oxford University Press, 1963), 21-23.

the Communist authority) and the subversive energies released by this historical reality with an impact on later [post-Communist] times." (334) Finally, Mícheál Mac Craith presents his new findings concerning the complex genesis of a group of very influential modern foundation texts, Macpherson's Ossianic poems. Providing persuasive evidence about Macpherson's effort to render the original Gaelic poetry into English verse reproducing typical features of Gaelic prosody, he examines the transformations in the earliest stage of the project (before the publication of *Fragments of Ancient Poetry* in 1760) caused by the influence of contemporary intellectual and literary authorities: John Home, Adam Ferguson, Hugh Blair, Charles Batteux, Thomas Gray, William Mason and William Shenstone. The resulting form of the Ossian poems seems to be much more a product of multicultural influences, which, apart from the original Gaelic poetry, include the Scottish Enlightenment, English Sentimentalism and French Neoclassical poetics. Mac Craith's conclusions demonstrate that the traditional notions of originality and mediation cannot be treated separately and that the search for sources, which would establish the authority of a foundation text, may lead to much more productive study of the composite and dynamic nature of the form of the text.

Although the essays in this collection are far from claiming to make a systematic and comprehensive representation of European myths, foundation texts and imagined communities, in many ways they register and explore the changes of their status, functioning and study in the second half of the twentieth and even at the beginning of the twenty-first century. Not unlike myths themselves, this volume is a *bricolage*, or better – in Deleuzean terms – an assemblage of transversally connected discourses[20] producing cultural memories of Europe as a set of interlinked fragmentary experiences, visions, identities, texts, objects and theories.

---

[20] Cf. Deleuze, *Proust and Signs*, 105-15.

I.

APPROACHES

LITERARY REITERATION OF MYTHS AND FOUNDATION TEXTS: THEORETICAL NOTES

Jean Bessière

To assert that rewriting myths and foundation texts institutes imagined communities may lead to an unexpected conclusion: Jacques Offenbach, whose operettas reiterate segments and symbols of many myths, should be considered one of the best candidates to exemplify the link between rewriting myths and imagining communities. Instead of affirming this conclusion, the reference to Offenbach should invite us to revisit the widely accepted thesis according to which repeating myths and foundation texts equals not only a designation and mapping of imagined communities but also the claim that they are relevant for the communities contemporaneous with the repetition. The focus has to be on what the reiteration of myths and foundation texts implies and how it works.

1. Myths and Foundation Texts: Paradoxes of their Reiteration

The title of the 2004 ACUME Prague colloquium, "Myths, Foundation Texts, Imagined Communities," should be read without interpreting the word "foundation" literally and without referring to the fallacy and illusion implied by the qualifier "imagined." The word "foundation," applied either to myths or to texts, cannot be interpreted literally, because a community is not founded by its myths: it elaborates them, instituting its social reality in time and history through language and symbols which can be shaped into myths. The word "imagined," because it connotes illusion and fallacy, does not take into account a specific feature of myths: any myth may be qualified as imaginary, but this qualification does not help to characterize its cultural function, namely that it allows the social institution of reality. Consequently, since by producing myths and texts communities institute their realities, by reiterating and altering these myths and texts the same communities institute their realities again in time and history. In doing so, they constitute their possible self-images and self-references, that is, images and references that include their own future transformation, designate the meaning that should be attached to this transformation, and bridge the gap between the new and the past meanings.

Because of its singularity, literary reiteration of myths and foundation texts, whatever epoch it belongs to – ancient, medieval, modern, or contemporary –, intensifies the play of myths and foundation texts and appears explicitly paradoxical. It does not found or institute anything, although it should recall or symbolize a community's institution of its own reality. It presupposes the discontinuity of the time sequence although it should figure its continuity. It is singular, even though it should display the kind of social relevance typical of myths and foundation texts in the past.

The relation of these singular reiterations to myths and foundation texts should be understood as *autopoiësis*. Reflecting on these texts, writers repeat them and refer them to current social and cultural symbols and discourses, thus making autonomous creations of them, since any work presenting these reiterations may be regarded as autonomous. As a result, whatever myth (or foundation text) is reiterated, the reiteration produces a discontinuity, which, however, does not erase their relations to the antecedent myth or text.

The word "foundation" appears to be ambiguous. On the one hand, it implies a community's specific origin and establishment; on the other, it designates the myths and foundation texts referred to only through specific works. This ambiguity is not difficult to interpret. Although individual works cannot aim at simulating the relevance of the myths and the foundation texts they repeat in part, they specifically mediate them through *autopoiësis*. In doing so, they assume the authority of these myths and texts and their capacity to provide comprehensive representations of many times and places, thus bridging the gaps between multiple dimensions of their meaning. This does not imply that the work reiterating these myths or foundation texts should be identified with a monologic representation of time, space and meaning. On the contrary, allowing a plural representation and many references to it enables it to permit the recognition of various historical moments.

Because these references and recognition are possible, the repetition of myths and founding texts has often been defined as a means to preserve and symbolize the community's memory and unity. However, it should be stressed that this repetition does not thematize this memory and unity: instead, it constitutes a code serving as a guide for thinking them. Consequently, it is no surprise that the repetition of myths and foundations texts should be singular: the code is always specifically designed and allows a differentiation of meaning, while it does not preclude its generalization. This generalization is both similar to that typical of myths and foundation texts and different from it, because of the singularity of the repetition on the basis of which myths and foundation texts are processed. The repetition work represents the community's ability to construct its own image in time and history. Since it turns references into myths and foundation texts into self-references, it cannot be equated with a foundation text or with the imagination that gives rise to an "imagined community."

The word "imagined" also appears ambiguous. On the one hand, it can be understood as denoting an imagination with its source in the symbols of and discourses about the origin, namely myths and foundation texts. On the other hand, it can refer to a community's image, which makes sense only by opening two irreconcilable alternatives: while repetition makes the image a part of the meaningful world in which these myths and foundation texts appear either true or false, it also controls itself as a self-referential system. Consequently, the outcome of repetition and *autopoïësis* is not difficult to define: rather than presenting an imagined community, they create an aporia. Myths and foundation texts are repeated to the extent that their repetition is not completely determined by the past referred to and identified with, as a reaction to the information generated by the texts.

This aporia is remarkably exemplified in Carlos Fuentes's novel, *Cristobal Nonato*.[1] The myths and the ancient history of Mexico are repeated and even equated to the Renaissance symbols presented in the conclusion of the novel. However, the narrator of the novel has not been born yet: he is a male embryo in his mother's womb. Repetition of myths demonstrates the continuity of the past and the present and shows it to be explicitly imagined. Fancying continuity cannot account for any determination by memory or history: rather, it expresses the need to interpret the information generated by myths and transmitted by ancient

---

[1] Carlos Fuentes, *Cristobal Nonato* (Mexico: Fondo de Cultura Economica, 1987).

history as referring to a present that designates a possible future – the narrator is not yet born.

The use of the word *autopoiësis* allows us to compare the singular reiteration of myths and foundation texts both with the process of memory and the literary creation. It leads to their differences being emphasized, which in turn enables us to specify the reiteration paradox and to explain why a singular text, which repeats myths and foundation texts although they are not transferable, reveals a distance between itself and the reiterated myths and foundation texts and characterizes this distance as justification of the need for unifying interpretations of community and history. The reiteration appears in fact as a generalization of the meaning of myths and foundation texts. On the one hand, it makes their meaning present without primarily thematizing it; on the other, it uses them to integrate multiple dimensions of meaning in the community reiterating the text, derived in particular from the complexity of this community and the difficulties of its definition and legitimization.

2. Reiteration of Myths and Foundation Texts: Time and Self-temporalization

Reiteration of myths and foundation texts is not essentially different from the memory process, either in its individual or cultural dimensions. This process includes the selection and autonomous representation of past data. It takes into account the difference between the past and the present, and, through this difference, it designates the past as a foundation for the individual's awareness of his or her situation in time. Which means that an individual becomes aware of the present only by identifying an originary past and relating the present to this. The memory process changes the existential experience of time – the sequence of the past, the present and the future – into the *autopoiësis* of time. Through the memory process, time becomes the locus of its own reflexivity: it is self-temporalized. It undergoes endless reiteration within itself, and needs a semantics which sets valid accents for specific moments. This definition of the memory process is implied by Paul Ricœur's notion of refiguration of the past, which he identifies with the function of any narrative. It explains why narratives at once mime the memory process and set up semantics of time. As collective creations that apply the function of narratives to various epochs, myths and foundation texts explicitly represented, in a community, the differentiation of meaning in relation to these epochs, and turned it into the representation of all meaning. They consequently allowed leaps in the time sequence, which made it possible to represent the origin of history. As a result, they could exemplify collective memory. The fact that the myths and foundation texts most often present singular agents proves the structural connection between the individuals' representations and collective memories.

By using myths and foundation texts, which constitute a semantics of time and, in principle, are not transferable because they are distant, the reiterating text at once gives the representation of time a self-referential dimension, stresses the need of time semantics and establishes the representation of history on the capacity of the narrative to leap within the time sequence: the transfer of what is not transferable (the myths and the foundation texts) amounts to this leap.

But there are obvious differences between the memory process attached to myths and foundation texts identified as the social *autopoiēsis* of the experience of time, and the representation of time implied by the reiteration of these myths and texts. First, the memory process the myths and foundation texts exemplify is collective. Their reiterations are singular. Second, these myths and foundation texts were created once for all, although their constitution or creation might have taken a long time. They were able to represent all dimensions of meaning once for all and for any epoch, which recognized the semantics of time they set up. When this recognition no longer exists, only singular authors can reiterate them in singular works. For this reason, the reiteration of myths and foundation texts is incompatible with the collective memory process. It makes the reiterated myths and foundation texts the locus for the work's self-reflexivity and expresses the need of a semantics of time which should set valid accents for specific moments and epochs. Consequently, the self-temporalization of time allowed by the reiteration of myths and foundation texts is similar to that of the works which do not process myths and foundation texts.

This is one way to specify the paradox of the reiteration of myths and foundation texts. On the one hand, the reiteration shows that the representation of myths and foundation texts is irrelevant; on the other, it emphasizes the need of a time semantics that should account for historical change. This duality is a constant feature of the literary works in Europe which reiterate myths and foundation texts, even if these works formulate a semantics of time related to religious beliefs or to ideological interpretations of history.

To illustrate this duality, it is useful to refer first to the medieval novels and epics. They comply with the Christian view of time and history and reinterpret ancient myths and foundation events according to this. However, this reinterpretation is possible only because all the dimensions both of meaning and the semantics of time of ancient myths and foundation events are represented: the reinterpretation at once recognizes the authority of Christian beliefs and turns ancient myths and founding events into a code making it possible to bridge various and distant meanings. Reinterpretation amounts to asserting the Christian view of history and taking into account historical transitions.

Another example may perhaps sufficiently demonstrate the permanence of this duality. Historical novels, which appeared at the end of the eighteenth century, are based on a probabilistic view of history. Simultaneously, they make many references to myths and foundation texts that contradict this view. But this contradiction is not their ultimate gesture. Thanks to the references to myths and foundation texts, the probabilistic representation of history makes it possible to bridge the gaps between individual dimensions of meaning in history. This bridging is necessary in order to point out historical change which justifies the probabilistic view.

To end this series of examples, it suffices to stress that the contemporary historical novel, which aims at defining a semantics of time that should be compatible with a sense of progress or future, identifies the myths and foundation texts with a kind of archaeology of its own semantics of time – *Christobal Nonato* exemplifies this play. Highlighting at once a sense of progress and its archaeology indicates an implicit argument: whatever sense of progress or of the future characterizes an epoch, it should not absolutize the reading of the semantics of time it implies. Even when the sense of progress or of the future is stressed, a two-dimensional relation between the past and the future, on the one hand, and the characterization of the present, on the other, should be preserved. The future is at once continuous and discontinuous with the past. The present is at once a reversible and an irreversible occurrence. The sense of progress and future cannot be dissociated from the presentation of transition.

The duality typical of medieval novels and epics, and of historical novels, is possible because reiterating myths and foundation texts represents the institution of a community's memory, and defines it as anachronistic. In other words, a singular work that reiterates makes the process of historical memory – i.e., recalling these myths and foundation texts – the means of a reflexive view of time and history. On the one hand, it shows how past communities created their own histories by setting up semantics of time. On the other, it proves that any semantics of time construed by an epoch presupposes the discontinuity and self-temporalization of time. Reiteration represents both these aspects.

3. The Community and its Singular and Fictive Symbolization

Individual works that reiterate myths and foundation texts are not essentially different from texts that do not reiterate them. These texts incorporate antecedent data they identify as their origins; they take hold of them and consequently present them as autonomous: this is what is meant by the term "intertextuality." The works reiterating myths and foundation texts operate in the same way. However, because these works do not erase their relation to the myths or foundation texts, they display a peculiar feature: they have to appear as justified and justifying as the myths and foundation texts they repeat, that is, to bridge the gaps among all dimensions of meaning. The reiteration has to appear as if it were founding or re-founding, although it cannot in fact do so since it is singular. This is another way of exemplifying the paradox of reiteration.

Myths and foundation texts imply and express meanings shared in a community. Any individual reiteration of one of these myths, texts, and meanings results in 'desymbolizing' them, making them external to the present community and its subjects or identifying the particular reiteration with the proof that they have become external. The rewriting of the Oedipus myth by Sophocles can be read both ways, namely as a singular reiteration causing the myths and the foundation texts to lose their projection and saturation functions, or one proving that these functions have become irrelevant. *Projection function*: because of the particular reiteration, the myths and foundation texts can no longer be considered as relevant for anyone at any time, in the past, in the present, or in the future, although a myth or a foundation text is, in principle, relevant for anyone who, in a community, refers to these texts. *Saturation function*: the particular reiteration deprives the myth or the foundation text of its ability to refer to any reality compatible with its symbols and discourses. Hence, any particular reiteration of a myth or a foundation text may be defined as a kind of play on these symbols and discourses. Since a play is always autotelic, the reiteration makes the myths and foundation texts belong only to this autotelic exercise. Leaving out of account the fact that the saturation and projection functions are lost makes it impossible to account for the sheer number of reiterations of myths and foundation texts in European literatures. These remarks are not difficult to sum up: even if it quotes the original moment or founding facts relevant for a community in the past and represented by the myths and foundation texts, the reiteration makes this quotation arbitrary.

However, because the reiteration implies that the projection and saturation functions are missing, or even denies them, it indicates a specific relevance. Since the places represented by these myths and texts are not disassociated from those identified by the reiterating work, the space this work delineates is encompassing. Because the times these myths and texts represent are not disassociated from the topicality of the reiterating work, they become an integral part of the present. As a result, the reiterating work provides a conspicuous and holistic representation of the past and the present, although it is only singular. Consequently, it enables any individual to face his or her community, its various epochs and spaces, and to view them. It still symbolizes the relation of the individual to his or her community and shows that an individual can qualify his or her community's past discourses and symbols as irrelevant; simultaneously, it makes his or her community readable by anyone through these discourses and symbols.

This paradoxical way of highlighting the past symbols and discourses of the community for a particular present and specific individuals leads us to read the reiterating work as a substitute for myths and foundation texts. Because the myths and foundation texts are shown to be external to the present and are deprived of their projection and saturation functions, they can be seen as potential possessions of any individual. Consequently, the times and places they represent can still be thought to be relevant as long as they are referred to the present and to a specific individual. Contemporary novels by the Martinican writers, Édouard Glissant and Patrick Chamoiseau provide excellent examples of this. Old traditions, beliefs, symbols and narratives are identified with dreams or with facts that cannot be documented. This is one way of suggesting that the projection and saturation functions are missing. However, these traditions, beliefs and symbols are rewritten and referred to individuals – the characters in the novels – who consequently seem to live according to these past symbols and beliefs as well as contemporary standards. On the one hand, this makes the past symbols and beliefs appear as a kind of excess, as a token of a fiction with which it is possible to equate the reiteration of myths and foundation texts. On the other hand, the individual – the character – can be identified with many past and present places and various locations in time. He bridges the gaps between the multiple dimensions of meaning in his community and contemporary world and designates this community in the same way as any other world. He also embodies the projection and saturation functions the reiterated myths and foundation texts have lost. These remarks can be reformulated and generalized. Myths and foundation texts can still be relevant if they are handled as an anachronism. Through this anachronism, the work reiterating them reenacts the social institution of reality they enabled in the past. Through the social institution of reality, a community at once symbolizes its realities and organizes its self-reference and self-abstraction: it imprints its realities and its identities onto the flow of experience and makes them function as reductive references at any given time. Myths and foundation texts represent this imprint: they can therefore be described as "founding" and equated with the social institution of reality in time. The reiteration of myths and foundation texts represents their past imprints. Because it is anachronistic and applied to an individual, it singularly reenacts the social institution of reality. The characters in Glissant's and Chamoiseau's novels exemplify the imprints of myths and foundation texts by means of identifying themselves, and being identified, with many times and places. The projection and saturation functions are not attached to the myths and foundation symbols which are mere legacies of the past but to these characters who individualize the myths and foundation symbols.

The reiteration of the myths and foundations texts neither constitutes their imitation nor is it one of their founding moments. It is a representation of the conditions of the foundation and its *autopoiēsis*. It allows the reader to be aware of what makes a community able to represent itself and to construe shared meanings. Through the social institution of reality a community makes available and evident to its members a synthesis of experiences and representations of time and space, as one of its members' relations to itself. By representing an excess of times and places, the work that reiterates myths and foundation texts makes, on the one hand, cultural symbols and discourses singular, and, on the other, links any epoch to the present, shaping the space so that it unifies representations of various places, and identifying the individual with an allegory of the community.

These remarks apply to medieval novels and epics, as well as eighteenth-century and contemporary historical novels. Because of the reiteration of myths and foundation texts, the characters in these genres belong both to the past and to the present. This does not mean that they refer simultaneously to the past of the myths and foundation texts and to the present and to the past which accounts for this present. In other words, they are not mere signs of reiterated myths and foundation texts.

By being what they perform (the two pasts and the present) the characters generalize the meanings of their acts, the present and the past that accounts for this present. Thus, they become specific meta-symbols to which the symbols of the Christian view of time and of the sense of progress and future in history can be referred without negating or denying them. Consequently, the work reiterating the myths and foundation texts demonstrates what any social and cultural symbolization does, namely, construing meta-symbols. Moreover, it deconstructs this construction, be it past or present, makes it contingent, and constitutes a basis for binding times and spaces, uniting the individuals and the community, and symbolizing this binding. Thus, the paradox attached to the reiteration of myths and foundation texts comes full circle: the reiteration allows the reiterating work to function as a substitute for the myths and the foundation texts, although it is singular and deconstructs meta-symbols.

4. The Reiterating Work as a Metatext or a Metalanguage, and its Authority[2]

To stress that the work reiterating myths and foundation texts deconstructs the meta-symbols they constitute means to qualify this work as a meta-symbol. It repeats the cultural symbols and discourses, presenting them as powerless: they are not granted any binding function in the representation of a community and of the social institution of reality. It uses their semantics of time and the links among their dimensions of meaning to reinforce the differentiation of meaning. Finally, it constitutes a meta-symbol because it simultaneously allows rejection and acceptance of the communication made possible by myths and foundation texts, their semantics of time and their dimensions of meaning. While it *rejects* the original relevance of these myths and foundation texts, it *accepts* the relevance given to these myths and foundation texts by the *autopoiësis* of the reiterating work. This work controls its references to the myths, foundation texts, cultural symbols and discourses, but does not turn them into sheer assertions. In doing so, it institutes the imagined power of literature and questions the available myths, foundation texts and cultural symbols to which it refers.

Since the reiterating work generalizes the meaning of its references to myths and foundation texts – despite the fact that it transforms them

---

[2] For references to "metatext" and "metalanguage" see Iouri Lotman, *La Sémiosphère* (Limoges: PULIM, 1999).

into self-references –, it bridges the gaps between the numerous dimensions of meaning in the community to which it belongs, especially the meanings attached to the complexity of this community and the problems of its legitimization and foundation. However, the reiterating work does not update this bridging. Consequently, the representation it constitutes should not be read as a continuation of the reiterated myths and foundation texts, the semantics of time and the dimensions of meaning that prevail in the context of the reiterating work. These remarks should be generalized: if, according to the tradition of literary criticism, a work is qualified as mimetic, imitating reality and past or present cultural symbols and discourses, it does not mean that it is faithful to the reality or to these symbols and discourses. As a result, mimesis cannot be separated from *autopoiésis* and from questioning what it reiterates.

This paradoxical mimesis can be found in works appearing to confirm the cultural symbols and discourses, the myths and the foundation texts as well as in those which express their discontinuity with them. The paradoxical mimesis makes the works of the first kind metatexts and those of the second kind metalanguages.

The first kind of works refers its recognition and its explicit representation of the myths, foundation texts and meta-symbols they constitute to the continuous link of individuals to the community and its shared meanings, either past or present. In Europe, from the Middle Ages to the eighteenth century, this linkage is exemplified by the mutual implication of their references to traditions, religious beliefs and cultural representations. Because of this link, the reiterating work explicitly thematizes the myths and the foundation texts it quotes, makes them reach a kind of saturation point, and consequently presents them as integrated in a long-term nexus of meaning which is more permanent than the meaning of the quoted myths and foundation texts. It becomes the text to which anyone can refer in the present or in the future. Its capacity of binding diverse meanings is higher than that of myths and foundation texts. The reiterating work represents them and, by developing its own semantics of time, it can be referred to by anyone in the present or in the future. This double determination makes the work a metatext. Such type of metatextuality characterizes the reiteration of myths and foundation texts up to the nineteenth century, and makes them explicit self-representations of the social institution of reality.

The other kind of works represents myths and foundation texts as explicitly external to the subjects referring to them, because the "tradition," whatever definition it is given, no longer justifies the continuous recognition of these myths and foundation texts. This type of works constitutes a metalanguage that provides a specific version of the myths and foundation texts and makes them external to their quotation. It perfectly exemplifies the fact that the projection and saturation functions are lost. Mallarmé's and T.S. Eliot's poems illustrate this status of the quotations. Because of the conditions they impose on quoting myths and foundation texts, these poems cannot present themselves as originating in these myths and in their shared meanings, and, at the same time, they are no longer referable to any individual. Repeating myths and foundation texts amounts to producing a double otherness – of these myths and texts and of the reiterating work. This is the reason why a modern text that identifies itself with a foundation text does not define itself correctly. Before one starts to read German Romantic poetry about ancient Greece and its myths as a search for the original grounds that should make it possible to imagine the modern German community, it should be stressed that the belief that it is in full control of its discourses and the cultural symbols it quotes is inherent in this poetry. This bias of modern reiterating works serves to teach one lesson: it is no longer indispensable to think that a unifying view of the world is needed. The substitute for this view intended to bridge the gaps between all dimensions of meaning is a work identifying its references to myths and foundation texts with a metalanguage and consequently interpreting the social institution of reality.

Both kinds of reiterating works illustrate their semiotic status by presenting the projection and saturation functions attached to myths and foundation texts in what is an explicit contradiction. Of the *reiterating works that constitute a metatext*, medieval epics and neoclassical tragedies are good examples. While *epic* represents myths, beliefs and cultural memory defining a community, it restricts the scope of this mimesis by stressing the entropy attached to its narrative – any epic is a story of disorder and violence – and making its characters non-referable to this mimesis. It shows both relevant and irrelevant aspects of the quoted myths and foundation texts. The projection and saturation functions of the myths, the beliefs and the cultural memory are all circumscribed by, and transferred to, the epic: this makes it an explicit metatext. As for the *neoclassical tragedy*, on the one hand, it represents the authority of the myths and cultural memory by submitting the hero to fate, on the other, the relevance of the myths and cultural memory is questioned because the hero does not accept his or her fate. As a result, in neoclassical tragedy there are means to limit the projection and saturation functions of the myths, which are quoted and updated in a specific context, and to identify the tragedy as a metatext. Of the *reiterating works which constitute a metalanguage*, the nineteenth-century literary utopias and science fiction narratives explicitly highlight the paradoxical presentation of the projection and saturation functions. They extend the representations of myths and foundation texts onto future epochs and places, and seem to confirm their saturation and projection functions. At the same time, the imagined future of science fiction belongs to an epoch no human being can reasonably conceive experiencing, while the utopias are presentations of imagined spaces, namely the de-realization of the saturation and projection functions. Therefore, the communities represented are explicitly imaginary. This contradiction demonstrates that the reiterating work neither thematizes primarily the contents of myths and foundation texts, nor repeats their power to reinforce and bridge the differentiation of meaning. It consequently appears to substitute its own language, which includes references to myths and foundation texts, for the language of these references. Therefore, it can be said to function as a metalanguage.

As a metatext or metalanguage, the reiterating work possesses a specific authority. This authority does not originate in the contents and symbols of what it reiterates but in its self-reference and self-identification. By presenting both aspects of its references to myths and foundation texts, it makes them the means of its self-identification, and finally equates their quotations with its self-references. This constitutes its power to bridge gaps between diverse meanings: it can quote myths and foundation texts and simultaneously account for them because it imposes a paradoxical representation of the projection and saturation functions.

5. The Reiterating Work and the Cognitive Representation of the Social Institution of Reality

If the outlined set of remarks is considered relevant, the reiterating work does not institute an imagined community: imagining a community cannot originate in the power of literature illustrated by the reiterating work. The reiterating work results in recognizing and representing the social institution of reality according to its *autopoiēsis*. It explicitly turns the representation of the collective memory process into its self-temporalization and refers it to a singular narrative. It symbolizes the community through the fiction of individuals. It paradoxically reenacts the projection and saturation functions denied to the myths and foundations texts it reiterates, and establishes the dimensions of meaning characterizing the community and the culture to which it refers. This makes the reiterating work a cognitive representation of the social institution of reality. The reiterating work shows that this institution is always arbitrary and that the order of meaning it founds in time and history is always improbable.

CONTINUITY AND DISCONTINUITY IN TRADITION

Riccardo Campi

Tradition is not to be abstractly negated, but criticized without naïveté according to the current situation: Thus the present constitutes the past.

Theodor W. Adorno[1]

At the beginning of *The Archaeology of Knowledge*, Michel Foucault outlines the task and, at the same time, the paradox of every discourse on the past:

> For history in its classical form, the discontinuous was both the given and the unthinkable: the raw material of history, which presented itself in the form of dispersed events […]; the material, which, through analysis, had to be rearranged, reduced, effaced, in order to reveal the continuity of events. Discontinuity was the stigma of the temporal dislocation that it was the historian's task to remove from history.[2]

Foucault's argument highlights the problematic relation between history and its object. From an entirely different historical perspective, however, Hans Georg Gadamer's hermeneutics has attempted to find a solution to the same problem.

---

[1] Theodor W. Adorno, *Aesthetic Theory*, ed. Gretel Adorno and Rolf Tiedemann, trans. Robert Hullot-Kentor (Minneapolis: University of Minnesota Press, 1997), 41.

[2] Michel Foucault, *The Archaeology of Knowledge* [L'Archéologie du savoir, 1969], trans. A.M. Sheridan Smith (London and New York: Routledge, 1991), 8.

Gadamer's avowed target is, first of all, historicism, or historicist positivism. In order to refute this doctrine, Gadamer claims that, strictly speaking, the object of historical research "clearly does not exist at all in itself."[3] For that very reason he distinguishes between "human sciences" (including history) and "natural sciences." (253) In the positivist perspective, only the latter constitute the paradigm for objective and scientific knowledge. To refute the objectivism on which historicism is founded might well be the means to avoid the paradox formulated by Foucault.

According to Gadamer, the object of "historical understanding" is not an "event," but rather the "meaning." (A similar conclusion can be found in Nietzsche, who also argued against positivism, maintaining that there were no "facts" but only "interpretations.")[4] The obvious aim of Gadamer's strategy is to suppress the difference between the past, where the historical object is placed, and the present of understanding. The task of the historian is no longer to capture the historical object "as it was" (according to the formula of Leopold Ranke), because there is no "historical object [...] in itself." For Gadamer, "the tradition reaching us speaks into the present and must be understood in this mediation – indeed, as this mediation." (293)

Consequently, hermeneutics may be said to upset the ontological fixity of the historical object. The "meaning" it claims to be the real object of historical understanding depends on a mediation that, by its very nature, can be nothing but essentially dynamic because each mediation is based on a relation between two poles. Gadamer's position is expounded and summarized in the following statement: "the true historical object is not an object at all, but the unity of the one and the other ["the true historical object" and "the true historical thinking"], a relationship in which exists both the reality of history and the reality of historical understanding." (267) This is the theoretical core of Gadamer's hermeneutics: Gadamer himself speaks in this connection of "the central problem of hermeneutics." (274) In fact, one of his basic concepts, that of "fusion of [...] horizons," (273) is intended to define precisely this

---

3 Hans Georg Gadamer, *Truth and Method*, ed. Garret Barden and John Cumming (New York: The Seabury Press, 1975), 253. Subsequent page references to this edition are given in parentheses in the text.
4 See Friedrich Nietzsche, *Nachgelassene Fragmente, Ende 1886-Frühjahr 1887*, 7 [60], in *Werke*, ed. Giorgio Colli and Mazzino Montinari (Berlin-New York: Walter de Gruyter, 1974), 8 (1): 323.

mediation between the present and the past through which the "meaning" of the historical object is constituted. The dynamic nature of every act of historical understanding seems to preclude the objectivist approach to history. From the theoretical perspective of hermeneutics, the cognition of the past is based on an interaction between two active entities and not on a one-sided relationship of an inert object to an active, understanding subject (according to the metaphysical concept of truth based upon *adaequatio rei et intellectus* that goes back at least to medieval scholastic philosophy). As a result, there is no truth of the past that is to be appropriated, but a "meaning" that should arise from the encounter (called "fusion" by Gadamer) between the two horizons, that of the past and that of the present. Thus, as Gadamer points out, "[i]n the process of understanding there takes place a real fusing of horizons, which means that as the historical horizon is projected it is simultaneously removed." (273) In other words, the fusion of horizons between the past and the present suppresses their difference and simultaneously becomes an object of historical knowledge. The "meaning" is finally produced by the fusion of horizons: it is not simply found but emerges within time and through time, because each mediation is essentially temporal.

This conclusion poses the problem of ascertaining the nature, or, more precisely, the structure, of the time produced by the fusion of horizons. The main feature of the time concept, that Gadamer's hermeneutics – though implicitly – puts at stake, is continuity.

Conceived by natural sciences (particularly by Newtonian physics) as a continuum, time is reversible and homogeneous, structured as an uninterrupted sequence, series, or a chain of causes and effects. Despite Gadamer's argument against historicist positivism, his notion of time may be recognized as an avatar of the positivist continuum. It is precisely this aspect of Gadamer's theory that makes the fusion of horizons possible. Gadamer insists that historical understanding "proved to be an event," which means that it is a continuing historical movement "situated within a process of tradition" (276), and also that "temporal distance is not an obstacle to be surmounted," adding that "[t]ime is no longer primarily a gulf to be bridged, because it separates, but it is actually the supportive ground of the process, in which the present is rooted." (264) As a result, Gadamer's notion of time informing the historical "process" (which is also the process of understanding, bridging the distance between past and present) is founded on continuity.

And the name of that continuity is tradition. Gadamer is unequivocal on this subject: understanding should be thought "as the placing of oneself within the process of tradition, in which the past and the present are constantly fused." (258) In spite of all Gadamer's affirmations of the necessity to respect the distance and the otherness that separate the past from the present of understanding, and all his claims that "[t]rue historical thinking must take account of its own historicality" (267), hermeneutics leads to an apology of tradition as a principle of temporal continuity. In fact, historical consciousness "is aware of its own otherness [...but], on the other hand, it is itself [...] only something laid over a continuing tradition." (273) As a consequence, hermeneutics suppresses the dualism between past and present, and, in so doing, it wipes out their distance and otherness by a fusion of horizons. Gadamer himself writes that historical consciousness "immediately recombines what it has distinguished, [...] in the unity of the historical horizon that it so acquires [by a fusion of horizons], to become again one with itself." (273) Gadamer takes care, and with good reason, to abstain from referring to empathy (*Einfühlung*), one of the keywords of historicism. But the fact is that he repudiates the dualist objectivism of historicist positivism only to supplant it with a subjectivism that disregards the otherness and distance separating the past from the present and reduces them to the unity and identity of a historical horizon where the awareness of the past is "again one with itself," finding itself (its identity) again in the past. Thus, the past loses its otherness and becomes a kind of a mirror in which the present can be reflected.

Hence, Gadamer's hermeneutics evades the paradox of the historian's task brought to light by Foucault. In doing so, it revives the reassuring notion of tradition, using it as a form of continuity principle, because it is precisely through tradition that discontinuity and continuity, though apparently irreconcilable, can be reconciled. Gadamer presents tradition as a process in which every contradiction, contrast, conflict, or rupture, in other words, all the differences emerging in the process of history, are lessened and even effaced. In his harangue in favor of tradition, Gadamer goes so far as to speak openly of the past as "a living continuity of elements that pile up to become a tradition."[5]

In this "living continuity," every otherness is effaced because

---

5 Hans Georg Gadamer, "Esquisse des fondements d'une herméneutique," in *Le problème de la conscience historique* (Louvain-Paris: Publications Universitaires de Louvain, 1963), 81.

[i]n our continually manifested attitude to the past, the main feature is not, at any rate, a distancing and freeing ourselves from what has been transmitted. Rather, we stand always within tradition, and this is no objectifying process, i.e. we do not conceive of what tradition says as something other, something alien. It is always part of us, a model or exemplar, a recognition of ourselves which our later historical judgement would hardly see as a kind of knowledge, but as the simplest preservation of tradition.

(250)

This long quotation allows us to assess the outcome of Gadamer's hermeneutics and to detect its weak point, that is, in a few words, the lack of a real dialectical mediation that would only allow to suppress and at the same time would preserve (in the Hegelian meaning of *aufheben*) the otherness of the past. When Gadamer speaks of mediation, what he means is an "entre-deux" (*zwischen*). As it is known, dialectical mediation has nothing to do with a compromise between the two sides, while that is precisely what seems to be the role of tradition: having, according to Gadamer, an "intermediate [...] place between strangeness and familiarity." (262-63) To reconcile contradiction between the two poles is the specific function of tradition. As is already clear, in Gadamer's hermeneutics, the true name of mediation (non-dialectical mediation) is "fusion:"

In a tradition this process of fusion is continually going on, for there old and new continually grow together to make something of living value, without either being explicitly distinguished from the other.

(273)

This apology of tradition brings about, finally, the triumph of historical continuity over all discontinuity, otherness and distance. Each rupture and each rift are joined inside tradition, which is essentially a fusion and fosters a historical understanding. It meets with no obstacles because it is nothing but "a way in which we recognize ourselves." It is indeed difficult to disentangle that self-recognition from historicist empathy. If hermeneutical mediation cannot refrain itself from leading to such an empathy (though it does not admit it), it is because it lacks the determinate negation, or, as Walter Benjamin puts it, that "destructive

element which authenticates both dialectical thought and the experience of the dialectical thinker."[6]
The dialectical thinker's experience with the past is the exact opposite of that described by Gadamer. To a dialectical historian

> [i]t is important [...], in the most rigorous way possible, to differentiate the construction of a historical state of affairs from what one customarily calls its "reconstruction." The "reconstruction," in empathy is one-dimensional. "Construction" presupposes "destruction."[7]

In this context, "destruction" means, first of all, to obliterate all continuity between past and present. According to Benjamin, this is necessary since the task of the historian is not to follow the series of causes and effects all the way back to an eternally unchangeable historical object which he is expected to know, describe, interpret and eventually quietly arrange in the museum of tradition, or, as Benjamin calls it, of "cultural heritage." On the contrary, a materialist hermeneutics should wrench the historical object from the continuity of the chain of causes and effects because here it could become a mere moment of an 'evolution' or an uninterrupted and infallible 'progress.' This would amount to falling into the "homogeneous and void" (as Benjamin puts it) temporality of history, where all the objects are displayed one after the other, one beside the other, like in the well-ordered rooms of a museum.

For Benjamin, instead, the historical object is seen as an "original phenomenon" (*Ur-phänomen*), a notion adopted from Goethe. It should not be forgotten that, in Benjamin, the words "original" and "origin" (*Ursprung*) designate something entirely different from a genesis, a primary cause, a root or a source, that is to say, something supposed to contain the germs of all elements of a tradition that would ensue from it. The "origin" is not plunged into the continuity of historical becoming, but, on the contrary, it represents the very element that disrupts that continuity. It is an empty space separating the pre-history and the "after-history" of the phenomenon. It could also be described as the breaking

---

6 Walter Benjamin, "Eduard Fuchs, Collector and Historian," trans. Howard Eiland and Michael W. Jennings, in *Selected Writings*, vol. 3, 1935-1938 (Cambridge, Mass. and London: The Belknap Press of Harvard University Press, 2002), 268.

7 Walter Benjamin, *The Arcades Project*, trans. Howard Eiland and Kevin McLaughlin (Cambridge, Mass. and London: The Belknap Press of Harvard University Press, 1999), 470 [No. 7, 6].

point of a sequence of historical events. Thus, the historicist pretension to reconstruct the historical object as it was runs into the stumbling block of what Benjamin calls "original phenomenon," as does the process of the fusion of horizons praised by Gadamer.

The "original phenomenon" has to be wrenched from the causal continuity of history to reveal what has been rejected by tradition, what has not found a place in it and what has been forgotten. In short, the "original phenomenon" embodies what has been repressed by tradition. However, it is not possible to speak of the Benjaminian notion of origin without at the same time mentioning the complementary notion of actuality (*Jetztzeit*, 'now'). The two notions are closely interconnected. As origin is not the starting point of a chain of causes and effects, actuality does not have to be understood as the terminal point at the opposite end of such a chain. Actuality is not the present as opposed to the past, but a transient instant, where a certain original phenomenon becomes readable and knowable, where finally what has been repressed by tradition is disclosed, and where the forgotten re-emerges into the memory. On the other hand, the phenomenon itself is original only through actuality. For the historical object, to be original is to break the homogeneous continuity and to bring to the surface what tradition has concealed by the monumentalization of the cultural heritage. Actuality is precisely what creates a short circuit between the two temporal layers. And, in time, the short circuit causes an explosion that reveals the hidden layer of the historical object.

According to Benjamin, there is no fusion, but a real shock, between the past and the present. He often uses the blast or the collision metaphor to underline the violence of the destructive moment inherent in each act of historical understanding. Thus, he points out the determinate negation proper to the dialectical method. Having denied the objectivity of the past and the possibility to reconstruct it, Benjamin is able to wrench the historical object off the continuity of tradition and rescue the otherness, which makes the original phenomenon a historical object. Moreover, the blast metaphor emphasizes the clash occurring between otherness and identity: the otherness of what has not found a place in tradition and the identity that establishes a possibility, for the present, of recognizing itself in the past celebrated by tradition. It is not empathy with the historical object that is at issue here, as Benjamin has often explained:

> The historical object removed from pure facticity does not need any "appreciation" [again a reference to empathy]. It does

not offer vague analogies to actuality, but constitutes itself in
the precise dialectical problem [*Aufgabe*] which actuality is
obliged to resolve.[8]

The "dialectical task" referred to here is the rejection of the double myth
of the empathy with the past and of its reconstruction representing the
historical object as it has never been seen before. The task is not to write
a different history (that of its outcasts, that Benjamin calls the
"vanquished"), but to write the same history differently, the history that
is ours, the history that was enclosed by tradition in its museums to be
worshipped as cultural heritage. To see the past differently is to
rediscover what has been forgotten, what was believed to be lost forever.
It is to put at stake what was believed to be true and has expired. In
short, it is to see the historical object as an original phenomenon. This is
an essentially political task because actuality brings forth the need to free
history as it was transmitted to the present by tradition. Hence, the
"dialectical problem" to be solved by the historian is to present "a given
experience with the past – an experience that is unique," or "[t]o put to
work an experience with history – a history that is originary for every
present."[9] Once again, actuality is closely linked to the cognition of the
origin, determined as such by the unique experience of the past lived in
each present. It is only from the point of view of this experience that a
phenomenon can be interpreted as "originary."

To expound the nature of that unique and original experience,
which, due to its suddenness and violence, should also be qualified as
dazzlingly striking, Benjamin employs another metaphor in addition to
that of the blast. It is a metaphor of the awakening, allowing him to
point out the fleeting and disruptive nature of the original experience,
and, above all, to illustrate the dialectical reversal produced by that
experience with reference to the past transmitted by tradition.

To sum up, discontinuity in Benjamin is not an obstacle to
historical understanding, but the very condition that makes it possible:
"[i]n order for a part of the past to be touched by the present instant
[*Aktualität*], there must be no continuity between them."[10] Therefore, the
historian must come to grips with the discontinuity, the otherness and
the distance separating the present from the past. To use a phrase from a
very important essay by Adorno devoted to the notion of tradition and

---

8 Walter Benjamin, "Eduard Fuchs, Collector and Historian," 269.
9 "Eduard Fuchs, Collector and Historian," 262.
10 Benjamin, *The Arcades Project*, 470 [No. 7, 7].

evidently influenced by Benjamin's thought, the historian must not ignore "the need of distance."[11] When Benjamin warns that "[t]here is a tradition that is catastrophe,"[12] he implies that there is a tradition that ignores the distance, deadens all the differences, effaces all the otherness separating us from the historical object, to praise the continuance of would-be universal values through the centuries. Contrary to this, actual continuity is a product of a historical conflict and of a tension that no fusion of horizons can reconcile.

Like any real paradox, Foucault's paradox has no solution. No hermeneutics can take the liberty to cancel or reconcile it by means of a compromise such as Gadamer's act of fusion. The only way to save tradition, and also historical understanding, is to acknowledge that it is neither a ready-made heritage, nor, even worse, something to be appropriated, monumentalized or worshipped. If a 'good' tradition exists, as opposed to the tradition that is a "catastrophe," then it is a "critical transmission."[13] Neither a celebration of a cultural heritage to be jealously guarded, nor an immersion into a living continuity belonging to us, or to which we always belong, a transmission of the past that would be "critical" has therefore to take upon itself the construction of its object. Benjamin's materialist and dialectical hermeneutics takes seriously the statement that there is no historical object in itself. To transmit is therefore to construct a "constellation" (Benjamin's term), where the scattered, fragmentary, heteroclite elements of the past, or simply its contradictions and its discontinuity, arrange themselves around the empty core Benjamin calls the "origin." The outcome is a "dialectical image" (again, Benjamin's term), making it possible to grasp the historical object as an original phenomenon and therefore to see it as it has never been seen before. In contrast to Gadamer's mediation by means of fusion, it will be the dialectical principle of mediation by antithesis that will govern the construction of that image or constellation.

To conclude, while tradition neutralizes the historical object, reducing it to a moment of historical evolution, to a single cause among others in the continuity of historical becoming, a dialectical

---

[11] Theodor W. Adorno, "Über Tradition," in *Ohne Leitbild; Gesammelte Schriften* (Frankfurt a. M.: Suhrkamp Verlag, 1996), 10.1: 316: "Das jedoch stiftet eine Tradition der allein noch zu folgen wäre. Ihr Kriterium ist correspondance. Sie wirft, als neu Hervortretendes, Licht aufs Gegenwärtige und empfängt von Gegenwärtigen ihr Licht. Solche correspondance ist keine der Einfühlung und unmittelbaren Verwandtschaft, sondern Bedarf der Distanz."

[12] Benjamin, *The Arcades Project*, 473 [No. 9, 4].

[13] Daniel Payot, *Après l'harmonie* (Belfort: Circé, 2000), 65.

understanding of the past is critical only if it is able to generate a hidden force, a "disturbing strangeness," still capable of calling our present into question. Tradition in itself is not a value. Its value lies in the fact that it forces us to think critically and construct incessantly and repeatedly our past as well as our present.

Translated by Alessandro Zabini.

MEMORY, DESIRE AND UTOPIA: A NEW PERSPECTIVE ON THE NOTION OF CRITICAL UTOPIA

Vita Fortunati

To a nostalgic friend who prompted my imagination.

Why should one be interested in nostalgia, a type of feeling, of passion, which is felt to be rather old fashioned and discredited, nowadays? The answer to this question involves strong personal, autobiographical reasons, as well as political and historical ones. The former are tightly bound to my generation, a generation that has witnessed great, epochal events and experienced moments of passionate utopian hopes, followed by burning disillusionments: a generation of intellectuals who could not avoid a critical reassessment of their past and had to painfully come to terms with the ideals they had believed in.

The start of the new millennium, the recent tragic events born from the rise of ferocious nationalism and carried out in the name of the reconstruction of a lost homeland, the phenomenon of the revival of postmodernity have foregrounded this feeling which we thought we had now left behind us forever. The massive and violent emigration processes make us aware how painful and upsetting it is for poor, indigenous populations to leave their birthplace. The tragic historical events of the twentieth century and in particular its many dictatorships have shown how deeply solitary the exile's position is; it is the position of human beings bereft of the cultural experience or the potential space that any person shares with his/her friends and compatriots, a place of negotiation between private and public memories. These are just a few of the reasons to explain why this feeling is still so strong today.

Nonetheless nostalgia – and this is one of the many contradictions of our times – has become the object of commercial exploitation, manipulated and abused as it is by the media and popular culture, as Linda Hutcheon has rightly underscored in her essay.[1] The Russian scholar Svetlana Boym assumes that in periods characterised by a heightened technological acceleration there is a strong resurgence in popular imagining of nostalgia for origins, which generates archaic mythologies.[2] Nostalgia appears as a defence mechanism of sorts, a feeling that charms and attracts because, as Lee Quinby maintains, it is a type of escape from what he describes as "a technological apocalypse."[3] However, this regressive flight to the past is paradoxically achieved, for instance in many contemporary films, with the aid of very refined technology, as is the case in the recent movie *Hero* (2003), by Chinese director Zhang Yimou, produced by Quentin Tarantino. An archaic, epic story, linked to ancient martial arts, is told using highly elaborate, astounding special effects. In the same way, the information technologies promoting globalisation also encourage and lead to a strong attachment to 'localisms.'

I intend to divide my contribution into three parts: in the first, I would like to identify, through the history of this feeling, certain conceptual connections which make nostalgia a complex feeling and partly explain the difficulties in its possible rehabilitation. In the second part, I will define the links between utopia, dystopia and nostalgia, introducing the concept of 'critical nostalgia.' This concept has been developed by various important studies published in the last two decades. It becomes an interpretative framework for a comparison and critique of the past, while the process also aims at the construction of a new, different future. In the third part, I would like to exemplify this concept through the reading of a critical dystopia, *The Telling* (2000), by Ursula Le Guin, and *Buongiorno, Notte* (2003), the film by Italian director Marco Bellocchio.

[1] Linda Hutcheon, "Irony, Nostalgia and the Postmodern," http://www. library.utoronto.ca/utel/criticism/hutchinp.html. See also Christopher Lasch, "The Politics of Nostalgia," *Harper's* (November 1984): 65-70.

[2] Svetlana Boym, *The Future of Nostalgia* (New York: Basic Books, 2001), 33-35.

[3] Lee Quinby, *Anti-Apocalypse: Exercises in Genealogical Criticism,* (Minneapolis: University of Minnesota Press, 1994), xvi.

1.

The history of nostalgia highlights the complexities and the ambiguities that nestle in this feeling. Nostalgia is a word that has stratified in time, assuming different connotations. It was born in the seventeenth century in the context of medical terminology and was used to define, as we shall see, a particular pathology of memory, causing physical symptoms. Subsequently, the notion ceased to be understood in this interpretive framework. By the end of the eighteenth century, and during the whole of the nineteenth century, nostalgia would be firmly ensconced in the realm of feeling, to the point that today its medical origin has been forgotten. After its exploitation by the Romantic movement and literature, it has become a vague expression with indefinite semantic contours.

The term, coined by the Alsatian doctor Johannes Hofer in 1688, derives from the Greek *nostos*, meaning return, and *algos*, pain. Each national language expresses this nostalgic feeling towards the country of origin by a specific term with different shades of meaning in different geographical contexts: *Heimweh* in German, *maladie du pays* in French, *mal de corazón* in Spanish, *saudade* in Portuguese, *rimpianto* in Italian, *stesk po domovu* in Czech, to cite a few examples. The various terms, despite being synonymous, maintain the rhythm of the respective languages and are as a matter of fact untranslatable, because the underlying desire expresses a different *Weltanschauung*, constituting the uniqueness and the peculiarity of each nation. The history of the pathology of this "perturbation of memory" has been skilfully studied by Jean Starobinski, who reminds his readers of how this disease was acknowledged, since Swiss soldiers actually died of it after living in faraway countries with customs and languages different from those of their native land.[4] Seventeenth-century treatises on the subject explain that the causes of this perturbation of memory were to be found in the anguish resulting from separation, or severance, in the feeling of being alien or uprooted and in the yearning to go home: feelings which provoked strong physical pains such as loss of appetite, nausea, hysterical weeping, delirium and hallucinations. An illness born in a specific, military, milieu, which then spreads to other social spheres and classes. Nostalgia, unlike melancholy – with which it shares many affinities and to which it is often compared – develops amongst the poorer and less literate classes.

---

[4] Jean Starobinski, "Le concepte de nostalgie," *Diogène*, 54 (1966): 92-115.

There are two aspects I would like to stress in the description of the causes of this particular illness: the pernicious obsession with everything that is familiar and the uncanny aspect, since the obsession leads to evoking ghosts and figures linked to home in an alien, unfamiliar environment, amongst strangers (cf. the German term, *Heimweh*). Nostalgia can thus be understood as the condition of dangerous and disquieted remembrance, caused by the senses of smell and hearing. In seventeenth-century medical treatises, the insurgence of such a perturbation provoking deep yearning is connected to *arias* (songs) or to the smell of a particular food. In the young conscripted soldiers, these songs evoked the longing for their faraway homeland with such strength that they had to be forbidden.

Nostalgia was thus considered a perturbation linked to a mnestic phenomenon. From this point of view, the theory of associative memory can be linked to nostalgia. In a letter of 20 January 1773 and in his *Dictionary of Music* (1779), Rousseau explains the effect these songs, in particular the ditty called *ranz-des-vaches*, had on the Swiss soldiers stationed in foreign lands: in this case the song "does not act precisely as music itself, but as a 'memorative sign.'"[5]

In the nineteenth century, when nostalgia becomes a recurring *topos* of poetry and literature, it expands to include a wide range of meanings and incorporate various semantic areas, from those linked to feelings to those connected with politics. The re-evaluation of the motherland during the Romantic period becomes pivotal to the actions for freedom and independence undertaken by exiles who had been forced, by political reasons, to leave their own countries. In this perspective, nostalgia is tied to the principle of nationalities and to modern forms of patriotism. It is not by chance that in Italy, in the *Vocabolario degli Accademici della Crusca* of 1832, nostalgia is defined as "the tormenting desire for one's distant motherland" and that Mazzini, in his writings, uses this term widely.[6]

When nostalgia enters the sphere of feeling, it acquires existential connotations that range from the Romantic notion of *spleen* to nostalgic *otiosity*. The object of nostalgic desire, the *elsewhere* as the native land or land of origin, appears in much Romantic European literature as an idealised and mythical place, an imaginary and utopian other place. The

---

[5] Jean-Jacques Rousseau, *Dictionary of Music*, trans. W. Waring (London: J. French, 1779), 267.

[6] Antonio Prete (ed.), *Nostalgia. Storia di un sentimento* (Milano: Raffaele Cortina, 1992).

Romantic era marks the beginning of the concept of "open nostalgia,"[7] a notion that highlights the paradoxical aspects of this feeling. Through the re-reading of the Ulysses myth, Jankélévitch suggests that one cannot be cured of nostalgia, because this desire for *elsewhere* triggers off in the traveller Ulysses a continuing and untiring search that homecoming, far from putting an end to, actually heightens: "Nostalgia oscillates between two regrets: the regret, from afar, of a lost fatherland; the regret, upon return, of missed adventures."[8] It is not possible to recover from nostalgia, because paradoxically it is the cause of its own cause, it is at the same time a cause and an effect: "The cause is contradictorily the effect of its own effect, and the effect the cause of its own cause; the *because* refers thus to the *why* and responds to the question with a question."[9]

There is an important twist in the concept of nostalgia in Kant's *Anthropologie in pragmatischer Hinsicht abgefaßt* (1798), where the object of nostalgia is not the physical place of origin any more, but youth itself that cannot be retrieved any longer, because it is lost forever. The object of desire is interiorised and, as Starobinski states, "[i]t is in his personal past that the nostalgic seeks to accomplish a movement of return."[10] The idea of an irretrievable time triggering the movement of remembrance and of regret thus creeps in. Nostalgia becomes a silent and painful dialogue with the haunting images of what has already been.

All the above suggests that nostalgia changes, from a disease, objectively described in the medical treatises of the seventeenth and eighteenth centuries, into a psychic state in the nineteenth century, and in the twentieth century it becomes an object of study for psychoanalysis. In the course of time, nostalgia has incorporated many semantic areas. As Antonio Prete reminds us, its object might be Ithaca, Eden, the pre-Babel tongue, childhood, good old times, bygone frugal habits, and, using a blatant oxymoron, even the future.[11] In the current usage, nostalgia normally has derogatory connotations, as it designates useless regret for an outdated social order or lifestyle.

Why is nostalgia a controversial feeling, a feeling that can arouse opposite responses? It has been compared to two-faced Janus exactly

---

7 This definition was introduced by Vladimir Jankélévitch in *L'irreversible et la nostalgie* (Paris: Flammarion, 1974).
8 Jankélévitch, *L'irreversible et la nostalgie*, 366.
9 *L'irreversible et la nostalgie*, 356.
10 Starobinski, "Le concepte de nostalgie," 115.
11 Prete, "L'assedio della lontananza," in *Nostalgia. Storia di un sentimento*, 17.

because of its oxymoronic characteristics. Two great myths of Western culture express its intrinsic ambivalence: on the one hand, the nostalgia of Ulysses who finds a conciliatory solution to his homecoming after endless peregrinations, on the other, the biblical character of Lot's wife who, because of her disobedience of the divine order not to look back, shall be turned into a pillar of salt.

Nostalgia, far from being a reassuring feeling, is a disquieting one, because it foregrounds the subject and its emotional involvement. Linda Hutcheon, trying to understand why certain "artefacts" of postmodern culture are at the same time nostalgic and ironic, points out the affinity between irony and nostalgia: "I want to argue that to call something ironic or nostalgic is, in fact, less a *description* of the ENTITY ITSELF than an *attribution* of a quality of RESPONSE."[12] As a result, nostalgia is not something perceived in the object, but rather it signals the feeling generated, the emotional reaction, when two distant temporal moments, past and present, are drawn close to each other. It is precisely because nostalgia always implies an "active attribution" on the part of the subject that it is "trans-ideological:" it is the subject that attributes a meaning, a political content to his/her attitude towards history and the past. From this point of view, the critique addressed to orthodox Marxist thinkers, such as Raymond Williams,[13] and Fredric Jameson,[14] has a strong ideological undertone, since they define nostalgia with derogatory adjectives, such as "reactionary," "escapist," "inauthentic," "unreflexive," and, above all, as a feeling fostering a simplification if not a falsification of history. To its detractors, nostalgia is reactionary, contrary to progress: "Nostalgia is to memory as kitsch is to art;"[15] a feeling that results in political detachment and a lack of responsibility towards history.

Instead, my working hypothesis – founded on the thought of Nietzsche, Benjamin and Bloch – aims to redefine and relocate this feeling by freeing it from the negative meanings that had made nostalgia a taboo to be repressed. The backdrop of what is currently termed "critical nostalgia" is the idea of history as non-linear and fragmented. Modernity has lost the certainties of continuity, identity and connection in the processes of recollection. The ideas, developed by Benjamin in his

---

[12] Hutcheon, "Irony, Nostalgia and the Postmodern," 5.

[13] Raymond Williams, *The Country and the City* (New York: Oxford University Press, 1974).

[14] Fredric Jameson, *The Seeds of Time* (New York: Columbia University Press, 1994).

[15] Charles Maier, "The End of Longing? Notes towards a History of Postwar German National Longing," a paper presented at the Centre for German and European studies, University of California at Berkeley in December 1995.

Theses on the Philosophy of History, clarify how much his position is in contrast to historicism and historical materialism and particularly to the idea that time appears as a "linear and rectilinear course" lacking qualitative leaps and unrepeatable emergencies. Against the social democratic conception of progress as a linear and unavoidable process, Benjamin pitches the image of a bewildered Angel, a kind of allegory of history, its gaze directed to the Past where ruins, unfulfilled hopes and happiness never found are still waiting, in a sense, for some sort of achievement. The Angel's nostalgia coincides with the dream of *another history*, with the hope for change.

Leo Spitzer sustains the positive role of nostalgia amongst Jewish refugees from Central Europe in Bolivia during the Second World War.[16] Referring to Maurice Halbwachs's studies, Spitzer revaluates nostalgia, since, by freeing individuals from the constraints of time, it allows them to select and appreciate not only the positive sides of the past, but also its unfulfilled opportunities. Nostalgia has a strong heuristic value because comparison between the past and the present stimulates the subject to find in the past potentialities and models in order to develop the future. Thus, the nostalgic gaze is not only "retrospective" but also "prospective."[17] It is important to stress that nostalgia functions as a kind of hinge, a bridge between personal and collective memory. Nostalgia, establishing a link between the 'I' of the present and its image in the past, plays a fundamental role in the reconstruction and maintaining of individual and collective identity. In this sense, the melancholic attitude differs from the nostalgic one: the former is essentially individualistic because it is centred on the melancholic individual's mood, while the latter can be construed as a feeling that ties the private to the public sphere. Consequently, nostalgia must go together with a critical vision; it must not mystify the past and create false idealisations. The meaning of nostalgia as a regressive escape to the past is underpinned by a static notion of memory because the retrospective gaze fixes the past in an idealised image. In a dynamic conception of the act of remembering, nostalgia assumes a different connotation, since it does not involve flying back towards the past, but rather retracing it in order to change the present.

---

[16] Leo Spitzer, "Back Through the Future: Nostalgic Memory and a Critical Memory in a Refugee from Nazism," in Mieke Bal, Jonathan Crew and Leo Spitzer (eds.), *Acts of Memory. Cultural Recall in the Present* (Hanover: University Press of New England, 1999), 87-104.

[17] Boym, *The Future of Nostalgia*, 41-49; see also Chapter 5.

Svetlana Boym distinguishes between two types of nostalgia: while "restorative nostalgia" emphasises return, the possibility of rebuilding the lost home and reconnecting the rifts of history, "reflective nostalgia" thrives on the concept of pain, desire and loss, and on the process of memory, which is always imperfect. Whereas in the course of history "restorative nostalgia" has assumed negative connotations, having been exploited by right-wing ideologies and employed by dangerous nationalisms, focused on the search for origins and lost homeland, "reflective nostalgia" is based, as the adjective indicates, on reflection: it is a critical meditation on the past and does not aim at retrieving it in its integrity.

"Critical nostalgia" does not include regressive and apocalyptic attitudes: rather, it is a critique of and a rebellion against the efficiency-based acceleration of time in capitalist society. In our postmodern era, nostalgia signals the desire for a different concept of time, an inner time which leaves room to think, reflect and build human relationships in everyday life.

Rereading history in the light of this meaning implies considering and illuminating not the master narratives of the twentieth century, but apparently marginal events, leaving the main roads in order to follow back alleys, not trailed by the winners of history, but by its losers. Benjamin's thought, and especially his concept of "remembrance" (*Eingedenken*), becomes central here because it focuses on the kind of memory dedicated to victims, to the oppressed, to those who apparently have left no trace, those swept away by history's 'triumphal chariot.' Thus, one can understand how nostalgia has played a central role in nations and cultures which have been, for historical reasons, crushed by hegemonic nations: in Eastern Europe and in Latin America, nostalgia has never been a mere artistic device, but a strategy for survival.

2.

Very few studies have attempted to investigate the relation between memory, nostalgia and utopia.[18] Unfortunately, the format of this article does not provide sufficient space for a thorough analysis of this line of

---

[18] Tom Moylan and Raffaella Baccolini (eds.), *Dark Horizons. Science Fiction and the Dystopian Imagination* (New York and London: Routledge, 2003); Vincent Geoghegan, "Ernst Bloch: Postsecular Thoughts," in Lawrence Wilde (ed.), *Marxism's Ethical Thinkers* (Basingstoke: Palgrave, 2001), 51-70.

thought in utopianism[19] that has highlighted the importance of memory as a repository of experience and value, maintaining that a society which is unable to remember has no hope for the future. In Bloch's thought, the link tying the past, the present and the future is produced by "emancipatory memory," memory not as simple recollection (*anamnesis*), but as recognition (*anagnorisis*) which involves judgement and leads to knowledge. According to Bloch, there is never a simple correspondence between past and present, and the power of the past resides in its complicated relationship of similarity/dissimilarity to the present. In order to become an active force and to acquire this "emancipatory function," memory must critically address the past and set up a dialogue that always departs from the present. As Tom Moylan puts it: "Memory helps to break hegemonic historical discourse, the master narratives that have managed to erase historical memory so that it is impossible to see that what is going on around us was not always the same."[20] Memory, then, like utopia, must be viewed not as a static unit, but a dynamic one, a process in continuous motion.

So, what is the link between utopia and nostalgia, what are their points of contact? Utopian and nostalgic tension are both born of a sense of unease, a critique of a present perceived to be unsatisfactory and inadequate. Both these attitudes are consequently dominated by desire. Utopian projects are born from the desire for a better world; in the same way, the nostalgic gaze is fuelled by the desire for a lost place or time. Utopia and nostalgia presuppose a spatial or temporal displacement: the utopian traveller experiences a sense of estrangement in the process of discovering *another* reality; similarly, the nostalgic visionary feels disoriented and dislocated during the reconstruction of the past. Movement backwards and forwards in time never occurs in a straight line but proceeds by leaps and bounds; nostalgic imagination is like the lens of a telescope, making people and places who really are far away seem very near in time and space. "Critical nostalgia" thrives on pain, which is an essential part of this complex feeling; it acquires cathartic value especially when the past is interwoven with traumatic and conflictual memories. As Boym rightly asserts: "Longing and critical thinking are not opposed to one another, as affective memories do not absolve one from compassion, judgement or critical reflection."[21] Thus,

---

[19] See Ernst Bloch, Theodor Adorno, Herbert Marcuse.
[20] Tom Moylan, *Scraps of the Untainted Sky: Science Fiction, Utopia, Dystopia* (Boulder: University of Colorado Press, 2000), 26.
[21] Boym, *The Future of Nostalgia*, 49-50.

the stimulus for change inevitably involves suffering because the critique of the past and of the present unavoidably brings pain.

3.

Before concluding, I would like to offer two examples of critical nostalgia: Ursula K. Le Guin's dystopia, *The Telling*,[22] and Marco Bellocchio's 2003 film *Buongiorno, Notte* contain elements of suffering, but also of utopian hope.

The Telling is a critical dystopia, a term that utopian scholars have chosen to characterise a series of fictions published since the end of the 1980s, after the fall of the Berlin Wall, in order to distinguish them from George Orwell's and Aldous Huxley's classical anti-utopias. Earlier twentieth-century anti-utopias were characterised by a totally negative outlook on the present and by a nostalgic, regressive vision of the past (see, for instance, the mythical Golden Country in Orwell's *1984*). Critical dystopias, although articulating a deconstructive reflection on our reality, present elements of utopian tension. Hence, this new dystopian writing is characterised by a hope of the unfulfilled, unachieved utopia, showing the reader a road that must start in the present, a dialectic that must begin from the here-and-now.

The Telling is pervaded by the nostalgia of the heroine Sutty, who travels far from Earth to study the newly discovered planet Aka whose culture has been erased while she was on her way there. Sutty feels a deep longing for the colours and smells of her home on Earth, for her loved ones and in particular for her deceased companion, Pao. But this painful nostalgia does not make her idealise and mythicise her past on Earth because – although she was happier due to the presence of her family and lover – she lived in a theocratic regime, dominated by violent fanaticisms and terrorism. Nostalgia, memory, and recollection of the Akan poem learned when she was young do not cause Sutty to withdraw into herself and give way to depression; instead they have a cathartic function because they reactivate her desire and hope. There are two central themes in *The Telling*: nostalgia as a link connecting individual and collective memory, and the word becoming a tale and thus developing into an essential tool to start the redeeming journey through memory. Sutty travels upriver to a remote mountain region where she finds the remnants of the suppressed culture, called The Telling, and having won the confidence of its people, she joins a pilgrimage to Silong, the sacred

---

[22] Ursula K. Le Guin, *The Telling* (New York: Harcourt Brace, 2000).

mountain where books and fragments of the suppressed culture are preserved. In order to understand the Akan past and to see how she can help in the preservation of its culture, Sutty must come to terms with her nostalgia, particularly the painful memories of her lover Pao. Sharing the pain of their past enables the inhabitants to reach a deeper understanding of themselves, their personal and collective histories. They engage in a utopian process of memory and storytelling that moves from a nostalgic recollection of their childhood homes through that of the loss of their loved ones and, ultimately, to an awareness and acceptance of responsibility.

Marco Bellocchio's controversial film is based only partly on *Il prigioniero* (The Captive), a memoir co-written by Anna Laura of the Italian Red Brigades and a journalist, Paola Tavella. *Buongiorno, Notte*, as the director himself has declared in many interviews, does not aim at a faithful historical reconstruction of such a complex moment of Italian history as terrorism and the Red Brigades, and in particular the fifty-five days of Aldo Moro's imprisonment after he was kidnapped. Rather, Marco Bellocchio wanted to tell his story "with the fervor of the possible, not the implacability of truth-telling."[23] The film portrays a sense of nostalgia for an irretrievable past. This past is not missed, yearned for or seen as better than the present; rather, a painful feeling is shown for a past that cannot be changed or for the suffering that cannot be eased: a nostalgia for what could have been. I choose to concentrate on the ending of the film because it contains, in my opinion, utopian elements, and the director has provocatively chosen a utopian ending.

Chiara, the character partly modelled on the *brigatist* Brighetti, is the only one who does not agree with her companions' decision to kill Moro. The director does not fully develop this point, but shows Chiara going to bed without locking the prisoner's door. In her dream, Chiara sees Moro leave his prison while the terrorists sleep, and at daybreak walk freely in the empty streets of Rome. But the following sequence shows Moro, blindfolded and escorted by three terrorists, about to be executed. The film concludes with the following sequence: the title, *Good Morning, Night*, appears in red script that evokes the infamous five-pointed red star of the Red Brigades, followed by real footage of Moro's funeral which shows a great number of Italian politicians who were more or less responsible for the line of no negotiation, and then comes a final image. Two elements contribute to opening up the utopian space in the film here: the extremely effective use of music and the final shot. The

---

[23] Elspeth Probyn, *Outside Belongings* (New York: Routledge, 1996), 116.

dream and the funeral are accompanied by the introduction of the famous Pink Floyd song "Shine on, You Crazy Diamond," with the crescendo of the music (the drums) coinciding with the end of the dream and the realisation of the politician's death (and the appearance of the title). While the images of the politicians of the time and of the Pope fade, the psychedelic, nostalgic, and haunting music of Pink Floyd fades as well, to be replaced, or nostalgically displaced by another sequence, accompanied by much lighter, utopian music of Schubert's "Moments Musicaux" Op. 94. The final image of Moro alive and free breaks away from the darkness of the film and of the time in which it takes place, thus representing a return to life, a realisation, though only imaginative, of not only a desire but an actual possibility of escaping from this blackness.

At the beginning of my essay, I asked why it was important to reconsider the concept of nostalgia and to propose a new notion of critical nostalgia. The notion of critical nostalgia can help us explain the bereavement felt for the traumatic past full of conflicts, the past which concerns all Europe and with which we must come to terms. In this context, critical nostalgia acquires an ethical dimension: only through the knowledge and evaluation of the past can memory acquire the utopian dimension that allows change.

CLOSENESS AND DISTANCE OF MEMORY TO JOAN OF ARC: A NATIONAL MYTH IN TRANSNATIONAL IMAGINED COMMUNITIES

Stephanie Wodianka

The myth of Joan of Arc is surely one of the best-known French national myths.[1] In France, schoolchildren become acquainted with it at an early age, through textbooks, and beyond French borders, Joan of Arc is a topic in German dramas[2] and Russian films,[3] in Japanese comics and in commercials for cosmetics,[4] as well as in characterizations of 'heroic-patriotic' female soldiers in the Iraq war.[5]

---

[1] Dietmar Rieger, "Jeanne d'Arc oder das engagierte Engagement," in K. Knabel, D. Rieger, S. Wodianka (eds.), *Nationale Mythen und kollektive Symbole. Funktionen, Konstruktionen und Medien der Erinnerung* (Göttingen: Vandenhoeck & Ruprecht, 2005), 177. For general information about Joan of Arc, see Régine Pernoud, Marie-Véronique Clin, *Jeanne d'Arc* (Paris: Fayard, 1986), and Gerd Krumeich, *Jeanne d'Arc in der Geschichte* (Sigmaringen: Jan Thorbecke Verlag, 1989).

[2] See, e.g., Friedrich Schiller's *Die Jungfrau von Orléans* (1801) and Bertolt Brecht's *Die Gesichte der Simone Machard* (1957).

[3] Gleb Panfilov, *Načalo* (1970).

[4] Stephanie Himmel, "Von der bonne Lorraine zum globalen magical girl. Wandlungen Jeanne d'Arcs in populären Medien," in Knabel, Rieger, Wodianka (eds.), *Nationale Mythen und kollektive Symbole*, 265-86.

[5] The US American soldier Jessica Lynch, who was taken hostage by Iraqis during the war in 2003, was declared a heroine on an American webpage and compared with Jeanne d'Arc – which led to protests, however, among some of her countrymen, who did not want to see 'her' put on a level with a mythical figure of 'Old Europe.' See www.windofchange.net/archives/003668.php and www.antiwar.com/gancarski/gan 111403.html).

But why is it that such an 'old' myth as that of Joan of Arc survives in 'modern' cultures of memory? How did it make it into our present, and what are its prospects for the future? There are at least two critical questions, two moments of doubt, in the face of the persistence of the mythic Pucelle: firstly, do myths not belong to the 'anachronistic' forms of memory that presuppose the existence of a cultural memory, which is no longer shared by anyone? These forms had, or have, the role of transmitting norms and commitments, and yet they tend towards the miraculous, having not reasoning but narration as their principle.[6] And secondly, how does an old *national* myth persist in modern cultures of memory, where phrases such as 'our common European house' and 'the global village' are perhaps more widespread than flag-waving and chanting of a national anthem? What happens to a national myth at a time when the nation as a community of identification is combined or even confronted with the idea of Europe or other transnational contexts, and when their recipients are European citizens and global players? I would like to address these questions through a comparative analysis of Joan of Arc – comparative insofar as I will look for the common features in mythical re-narrations at the millennium, in order to offer an explanation as to how and why this myth has survived in modern cultures of memory, within and beyond the borders of France, in literature and film.

Against the first reservation that mythical forms of narration and memory are not of current concern, it has to be said that myths obviously remain in fashion, now, at the time of, and after, the millennium. Besides Joan of Arc, there is Arthur and the Knights of the Round Table, Merlin and the quest for the Holy Grail, which people are encouraged to see in supersized movies and read about in bestsellers – see, for instance, the recent American-Irish movie *King Arthur*.[7] Within these contemporary re-narrations in literature and film, there are some features, or tendencies, that I would like to highlight, using Joan of Arc as an example. These features indicate that the two critical doubts mentioned above are not mere phantasms of cultural pessimism; and that mythical narrative and memory at the time of the millennium react and respond to these doubts.

Firstly, as far as the relation of myth and history is concerned, a historicization of the Joan of Arc myth is apparently taking place. This

---

[6] Harald Weinrich, "Structures narratives du mythe," *Revue poétique*, 1 (1970): 25-34.

[7] Antoine Fuqua, *King Arthur: The Truth behind the Legend* (USA/Ireland: Touchstone Pictures / Jerry Bruckheimer Films, 2004).

phenomenon not only leads to the problem of conceptualizing the difference between history and myth,[8] but also raises questions about the functions of this hybrid mode of memory.

Secondly, although the common categorization of myths as cultural memory is accurate in some respect for the re-narrations of the Joan of Arc myth, some observations show characteristic features of communicative memory.[9] There are signs that the modern and contemporary representations of the Pucelle myth have to be classified as hybrid forms of memory in this respect, too.

Thirdly, a prevalence of the themes of time and time concepts in the mythical narratives surrounding Joan of Arc in contemporary literature and film is notable. At first sight, these only seem to be the consequences of common modern or postmodern trends.[10] Yet, I would like to show that they are in fact, beyond the cliché, a phenomenon specific to Joan of Arc. This phenomenon may provide insight into the relation of time, myth, and memory; moreover, it can be linked to the hybridity of the Joan of Arc myth.

The last part of this essay presents my model of closeness of memory and distance of memory, which will help to describe and explain the function of these three phenomena. It is based on the presumption that cultures of memory[11] are "imagined communities" insofar as members will never know most of their fellow-members, yet in the minds of each lives the image of their communion.[12] This constitutive

---

[8] See, e.g., Jan Assmann, *Das kulturelle Gedächtnis. Schrift, Erinnerung und politische Identität in frühen Hochkulturen* (Munich: Beck, 1992), 56, who declares that "[...] im kulturellen Gedächtnis faktische Geschichte in erinnerte und damit in Mythos transformiert wird. Mythos ist eine fundierende Geschichte, eine Geschichte, die erzählt wird, um eine Gegenwart vom Ursprung her zu erhellen. [...] Durch Erinnerung wird Geschichte zum Mythos. Dadurch wird sie nicht unwirklich, sondern im Gegenteil erst Wirklichkeit im Sinne einer fortdauernden normativen und formativen Kraft." See also Ernst Cassirer, "Das mythische Denken," in *Gesammelte Werke*, ed. B. Recki, 15 vols. (Hamburg: Felix Meiner, 2002), 12:125, 130.

[9] See Assmann, *Das kulturelle Gedächtnis*, 56, where the terms "cultural memory" and "communicative memory" are defined.

[10] See, e.g, Ursula K. Heise, *Chronoschisms. Time, Narrative and Postmodernism* (New York: Columbia University Press, 1997).

[11] Cf. the "Collaborative Research Centre 'Cultures of Memory'" ("Sonderforschungs-bereich 434 'Erinnerungskulturen'") at the Justus-Liebig-Universität Gießen. The members of the interdisciplinary research centre chose the term 'cultures of memory' in order to accentuate the plurality and dynamics of memory (www.uni-giessen.de/erinnerungskulturen).

[12] Benedict Anderson, *Imagined Communities. Reflections on the Origin and Spread of Nationalism* (London and New York: Verso, 1998), Chapter 1.

fact of 'imagination' recurs in the individual member's awareness of closeness and distance of memory in a temporal, identificatory and modal dimension that will be differentiated according to the model.

In the following, I would like to comment on the three above-mentioned observations concerning representations of the Joan of Arc myth, that is: 1. its position between myth and history; 2. its position between cultural and communicative memory; and 3. the recurrence of the themes of time and concepts of time.

It is possible to speak about the historization of the Joan of Arc myth insofar as in many of its representations around the millennium, special consideration is given to the history 'behind' the myth, and there is an emphasis on staging it in a way that appears to be historical and even historiographical. Of course, the assurance to tell 'not only a myth' is one of the topoi of mythical re-narration. Following Roland Barthes, it might be said that the belief in the truth of the myth, or in the representation of the myth, are constitutive of any mythopoiesis.[13] However, the features described go further because they obviously seem to have lost the trust typical of myth in the convincing power of tradition and collective faith, and instead prefer the rational or logical reasoning of historical discourse. This is done, for instance, by including footnotes into the text of a novel that point out the 'objective truth,' or the historical verifiability of the production process of the literary description of Joan of Arc.[14] Furthermore, timetables, geographical maps, genealogical trees or other historiographical documents are integrated as scholarly tools into the literary text,[15] as well as learned remarks reflecting on the inaccuracy of competing 'wrong' representations of the mythical story.[16] Eventually, it is also the references to the author's professional authority in prefaces and on book covers that reveal his or her academic work on the Middle Ages in general, and on Joan of Arc in particular as the incentive and legitimation of literary production.[17] Recently, a growing number of historians and

---

[13] Roland Barthes, "Le mythe, aujourd'hui," in *Mythologies* (Paris: Éditions du Seuil,1957), 265ff.

[14] See, e.g., Colette Beaune, *Jeanne d'Arc* (Paris: Perrin, 2004).

[15] Pierre Moinot, *Jeanne d'Arc. Le pouvoir et l'innocence* (Paris: Flammarion, 1988).

[16] Florence Trystram, *Moi, Jeanne obéissance* (Paris: Flammarion, 1984).

[17] E.g., Paul Mourousy, *Jeanne d'Arc et son double* (Paris: Éditions du Rocher, 2003).

professors of literature seem to be earning extra income through the literarization of their academic publications.

These phenomena, which may also be observed with regard to other myths, such as King Arthur,[18] acquire an additional significance in the case of Joan of Arc. The self-doubting, self-reflecting dimension of the representation of myth is specific to the Joan of Arc myth, insofar as critical inquiry, calling into question, and self-observation are already part of the myth's inventory.[19] The reflections of Joan's contemporaries upon her trustworthiness stand at the beginning of the distancing and self-reflexive dimension of the Joan of Arc myth. The virginity test in Poitiers, her secret signs of veracity for Charles in Chinon, the natural and supernatural explanations of her 'voices,' the contested motivations for her burning, and the re-interpretation of Joan by the Church (burning, reconciliation, and sainthood) all show that the calling into question of Joan is one of the integral parts of the myth's inventory.

The second observation, the hybrid character of the Joan of Arc myth, results from the attempt to describe mythical re-narration and its function in terms of cultural memory. Although this category seems to provide promising lines of interpretation to explain the obvious popularity of the Pucelle beyond French borders, as it succeeds in pointing in the right direction, there is always a caveat, a 'yes but,' to be inserted. Recent films and novels with the Joan theme, for instance, are mythical narratives that embody the features of cultural memory, as is proper for myths, according to Jan Assmann.[20] They are set in a remote temporal horizon. Commonly, the temporal frame is unspecific, the dates in the Middle Ages are blurred, for instance, through the lack of fixed temporal points of reference, or through a retrospective opening of the temporal horizon into the past. One example of this is the connection of the Joan myth with 'pre-myths,' such as the mythical narrative on the sorcerer Merlin, for instance in the film *The Messenger: The Story of Joan of Arc* by the Francocanadian Christian Duguay (1999). A further indication of the subsumption under cultural memory is that the texts on the book covers and textual passages in films commonly claim that Joan of Arc and her companions are old acquaintances, whom

---

[18] See, e.g., the triology of the novels entitled *Merlin, Arthur* and *Morgane* (Paris: Éditions du Seuil, 1989-2001) by Michel Rio, and Michel Zink, *Déodat ou la transparence: un roman du Graal* (Paris: Éditions du Seuil, 2002).

[19] On the term the "inventory of myth," see Claude Lévi-Strauss, "La structure des mythes," in Claude Lévi-Strauss, *Anthropologie structurale* (Paris: Éditions du Seuil, 1958), 242.

[20] Assmann, *Das kulturelle Gedächtnis*, 56.

everybody knows or should know.[21] On the other hand, certain
characteristics of cultural memory are absent, or run contrary to it, for
example, the untypical abstention from hegemony and exclusiveness, and
the defusing of the tension between competing memories – as in the
novel *Jehanne* by Violaine Bèrot, where the author constantly remarks on
the constructed nature of the mythical story,[22] as in *La conjuration de Jeanne*
by Michel de Grèce who speculates carefully "Et si c'était vrai?"[23] or in
Florence Trystram's novel *Moi, Jeanne obéissance*, which is preceded by the
remark that Jeanne's 'truth' is "peut-être introuvable, à tout de moins
variable avec les époques."[24] What is striking here is a lack of
commitment, which is rather unusual for cultural memory and goes
together with an element of self-reflection of the process of
remembering. Also, normative demands are reduced or passed over,
while a staging of a 'generally human' experience, which is not at all
exclusive, takes place. This allows the recipient to make the connection
with his or her own experience, and recalls the characteristics of
communicative memory; it appears as if the recipient were really an old
friend or buddy of Jeanne's, a member of a band of brothers or sisters.
This phenomenon was already very explicit in Otto Preminger's film
Saint Joan (USA, 1957), and particularly in the Russian film *Načalo* (1970)
by Gleb Panfilov, and in the French movie *Jeanne la Pucelle* by Jacques
Rivette (1994).

    As to the third point, the themes of time and concepts of time, it is
notable that in many recent adaptations of the Joan of Arc myth, Jeanne
is characterized through her problematic relation with time which
collides with other concepts of time, and not only in the sense of the
modern or postmodern trend. This is another common feature in the
national and the transnational or even 'global' formation of this myth.
Time is the "maître mot," as it is called in the novel *Moi, Jeanne
obéissance.*[25] Similarly, the protagonist in Luc Besson's international
blockbuster *Joan of Arc* (France, 1999) is driven towards her mission not
by voices but by various experiences of time (subjective temporal planes
articulated through acceleration and other technical effects) and, most
recently, the British production, not yet completed, *Jeanne d'Arc – Fille de*

---

[21] Mourousy, *Jeanne d'Arc et son double* and Roger Caratini, *Jeanne d'Arc. De Domrémy à
    Orléans et du bûcher à la légende* (Paris: L'Archipel, 1999).
[22] Violaine Bèrot, *Jehanne* (Paris: Éditions Denoël, 1995).
[23] Michel de Grèce, *La conjuration de Jeanne* (Paris: XO Éditions, 2002).
[24] Trystram, *Moi, Jeanne obéissance*, dédicace.
[25] *Moi, Jeanne obéissance*, 159. Subsequent page references are given in the text.

Dieu by Ellis Sanford advertises on its elaborate Internet home page that it offers "[...] a truly remarkable story […] which totally replaces all concepts of [...] time."[26]

Trystram's novel *Moi, Jeanne obéissance* might give the reader the impression that Jeanne's story is less driven by the fight against the English who threaten France than by the conflict with competing concepts of time. Jeanne is constantly concerned with thoughts about time. Jeanne's fight is less a fight against the English occupiers than a fight with or against time – the obstacles she faces are systematically made manifest as conflicting concepts of time. When she exclaims "Il n'est plus temps" and drives her companions to move, others intervene: "Laissez-leur le temps." (180) Conversely, when others think that the day for battle has come, Jeanne must be urged: "Venez, Jeanne, il est temps. Nos hommes nous attendent." (183) Thus, Jeanne herself recognizes her failure as a failure against time: "J'ai marché à la tête d'une armée merveilleuse, animée d'une foi telle qu'elle a pu, un moment, renverser le cours du temps. J'ai cru que ce serait possible." (181) While Jeanne, pressed for time, conceives the salvation of France a task of the present, Charles states: "La force de ma couronne est dans le temps qu'elle me donne. Le temps. Voilà le maître mot. [...] La France a le temps, si vous-mêmes ne croyez pas l'avoir. [...] La France, vous dis-je, a le temps." (159ff) According to Charles, after the fall of Orléans and his own coronation, Jeanne's time is now over. He dismisses her: "Jeanne est seulement arrivée à temps." (161) Jeanne's fate, so is his judgment, may now be resigned to the course of time: "Laissons faire le temps, amusons-la [Jeanne] avec quelques escarmouches, l'hiver n'est plus loin, où il faudra bien interrompre les combats, et au printemps prochain nous verrons mieux où nous en sommes." (163) In putting his trust in cyclical time, he declares Jeanne's time pressures and her attempt to 'reverse the times' meaningless and aberrant. Yet, Jeanne's final defeat at the stake in her fight against time only occurs on the surface, only seems to be the end. The mythical memory which is given form in the novel and which is carried by the recipient retroactively shows Jeanne's reversed clocks to have the right time.

In Luc Besson's film *Jeanne d'Arc* with Milla Jovovich, John Malkovich, and Dustin Hoffmann, there, too, are time contrasts which are articulated aesthetically and reflect the conflicts between different time concepts. Like the novel referred to above, it is also a French product, but one that addresses a transnational audience. The film was

---

[26] www.darc-queste.com.

shot in English, dubbed in French and German, and subtitled in more than 15 languages. Through the aesthetic means of the cinema, Jeanne is given her own time and an individual time consciousness.[27] Her 'voices' and visions normally begin with an image of ringing bells. This does not only call up an element of the mythical story, but also marks the boundary of an alternative temporal plane. This plane is articulated through acceleration and other technical effects, as Jeanne's subjective and anachronistic experience of time. Flashbacks allow the recipient to experience Jeanne's spatial and temporal disorientation; the sensation of a storm, rushing sounds, and rapidly moving clouds enable him to experience the accelerated time. They also emphasize the threatening nature of these temporal disharmonies between Jeanne's time and real time, and are moreover accompanied by musical disharmonies. In all of this Jeanne does not appear to be the one who controls this different form of time but instead to be thrown into a temporal maelstrom to which she has to submit. In her conversation with Charles at Chinon, Jeanne recalls and describes this experience of time and emphasizes the "fierce wind." She finds herself overwhelmed by the speed of things around her that is in stark contrast with her own immobility, which she experiences as threatening. In this scene, several of the temporal experiences of her life are presented in succession. The Christ figure ages during these encounters with Jeanne, and yet exhibits an impressive "presence" ("Il était si présent.").

These observations, too, cannot be reduced to the generic modern or postmodern trend because the theme and problematization of time are found in the myth of the Pucelle itself. The story of Joan of Arc implies elements dealing with time, time concepts, and time consciousness that appear to be inscribed in the myth itself, seem to be inherent. To name but a few, there is Jeanne's fascination for the ringing of the church bells, and her almost insatiable need for confession, which constantly sets off temporal retrospection. There are also Merlin's prophecies that France will be driven to misery by a woman and that it will be saved by a woman; these create a specific relationship between the past and the future in which they become interconnected and interwoven. As well, Jeanne's contacts with the heavenly 'transtemporal' voices point to her participation in another time. Also of significance are the endings of several parts of her mythical story: as they become turning points, points where fate and the times are turning, they also become the

---

[27] Luc Besson, *Jeanne d'Arc* (France: G.C.T.H.V., 1999), 47:20-51:50; 122:40-126:40; 203:20-206:00.

starting points for interpreting the past in retrospect and for future propositions. Such points are the end of the siege of Orléans, the disappearance of the voices at Paris, the stake, and sainthood. Last not least, the positioning of Joan at the threshold between the Middle Ages and Early Modern Times is one of the aspects that exhibit the mythical figure's special relationship to time.

But how are the three above phenomena related to the questions raised at the beginning of this essay? In what way are they evidence that the most recent re-narrations of the Joan of Arc myth take up and share the doubts about the place of old myths in modern cultures of memory, and the doubts about the meaning of national myths for imagined communities in the European, transnational, and global spheres?[28]

To answer this question, and to describe and clarify these connections, it may be helpful to use the model of closeness and distance of memory, which will be presented in the following. It takes some basic assumptions of recent cultural memory research as its starting point and develops them further with regard to the constitution and transformation of "imagined communities." According to Jan Assmann, it is especially the temporal structure that separates the cultural memory from the communicative memory.[29] While the communicative memory reaches back to a recent past, comprising no more than 80-100 years, the contents of the cultural memory are placed within a far-reaching temporal horizon: they are part of the 'absolute past' of mythical times. Astrid Erll has adjusted this model by drawing attention to a crucial point: she maintains that the criterion that allows a distinction between cultural and communicative frames of remembering is "not so much measurable time, the temporal distance of remembered events from the present in which the act of remembering takes place, but rather the kind of memory produced, the collective ideas about the meaning of the remembered events and about its location within temporal processes."[30]

---

[28] See also Dietmar Rieger, "Nationalmythos und Globalisierung. Der Sonderfall 'Jeanne d'Arc,'" in G. Oesterle (ed.), *Erinnerungskulturen interdisziplinär: kulturhistorische Problemfelder und Perspektiven* (Göttingen: Vandenhoeck & Ruprecht, 2005).

[29] Assmann, *Das kulturelle Gedächtnis*, 52; Jan Assmann, "Collective memory and Cultural Identity," in *New German Critique*, 65: 125-33.

[30] Astrid Erll, *Gedächtnisromane. Literatur über den Ersten Weltkrieg als Medium englischer und deutscher Erinnerungskulturen in den 1920er Jahren* (Trier: ELCH, 2003), 49: "[...] nicht die meßbare Zeit, der zeitliche Abstand der erinnerten Ereignisse von der Gegenwart des Erinnerungsaktes, sondern die Art der Erinnerung, die kollektive Vorstellung von der

Thus, the distinction between the two modes is "not based on a temporal structure (a universal, measurable category of observation) in the first place, but instead on a specific awareness of time (a culturally and historically variable phenomenon of collective mentalities)."[31]

The model of distance and closeness of memory augments these categories of cultural memory and communicative memory, which are distinguished through time (Jan Assmann) or better through the subjective time consciousness (Astrid Erll). It relates the distinctive feature of cognitive closeness or distance not only to the time consciousness of the subject of memory in his or her relation to the object of memory (as it is inherent in Assmann's theory of cultural memory), but also applies the two other dimensions of the constellation of remembering (see the scheme below). Closeness of memory and distance of memory are used as relevant categories for investigating the relation between the subject of memory and the process of remembering, and the relation between different subjects of memory (e.g. intra- as well as extra-literary). Thus, the terms "closeness of memory" and "distance of memory" imply not only a temporal but also a modal and an identificatory aspect. Thereby, the scheme permits firstly to differentiate between three dimensions that constitute the 'imaginative aspect' of cultures of memory as imagined communities: the vivid image of the past in each member of their communion is based on a subjective awareness of distance and/or closeness of memory in a temporal, modal and identificatory sense, that is imagined as shared with the other members. Secondly, the model makes it possible to visualize "hybrid" forms of memory – like the re-narrations of the Joan of Arc myth – that cannot be adequately described using the categories already at hand, and which seem to characterize imagined communities between national and transnational contexts.

Bedeutung des Erinnerten und von seiner Einbettung in zeitliche Prozesse." (My translation.)

[31] "[...] nicht in erster Linie auf der Zeitstruktur (eine universale, meßbare Beobachterkategorie), sondern auf dem Zeitbewußtsein (ein kulturell und historisch variables Phänomen der mentalen Dimension der Kultur)." Erll, *Gedächtnisromane*, 49. (My translation.)

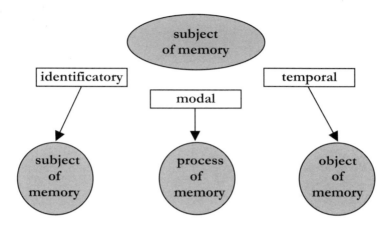

SCHEME: *"Closeness of Memory / Distance of Memory"*

Concerning the aspect "between myth and history" mentioned above, I would like to argue as follows: myth and history – as may be illustrated by the model – are two different forms of memory which imply different constellations of closeness or remoteness of memory in relation to the subjects, objects, and processes of remembering. Myths are characterized by the fact that, on the one hand, their object of memory is located in the temporal or transtemporal remote horizon,[32] but, on the other hand, they are brought into the proximity, the closeness of memory, into the present through repetition and actualization;[33] their meaning is experienced in the present, is being made present[34] (we can call this an 'elastic arrow'). Recipients participating in the myth are, as remembering subjects, in a known closeness of memory to each other; this results in the potential for the foundation of collective identity that is specific to myths.[35] Myths are also characterized by an extremely small distance of memory between the remembering subjects and the process of remembering. Only those who 'believe' in the myth,

---

[32] Assmann, *Das kulturelle Gedächtnis*, 59.

[33] Dietmar Rieger, Stephanie Himmel, Stephanie Wodianka, "Heilige, Nationalheldin und Superwoman – die Gesichter der Jeanne d'Arc. Zum Platz eines alten Mythos in einer neuen Erinnerungskultur," *Spiegel der Forschung. Wissenschaftsmagazin der Justus-Liebig-Universität Gießen*, 2 (2003): 146-53.

[34] Barthes, *Mythologies*, 265ff.

[35] See Andreas Dörner, *Politischer Mythos und symbolische Politik. Sinnstiftung durch symbolische Formen am Beispiel des Hermannmythos* (Opladen: Westdeutscher Verlag, 1995).

who do not decipher it as symbolic, really take part in it.[36] Historical, or historiographical, memory has to be located at the other end of the scale. It is based on the explicitly stated, supposedly 'objective' distance to the subject of memory, on the relativizing positioning of the self in relation to other subjects engaged in historiography, and on the methodical self-reflecting distance to the mode of remembering. This historical or even historiographical memory is also characterized by the stasis of the temporal closeness or distance. Indeed, the temporal arrow can be either long or short – this depends on the objective measurable distance to the historical event – but the arrow is never 'elastic,' because historical memory does not imply the subjective awareness of time that characterizes mythic memory.

Applying the concepts of closeness and distance of memory, the observed historicization of the Joan of Arc myth could be described as follows: by integrating 'scientific' footnotes, historiographic tables, and lists of the author's credentials in medieval studies into the text, the closeness between the remembering subject and the process of memory that is specific to myth is (at least for a time) suspended and weakened. The process of remembering as such is brought to attention; the recipient is placed at some critical distance from it. Thus, tension is created between extra-literary reality and intra-literary illusion: despite historiographical or scientific 'objectivity,' the text continues to be read as fiction. This tension in turn carries some semantic surplus value, because ultimately, the myth's mythifying effect is actually enhanced: the short-term historization makes the recipient 'believe' more intensively in the myth; the closeness to the process of memory is even enhanced in the long term.

Furthermore, the weakening and calling into question of norms and commitments, which is rather untypical of cultural memory, creates a distance of memory between the subject and the process of memory, through self-reflection. This modal distance of memory, on the other hand, may create a greater closeness between the intended subjects of memory. It will then serve the purpose of identification; it turns the novel's readers into an imagined community. The recipients find themselves (and maybe also the novel's narrative voice) united in a posture of self-reflexive, critical remembering – a posture which may make the anachronistic forms and objects of cultural memory bearable, and even attractive again. Thus, the power of myth today depends less on the original mode of mythical memory (authoritative values, non-

---

[36] Barthes, *Mythologies*, 265ff.

rational belief in myth). This lack, however, is at least partially compensated by the shared critical distance from the remembering process, which performatively creates a new, reflecting mode of remembering. The experience of the 'how' of remembering, as a reflexive mode, replaces the lost 'foundation-giving' certainty of the mythical content, thus creating modal and identificatory closeness.

The diminishing of normative, traditional commitments and the emphasis on the fictitious experience of generally human emotions and everyday situations may also be understood in terms of the closeness or distance of memory. When it is no longer possible to achieve the closeness necessary for cultural memory through exclusive norms and traditional common values (because the recipients of the novel or the film do not belong to one nation or culture, for instance), this lack is compensated by a closeness that is produced in a performative way in the act of reception itself. In literature and film, this may be achieved through strategies specific to the medium – strategies, for example, which heighten the effect of illusion (e.g., technical effects in Hollywood movies, or narrative techniques). These effects enhance, at least to some extent, the modal closeness of memory, that is, the closeness of the remembering subject to the remembering process. The set-up within the medium as such does not come into focus. General human feelings, pity, shared joy, shared suspense and excitement with Joan of Arc and with the entire intended circle of recipients create the basis for a common experience that in turn can be remembered as one's 'own experience' of the myth, in the sense of communicative memory.[37]

The third phenomenon, the prevalence of themes of time and time consciousness and their problematization, can also be related to the model of the closeness or distance of memory. On the one hand, the arrow that designated the temporal distance becomes the object of reflection. To the extent that the problematic time consciousness of the mythical figure Jeanne is used to characterize her, the recipient's own relation to the time of the myth can be associated, reflected upon, and 'co-remembered' – even (or especially) when it has indeed become problematic to share the typical twofold temporal experience of myth: its positioning in the remote horizon and its 'experience as present'. Consequently, 'time's arrow' becomes one of the myth's objects of memory. The remembered aspect of the myth that calls into question and problematizes Jeanne's consciousness of time thus moves closer to the recipient's memory and experience – he or she experiences this

---

[37] See Erll, *Gedächtnisromane*, 64.

object of memory on his/her own: the arrow, i.e., the distance between remembering subject and remembered object is diminished. And finally, the closeness of memory that is the foundation of identity typical of myths, between the myth's recipients as the subjects of memory, is created through an experience of time shared with Joan. This experience compensates for the formerly shared temporal relation of the remembering subjects to the mythical figure in her position in the remote horizon (in the sense of cultural memory) – a relation that has become doubtful to or even sometimes contested by the European, transnational or even global recipients and the (diverse) imagined communities they form.

We can summarize that firstly, the concepts of closeness and distance of memory in their three dimensions (temporal, modal and identificatory) help to describe how an old national myth is able to persist in transnational cultures of memory as imagined communities. The model illustrates the potentials and mechanisms of flexibility and compensation necessary to create or to confirm a living image of the communion between members of imagined communities which transcend national borders. Secondly, the modifications and shifts of the arrows demonstrated in the model are the expression and result of the doubts and self-doubts expressed in the critical questions at the beginning, concerning the relevance of (national) myths in modern, transnational cultures of memory. The re-narrations of the decades around the millennium (not only those that address an intellectual audience, but also those directed at mass audiences, like Luc Besson's film) reflect the awareness that national myths are not obsolete, but must be told and remembered differently today, because their recipients are (multiple) members[38] of imagined communities which are not 'only' national ones. The typical myth-specific constellation of the closeness and distance of memory must obviously be changed, compensated or reached by alternative means, as I have attempted to describe by means of my model. This is necessary because a reliable, predictable cultural memory, an unproblematic acceptance of the national model as well as the uninterrupted acceptance of mythical forms of remembering for the intended audiences have become less likely. Yet in the face of the numbers of mythical stories sold in the form of bestselling novels or blockbuster movies, there still seems to be a need to remember

---

[38] Cf. the contribution of Aleida Assmann in this volume.

mythically, as part of an imagined community, whether one is French or not.

The myth of Joan of Arc satisfies this need particularly well, because the self-doubting, self-reflexive moment and Jeanne's specific relation to time are part of the myth itself. The hybridity of the myth's re-narrations between myth and history, between cultural and communicative memory, and between temporal, identificatory and modal closeness and distance of memory is not merely a gratuitous postmodern play but is inscribed into the myth of Joan of Arc itself. The adaptation to the need of modern cultures of memory does not lead to the end of the myth, in the sense of a de-mythification, but instead allows it to transcend national and cultural boundaries and distances.

SLAVONIC COSMOGONIC MYTH AS A MATRIX FOR ENCODING MEANINGS[1]

Anna Brzozowska-Krajka

To paraphrase Gerardus van der Leeuw's idea: to understand myth means to penetrate to the hidden structures through which humans perceive and interpret reality.[2] The mythical system and its constituent representations enable comprehension of general laws governing the order of the universe, breaking through to archaic visions of being. They serve to establish relations of homology between natural and social conditions (e.g., interaction between an individual and social heritage), and precisely to define the law of balance of multi-layered opposites. These contradictions form a semantic chain connected by the principles of opposition, correlation or analogy. The proto-source of all these is the paradigm of cosmogony which reflects the mythical act of creation, the process of structuring and the formation of the ordered world from its chaotic proto-state, achieved through violation of pre-creational unity of all things, when light was separated from darkness, and night and day were formed, and when the world saw the light of day for the first time.

---

[1] This article is based on Chapter II ("The cosmogonic myth and the folkloric opposition of Night-Day") of my book *Polish Traditional Folklore. The Magic of Time*, trans. Wiesław Krajka (Boulder: East European Monographs; Lublin: Maria Curie-Skłodowska University; New York: Columbia University Press, 1998).

[2] G. van der Leeuw, "L'homme primitif et la religion," quoted after R. Tomicki, "Słowiański mit kosmogoniczny," *Etnografia Polska* (1976) 1:47.

In Polish and Slavonic folklore, the principal explanatory function attributed to the structure of the fundamental myth[3] (both as officially accepted Judeo-Christian cosmogony and as syncretic cosmogonic myths, formed at least partly from original elements of Christian religion or their transformations) leads to distinguishing the basic binary oppositions that originate in the dual nature of the Slavonic cosmogonic myth.

The antagonism of the two creators – God and the Devil – is an instrument of semantic differentiation of various levels of reality, and thus the whole process of creation rests essentially on establishing this dichotomic classification. The God-Devil oppositions can be represented as follows, creating a mythical 'Mendeleyev table:'[4]

	GOD	DEVIL
ELEMENTS	heavenly fire	cosmic waters
SPACE	up	down
	east	west
	right	left
TOPOGRAPHY	plains	mountains
TIME	day	night
	morning	evening
	summer	winter
SUPERNATURAL BEINGS	Archangel Michael or Elijah (angels)	devils (demons)
STATES OF BEING	metaphysical life (immortality)	metaphysical death (eternal death)
COLOURS	white	black
	light	dark
NUMBERS	odd	even
ETHICAL VALUES	good	evil
QUALITIES	fertility (arable land)	barrenness (waste land)
	functionality	non-functionality
	intelligence	stupidity

---

[3] See, e.g., E. Mieletinski, *Poetyka mitu*, trans. J. Dancygier (Warszawa: Państwowy Instytut Wydawniczy, 1981), 288 and passim.

[4] On the application of the concept of the Mendeleyev table to anthropological studies of Polish folk culture, see L. Stomma, *Antropologia kultury wsi polskiej XIXw.* (Warszawa: Instytut Wydawniczy PAX, 1986), 151-203. In this article, I applied this concept to mythical ordering of the universe.

FLORA	useful plants	useless plants
	edible plants	poisonous plants
FAUNA	domesticated animals	wild animals
	edible animals	inedible animals
ANTHROPOLOGY	humans	demons
AND SOCIOLOGY	insiders	outsiders
	man	woman
COSMOLOGY	heaven	earth
	earth	underworld
ASTRONOMY	sun	moon

The above list of elementary semantic oppositions has a paradigmatic character and makes it possible to describe the universe (its various levels) in dualistic categories.[5] The construction of the mythical 'Mendeleyev table,' i.e., a set of evaluating binary oppositions of the cosmogonic myth, reveals universal, archetypal, paradigmatic mental structures inherent in texts of both folklore and literature of particular Slavonic cultures. One of these oppositions – Night vs. Day – will be considered in detail here to disclose a fundamental dualism in nature: darkness vs. light and the symbolic moral opposition of evil vs. good along with all their attendant qualities correlated in a series of equivalent notions.

The dialectic of night and day constitutes the basis of human existence. Humans perceive and interpret the world in terms of a set of categories that guarantee the success of their actions and create the most profound level of their life. The cosmogonic myth about separation of light from darkness, about the creation of day and night, performs the function of such a symbolic universe, regulating and sanctioning nature. This myth provides the assumptions for the semantics of registered symbolic actions, the logical model for resolving contradictions manifest in folkloric texts-behaviors that are key forms of psychosocial expression.[6] This interpretative essence of myth derives from its nature

---

[5] R. Tomicki, "Religious Dualism in the Slavic Cosmogonic Myth," in J. Burszta (ed.), *Poland at the Tenth International Congress of Anthropological and Ethnological Sciences*, trans. J. Sehnert (Wrocław: Ossolineum, 1978), 61.

[6] See, e.g. H. Podbielski, *Mit kosmogoniczny w "Teogonii" Hezjoda* (Lublin: Katolicki Uniwersytet Lubelski, 1978); R. Tomicki, "Słowiański mit kosmogoniczny," *Etnografia Polska*, (1976). 1:47-97; Tomicki, "Religious Dualism," 59-67; Mircea Eliade, *The Myth of the Eternal Return*, trans. W.R. Trask, Bollingen Series XLVI (New York: Bollingen Foundation, 1954); V.N. Toporov, "Kosmogonicheskiye mify," in *Mify narodov mira*, ed.

as a secondary modeling system that produces its own system of designata, notions and values: not as a copy but as a model of the world.[7] As such, it interprets, orders, organizes and creates the reality surrounding humans. The cosmogonic myth also constitutes a kind of language that communicates a specific vision of the universe. As a secondary modeling system, it is a complex composition: it is created through superimposing a number of interrelated structures (religious, ideological, magical, ethical, social, etc.) on the natural language. This conglomerate of sign systems comprises many strata: from the micro-sphere of *anthropos* to the macro-sphere of *cosmos*. Its meanings arise from mutual internal coding of these sign systems as well as their external coding with systems situated outside the myth.

The symbolism of the alternation of night and day, as a set of constant qualities derived from the observation of the interplay of cosmic powers, comprises antithetical meanings (see the proverb: "similar as night and day").[8] As in the case of the annual cycle, they lead to reconstruction of the traditional vision of man and the universe.

The present reconstruction of this 'philosophy' poses considerable difficulties; in many cases, it is grounded on mere speculation. Its system of evaluation concerned primarily the real foundations of being (the folk knowledge of the world and philosophy of nature and the universe, created laboriously from the experience of many generations, explained principally life); it only marginally referred to the abstract conception of the cosmos, man and nature. This 'philosophy' was based on the logical association of certain facts compared by Claude Lévi-Strauss to the kind of creation called *bricolage* in which the creator-constructor used various substitutes as his substance, which composed a non-homogeneous, even accidental set. Its production was subordinated to no initial plan but to a mere instrumentality of means.[9] In folk symbolic imagination, and

---

S.A. Tokaryev (Moskva: Sovetskaya Enciklopediya, 1988), 2:6-9; M. Leach, *The Beginning. Creation Myths around the World* (New York: Funk & Wagnalls, 1956).

[7] J. Łotman, *Struktura tekstu artystycznego*, trans. A. Tanalska (Warszawa: Państwowy Instytut Wydawniczy, 1984), 70 and passim; J. Łotman, "O znaczeniach we wtórnych systemach modelujących," *Pamiętnik Literacki* (1969), 1:279-94; J. Łotman, "Wykłady z poetyki strukturalnej," in H. Markiewicz (ed.), *Współczesna teoria badań literackich za granicą* (Kraków: Wydawnictwo Literackie, 1976), 2:138-53; R. Tomicki, "Mit," in Z. Staszczak (ed.), *Słownik etnologiczny. Terminy ogólne* (Warszawa: Państwowe Wydawnictwo Naukowe, 1987), 245.

[8] J. Krzyżanowski (ed.), *Nowa księga przysłów i wyrażeń przysłowiowych polskich* (Warszawa: Państwowy Instytut Wydawniczy, 1969), 1:536.

[9] C. Lévi-Strauss, *Myśl nieoswojona*, trans. A. Zajączkowski (Warszawa: Państwowe Wydawnictwo Naukowe, 1969), 33.

specifically in myth (understood as the proto-source, as general etiology, as a superior reality revealing the strict order of the world), this specific *bricolage* assumes the shape of a logical, coherent vision of the world.[10] It resembles the order of the clock in which, as Lévi-Strauss stated in his conversation with G. Charbonnier, all pinions harmoniously participate in the same action – unlike those mechanisms which seem to contain a secret antagonism between the source of energy and the cooling part.[11]

Elements of folk culture are never separate, isolated, fortuitous, unrelated. All attempts at their explanation lead to broad reflection pertaining to diverse and extensive areas of culture. This entails permanent interpenetration of empirical reality and myth, of rational and mythical thinking, of observations of the macrocosm and a vision of the microcosm. Reality becomes incorporated in myth and acquires universal, exemplary meanings; eternal laws and instinctive convictions start to function in the realm of culture.[12]

According to the principles of mythical thinking, the diptych of darkness and light symbolizes the cosmic night (its darkness being the original state) and the cosmic day.[13] The night precedes the creation of all things, it "gives birth" to the day; like water, it denotes fertility, potentiality, the power to produce. Thus, darkness precedes light, the light of day emerges gradually from the darkness of night and the falling night does not emerge from the light of day but covers it. This regularity is sanctioned by the epic Night-Day formula. The day is born from the night (not vice versa), as it represents the more developed state of the cosmos: shaped and inhabited by human beings. The Night-Day transformation is progressive, whereas the Day-Night transformation is regressive.

Thus, every alternation of night and day re-actualizes the cosmogonic myth: it recreates the transition from the state of chaos to the state of cosmos. This repetition of the mythical act of creation follows the belief in the original existence of the cosmic Night, darkness – the amorphous state of the cosmos identified with waters symbolizing

---

[10] S.E. Hyman, "The Ritual View of Myth and the Mythic," in T.A. Sebeok (ed.), *Myth. A Symposium* (Bloomington: Indiana University Press, 1974), 136-53.

[11] G. Charbonnier, *Rozmowy z Claude Lévi-Straussem*, trans. J. Trznadel (Warszawa: "Czytelnik," 1968), 30.

[12] L. Stomma, *Słońce rodzi się 13 grudnia* (Warszawa: Ludowa Spółdzielnia Wydawnicza, 1981), 8.

[13] J.A. MacCulloch, "Light and Darkness (Primitive)," in J. Hastings (ed.), *Encyclopedia of Religion and Ethics* (New York: Scribner's, 1961), 7:47-51.

chaos, the larval modality of existence.[14] This state preceded the creation and evolution of all things that emerged after the appearance of the light of day and the re-establishment of forms and borders. This idea was reflected in the oldest tales which depict the setting sun as "hiding in some unknown sea"[15] through which it travels to another world to shine for the whole night and returns to our world on the following day as the tired, red rising sun.[16] Thus, light creates forms of existence. A similar exegesis is given in the well-known passage from *The Book of Genesis*:

> And the earth was without form, and void; and darkness *was* upon the face of the deep. And the Spirit of God moved upon the face of the waters.
> And God said, Let there be light: and there was light.
> And God saw the light, that *it was* good: and God divided the light from the darkness.
> And God called the light Day, and the darkness he called Night.
>
> (*Gen* 1.2-5)

The antithesis of the productive force of light and the destructive force of darkness lay at the basis of the primordial dualism in Slavonic mythology: it gave birth to the dualism of the superior realm of light and the inferior realm of darkness, of the two divinities worshipped by Western Slavs: the White God (of light and day) and the Black God[17] (of darkness and night). In the language of folklore, this opposition assumes the shape of such well-known *loci communes* as "white/bright day" and "black/dark night."

In Polish and Slavonic dualistic cosmogony, the symbolic dichotomy of the universe is intensified by the struggle of the pair of antithetical uranian-chthonian demiurges: God (representing the fire as

---

[14] Toporov, "Kosmogonicheskiye mify," 2:7-9.

[15] A. Petrow, "Lud Ziemi Dobrzyńskiej, jego charakter, mowa, zwyczaje, obrzędy, pieśni, przysłowia, zagadki," *Zbiór Wiadomości do Antropologii Krajowej*, 2 (1878): 126, No. 15; O. Kolberg, *Dzieła wszystkie. Krakowskie* (Kraków: Polskie Wydawnictwo Muzyczne, 1962), 7.3:193-94.

[16] K. Mátyás, "Nasze sioło. Studium etnograficzne," *Wisła*, 7 (1893): 119.

[17] See A.N. Afanasyev, "Svet i t'ma," in A.N. Afanasjev, *Zhivaya voda i veshtcheye slovo* (Moskva: Sovetskaya Rossiya, 1988), 124-26. A. Brückner opposes the theory of the Slavonic provenance of these gods: he claims their origin was Christian – see S. Urbańczyk (ed.), *Mitologia słowiańska i polska* (Warszawa: Państwowe Wydawnictwo Naukowe, 1985), 198-99.

the essential attribute of the sun and the heaven) and the Devil (representing the cosmic waters) who jointly create the universe (the Russian folk saying claiming that the universe was born from the tsar-fire and the tsarina-water is assumed to be the shortest version of the cosmogonic myth).[18] Each version of Slavonic cosmogonic myth reveals a sharp antagonism of these two elemental forces. This may be exemplified by the story of the beginning of the world from the region of Kraków which resembles the Judeo-Christian cosmogony.[19]

Further reconstruction of the myth would broaden the God/Devil polarity by including the opposition of specific features and qualities connected with the creation of the Earth, the structuring of the cosmos and anthropogenesis (its folk version was close to the Biblical one). The co-operation and rivalry of two kinds of antithetical deities – the ruling and the defeated – became *sine qua non* for ordering and evaluating the universe, based on acts of separation and division. They also comprised spatial stratification of the universe into heaven, the earth and the underworld. This entailed a representation of the underworld as the place of habitation of dead and chthonic demons, and of the upper world as the seat of gods and, later, also of the chosen people (after death). This traditional tripartite verticality may be reduced to a dichotomy: This World (i.e., the physical cosmos, the solar system; in its folk version it is reduced to the sun, the earth, the moon and the stars) and the Other World (consisting of Heaven[20] as the seat of God and of Hell as the hypostasis of evil, the image of impending punishment).

Symbolic recreation of cosmogony – the emergence of the white day from the dark night (a sign of cosmic and moral order) – was made possible by God's rule over the world, by the victory of light over darkness, the appearance of divine light, of heavenly, divine fire. It was also represented by God's eye or face, the sun, regarded as the highest heavenly hierophany of the day.[21] The concepts of light and divinity were joined already in pre-Christian times, yet this combination reached its apogee in the medieval philosophy of light (*vera lux* – God). According

---

[18] A.N. Afanasyev, *Poeticheskiye vozzreniya Slavyan na prirodu. Opyt sravnitelnogo izucheniya slavyanskich peredanii i verovanii v svyazi s mificheskimi skazaniyami drugich rodstvennych narodov* (Moskva: Soldatyenkova, 1868), 2:468.

[19] Kolberg, *Dzieła wszystkie*, 7.3:3-4.

[20] See M. Niewiadomska, "Ludowa wizja kosmosu w gminie Głuchów," *Łódzkie Studia Etnograficzne*, 23 (1981): 141.

[21] See Tomicki, "Słowiański mit kosmogoniczny," 70.

to the Gospel of St John, God is pure light and no darkness.[22] This inspired the Augustinian idea that *Deus veritas est; hic enim scriptum est; quoniam Dei lux est*.[23] It is derived from the primitive myth about the solar Demiurge, directly connected with fertility and the vegetation of plants. This justifies the use of the metaphor of sun-oak, for instance in Polish folk riddles: "an oak tree stands in the middle of the village (the world); its twigs peep into every cottage."[24] In Slavonic culture, the oak was considered to be a tree of divine attributes: good, pure and holy.[25]

Clear Christian theological evaluation of the solar symbolism points to the solar structure of God, the Cosmocrator who creates and gives life on both cosmic and social levels. In the Old Testament, God's light appeared together with life, to express His powerful blessing for people on Earth. The very first Christians faced east during their prayers to worship Christ the Lord as "the light of the world" or "the sun of justice." It was believed that the sunset was darkness, as was Satan, whose power is in darkness. Symbolically, facing east means renunciation of darkness and its dismal ruler.[26]

In the course of the expansion and consolidation of Christianity, the former solar cult (which played a very significant role in Slavonic magico-cultic systems) assumed the shape of the cult of *Lumen Christi* which either directly identified the sun with the Christian God or showed it as indirectly derived from God (whereas primordial somatic formulae and verbal magic aimed at casting a spell over the "newly born" sun – a kind of inceptive magic).[27]

---

[22] According to R.M. Dorson, the mythical man always, in all prehistoric cultures, constructed his pantheon around solar phenomena. "The Eclipse of Solar Mythology," in A. Dundes (ed.), *The Study of Folklore* (Englewood Cliffs, N.J.: Prentice-Hall, 1965), 64.

[23] Quoted after W. Schöne, *Über das Licht in der Malerei* (Berlin: Gebr. Mann, 1954), 59; see also M. Rzepińska, *Studia z teorii i historii koloru* (Kraków: Wydawnictwo Literackie, 1966), 148.

[24] B. Gustawicz, "Zagadki i łamigłówki ludowe," *Zbiór Wiadomości do Antropologii Krajowej*, 17 (1893): 241, nos. 392-94.

[25] K. Moszyński, *Kultura ludowa Słowian* (Warszawa: "Książka i Wiedza," 1967), 2.1:528.

[26] See E.B. Tylor, *Primitive Culture. Researches into the Development of Mythology, Philosophy, Religion, Language, Art and Custom* (London: John Murray, 1929), 2:428.

[27] See the old prayer to the sun recited throughout the region of Polesie on All Souls' Day in spring: in C. Pietkiewicz, "Kultura duchowa Polesia Rzeczyckiego," *Prace Etnologiczne*, 4 (1938): 295.

In Slavonic myths, the sun was anthropomorphized, for example, as a man walking, looking about and eating honey.[28] It was believed to be born every morning, then to pass through childhood, manhood, old age and to die in the evening. According to the principle of semantic proportion, isomorphism, this cosmic cycle could be transferred onto the stratum of anthropogenesis, the birth of the mythical ancestor, the creation of man. In the beauty of daybreak, in the glory of noon, and in the evening death, the sun's 'life' during the day represents human life.[29] According to proverbs, the evening is to the day what old age is to life (hence, the evening may be called the old age of day, and old age the evening of life), life is like a flower in May that blooms in the morning and withers in the evening.[30] The mythical foundations of this idea were expressed already in the riddle of the Sphinx: which animal has a voice, moves on all fours in the morning, on two legs at noon, and on three in the evening?[31] Thus, the cosmogonic calendrical and diurnal-nocturnal cycles are very close, representing the same mythologem: dawn – spring – birth; zenith – summer – maturity; sunset – autumn – old age; night – winter – death.

Medieval etymologies, penetrating mysteries of the universe, derived the notion of the sunset not from *occidĕre* (from *ob* and *cadere*) – "to set," but from *occidēre* (from *ob* and *caedere*)[32] – "to kill." Hence comes the saying "his sun is already set," i.e., he has lost his happiness, fortune or life.[33] However, this was not a real death but one implying rebirth, represented by the Christian ceremony of Resurrection (hence the cult of the dead was identified with the solar cult – through the symbolic promise of protection and salvation). The sunset was associated with the underworld, with death, and the sunrise with new life: hence, the practices of placing the dead on the axis of the sun (east-west), of saying

---

[28] O. Kolberg, *Dzieła wszystkie*, 7:28; S. Udziela, "Świat nadzmysłowy ludu krakowskiego," *Wisła*, 14.54 (1900): 467.

[29] Tylor, *Primitive Culture*, 48.

[30] J. Krzyżanowski (ed.), *Nowa księga przysłów i wyrażeń przysłowiowych polskich*, 3:971, No. 37.

[31] Man moves in the morning, i.e., in his childhood, on all fours, when adult – he becomes a two-legged animal, and in his old age, the evening of his life – he uses a stick which is like his third leg. J. Parandowski, *Mitologia. Wierzenia Greków i Rzymian* (Poznań: Wydawnictwo Poznańskie, 1990), 150-51.

[32] See A. Guriewicz, *Kategorie kultury średniowiecznej*, trans. J. Dancygier (Warszawa: Państwowy Instytut Wydawniczy, 1976), 298.

[33] G. Jobes, *Dictionary of Mythology and Symbols*, vols. 1-2 (New York: Scarecrow, 1961), 1508.

prayers during sunrise.[34] The sun – the greatest power in the universe, the heart of the cosmos, the transcendental archetype of light – symbolizes both life and death, and regeneration of life through death, as it constantly rises and sets, as its rays have the power of both animation and destruction. Every night it passes through the empire of death to reappear every morning. Thus, it may bring people to life and put them to death, as well as pointing their soul's way through subterranean regions to bring them to light the next day. Mircea Eliade views these phenomena in terms of the ambivalent function of the psychopomp (putting souls to death and guiding them) and the initiating hierophant.[35] On the earthly scale, on the temporal stratum of the everyday, the opposition of Day-Night refers to the dualism of God and the Devil: it assumes a solar-funerary and chthonian structure and connotes the antithesis of life and death. Each immersion in the darkness of night denotes a symbolic encounter with death, a ritualistic annihilation of existence, assuming that darkness without light is synonymous with death, as God assigned the day to the living and the night to the dead (Thietmar of Merseburg).

In the annual sequence (structurally parallel to the diurnal-nocturnal sequence), the same significance is acquired by the opposition of summer and winter, which makes the microcosm a replica of the macrocosm. Thus, the Earth is the area of confrontation between two antagonistic forces, the cosmic sphere where brightness, day and summer alternate with darkness, night and winter. The mediating position of the Earth in the spatial configuration of the universe is rendered by R. Tomicki's mythical construction:

State A	– Heaven	– God	– metaphysical life
State A and non-A B and non-B	– the Earth	– Man	– biological life (the rhythm of life and death)
State B	– the Underworld	– the Devil	– metaphysical death[36]

Thus Man, placed in the mediating position, is exposed to the influence of both these contradictory powers that determine his life and death. Agrarian cults developed the cosmic religion based on the principle of

---

[34] See Tylor, *Primitive Culture*, 422.

[35] M. Eliade, *Traktat o historii religii*, trans. J. Wierusz-Kowalski (Warszawa: "Książka i Wiedza," 1966), 138-39; see also J.C. Cooper, *An Illustrated Encyclopedia of Traditional Symbols* (London: Thames, 1978), 162.

[36] Tomicki, "Religious dualism," 66.

periodical regeneration of the world. Since human life and the world are understood in terms of the life of nature, the cosmic and anthropogonic cycles infinitely repeat the same rhythm: birth – death – birth – death. In folkloric texts-behaviors, symbolic meaning is attributed principally to the dynamic opposition of the passage from the phase of diurnal activity to the phase of nocturnal passivity, non-existence (followed by the restoration of existence with the re-emergence of light). The liminal structure of the night acquired complete autonomy in the model of the rites of passage of this fundamental cycle. This individual ritual is structuralized in a tripartite pattern: 1. separation and destructuralization, 2. the liminal (marginal) phase (*limen*), 3. restructuralization (organization into new relationships). In this scheme, the place of night is central: it liberates humans from their former social structural roles and makes them assume new symbolic roles.[37] This liminality does not presuppose structural contradictions, but rather what is essentially unstructured, i.e., simultaneously destructured and prestructured. Nocturnal structural invisibility of liminal persons has a dual nature: they are at once no longer classified and not yet classified, neither alive nor dead from one perspective, and both alive and dead from another perspective. They are posed "betwixt and between,"[38] in an ambiguous state; they mix all regular categories. Thus, logically, antithetical processes of symbolic death and life may be represented by the same signs as pre-natal and funerary darkness. In contemporary psychology and history of religion, these motifs are denoted by the common name of *regressus ad uterum* and *descensus ad inferos*[39] – the process of life from death and towards death.

Jacob Boehme, the German mystic whose writings inspired Hegel to formulate his famous dialectical triad, used to say that everything is comprised of "yes" or "no."[40] Liminality may be thus treated as a "no," as negation of all positive structural statements, but also, in a sense, as their source, and even more – as the realm of pure possibility from which new configurations of ideas and relations may arise (according to

---

[37] See e.g., D. Zadra, "Symbolic Time," in M. Eliade (ed.), *The Encyclopedia of Religion* (New York: Macmillan, 1987), 14:196.

[38] V. Turner, "'Betwixt and Between:' The Liminal Period in Rites de Passage," in V. Turner, *The Forest of Symbols. Aspects of Ndembu Ritual* (Ithaca: Cornell University Press, 1967), 93-111.

[39] See M. Eliade, *Aspects du mythe* (Paris: Gallimard, 1963), 102; M. Eliade, "L'initiation et le monde moderne," in C.J. Bleeker (ed.), *Initiation. Contribution to the Theme of the Study-Conference of the International Association for the History of Religions* (Leiden: Brill, 1965), 3.

[40] Quoted after V. Turner, "'Betwixt and Between,'" 97.

Victor Turner).[41] The status of man at home at night, situated symbolically in the center of the world, in the cosmological point of communication between Heaven, Earth and Hell (symbolic assimilation of home to the center of the world) acquires features of magico-cultic inclusion. This situation normally models a definite cosmic principle and causes a true ontological transformation: through symbolic or biological death of one state, it leads to rebirth in a new mode of existence. The symbolism of night and darkness, a paradigmatic reflection of cosmogonic myths, discloses its initiatory nature: a structural link between the pre-cosmic, pre-natal darkness and death, rebirth and initiation. (As mentioned above, here the contrast between night and day is isomorphic with the contrast between death and birth). Human life progresses as a sequence of periods; according to C.J. Bleeker, it always denotes initiation into a new reality, a new truth.[42] This passage takes place in each kind of cosmic existence, analogous to man's passage from pre-life through life to death, reflecting the mythical ancestor's sun's transition from darkness to light. This movement is a variant of a larger, more universal process, in which the moon is the archetype of cosmic becoming, and plants – the symbol of permanent rebirth. Therefore, according to Mircea Eliade, the cosmos was represented as an immense tree:[43] its capabilities of rebirth being symbolically expressed by the life of the tree (see the riddle: "there stands a sycamore in the middle, it has twelve boughs, four nests on each bough, and seven eggs in each nest").[44]

Initiatory nocturnal symbolism is bound up with the Christian conception of anthropological dualism (comprising the antithesis of the top and the bottom) widespread in nineteenth-century folk outlook. This ideology was developed in particular by St Augustine and many later outstanding theologians in the first millennium of Christianity.[45] According to this theory, death consists in the separation of the soul from the body: from this moment, the fate of the soul is independent of the fate of the body, the temporary abode the soul abandons in order to

---

[41] ibid., 97.

[42] C.J. Bleeker, "Some Introductory Remarks on the Significance of Initiation," in C.J. Bleeker (ed.), *Initiation*, 19.

[43] Eliade, *Traktat o historii religii*, 262.

[44] Years, months, days. G. Smólski, "Zagadki i łamigłówki górali polskich w Tatrach i Beskidach," *Lud* 17 (1911): 83, no. 25.

[45] See E. Potkowski, *Dziedzictwo wierzeń pogańskich w średniowiecznych Niemczech. Defuncti vivi* (Warszawa, 1973), 95; A. Kowalska-Lewicka, "Ludowe wyobrażenia śmierci," *Polska Sztuka Ludowa*,1-2 (1986): 24.

pass to the superior, spiritual existence. The motif of separation of the soul from the body and its journey into the supernatural world belonged to popular visionary motifs not only in Poland but also in the eschatological imagery of most religious systems and mythologies. These themes were current in exempla from the turn of the fourteenth century.[46]

The equivalence of sleep to symbolic death and of biological death to sleep (falling asleep as an euphemism for dying) is closely connected with the visionary code based on the journey into the Other World of the soul that has left its body[47] – a journey with a clearly specified cognitive aim. This initiation pertains particularly to places of eternal punishment and reward, and the experience is meant to serve many of the living. This type of contact with new, esoteric knowledge, within the equivalence of sleep to symbolic death, occurred in dreams treated as mysterious adventures of the soul during sleep – in folk mentality, they were connected with ghosts of the dead as well as with wandering ghosts of other people. Hence, dream visions were significant for people (see the interethnic proverb: "Night is the mother of advice.").[48] A powerful dead man appeared in them as a herald of the future (most often foreboding death or misfortune).[49] In folk mentality, dreams were interpreted as "relationships of people with saints or spirits of the dead. In this way people blessed by God acquire numerous pieces of advice, many dead wrong-doers request forgiveness, many mysteries are explained"[50] – particularly if a dream is repeated for two consecutive nights, which is a signal confirming the imparted information.[51] Thus,

---

[46] See T. Michałowska, "'Dusza z ciała wyleciała.' Próba interpretacji," *Pamiętnik Literacki*, 2 (1989): 19.

[47] See ibid., 3-26. The oldest trace of this song is preserved in the Wrocław manuscript from the beginning of the fifteenth century as a supplement to the poem "Skarga umierającego." See S. Vrtel-Wierczyński (ed.), *Średniowieczna poezja polska świecka* (Wrocław: Ossolineum, 1952), 49.

[48] J.S. Gluski (ed.), *Proverbs. A Comparative Book of English, French, German, Italian, Spanish and Russian Proverbs with a Latin Appendix* (Amsterdam: Elsewier, 1971), 18.

[49] On oneiromancy and its significance in human life, see S. Oświecimski, *Zeus daje tylko znak, Apollo wieszczy osobiście. Starożytne wróżbiarstwo greckie* (Wrocław: Ossolineum, 1989), 75-83. See also "Dreams," in M. Leach, J. Fried (ed.), *Funk and Wagnalls Standard Dictionary of Folklore, Mythology and Legend* (New York: Funk and Wagnalls, 1972), 324-25.

[50] O. Kolberg, *Dzieła wszystkie,* vol. 48, *Tarnowskie – Rzeszowskie,* ed. J. Burszta (Warszawa: Ludowa Spółdzielnia Wydawnicza, 1967), 277.

[51] R. Lilientalowa, "Wierzenia, przesądy i praktyki ludu żydowskiego," *Wisła*, 19 (1905): 152.

dreams revealed the superhuman world, introduced into the unknown, hidden and fascinating realms of thought and feeling. The nocturnal initiation ensured man's spiritual development, his cognition of a new truth, a new sphere of reality (the didactic element of initiation).

The value of this internal, esoteric aspect of nocturnal initiation was connected with the common belief in the existence of communication between the microcosm and the macrocosm, which revealed its mysteries to humans in various ways (also through manifold secret activities). This knowledge was also deciphered by means of cosmogonic-initiatory signs and symbols that defined the alternation of night and day. The time of dreams, wrapped up in the nocturnal darkness, deprived of the logic of diurnal ordering and anomalous, most often presupposed explication through reverse ordering. There is a proverb which says that reality is always reversed in dreams.[52] Inversion (for instance, replacing the right with the left, the top with the bottom, the front with the rear, etc.) belonged to features characteristic of the Other World. The principle of reversal, ordering the realm on the other side of the mirror, was essential to the space which was unsafe, remained beyond the sphere of human activity, to the time of the unconscious. The nocturnal condition of the man remaining outside the community of the living, outside his social structure, in the natural state, deprived of possessions, evokes the initiatory scenario.[53]

The mystical, pre-logical imagination manifest in folk communication, both verbal (texts) and non-verbal (patterns of behavior preserved in inter-generational transmission), combined specific, real phenomena with the occult power of their origin. This mentality displayed a peculiar interaction of the ontological-cosmological and ontological-anthropological strata centered upon the dualism of darkness and light contrasted in the Night-Day formula. On the anthropological-ethical-axiological level, this dualism assumes the form of another dichotomy: Night (*civitas Diaboli*) vs. Day (*civitas Dei*). It generates a series of symbolic sign systems: potentiality, shapelessness, chaos, destruction, death, the Other World, the subconscious, passivity, immobility, silence, the horizontal. And in the realm of Day (light), as *civitas Dei*, it respectively engenders hierarchical order, shape, creation, life, This

---

[52] S. Gonet, "Opowiadania ludowe z okolic Andrychowa," *Materiały Antropologiczno – Archeologiczne i Etnograficzne,* 4 (1900): 235.

[53] See, e.g., V. Turner, "Liminality and Communitas," in V. Turner, *The Ritual Process. Structure and Anti-structure* (Chicago: Aloline, 1969), 94-130.

World, consciousness, activity, work, movement, noise, the vertical.[54] The everyday symbolic re-creation of the cosmogony, i.e., the emergence from the nocturnal darkness of the white day, the sign of cosmic and moral order, only became possible due to the victory of light (God) over darkness (satanic forces), of life over death, of good over evil. Attempts at a constant renewal of this rhythm lay at the foundations of folk ontology comprised in its principal explicatory systems: folkloric texts-behaviors connected with Catholicism, traditional systems of beliefs and folklore. These systems, both verbal and non-verbal, provided simple rules enabling an individual to live in harmony with the surrounding reality, as its integral component.

Translated by Wiesław Krajka.

---

[54] On the application of these symbolic signs to an analysis of Polish traditional culture, see Chapter III (*"Civitas Dei* and *Civitas Diaboli*, or Diurnal Active Symbols and Nocturnal Inactive Symbols"*) of Brzozowska-Krajka, *Polish Traditional Folklore*, 51-72.

BEYOND THE RATIONAL: JOSEPH CONRAD'S PORTRAYAL OF THE SEA[1]

Wojciech Kozak

1.

The assumption that an all-pervasive crisis of values in Western culture gave rise at the turn of the twentieth century to the modernist mode of writing has now become a critical platitude. Yet we constantly need to mouth this platitude in order to account for the revival of interest in myth among the most prominent authors of the time. The inspiration may have come from anthropological and ethnological studies, which had been rapidly developing from the mid-nineteenth century and were crowned by Sir James Frazer's *The Golden Bough* – a monumental study in mythical beliefs and rituals of primitive peoples all over the world. However, Frazer's work itself, which many modernist writers such as Eliot, Joyce, Lawrence and Yeats knew and appreciated, had been a manifestation of the Victorian belief in the progress of science. Very much in accordance with the post-Darwinian notion of social evolutionism, it discredited the mythical world view altogether as a 'relic

---

[1] The article borrows some of its ideas from two earlier texts: Wojciech Kozak, "Spatial Axiology of the Sea, the Land and Ships in Conrad's Sea Fiction," in Wiesław Krajka (ed.), *Joseph Conrad: East European, Polish and Worldwide*, East European Monographs (Boulder, Lublin and New York: Maria Curie-Skłodowska University Press and Columbia University Press, 1999), 185-99; Wojciech Kozak, "Some Aspects of Myth in Joseph Conrad's Fiction," in Elena Lamberti (ed.), *Interpreting/Translating European Modernism: A Comparative Approach* (Bologna: University of Bologna Press, 2001), 107-32.

of the past,' a state of the benighted mind ignorant of the true nature of the workings of the universe.

The tenets of such reasoning were soon to be undermined by science itself, most notably by the work of Freud, whose *Totem and Taboo*, published in 1913, aptly, if controversially, argued for a close analogy between archaic consciousness and neurotic states of mind in contemporary man. In the aftermath of this theory, and not infrequently prior to it, the importance of myth had been gaining wide currency with many modernist writers. For them, it was not only the acceptance of the continuity of human thought that was particularly appealing but also, and more significantly, the belief that exploring and incorporating the mythical material in a literary work was of an obvious artistic advantage, that it provided a useful tool for bringing literature closer to life. If, as some critics put it, "at the heart of the modernist aesthetic lay the conviction that the previously sustaining structures of human life, whether social, political, religious, or artistic, had been either destroyed or shown up as falsehoods or fantasies,"[2] reliance on the mythical was supposed to offer an alternative, axiologically oriented model of reality which could provide a counterbalance to the shattered world of values in the contemporary time, in this way transcending, to use Stephen Dedalus's phrase, "the nightmare of history," as well as reflect in a more true-to-life manner the essentially intuitive and subjective nature of the cognitive process. As James McFarlane argues,

> "myth" commended itself as a highly effective device for imposing order of a symbolic, even poetic, kind on the chaos of quotidian event, and offering the opportunity – to use a phrase of Frank Kermode's – to "short circuit the intellect and liberate the imagination which the scientism of the modern world suppresses" [...] Born of the irrational, and obeying a logic much closer to the subjective and associative promptings of the unconscious mind than to the formal progression of scientific thought, myth offered a new kind of insight into the wayward realities of social phenomena, gave – as Eliot was to say of Joyce's myth – "a way of controlling, of ordering, of

---

2 Nina Baym and Lawrence B. Holland, "Introduction: American Literature between the Wars, 1914-1945," in *The Norton Anthology of American Literature*, ed. Nina Baym, et al. (New York: W.W. Norton and Co., 1989), 2:932.

giving a shape and a significance to the immense paradox [sic] of futility and anarchy which is contemporary history."[3]

Thus, what needs to be borne in mind about the modernist practice of mythopoeia is not only its highly ironic function but also its highly normative one. While confronting the ordered and timeless world of myth with the history-ridden panorama of "futility and anarchy" inevitably leads to the parody of the contemporary wasteland – a godless world inhabited by unheroic mediocrities – at the same time, it elevates myth to the status of a world view reaching beyond the paralysing limitations of the present, and thus providing an answer to the agonising modernist question of 'how to be.' To paraphrase a distinguished Russian student of myth, Eleazar Meletinski, the value of myth-making in the twentieth century lies not so much in unmasking the stunted and hideous contemporary world but primarily in bringing to light the timeless nature of myth and setting it against the flux of historical change.[4]

2.

It would be highly unjustified to rank Joseph Conrad among the greatest myth makers of British modernism, such as Eliot, Joyce, Lawrence and Yeats. The main reason is that the substantial part of his oeuvre had been produced before mythopoeia reached the status of conscious literary practice and that his writing, for all its modern character, clearly acknowledges an affinity with the tradition of nineteenth-century fiction and rarely expresses 'a flight from history,' recognising the importance of facing the here-and-now of the historical moment. Nonetheless, some of Conrad's texts provide enough evidence for discussing them as representative of the myth-oriented spirit of his epoch.

For the author of *Lord Jim*, drawing on myth provided a way to explore the intuitive and subjective character of human perception of reality, offered some normative meaning to his vision of existence and became a fruitful source of parody and irony. In the present paper, I would like to focus on Conrad's portrayal of the sea as the primordial chaos, which owes much to the primitive perception of the natural

---

[3] James McFarlane, "The Mind of Modernism," in Malcolm Bradbury and James McFarlane (eds.), *Modernism: A Guide to European Literature, 1890-1930* (Harmondsworth: Penguin, 1991), 82-83.

[4] Eleazar Mieletinski, *Poetyka mitu*, trans. J. Dancygier (Warsaw: PIW, 1981), 366-67.

phenomena, and then highlight the possible ways in which the writer's transformation of the other major elements of the sea universe – such as the sailors and the ship – could be read as a normative, myth-based vision of life, furnishing Conrad the man with an alternative to the pessimistic outlook on life he is known for among most Conradians.[5]

Although the writer's reluctance to be called an author of marine literature has often been stressed by his biographers,[6] and there are only two texts that Conrad himself defined as books about the sea, *The Mirror of the Sea* and *The Nigger of the "Narcissus,"* his professions are not to be taken at face value. It was only in the nineteenth century, most notably in the works of Melville and Conrad, that the sea started to occupy the central position in a literary work, changing its status from the marginal setting to a deeply symbolic embodiment of the truth about man and universe.[7] Life at sea, as the writer would frequently stress, belonged to Conrad's most formative years, shaping his artistic sensitivity and providing him with an ethics that became an alternative to the modernist crisis of values. Bearing in mind the frequently ambiguous nature of the 'briny' in his works, it nonetheless seems justified to infer that Conrad's sea is first of all a challenge which, once accepted, makes it possible for man to uphold his belief in 'a few very simple notions' constituting the tenets of the marine ethos – a means of achieving a *modus vivendi* with the surrounding world.

In the essay called "Well-Done," Conrad posed the question about the nature of the sea, although at the same time, aware of its essentially enigmatic nature, he refrained from coming up with a ready answer:

> And then, what is this sea, the subject of so many apostrophes in verse and prose addressed to its greatness and its mystery by men who had never penetrated either the one or the other? [...] At any time within the navigating centuries mankind

---

[5] For a discussion on Conrad's pessimistic world view, see, for instance, C.B. Cox, *Joseph Conrad: The Modern Imagination* (London: Dent and Sons, 1974); Zdzisław Najder, *Nad Conradem* (Warsaw: PIW, 1965), 185-203; Zdzisław Najder, "Introduction," in *Joseph Conrad. Listy*, trans. Halina Carroll-Najder, ed. Zdzisław Najder (Warsaw: PIW, 1968), 9; Michał Komar, *Piekło Konrada* (Warsaw: Czytelnik, 1978); Józef Ujejski, *O Konradzie Korzeniowskim* (Warsaw: Dom Książki Polskiej, 1936), 87-102.

[6] See, for instance, Jocelyn Baines, *Joseph Conrad: A Critical Biography* (London: Weidenfeld and Nicolson, 1960), 184; Adam Gillon, *Joseph Conrad* (Boston: Twayne Publishers, 1982), 53.

[7] For a comparison of the two writers, see Leon F. Seltzer, *The Vision of Conrad and Melville: A Comparative Study* (Athens: Ohio University Press, 1970).

might have addressed it with the words: "What are you after all? Oh yes, we know. The greatest scene of potential terror, a devouring enigma of space. But our lives had been nothing if not a continuous defiance of what you can do and what you may hold; a spiritual and material defiance carried on in our plucky cockleshells on and on beyond the successive provocations of your unreadable horizons."[8]

The rhetoric of the quoted passage points to the close relationship between the natural and human world as well as the two-faceted character of the perception of the former. Conrad's vision of the sea, a far cry from the romantic, pantheistic unity of man and nature, entices the reader to perceive it as an autonomous empirical reality but also, in accordance with the primordial, intuitive perception of natural phenomena, leads to its personification (the ocean is the addressee of the sailing mankind). The detached authorial comment is given some emotional colouring – the human voice takes on the function of apostrophe. It can be argued that such a juxtaposition of two opposing ways of perceiving reality is expressive of the spirit of the epoch.

In his classic essay "The Mind of Modernism," James McFarlane stresses two apparently incongruous ways of understanding the notion of the modern: on the one hand, it can mean a rational analysis, on the other, a purely intuitive vision. It was only in modernism, McFarlane argues, that these two contradictory notions came to interpenetrate, contributing to the rise of a specific form of artistry, amalgamating the conscious and unconscious workings of the human mind. What we need to realise is

> the subsumption, within a single, newly emerging and as yet semantically unstable concept of the 'modern,' of two distinct *Weltanschauungen* — the mechanistic and the intuitive - which the earlier nineteenth century had so productively kept separate. The century's intellectual achievement had largely derived from the creative rivalry between these two anti-thetical modes of intellectual inquiry; now the new concept brought them into a relationship of novel and unexpected intimacy.[9]

---

[8] Joseph Conrad, *Notes on Life and Letters* (London: Dent and Sons, 1923), 184-85.
[9] McFarlane, "The Mind of Modernism," 71-72.

The "two anti-thetical modes of intellectual inquiry" point to one of the crucial modernist precepts concerning the nature of the cognitive process: with the collapse of many of the sustaining structures of nineteenth-century science and the professed 'bankruptcy of science' in sight, our epistemological stance needs to be modified. Because we can reach no real knowledge of *what* we actually see, it is *how* we see it that becomes of utmost importance. The line between science and art must be drawn and, in a final confrontation, the latter is given priority as reflecting a 'truer' world.

In his little known essay called "The Ascending Effort," which borrows its title from George Bourne's book, Conrad questions the author's assumption about the great role art is supposed to play in propagating science. For Conrad, art arises from sentiment and emotion, which belong to an essentially irrational sphere of understanding. It "issues straight from our organic vitality, and is a movement of life-cells with their matchless unintellectual knowledge."[10] Much as this knowledge seems to be at odds with empirical cognition, it nevertheless gives testimony to the truth of human experience, and, not aspiring to lay bare the workings of the universe, it is the only way to get to know the human mind. As an example, Conrad gives the scientifically verified Copernican theory:

> Many a man has heard or read and believes that the earth goes round the sun [...]. This is the Copernican system, and the man believes in the system without often knowing as much about it as its name. But while watching a sunset he sheds this belief; he sees the sun as a small and useful object, the servant of his needs and the witness of his ascending effort, sinking slowly behind a range of mountains, and then he holds the system of Ptolemy. He holds it without knowing it. In the same way a poet hears, reads, and believes a thousand undeniable truths which have not yet got into his blood, nor will do after reading Mr. Bourne's book; he writes, therefore, as if neither truths nor book existed. Life and the arts follow dark courses, and will not turn aside to the brilliant arc-lights of science [...]. Art has served Religion; artists have found the most exalted inspiration in Christianity; but the light of Transfiguration which has illuminated the profoundest mysteries of our sinful souls is not the light of the generating

---

[10] Conrad, *Notes on Life and Letters*, 73.

stations, which exposes the depths of our infatuation where our mere cleverness is permitted for a while to grope for the unessential among invincible shadows.[11]

Being itself at variance with 'common sense,' such an intuitive and pre-scientific outlook of the artist owes much to the highly subjective, man-oriented mythical world view in which natural phenomena may be interpreted as part of a timeless model of the universe. In this world view, water symbolism plays an important part: "The waters symbolize the universal sum of virtualities; they are *fons et origo*, 'spring and origin,' the reservoir of all the possibilities of existence [...]"[12] They were preset at the beginning of time and they return at the end of every historical or cosmic cycle. Thus, the water element embodies the mythical Chaos that precedes the creative act of gods and terminates any mythical cycle. As Mieletinski puts it, the notion of the primordial sea, out of whose depths the earth emerges, is of universal character and can be found in almost every mythology.[13] The mythical waters stand for the whole creative potential – prior to all forms of existence, they lie at the heart of any creative act. Water, therefore, is part and parcel of cosmogonic myths. In such stories the transformation of Chaos into Cosmos is narrated as the passage from water to earth, from vacuum to objects, from darkness to light, or from formlessness to form.[14] In the Bible, water and darkness represent non-existence and the creative act of God, through separation of the previously indistinguishable phenomena and grouping them into binary oppositions, makes for the order of the universe.[15]

Water, which is identified with nascent forms of existence, is believed to have regenerative properties and to be a source of spiritual purification. In Christianity these properties of water are most fully

---

[11] *Notes on Life and Letters*, 73-75.

[12] Mircea Eliade, *The Sacred and the Profane: The Nature of Religion*, trans. Willard R. Trask (New York and Evanston, Ill.: Harper Torchbooks, 1961), 130.

[13] Mieletinski, *Poetyka mitu*, 256.

[14] ibid.

[15] "In the beginning God created the heaven and the earth. And the earth was without form, and void; and darkness was upon the face of the deep. And the Spirit of God moved upon the face of the waters. And God said, Let there be light: and there was light. And God saw the light, that it was good; and God divided the light from the darkness. [...] And God said, Let the waters under the heaven be gathered together unto one place, and let the dry land appear: and it was so. And God called the dry land Earth, and the gathering together of the waters called he seas; and God saw that it was good." (Genesis 1.1-4, 9-10) The quotation is taken from the Authorised King James Version.

embodied in the sacrament of baptism. To quote Eliade again, "just as Noah had confronted the Sea of Death in which sinful humanity had been destroyed, and had emerged from it, so the newly baptized man descends into the baptismal piscine to confront the Water Dragon in a supreme combat from which he emerges victorious."[16]

A continual clash of two authorial perspectives is evident in Conrad's presentation of the sea. One can be defined as an objective, detached and realistic view of fact, not infrequently rooted in the historical context; the other, in turn, is based on a highly subjective and intuitive perception of natural phenomena, bearing a close resemblance to the mythical world view. This is most discernible in the collection of essays entitled *The Mirror of the Sea*, which is a kind of tribute the writer paid to almost twenty years he spent on board English ships.

Conrad makes it clear that any attempt at understanding the true nature of the 'briny,' however unsuccessful and incomplete it may turn out to be in the end, must be preceded by a critical reassessment of a naive, post-romantic glorification of the sea as a source of poetic inspiration:

> For all that has been said of the love that certain natures (on shore) had professed to feel for it, for all the celebration it had been the subject of in prose and song, the sea has never been friendly to man. [...] As if it were too great, too mighty for common virtues, the ocean has no compassion, no faith, no law, no memory. [...] Impenetrable and heartless, the sea has given nothing of itself to the suitors for its precarious favours.[17]

Even if, as the passage quoted here shows, there is an unbridgeable gap between the world of nature and the world of man, the ocean being deprived of any human features, a 'sober,' positivist awareness of the fact is not something Conrad is ultimately striving for in his artistic vision. Indeed, a few pages later, he makes the following, somewhat different confession: "And I looked upon the true sea – the sea that plays with men till their hearts are broken, and wears stout ships to death. Nothing can touch the brooding bitterness of its soul." (129) What is noticeable about this description is that in contrast to the previous one in which the

---

[16] Eliade, *The Sacred and the Profane*, 134.

[17] Joseph Conrad, *The Mirror of the Sea* (London: Dent and Sons, 1923), 118-19. Subsequent references are given in the text.

sea is "heartless," here it comes equipped with an essentially human 'component' – a soul. It is possible to account for this apparent incoherence by referring to the assumptions made in "The Ascending Effort," discussed earlier in this paper. Science may have taught us to discredit mythical beliefs as essentially fallacious, yet to make an artistic discourse suggestive, the writer frequently has to rely on the intuitive and irrational, that is, on the mythical. Making the reservation that "after all, a gale of wind [...] is inarticulate," that "it is a man, who, in chance phrase, interprets the elemental passion of his enemy" and that "it is, after all, the human voice that stamps the mark of human consciousness upon the character of the gale" (84-85), Conrad feels justified in introducing imagery highly reminiscent of the mythical interpretation of natural phenomena, thus raising some of his essays to the status of strictly literary texts.

A good example of this is the piece called "The Character of the Foe," in which the suggestiveness of the depiction of a sea storm is achieved through a symbolic reference to the mythical waters of Chaos preceding the act of creation:

> If you would know *the age of the earth*, look upon the sea in a storm. The greyness of the whole immense surface, the wind furrows upon the faces of the waves, the great masses of foam, tossed about and waving, like matted white locks, give to the sea in a gale an appearance of *hoary age*, lustreless, dull, without gleams, as though it *had been created before the light itself.*
>
> (62; emphasis added)

The mythical sources of such a perception of natural phenomena are underlined in the next paragraph, where the personified ocean raging in a storm evokes archetypal fear of the forces of nature, typical of primeval man: "Looking back after much love and much trouble, the instinct of primitive man, who seeks to personify the forces of Nature for his affection and for his fear, is awakened again in the breast of one civilized beyond that stage even in his infancy" (65).

In the discussed collection, personification of natural phenomena is the central artistic device the writer employs in his presentation of the sea and the storm. The latter is described as follows:

> Gales have their personalities, and after all, perhaps it is not strange: for, when all is said and done, they are adversaries whose wiles you must defeat, whose violence you must resist,

and yet with whom you must live in the intimacies of nights
and days.

(62)

[...] gales have their physiognomy. You remember them by
your own feelings, and no two gales stamp themselves in the
same way upon your emotions. Some cling to you in
woebegone misery, others come back fiercely and weirdly, like
ghouls bent upon sucking your strength away [...] some are
unvenerated recollections, as of spiteful wild-cats, chewing at
your agonized vitals [...]

(66)

In a similar manner, the chapter "Rulers of East and West" depicts sea
winds as possessing human features *par excellence*. They are portrayed as
despotic monarchs, in full control of the infinitude of the sea and time,
imposing their absolute rule over generations of seamen unsuccessfully
trying to conquer the natural world. Like mythical weather gods, they
direct the fate of the seamen and their ships, not allowing for any kind of
protest and mercilessly exposing all human weaknesses. The description
of the west wind is particularly evocative here:

The magnificent barbarian sits enthroned in a mantle of gold-
lined clouds looking from on high on great ships gliding like
mechanical toys upon his sea and on men who, armed with fire
and iron, no longer need to watch anxiously for the slightest
sign of his royal mood. He is disregarded; but he has kept all
his strength, all his splendour, and a great part of his power.
Time itself, that shakes all the thrones, is on the side of that
king. The sword in his hand remains as sharp as ever upon
both of its edges; and he may well go on playing his royal game
of quoits with hurricanes, tossing them over from the
continent of republics to the continent of kingdoms, in the
assurance that both the new republics and the old kingdoms,
the heat of fire and the strength of iron, with the untold
generations of audacious men, shall crumble to dust at the
steps of his throne, and pass away, and be forgotten before his
own rule comes to an end.

(106)

The lofty style of the quoted passage is pervaded by the author's awareness of inevitable historical change, which imbues the description with overtones of epic nostalgia. The "mechanical toys" stand for the modern, 'degenerate' kind of ship, the steamer, which is a product of mechanised life. In a manner typical of a modernist writer, Conrad is very wary of identifying history with progress. On the contrary, he will occasionally pick up an ancient mythological motif and discuss its noble character only to set it against the unheroic background of the present, thus achieving an ironical effect.

Such is the case, for instance, in his description of the Mediterranean Sea as the cradle of Western marine literature originated from the Homeric epic:

> Happy he who, like Ulysses, has made an adventurous voyage; and there is no such sea for adventurous voyages as the Mediterranean — the inland sea which the ancients looked upon as so fast and so full of wonders [...] The dark and fearful sea of the subtle Ulysses' wanderings, agitated by the wrath of Olympian gods, harbouring on its islets the fury of strange monsters and the wiles of strange women; the highway of heroes and sages, pirates and saints; the workaday sea of Carthaginian merchants and the pleasure lake of Roman Caesars, claiming the veneration of every seaman as the historical home of that spirit of open defiance against the great waters of the earth which is the very soul of his calling.
>
> (157-58)

Conrad compares his own voyages to the wanderings of the mythological hero, but soon discredits the legitimacy of such a comparison:

> Such was my abominable luck in being born by the mere hair's breadth of twenty-five centuries too late into a world where kings have been growing scarce with scandalous rapidity, while the few who remain have adopted the uninteresting manners and customs of simple millionaires.
>
> (160)

3.

The author of "Typhoon" does not turn his back on history and it would be a far-fetched assumption to call his artistic vision a flight into the world of myth. Yet there is enough textual evidence to assume that the mythical world view provided him with an ethics which offered a meaningful alternative to the crisis-ridden world of the present.

In one of his books on Conrad, Zdzisław Najder characterises the writer's *Weltanschauung* as follows: although everything is questionable, one needs to cling to some norms of conduct, irrespective of the fact that they cannot be corroborated from a scientific point of view. These norms of conduct may have no meaning for the universe; still, they have some meaning and are indispensable for man.[18] Here, Conrad, himself defined by one of his critics as "the restless seeker after normative vision,"[19] departs from other modernist writers, most notably Eliot and Joyce, who held the extremely aesthetic belief that if the lost order is to be regained, it is to be regained in the order of a literary work and literary work only.

It would take another paper to discuss how Conrad's mythologising discourse aims at creating an order of a different, axiological kind and how it develops in his presentation of the other crucial elements of his universe, that is, the men and the ships.[20] Here, it can only be stated that by constantly drawing a parallel between a primitive tribe whose life is sanctioned by specific social structure, regulated by myth and ritual, and the imagined community of seamen centred around the *imago mundi* of the ship, the writer arrives at a normative artistic vision of human existence.

In the closing passage of *The Nigger of the "Narcissus,"* looking at the ship's crew vanishing from sight once the voyage has been completed, the narrator asks a rhetorical question, "Haven't we, together and upon the immortal sea, wrung out a meaning from our sinful lives?"[21] As a writer of 'sea stories,' Conrad always attempted to answer this question in the affirmative.

---

[18] Najder, *Nad Conradem*, 193-94.
[19] Edward W. Said, *Joseph Conrad and the Fiction of Autobiography* (Cambridge, Mass.: Harvard University Press, 1966), 15.
[20] For a discussion of these, see Note 1 to the present article.
[21] Joseph Conrad, *The Niger of the "Narcissus"* (London: Dent and Sons, 1923), 173.

JUST SO STORIES BY RUDYARD KIPLING AS A MYTHOLOGICAL-AESTHETIC FOUNDATION TEXT FOR CHILDREN

Wiesław Krajka

Just So Stories are the most charming and interesting of Kipling's stories for children; they have also been the most popular of his books among the child readers to date.[1] They are a collection of twelve short tales published by Rudyard Kipling in 1901. Each of them asks a mythical question about the origin of something[2] and gives an answer to the question. (Some of these questions are even formulated directly in the titles of the respective stories: "How the Whale Got His Throat," "How the Camel Got His Hump," "How the Rhinoceros Got His Skin," "How the Leopard Got His Spots," "How the First Letter Was Written," and "How the Alphabet Was Made").

---

[1] See, e.g., Gillian Avery, "The Children's Writer," in J. Gross (ed.), *Rudyard Kipling, the Man, His Work and His World* (London: Weidenfeld and Nicolson, 1972), 114. Many critics point to the existence of the child addressee in the collection.

[2] Some critics regard these questions as mythical: e.g., Robert Escarpit, *Rudyard Kipling. Servitudes et Grandeurs Impériales* (Paris: Hachette, 1955), 211, 228; Cornelia Meigs et al., *A Critical History of Children's Literature* (New York: Macmillan, 1953), 341; R. Hildebrandt, *Nonsense-Aspekte der Englischen Kinderliteratur* (Hamburg: Beltz, 1962), 187; Witold Chwalewik, "Kipling," in *Z literatury angielskiej. Studia i wrażenia* (Warsaw: Państwowy Instytut Wydawniczy, 1969), 248-49; R.L. Green, *Kipling and the Children* (London: Elek Books, 1965), 178; Wiesław Krajka, Andrzej Zgorzelski, "R. Kipling, 'The Butterfly that Stamped' – Sample Analysis," in *On the Analysis of the Literary Text*, trans. A. Blaim (Warsaw: Państwowe Wydawnictwo Naukowe, 1984), 166.

The thesis of my essay is that the questions posed are the mythical, etiologic questions of a foundation, cosmogonic myth, yet the answers provided are not mythical but fictional: a product of literary creativity, fantasy and imagination.

Here are some examples of the questions asked and the answers given in Kipling's *Just So Stories*:

1. "How the Whale Got His Throat:"

   The Whale swallowed a shipwrecked mariner. The mariner cut up a raft into a little square grating, tied it firm and put the grating tight into the Whale's throat. And since that time, the grating has prevented whales from eating anything except very small fish, which is why whales never eat very small children.

2. "How the Camel Got His Hump:"

   At the beginning of time, the Camel was the only animal who refused to work for Man and when anyone requested him to work or help, he refused and said "Humph." In order to punish him for his idleness, a Djinn put an ugly hump on his back. And ever since that time, camels have had humps.

3. "How the Rhinoceros Got His Skin:"

   The first Rhinoceros's skin was smooth and he did not have any manners. A Parsee decided to punish him for that. One day the Rhinoceros took his skin off, left it on the shore and went bathing. The Parsee rubbed cake-crumbs into his skin to punish him for his lack of manners. The Rhinoceros put his skin on and the skin with the cake-crumbs inside tickled him. In order to stop this, the Rhinoceros rubbed his skin against various objects. And from that day on, every rhinoceros has had folds in his skin and a bad temper on the account of the cake-crumbs in his skin that tickle him.

4. "The Elephant's Child" (how the elephant got his trunk):

   The first Elephant's Child was full of insatiable curiosity: he asked many questions and poked his nose into everything. Once he wanted to know what the Crocodile had for dinner: he asked the Crocodile, and the clever Crocodile asked the Elephant's Child to come closer and closer and finally caught him by his nose which was small then. In order to free his nose from the Crocodile's grip, the Elephant's Child started to pull it hard. When he freed himself from the Crocodile's grip, the Elephant's Child's nose turned into a long trunk. The Elephant's Child and all the other elephants found out the trunk had a few advantages over the nose. And all the other elephants went in a great hurry to borrow the new noses from the Crocodile. And ever since that day, all elephants have had trunks.

5. "The Sing-Song of Old Man Kangaroo" (why kangaroos hop on their
    hind legs):
    The first Kangaroo was a creature with four short legs; he was grey,
    woolly and extremely proud. He asked the gods to make him
    different from all the other animals. He wanted to be popular and run
    after. One of the gods, wanting to grant the first Kangaroo's wish,
    asked Dingo – Yellow-Dog Dingo – to run after him (but in the
    literal meaning of the word: to chase him). When they came to a river
    with neither a bridge nor a ferry-boat, the Kangaroo, in order to flee
    from the Dog following him, had to hop through it. Later, in order to
    make his escape more effective, he continued to hop. And each hop
    was longer and longer. And the hopping made his hind legs stronger
    and stronger, and longer and longer. And that is why all kangaroos
    have long hind legs and hop on them.

    To begin with, let us examine the fictitious image of cosmogony as
presented in the story "The Crab that Played with the Sea:"

> Before the High and Far-Off Times, O my Best Beloved, came
> the Time of the Very Beginnings; and that was in the days
> when the Eldest Magician was getting Things ready. First he
> got the Earth ready; then he got the Sea ready; and then he
> told all the Animals that they could come out and play. And
> the Animals said, "O Eldest Magician, what shall we play at?"
> and he said, "I will show you." He took the Elephant – All-
> the-Elephant-there-was – and said, "Play at being an
> Elephant," and All-the-Elephant-there-was played. He took
> the Beaver – All-the-Beaver-there-was – and said, "Play at
> being a Beaver," and All-the-Beaver-there-was played. He took
> the Cow – All-the-Cow-there-was – and said, "Play at being a
> Cow," and All-the-Cow-there-was played. He took the Turtle –
> All-the-Turtle-there-was – and said, "Play at being a Turtle,"
> and All-the-Turtle-there-was played. One by one he took all
> the beasts and birds and fishes and told them what to play at.[3]
>
> (157-58)

On the top of the hill you can see All-the-Elephant-there-was,
and All-the-Cow-there-was, and All-the-Turtle-there-was going
off to play as the Eldest Magician told them. The Cow has a

---

[3] All quotations are from Rudyard Kipling, *Just So Stories for Little Children* (London:
Macmillan, 1962). Further references appear in parentheses in the text.

hump, because she was All-the-Cow-there-was; so she had to have all there was for all the cows that were made afterwards. Under the hill there are Animals who have been taught the game they were to play. You can see All-the-Tiger-there-was smiling at All-the-Bones-there-were, and you can see All-the-Elk-there-was, and All-the-Parrot-there-was, and All-the-Bunnies-there-were on the hill. The other Animals are on the other side of the hill, so I haven't drawn them. The little house up the hill is All-the-House-there-was. The Eldest Magician made it to show the Man how to make houses when he wanted to. The Snake round that spiky hill is All-the-Snake-there-was, and he is talking to All-the-Monkey-there-was, and the Monkey is being rude to the Snake, and the Snake is being rude to the Monkey

(160).[4]

Just So Stories fall into the category of mythical-etiologic tales, which usually offer truthful, authoritative explanations of the origin of selected elements of the surrounding world. They apply the conventions of the cosmogonic myth, which explains the creation of the world, nature and life, accounts for the origins of certain elements of empirical reality and orders cosmic as well as social structures.[5] The cosmogonic myth concerns the time when the precedents and paradigms of objects and phenomena were created: the time that transformed chaos into cosmos and gave birth to the world still existing today. It is a sacred story that took place *ab initio, in illo tempore*, in the mythical time of the absolute beginning, or at an early stage of pre-history, before and beyond the historical, empirical time. The mythical proto-events were enacted by the first creatures – gods, supernatural beings or cultural heroes. The scale and consequences of their actions were universal, cosmic as they created the world, its living beings and inanimate objects. These events are totally outside the common range of perception and reason, outside ordinary human life, yet at the same time basic to it: they are paradigmatic, providing a symbolic code, a model for the natural and

---

[4] This quotation comments on a drawing that represents the actions of some of the First Animals created by the Eldest Magician.

[5] In this article, the general characteristics of the cosmogonic myth are based on Ryszard Tomicki, "Mit," in Zofia Staszczak (ed.), *Słownik etnologiczny. Terminy ogólne* (Warsaw-Poznan: Państwowe Wydawnictwo Naukowe, 1987), 244-48; *The New Encyclopedia Britannica*, 15th ed., Vol. 8, "Myth," 470-71; Vol. 24, "Myth and Mythology," 715-32; as well as on items listed in the bibliographies to these entries.

social order of the world. They put everything in its proper place, defending man from chaos and ensuring a sense of order and safety. The setting for these events is semi-divine, supernatural and sacred, neither realistic nor specific and historical.

Like real cosmogonic myths, Kipling's etiologic tales, fictional quasi-myths, reduce the essence, meaning and structure of the explained elements of reality to their origins. The significance of these paradigmatic events is not merely ontological but also axiological: they constitute models for human behavior, fundamental paradigms of norms and values, patterns of individual and social life to be followed – sanctified in this way, and sanctioning and supporting the existing order of the world.

However, the quasi-myths for children in Kipling's *Just So Stories* are aesthetically functioning products of literary imagination, devoid of the religious significance (sacred elements) and the social function of real myths. Their characters are neither gods nor cultural heroes, the etiologic explanations given in them are a matter not of faith but of artistic creation and imagination. In *Just So Stories*, the mythical etiologic paradigm has been transformed into artistic discourse. The ontological and axiological essence of actual myths has been replaced by aesthetic constructs requiring a certain paradigm of artistic imagination on the part of the small child addressee.

Unlike their mythic precursors (and like fables, parables or fairy stories), the stories of *Just So Stories* are fictitious, untrue.[6] Despite this, they answer the etiologic questions in terms of authoritative rhetoric. Although the narrator tries hard to make his small child addressee believe his fictional stories by appealing strongly to the child's emotions and power of imagination, the authority, validity and truthfulness of his stories are negated by their nature of quasi-judgements, a part of literary (artistic) fiction.

The solutions to these problems given in the unraveling of the action of the stories turn out to be quite simple and definite, thus suiting the intellectual powers of child readers. However, these solutions do not possess cognitive value with respect to empirical reality: they remain valid only within the sphere of literary fiction, in the world created by the writer. The denotative significance of these stories, unlike the denotative function of the problems posed in them, is hence almost non-existent in relation to the empirical world: owing to their fictitious character, these

---

[6] See also an analysis of "The Butterfly that Stamped," a sample story from the collection, in terms of the genre variants of the fairy-tale/fairy-story: Krajka, Zgorzelski, "R. Kipling, 'The Butterfly that Stamped' – Sample Analysis," 155-67.

stories do not increase children's knowledge of the empirical world so much as develop their imagination and creativity.

Just So Stories fulfill the cognitive function in a way that is typical of a literary work of fiction: not by explaining the true origins of the phenomena of the world but by merely drawing the small child addressee's attention to them, making him/her remember them, satisfying his/her curiosity. The very fact that such questions are posed is of great denotative value for the child addressee: it means he/she is reminded of such real facts as the elephant's trunk, the leopard's spotted skin or the long hind legs of the kangaroo.[7] And the choice of the naive etiologic questions asked in this collection is determined by the likely interests of the small child addressee for whom the origin of the elephant's trunk or the camel's hump are important issues and may be numbered among normal questions of a cognitive nature asked by every child interested in the world surrounding him/her.[8]

In order to help the small child addressee to understand the surrounding reality, Kipling anthropomorphizes animals in the ways typical of fables, parables or fairy stories. This coincides with the anthropomorphism of mythical thinking, emphasizing the essential unity of the world, of human beings and animals. Following the paradigmatic nature of cosmogonic myths, the characters of *Just So Stories*, who enact the quasi-mythical proto-events, are either gods or representatives of various classes of beings. They are made typical in the ways characteristic of fables, parables or fairy stories: they do not have individual names but are identified only by the name of the general class or species to which they belong, with the first letters of their names capitalized (e.g., Animal, Butterfly, Camel, Rhinoceros, etc.). As in myth, the actions of these characters take place at a time that is unspecified, existing beyond ordinary human experience; but this is the time of a work of fiction, as distinct from empirical, historical time. The setting for these actions is also unspecific and vague – as in a fable, parable, or fairy tale.

In *Just So Stories,* the axiological significance of myth (the transformation of chaos into an ordered and ethical cosmos) acquires the form of specific didacticism directed to the small child addressee of the collection, suited to his/her powers of comprehension and aimed at offering him/her prescriptions for appropriate behavior – for instance,

---

[7] On the denotative (cognitive) value of the etiologic questions and answers in *Just So Stories*, see Wiesław Krajka, "On the Dual Addressee of the 'Just So Stories,'" *Essays in Poetics. The Journal of the British Neo-Formalist Circle*, 3.2 (September 1978): 77-78.

[8] Jean Piaget, *Mowa i myślenie u dziecka* (Warsaw: PWN, 1992), 185-266.

"one should not be lazy," "unmannered," "too curious," "proud" – as in the stories summarized at the beginning of this paper. These connotative meanings show close affinities with the didacticism of the fairy tale (the concept of justice according to which an evil character is always punished) and the fable (connotative meanings put in terms of simple ethical values as well as ending up a story with a moral). But the didacticism of *Just So Stories* is significantly transformed above all for their child addressee. In order to make such ideas easier to understand for the child addressee, a moral is normally communicated very clearly and explicitly. For example, commenting on the picture presenting the Whale and the 'Stute Fish trying to hide, the narrator says: "I have drawn the Doors of the Equator. They are shut. They are always kept shut, because a door ought always to be kept shut." (6) To strengthen the didactic effect of these stories, their morals are connected with punishing one of the characters for some vice. Thus, both the moral and the punishment are a kind of warning and a lesson to the child addressee. The stock of vices appearing in these stories is limited to such basic evil features of human character as laziness, unkindness, pride, selfishness – features that many of the child readers might possess. The punishment is very specific and therefore easy for the child addressee to imagine and understand: e.g., the crab is punished for his pride by having his power taken away from him; the little elephant's excessive curiosity is punished by his nose being pulled to the length of a trunk.[9]

Thus, in Kipling's *Just So Stories* the fusion of the mythical-etiologic and the aesthetic-fictional elements created the mythical-etiologic fairy stories for small children. The narrator of the collection assumes the role of the originator of cosmogonic myths and, following their fundamental patterns, creates fictional quasi-myths, mythological-aesthetic foundation texts for small children. Due to Kipling's transformation of true cosmogonic myths, their original ontological and axiological nature has been transformed into the aesthetic function determining a certain type of artistic imagination specific for the small child addressee. Similar quasi-myths, but for the older child addressee, appear in the famous *Jungle Books* by the same author.

However, *Just So Stories* should primarily be considered as a literary work of art, as a masterpiece of literature for children, or rather literature

---

[9] On transformation of the didacticism of *Just So Stories* by the small child addressee, see also Krajka, "On the Dual Addressee of the 'Just So Stories,'" 78.

with a double addressee: the child and the adult.[10] The child addressee exerts a tremendous influence on the way the fictional world of *Just So Stories* is shaped – its considerable schematization functions through facilitating its perception by the child addressee.[11] Such an attitude is discernible on the part of the narrator who presents the fictional world in the simplest possible way. His stories are very short and their plots simple. For example, the action of "How the Whale Got His Throat" presents only one adventure. The characters of *Just So Stories* embody some definite, elementary ethical notions: e.g., Elephant's Child – excessive curiosity; Baboon – wisdom; Kangaroo – vanity. The presentation of the setting in these stories is also very sketchy and schematic: in most of them, it is limited to only a few clearly indicated objects. For example in "How the Whale Got His Throat" it consists of the sea, the raft, the mariner's suspenders and a few of his necessities, which are only mentioned but not characterized precisely by means of epithets or descriptions.

Frequently, the particular elements of the setting and characters are carefully enumerated by the narrator: e.g., "The Dog was wild, and the Horse was wild, and the Cow was wild, and the Sheep was wild, and the Pig was wild – as wild as wild could be – and they walked in the Wet Wild Woods by their wild lones. But the wildest of all the wild animals was the Cat." (181) In this passage the narrator repeats the word "wild," thus persistently drawing the addressee's attention to the "wildness" of the fictional world of the story which is one of its most important characteristics. This device is used in nearly every story in the collection; e.g., telling the addressee about the mariner's suspenders, the camel's hump, the elephant's excessive curiosity, the graciously waving tail of the jaguar's mother, the wisdom and nobility of king Suleiman. Such motifs are constantly and persistently recalled by the narrator who in this way focuses the child addressee's attention on them.

The general tendency of the narrator to aim at facilitating the perception of the fictional world by the child addressee is also manifested by the inclusion of illustrations and comments accompanying them in the text (most stories contain two pictures and comments); they usually present only the most important and characteristic motifs of the story. For example, one of the pictures in "The Sing-Song of Old Man

---

[10] The following part of this article is based on Krajka, "On the Dual Addressee of the 'Just So Stories,'" 78-84.

[11] See an analysis of this tendency as manifest in "The Butterfly that Stamped:" Krajka, Zgorzelski, "R. Kipling, 'The Butterfly that Stamped' – Sample Analysis," 158-62.

Kangaroo" depicts only the kangaroo dancing on a rock, the God Nqa talking to him, and the rising sun indicating the precise time. In addition, the meaning of an illustration is fully explained in the comment on it. Thus, the narrator makes a triple presentation of parts of stories (in its text – in the picture – in the comment on it); the repeated presentations additionally focus the addressee's attention on some, normally the most important, motifs.

It also seems that the triple presentation of certain sections of the fictional world results in the imposition upon the addressee of some patterns of reception: the pictures and comments indicate how it should be imagined. These patterns accurately fit the mentality of the child addressee. For example, in order to suggest that the 'Stute Fish succeeded in hiding herself from the Whale, the equator is depicted as a line with closed doors guarded by giants Moar and Koar and the 'Stute Fish is hidden deeply in the roots of some seaweed under the equator. In the comments to these black-and-white pictures, the narrator also encourages the child addressee to complete the sketchy pattern of reception presented there, leaving it to him/her to paint them with colored pencils. For example, commenting on the depiction of Elephant's Child trying to reach bananas with his trunk, the narrator says: "I think it would look better if you painted the banana-tree green and the Elephant's Child red." (72) Similarly, discussing the Baboon he has drawn, he pretends to be interested in painting this picture with colors, thus prompting this idea to the child addressee: "I should like to paint him with paint-box colours, but I am not allowed." (44)

The child addressee also exerts a considerable influence on the shaping of narration and the language of *Just So Stories*. The tendency, described above, for the narrator to schematize the fictional world and facilitate its perception by the child addressee, brought about the use of such devices of language as enumerations, set epithets and recurring phrases. Apart from this, the language organization of *Just So Stories* primarily focuses the addressee's attention on the actual shape of itself. This is done mainly by using the following language devices:

1. Rhymed neologisms: e.g., "Stickly-Prickly," "speckly-spickly," "patchy-blatchy;"
2. Neological epithets: e.g., "hissy-snake," "deserty-desert;"
3. Emphases: e.g., "girl-daughter;"
4. Onomatopoeias: e.g., "Shu-shu-u-u-u!," "Humph;"
5. Alliteration: e.g. "Wet Wild Woods," "a nasty nosy noise," or "I hate helping to hang heavy, hot, hairy hides on them;"

6. Rhythmical prose: e.g., "he stumped and he jumped and he thumped and he bumped, and he pranced and he danced, and he banged and he clanged, and he hit and he bit, and he leaped and he creeped, and he prowled and he howled, and he hopped and he dropped, and he cried and he sighed, and he crawled and he bawled, and he stepped and he lepped [...];" (9)
7. Enumerations: e.g., "The Dog was wild, and the Horse was wild, and the Cow was wild, and the Sheep was wild, and the Pig was wild – as wild as wild could be – and they walked in the Wet Wild Woods by their wild lones;" (181)
8. Repetitions of words and phrases within a single sentence: e.g., the word "wild" in the example quoted above, "And after thousands and thousands and thousands of years," "Pau Amma grew smaller and smaller and smaller," "for always and always and always;"
9. Almost exact repetitions (usually triple) of some section of a story (e.g., the first part of "How the Camel Got His Hump");
10. Recurrent phrases: e.g., "Dingo – Yellow-Dog Dingo," "and he was a Tewara," or "'*Kun*?' [...] '*Payah kun!*'"

The above examples illustrate that linguistically highly organized elements of these stories are frequently redundant as far as informing the child addressee about the course of action or the detailed shape of the fictional world is concerned.[12] They simply have a different semantic function – that of fascinating the child addressee with exotic names and the very shape of an utterance, stylized at times by an analogy with children's speech. Seemingly nonsensical poetic phrases are peculiarly fascinating to the child addressee since the language of children also contains such 'ungrammatical' words and sentences and 'meaningless' neologisms and phonetic associations. The language of these stories casts a spell of literary fiction upon the child addressee and serves to develop his/her aesthetic tastes and feelings.

All these linguistic devices (rhythm, rhyme, parallelism, refrain quality, alliteration, or even stanzaic patterns), applied abundantly, turn the language of *Just So Stories* into poetic prose, a poetically organized utterance giving information about itself and providing the reader with a tremendous range of semantic and aesthetic associations. But these

---

[12] In view of the evident modeling of the narration of *Just So Stories* after the oral fairy tale yarn, enumerations, recurring phrases, repetitions of a part of action with the use of the same expressions and set phrases, might have helped Kipling the storyteller by indicating certain typical patterns in his oral improvisation of these stories to his children listeners.

qualities of the text are impossible for the child addressee to grasp and understand: they are directed at the adult addressee of *Just So Stories*.

The last story in the collection ("The Butterfly that Stamped") is an example of such double communication. For the small child addressee, the enumeration of the titles of Queen Balkis ("Queen that was of Sheba and Sabie and the Rivers of the Gold of the South – from the desert of Zinn to the towers of Zimbabwe;" 225) is nothing more than a fairy tale accumulation of meaningless exotic names. Yet the main function of this enumeration in *Just So Stories* is to convey information about the extraordinary power of the Queen and, what makes her more praiseworthy, about her modesty and generosity that match her power. Similarly, in order to render how powerful a ruler King Suleiman-bin-Daoud was, the narrator enumerates the 'languages' of animals and objects which he understood; in order to emphasize the King's tremendous fame, he enumerates the titles of some widely known stories about Suleiman-bin-Daoud before beginning to tell the story about the butterfly.

At the level of connotative (didactic) meaning directed at the child addressee, "The Butterfly that Stamped" condemns pride and vanity: "After that he [King Suleiman-bin-Daoud] never forgot that it was silly to show off" (209), "he turned the ring on his finger – just for the little Butterfly's sake, not for the sake of showing off." (219) However, the story also communicates meanings that are directed at the adult addressee. King Suleiman-bin-Daoud and Queen Balkis are ideal and almost god-like rulers, and yet they address the butterflies as their brother creatures, calling them "Little brother" and "Little sister" and thus expressing brotherly affection toward not only the butterflies but also any fellow creature, even the weakest and tiniest. Parting with his small animal friends, Suleiman-bin-Daoud kisses their wings and says: "Go in peace, little folk!" (226) His speech signifies not only a blessing given by a powerful ruler but also the godlike joy of making weak and tiny creatures happy, although they may not always deserve it (the narrator says that the King "laughed […] at the impudence of the bad little Butterfly;" 216). This illustrates how a single short sentence implies an infinite range of meanings and associations. In this short story, the communication to the adult addressee also consists in the comic element, the parody of the fairy tale style, and the motif of the "war of the sexes."[13]

---

[13] Krajka, Zgorzelski, "R. Kipling, 'The Butterfly that Stamped' – Sample Analysis," 162-65.

In the poem at the end of "How the Camel Got His Hump," one of the levels of meaning is constituted by a set of connotative (didactic) ideas: the child addressee is instructed that laziness should not be encouraged since a lazy person may be given an ugly hump. On the other hand, the word "hump" functions metaphorically by introducing a whole gamut of additional meanings. For example, it implies not only a person's distorted outward appearance, but also a deformity of the psychological and ethical aspects of his/her personality (mainly in the first stanza of the poem which says that the hump given as a punishment for laziness is much uglier than the ordinary hump of a camel from a zoo). This type of deformity is universal: everybody has a hump since everybody is inclined to laziness. Isolating the phrase "We get the hump" as a separate line functions as an additional generalization of the metaphor. In ordinary speech, this phrase evokes associations implying that all of us have some flaws (psychological, physical), complexes, deeply hidden troubles, etc. Still further universalization is reached by evoking the biblical notion of expulsion from Paradise (the hump-work is the burden of humanity and its everlasting doom).

The poem at the end of "How the Alphabet Was Made" communicates meanings that are impossible for the child addressee to understand. The first stanza introduces the pensive mood of the lyrical "I" reflecting upon the transience of human societies as contrasted to unchanging nature: the tribe of Tegumai became extinct a long time ago, and the cuckoo, the sun and silence constitute everlasting attributes of the never-changing nature of the Merrow Down region. This contrast is emphasized by the rhyme of the second and fourth lines of the first stanza ("none remain,– " vs. "The silence and the sun remain.") because of the repetition of the same word, "remain," in the contrasted semantic messages: nothing remains – something remains; none of the tribe of Tegumai remains – the nature (silence, the sun) remains. The next three stanzas present the character of Taffimai as embodying spring, abounding in freshness, vigor and vitality. The image of the girl is very dynamic: she dances, flits (the importance of this word is emphasized by using it twice in the rhymed positions in the second and fourth lines of the fourth stanza) as quickly as a deer (she is dressed in a deer-skin cloak). She is also conventionally beautiful: "Her eyes are bright as diamonds / And bluer than the sky above." This dynamism and idealization turn Taffimai into an epitome of youth, health, happiness, joy and life – make her symbolically identical with the spring that comes with her. This symbolism turns the last stanza of the poem, expressing her father's (Tegumai's) love for her, into an expression of general human desire for such values. The power of this feeling is enhanced by Tegumai's separation from his daughter: in the first two lines of the last stanza, the word "far" is repeated three times with a gradation of meaning and effect: "far–oh, very far behind, / So far she cannot call to him." The emphasis is put here on the abstract sense of this word: it means here not only physical distance, but also, and primarily, unattainability of a desired object. This makes the two principal characters of the poem (Taffimai and Tegumai) signify a human being's desire for happiness and youth, the sad and melancholy mood of transience, etc. – meanings which are beyond the power of intellectual understanding by the child addressee.

Many other poetically organized samples from *Just So Stories* might be discussed here to further prove the existence of the adult addressee in the collection and the considerable degree to which it modifies its language. This kind of addressee would indeed appear focal when applying many of the possible intercultural readings of this collection of short stories: e.g., those focusing on intercultural dialogue of elements of various civilizations (Islamic, Hindu, Buddhist, European), on ways of assimilating otherness, on universal iconography, etc.

To sum up, *Just So Stories* by Rudyard Kipling is a masterpiece both as a literary text addressed to a small child and an adult addressee and as a unique collection of highly imaginative quasi-mythical etiologic tales for very small children. They are indeed a mythological-aesthetic foundation text for children.

IMAGINED COMMUNITIES REVISITED: BEYOND ROMANTIC AND TECHNOLOGICAL APPROACHES TO CULTURAL IDENTITY AND DIVERSITY

Martin Procházka

This essay is an attempt to view the study of myths from an unusual angle. I do not approach them as objects of study, semiotic structures, or mere constituents of cultural heritage, obsolete or anachronistic cultural forms. I see them as discursive practices shaping collective memories and influencing social behavior, particularly identifications with certain values, however mundane, commercial, trite or dangerous they may seem. Similar to Clifford Geertz[1] or Roland Barthes,[2] I do not think we can reliably distinguish between the traditional symbolism of myth or ritual on the one hand, and ideologies, advertising strategies or patterns of pop culture on the other. The questions I will attempt to answer are to what extent these discursive practices can produce what Benedict Anderson has called "imagined communities," that is, communities which "are to be distinguished, not by their falsity/genuineness, but by the style in which they are imagined,"[3] and to what extent Europe can be

---

[1] Clifford Geertz, *The Interpretation of Cultures* (New York: Basic Books, 1973), 143-69, 193-234.

[2] Roland Barthes, *Mythologies*, trans. Anette Lavers (New York: Hill and Wang, 1972), 111-59.

[3] Benedict Anderson, *Imagined Communities: Reflections on the Origin and Spread of Nationalism*, revised edition (London and New York: Verso, 1991), 6.

imagined as such a community, however heterogeneous and incomplete it may appear. Although this view of collective imagination may be tempting, I am also aware of its risks especially at a time of resurgent nationalism, racism and religious fundamentalism.

Despite these threats, Anderson's emphasis on the "style" of imagining communities seems a salient prerequisite for understanding contemporary cultural as well as political differences. It points out the advantages of functionalism over essentialism in comparative study of cultures and prevents scholars from absolutizing the values of their own culture, or of a general "affirmative culture,"[4] such as Shakespeare's universal humanism.[5]

Another, equally important and closely related question is how myths can be grasped in the flux of time: not in their hypothetical evolution from ancient oral forms to ambiguous symbolic patterns of modernist art, but in their social functioning as "machines:" "fuzzy aggregates" whose operation resembles musical "synthesizers" that do not merely repeat (or represent) sounds of individual instruments but "unite disparate elements" (tones and noises) and transpose "the parameters from one formula to another."[6] This approach prevents reducing myths to a mathematical formula, a set of general rules of combination for narrative elements and value patterns.[7] In contrast to Deleuze and Guattari, who sharply distinguish between the mass media as "machines for reproduction [...] that effectively scramble all terrestrial forces of the people" and modern artistic creation open to cosmic powers and anticipating as its audience some deterritorialized "cosmic people" of the future,[8] I see a link between these two activities in *myths functioning as machines*, for instance, in the form of historical films, TV adaptations of well-known novels, travel films and commercials. These machines do not merely *reproduce* sentiments, desires or values, they also *produce* them, making people imagine their communities, cultural identities, and their diversities.

---

[4] Herbert Marcuse, "The Affirmative Character of Culture," in *Negations: Essays in Critical Theory*, trans. Jeremy Shapiro (Boston: Beacon Press, 1968), 95.

[5] Michael Bristol, *Shakespeare's America, America's Shakespeare* (London and New York: Routledge, 1990), 39-41.

[6] Gilles Deleuze and Félix Guattari, *A Thousand Plateaus: Capitalism and Schizophrenia*, trans. Brian Massumi (Minneapolis: University of Minnesota Press, 1987), 343-47.

[7] Claude Lévi-Strauss, *Structural Anthropology*, trans. Claire Jacobson and Brooke G. Schoepfe (New York: Basic Books, 1963), 228.

[8] Deleuze and Guattari, *A Thousand Plateaus*, 345-46.

One good example of this production is a recent Czech television commercial transposing a generally known narrative about the arrival of the tribe of the Czechs to their homeland, first told by the chronicler Kosmas at the end of the eleventh century. With a good deal of humor and irony, the story of the origin of the Czechs is told in a characteristic dialect spoken in Brno, the capital of Moravia, a distinct historical and cultural region of the Czech Republic (or, historically, the Kingdom of Bohemia). Together with a language shift, there are also shifts in place names and references, making the narrative a typical Brno story. Its cultural otherness is emphasized by the use of subtitles, translating the local dialect into literary Czech. This "fuzzy aggregate" of mythical travesty, oral culture and cinematic technique is used both to sell an allegedly 'local' beer, and to express (as well as control) patriotic sentiments. It is a "machine," producing desire and consumption, cultural identity and diversity.

As a consequence, the understanding of myths as "machines" does not only emphasize their heterogeneous and fragmentary nature (earlier described by Lévi-Strauss as *bricolage*)[9] but also their capacity to produce desires or affects[10] and to give rise to economic processes, such as production or consumption,[11] along with cultural processes, such as formation or dismantling of stereotypes, identification or disidentification with certain values.

Combining the continuity of processes with a structural and functional heterogeneity, myths as "machines" do not exist in a temporal continuum. This is also true of "imagined communities" but, as Anderson shows, some ways of imagining assert or even impose continuity in time, while others focus on the unity of a present moment, no matter how ephemeral it may be. Recent analyses of time, especially those by Deleuze or Derrida, have shown that no fundamental distinction can be made between these approaches: they are two versions of the same philosophical problem, namely, whether the essence of time is continuity, or radical, irreducible difference.[12] Similarly, in cultural studies, particularly when tracing the development of modern

---

[9] Claude Lévi-Strauss, *The Savage Mind* (London: Weidenfeld and Nicholson, 1966), 17.

[10] Deleuze and Guattari, *A Thousand Plateaus*, 399-400.

[11] Gilles Deleuze and Félix Guattari, *Anti-Oedipus: Capitalism and Schizophrenia*, trans. Robert Hurley, Mark Seem and Helen R. Lane (New York: Viking Press, 1977), 20.

[12] See, e.g., Gilles Deleuze, *The Logic of Sense*, trans. Mark Lester, ed. Constantin V. Boundas (New York: Columbia University Press, 1990), 5, 61-65, 162-68; Jacques Derrida, *The Specters of Marx: The State of the Debt, the Work of Mourning, & the New International*, trans. Peggy Kamuf (New York and London: Routledge, 1994), 27.

nationalism, these two ways of imagining are often found to intermingle and the "style" of imagining a community resembles the Deleuzean "machine."

Given all this, the main problem of Anderson's approach seems to consist in the radical, fundamentalist separation of the two ways of imagining. This strategy is not of Anderson's own making: it can be traced back to Walter Benjamin's notion of "art in the age of mechanical reproduction,"[13] or even to Auerbach's two concepts of temporality in Homer's epic and the Old Testament.[14] What connects these two approaches is a nostalgia for a strong, central power organizing collective imaginings in a temporal continuum.[15] The primary aim of my critique is not to point out the schematic nature of Anderson's "styles" in which communities are imagined, but to overcome this hereditary yearning for the lost spiritual power of myths.

According to Anderson, communities are imagined either in a temporal continuum, which can be described as "simultaneity-along-time," or in "transverse, cross-time" linkages between fragmentary and disparate discourses in heterogeneous historical and social circumstances.[16] The former way of imagining is typical of religious communities based on the existence of a sacred language, a canon of sacred texts, which can be interpreted as a sacred history. The latter way is symptomatic of the rise of modern nations, caused, as Anderson points out, by a simultaneous expansion of administrative vernacular languages, printing press and newspapers.

One rather problematic aspect of Anderson's approach lies in his belief that modern nations as imagined communities are articulated by mostly technological forces of "democratic anonymity" which produce a semblance of cultural homogeneity. In contrast to this assertion, it can be pointed out that under the influence of Romanticism, nations are often imagined, and invented, as religious communities, and the printing press (and mechanical reproduction in general) may be used to monumentalize their (often invented) oral mythologies.

This is certainly the case of the graphic design used on the cover of this book. The woodcut made circa 1857 by Josef Mánes (1820-71)

---

[13] Walter Benjamin, *Illuminations*, trans. Harry Zohn (New York: Schocken Books, 1969), 263-65.

[14] Erich Auerbach, *Mimesis: The Representation of Reality in Western Literature*, trans. Willard R. Trask (Princeton: Princeton University Press, 1953), 4-23.

[15] Auerbach, *Mimesis*, 542 and passim.

[16] Anderson, *Imagined Communities*, 24.

represents a scene from an allegedly archaic Czech epic poem entitled "Záboj, Slavoj and Luděk." This text is a part of a monumental literary forgery, *The Manuscript of Dvůr Králové*, 'discovered' by a Czech nationalist Václav Hanka in 1817. The empty space in the engraving (now displaying the title of this volume) was reserved for the printed text of the poem, which, together with the graphic design, facilitated the imagining of the nation as an archaic, almost entirely male community, similar to Ossian's *fianna*. It is clear from the design that the two ways of imagining, let us call them *romantic* (referring obliquely to Hegel's comparison of Romanticism and Christianity), and *technological*, are interlinked by specific discursive strategies. The assemblage of a visual image and a monumentalized, printed version of an (invented) oral epic functions as a Deleuzean "machine," synthesizing a semblance of an old myth, with militant as well as erotic sentiments (the poem's text was meant to touch the seductive body of a young woman, the only female in the picture) and the nostalgic desire for primitive life in the bosom of nature.

Apart from a good deal of schematism, Anderson's approach also has other disadvantages. Homi Bhabha has alerted us to the duality between the "pedagogy" of the narratives engendering the "cross-time" imaginings in individuals, and the performative act of speech in which the individual identifies herself with the imagined "inscribed in a sudden primordiality of meaning that 'looms up *imperceptibly* out of the horizonless past.'"[17] To cover up this difference between the "modern" construction of imagined communities, and the "primordialist"[18] approach to language, signification, and – indeed – national identity, Anderson invokes "the selfless [...] unisonance" in language and poetry (in ritual utterances, popular songs and national anthems) as the power responsible for the emergence of the imagined communities. As Bhabha points out, in doing so, Anderson confuses the *act of imagination* with the *act of will* unifying "historical memory" and securing "present-day consent," thus making individuals forget history as past violence.[19] In other words, Anderson does not recognize the actual heterogeneity of myths in time, which is not "empty" but exceedingly complex, integrating fragmentary discourses, representations, desires, affects and intensities, into assemblages or machines whose parts move as if at

---

[17] Homi Bhabha, *The Location of Culture* (London and New York: Routledge, 1994), 159; cf. Anderson, *Imagined Communities*, 144.

[18] See Anthony D. Smith, *The Nation in History: Historiographical Debates about Ethnicity and Nationalism* (Oxford: Polity Press, 2000), 4, 5.

[19] Bhabha, *The Location of Culture*, 160.

different speeds. Moreover, he disregards what Bhabha points out, namely that the imagining of the homogeneity of modern nations has for a long time been disrupted by "a more instantaneous and subaltern voice of the people, minority discourses that speak betwixt and between times and places."[20]

This is particularly important for the imagining of Europe, a process that may be said to have a similar dynamism as the imagining of individual nations. I will first demonstrate the aspects of this process that resemble the imagining of sacred communities. Then I will discuss an example of the *technological* way of imagining. In both cases, I will focus on the transformative power of myths functioning as "machines" in two canonical works of modern European literature: Novalis' essay "Christianity or Europe" (Christenheit oder Europa, 1799)[21] and Kundera's novel *Immortality* (1990; L'Immortalité, 1989; Nesmrtelnost, 1993).[22] The choice of these texts is motivated by their relations to the central spiritual values of the Christian myth – the sacrificial love and unity of the church in Christ – and by their transformation of these values into individual desires and sentiments, used, as Kundera shows, not only for the assertion of individual identities, but also in advertising and forms of contemporary popular culture. In this way, the "minority discourses that speak betwixt times and places," described by Bhabha, are not merely repressed but also articulated.

In Novalis' essay, medieval Europe is united by "a great communal interest:" the Christian faith supported by the papal authority. The Church, represented by the elite of "holy men" is imagined as an all-inclusive corporation, "a guild to which everyone had access." (327) Its unity, however, does not consist in a sacred language and texts known only by its elite, but in an originally homogeneous organization based on love, spiritual authority, beauty of rituals and ceremonies, and also on the economic and cultural power of the new center – Rome, that had supplanted the destroyed Jerusalem.

It is not surprising that Novalis' imagining of European unity initially uses the 'body' metaphor developed in the First Letter of St. Paul to the Corinthians:

---

20 *The Location of Culture*, 158.

21 Novalis, "Christenheit oder Europa," in *Werke in einem Band* (Berlin and Weimar: Aufbau Verlag, 1980), 327-46. Subsequent references to this edition are given in the text. All translations are my own.

22 Milan Kundera, *Immortality*, trans. Peter Kussi (New York: Grove Weidenfeld, 1991). Subsequent references are given in the text.

> For Christ is like a single body with its many limbs and organs,
> which, many as they are, together make up one body. For
> indeed we have all been brought into one body by baptism. [...]
> A body is not a single organ but many [...] God appointed each
> limb and organ to its own place in the body, as he chose.
>
> (1 Corinthians 12.12-13,18-19)[23]

But Novalis soon moves beyond this representation. Although the unity
of Europe seems initially to be secured by the simultaneity of spiritual
time, represented by the collective body of believers bound together by
the power and purpose of a sacred ceremony (baptism), the secular
process of amassing riches and concentrating power disrupts the
coherence of the corporation. The simultaneity of the spiritual time gives
way to the disintegration caused not only by economic and political
forces, but also by the internal dynamism of culture, where the
"immortal sense" ("unsterbliche Sinn") of the Invisible is "obscured,
paralyzed" and "suppressed by other senses." (329-30) This is the case of
the Reformation, which replaced religious fervor and authority with the
power of the vernacular Biblical text imposing "the raw abstract scheme
of religion" (333) and converting Protestantism into a secular ideology of
territorial fights and a manifestation of the independence from Rome.
Although Lutheranism and its sequel "the secular Protestantism" (339)
of the French Enlightenment, had threatened to destroy Christian
spirituality, in Germany, enjoying a short period of peace, they produced
a reversal, marked by "a higher religious life" (340) in all branches of
sciences and arts.

This dialectical process of growth and perfection seems to lead to
the restitution of Christianity as the integrating power of Europe.
However, here Novalis emphasizes the cultural diversity, instead of
identity: while other European nations are absorbed in "war, speculation
and factions," the Germans are making every effort to become a new
community establishing "the higher epoch of culture." No wonder that
this progress must ultimately lead to the "great preponderance" of
Germany and its culture over European countries ("muß ihm
[Deutschland] ein großes Übergewicht über die anderen [Länder] im
Lauf der Zeit geben;" 340). The new Christian Europe is imagined as
German cultural hegemony based no longer on generalizing structural
and value patterns but on "holy particularity" and individuality ("den

---

[23] The quotation is taken from *The New English Bible. Standard Edition* (London: Oxford
University Press and Cambridge: Cambridge University Press, 1970), 220.

heiligen Eigentümlichkeit") and the "omnipotence of inner humanity."
(340) As a result, Novalis' imagining of Europe is characterized by
surprisingly divergent tendencies: apart from the integrating power of
national culture, there is also the diversifying force of individual
creativity.

At the end of Novalis' essay, this diversifying force is substituted by
an individualizing love with some features of erotic desire as well as a
spiritual dimension: the unity of Europe no longer resembles that of a
collective body, corporation or fraternity. The "brother" to whom
Novalis wishes to lead the representatives of Enlightenment universalism
("Philantropen und Enzyklopädisten") is the feeling of the "pulse of the
new age" which creates a "new community of apostles." (342) Apostles
of what? Of the new spirituality that blends in the infinity of imagination
erotic desire and the mystical mute language, or rather "music" of secret
symbols ("Chiffernmusik;" 342) of the Annunciation. This mysterious
"music" is represented in a complex image of "an endless play of the
folds" ("das unendliche Faltenspiel;" 342) of a semi-transparent veil
stretched tight over the face of a virgin. In symbolical terms, the folds of
the veil do "not conceal the formal element,"[24] "the structure of her
heavenly body" (340), but they effectively prevent its attainment, since it
can appear fully only "with infinity."[25]

In Deleuzean terms, the unity of the new Europe in Novalis' essay
emerges in a typical Baroque manner, being invented as "the infinite
work or process", which "moves between matter and soul," between
"the high and the low," and includes "unfolding" in its constant play of
folds, making the new object inseparable from "the different layers that
are dilating," due to which "matter becomes a matter of expression."[26]
However, in other (and also Deleuzean) terms, Novalis' imagery can be
read as a heterogeneous aggregate, which comprises "a desiring
machine," processing (in the metonymical connection between
"brother," "heartbeat" and "bride") the relations of kinship and bodily
feelings into erotic drives, and "a literary machine"[27] able to create a
unity out of fragments, a unity of style, which is fundamentally different
from the organic unity of the body of a medieval church.

---

[24] Gilles Deleuze, *The Fold: Leibniz and the Baroque*, trans. Tom Conley (Minneapolis and
London: University of Minnesota Press, 1993), 37.

[25] Deleuze, *The Fold*, 38.

[26] *The Fold*, 34-37.

[27] Gilles Deleuze, *Proust and Signs*, trans. Richard Howard, 2nd ed. (Minneapolis: University
of Minnesota Press, 2000), 146-49 and passim.

This Baroque and hallucinatory form of European unity evidently differs from Novalis' description of revived Christianity as a cultural as well as political power: "a visible church" reaching beyond the boundaries of individual countries and organizing a peaceful reform of European states. (346) From other writings of Novalis, for instance, his *Blütenstaub* fragments, it is clear that this new community is conceived as a totalitarian, state-like organization, whose integrating force is "the instinctive global policy" of the German *Volk* leading to the hegemony of Germany as a country, which has justly succeeded Rome in its imperial mission. (Fragment 64; 289) Here, the discourse of nationalism with its pretence to universal power seems to have swallowed up the individualizing "minority discourses" of Baroque philosophy and Romantic poetry. Both of them can be understood as attempts to integrate the "subaltern voice of the people"[28] into the thought and art of the elites.

Contrary to Anderson, who deals with the emergence of modern nations only as the result of the "cross-time" simultaneity of imagining,[29] my reading of Novalis' essay on imagining Europe has shown both the importance of the interplay between the traditional representations of sacred community and its modern transformation, and also between universalism and nationalism.

The next step is a reading of a novel that takes the "homogeneous empty time [...] marked [...] by temporal coincidence"[30] as its point of departure. Unlike in Anderson's assumptions, the time at the outset of Kundera's *Immortality* seems "empty" with respect to two sign systems of different orders. The emptiness of time appears when the temporality of our existence is contrasted with the aesthetic value, the "charm and elegance" of a human gesture that seem to exist "outside of time." (4) Kundera's gestures are signs that make sense only in contrast to the homely, trivial meanings of other signs in the context of which they appear. Despite their randomness, they are not unique because they can be repeated by different individuals almost identically and have constant qualities or values. In this way, the relationship between the signifier and the signified is inverted: individuals become signifiers and gestures signifieds: "it is gestures that use us as their instruments, as their bearers and incarnations." (7) The other sign system representing the emptiness of time is, rather ironically, characterized by "a harmonious combination

---

[28] Bhabha, *The Location of Culture*, 158.
[29] Anderson, *Imagined Communities*, 24ff.
[30] *Imagined Communities*, 24.

of uniformity and freedom" (6) typical of the modern media and globalized consumerism. In contrast to the previous one, it privileges the diversity and proliferation of signifiers at the expense of the relative value of signifieds. The system does not make a difference between informing and entertaining and its signs may not even function as units of communication, since they are easily converted into dreamy associations, as happens at the outset of Kundera's book. Despite the variety based on the play of its signifiers, the system's effects are uniform. The narrator makes this clear when he observes that all the radio stations say "at precisely the same time [...] the same thing about the same things." (6)

According to Anderson, this understanding of signification and time derives from a belief in the unifying and homogenizing power of technology, trade, capital and media. Anderson explicitly connects this *technological* time with the new imagining when he says that "the novel and the newspaper [...] provided the technical means for 're-presenting' the *kind* of imagined community that is the nation."[31] Although *Immortality* appears to develop this idea both in its theoretical sources and its global implications, it uses different and more sophisticated patterns of temporality. In contrast to the "mechanical reproduction" attributed to the technological media by Benjamin and Anderson, Kundera uses the central metaphor of "the Creator's computer" where all complexities of human existence are generated at random as "a play of permutations and combinations within a general program, which is not a prophetic anticipation of the future [that is, does not reveal any simultaneity of communal life "along time"] but merely sets the limits of possibilities, within which all power of decision has been left to chance." (11-12)

This computer metaphor does not point to any specific social formation or technological condition. A parallel may be drawn between the use of this metaphor and Homi Bhabha's critique of Anderson's hypothesis. Bhabha demonstrates that it is the basic feature of any sign system – the arbitrary nature of the sign, "its separation of language and reality" – that "enables Anderson to emphasize the imaginary or mythical nature of the society of the nation." In "the separation of language and reality – in the *process* of signification [...] there is no epistemological equivalence of subject and object, no possibility of the mimesis of meaning."[32] Translated into Kundera's terms, on the one hand, there is a

---

[31] ibid., 25.
[32] Bhabha, *The Location of Culture*, 158.

sign language of the computer program and, on the other, there are specific events generated by the program's iterations.

In order to resist the reductive pressure of the computer metaphor, Kundera strives to "make reflection or meditation a natural part of the novel, and to create the way of thinking specific for the novel (that is, no abstract reasoning, but reflection connected with the situations of individual characters, no serious, theoretical thought but ironic, provocative, questioning leading eventually to a comical way of thinking)."[33] In simplified terms, Kundera combines reflections about reality with fictions (his "play of imagination") in the architectonic space of the novelistic world, where individual dreams, delusions of masses and diversely constructed realities reveal and mock one another.

For this purpose, he does not rely on the story and its development, but on the formal unity of the novel. "[T]he idea of the overall architecture," claims Kundera, "is part of my original idea from which the novel is born; though it is not a product of a formal calculation but of a compulsive, involuntary vision."[34] In other words, *Immortality* attempts to restructure the narrator's self and his perception of the world, while disclaiming the fabricated postmodern reality and supplanting it with a balanced aesthetic form. However, this process is not quite deliberate, being based on an involuntary formal drive, an "archetypal" formal pattern common to most of Kundera's fictions. The main purpose of this pattern is to supplant the causal unity of the story by the interplay of the main *themes* of the novel, or, to accomplish a synthesis of the reflection and the plot.

This synthesis does not lead to unification. Its main device is the diversification of narrative time and strategies. While the former allows Kundera to alternate between the microscopic images of moments in individual lives, and the telescopic panoramas of the historical development, the latter tend to produce a unity of individual stories despite the fortuitous character of individual events. This is especially evident in the fifth part of the novel, called "Chance." Although the three stories cannot be combined on the basis of probability, their random combination integrates the three different levels of the plot: 1. the fictional tale of Agnes and her life, 2. the parallel story of a young suicide as a part of the image of the world created by the media (the author heard it on the radio), 3. the 'metafictional' level where the author

---

[33] Milan Kundera, "Poznámka autora" (Author's Note), in *Nesmrtelnost* (Immortality) (Brno: Atlantis, 1993), 347. All translations are my own.

[34] Kundera, "Poznámka autora," 348.

tells his friend, Professor Avenarius, about his heroine. While in the former part of the novel, the levels of fiction, non-fiction (historical narrative and essay) and metafiction are more or less distinctly separated, in the latter parts, after the 'crisis' in the plot, they converge, which is evident in the description of the love affair between Rubens and the lute-player, later identified as Agnes.

Apart from transforming the initial computer metaphor into a reflection of the narrative structure of *Immortality*, Kundera makes another daring claim. In the afterword to the Czech edition, he implies that his effort was "to expand radically the time of the novel, so that it might grasp 'the time of Europe.'"[35] This rather cryptic statement needs some elucidation. The section of the novel most preoccupied with this *longue durée* of European modernity (starting, according to Hegel's definition of Romanticism, with the rise of Christianity) is the fourth part, entitled "Homo Sentimentalis." The problem of Europe is the problem of love in Christianity: in Europe, the criterion of good and evil ceased to be objective:

> Christianity turned this criterion inside out: love God, and do as you wish! said Saint Augustine. The criterion of good and evil was placed in the individual soul and became subjective [...] true love is always right, even when it is in the wrong.
>
> (192)

Kundera proceeds to quote Luther:

> love precedes everything, even sacrifice, even prayer. From this I deduce that love is the highest virtue. Love makes us unaware of the earthly and fills us with the heavenly; thus love frees us of guilt.
>
> (192)

Therefore, Kundera argues, the *homo sentimentalis* is defined "as a man who raised feelings to a category of value." (193) But how can the authenticity of feelings be demonstrated? As a result, Kundera claims, "as soon as we *want* to feel [...], feeling is no longer a feeling but an imitation of feeling, a show of feeling. That's why *homo sentimentalis* (a person who has raised feeling to value) is in reality identical to *homo hystericus*." (193) This irresolvable dilemma between sentiments as

---

[35] "Poznámka autora," 347.

emotional expressions and as *signs (or representations) of certain values* is an important feature of European identity, beginning with King Lear and Don Quixote, and culminating in Romanticism.

As Kundera shows in the case of Bettina Brentano, romantic love is "extra-coital." It does not identify the emotion with the intensity of feeling but rather with specific signs or representations, namely, abstract and absolute concepts, such as Eternity, Immortality, and so on. This is an oblique reference to all utopias of romantic nationalism and universalism (including Novalis' essay on Christianity), relying on love as the chief principle of imagining and shaping the new community.

What, however, is more important in the context of Kundera's novel, is the fact that this 'high' romantic love has been trivialized in the illusions and phantasms of pop culture, including commercials. Contemporary society uses sentimentality as a power of aggression. An important consequence of this, claims Kundera, is that people no longer seem to be interested in reflecting on the relationship between their self and their own image. This, of course, is one of the main themes of the novel, articulated in the story of Agnes. To what extent is our image really a part of our own identity? What if it is composed of impersonal and repeatable gestures generated by some structural model or matrix, some general program running on the "cosmic computer?" Instead of asking these questions, most individuals are intent on imposing violently the phantasms of their own self, produced by the media, advertising, fashions, etcetera, on others. In this respect, their imaginings are generated by means of technical reproduction.

As Kundera indicates, this degenerate world cannot be resisted through aggressive acts. Professor Avenarius, who entertains himself by slashing car tires, is nauseating rather than comical, as are Bettina Brentano and Agnes' sister Laura. The only reliable way of dealing with the decay of the world is through its aesthetic transformation into a novel. The novel which is no longer a representation of this world but a self-contained musical structure producing different feelings than those of the *homo hystericus* (typical of Romanticism) and balancing them with rational impulses, thus leading us to discover structuredness in fiction as well as in reality. "The magic of art is the beauty of form," claims Kundera, "transparence, and clarity, explicability and understandability."[36]

By privileging music as the model for all arts, Kundera continues in the Romantic tradition, but by stressing the architectonic, structural

---

[36] ibid., 350.

value of music, he avoids the frequent Romantic error of identifying music with passionate emotionality. The feelings produced by music are of a different kind: the aesthetic pleasure of harmonious forms. In this pleasure, Kundera seems to seek an antidote to the decayed Romanticism, hysteric sentimentality, that threatens to undermine the grounds of European culture.

When *Immortality* was completed in 1988, the Czech draft text was still unfinished. According to Kundera, it had been abandoned

> in such a condition that it would require at least a month to put it in order. It was necessary to read it slowly sentence after sentence and to incorporate all the corrections and changes made in the process of my work on various translations.[37]

If this is true, the temporal hierarchy of the original text and its translations has been unsettled: the alleged 'original' was completed only after several translations had been published. As a result, the final version of this 'original' is no longer original: it incorporates a number of revisions made in the previous translations. In this way, Kundera's novel can be said to have no original text: it is an *intertext composed of drafts and translations*. The Czech text then, is similarly derivative as the French or English 'translations' are.

This establishes a different standard of novel writing and a different vision of Europe. No longer as a *site* of competing national cultures (as imagined in the age of Romanticism and also throughout the rest of the nineteenth and in the twentieth centuries), but as a *process* of a horizontal, or transversal, integration, in which fairly remote cultures (French, Czech, English and German) are interlinked by a text. This text is no longer a unity of meaning in one language, but rather a multiplicity of meanings based on different cultural resonances of the story, of Kundera's reflections, and of the novel's aesthetic form. While the Czech reader may identify the novel with a vague notion of "cosmopolitanism," the French will be looking for the echoes of the *esprit* of the Enlightenment, or for metafictional features, German readers may reflect on Schiller's distinction between the "naive" and the "sentimental" in culture, and so on.

As a result, *Immortality* displays an effective aesthetic way of imagining Europe, reaching beyond the *romantic* and *technological* ways of imagining communities. It should be noted, however, that Kundera's

---

[37] ibid., 345.

specific perspective of an expatriate, based on his admiration of the international "Republic of Letters" created by the French Enlightenment, can hardly work as a universally valid model for such imagining. The *aesthetic of the picturesque*, which changed the attitude towards landscape at the close of the Enlightenment period, is another and perhaps more feasible way of imagining Europe. Taking the regional specificity and local variety as a point of departure, it succeeds in integrating both local and universal, mythological, literary and artistic *topoi* into a specific landscape design. The aesthetic of the picturesque is based on "accidental" (irregular, mobile or ephemeral, yet locally and temporally specific) distributions of singularities – natural as well as cultural objects.[38] It also asserts the general importance of "those bonds of union by which the different parts of landscape are so happily connected."[39] According to John Dixon Hunt, these connections are based on "a mixed economy of design and land use to mirror a similar diversity of human existence."[40] In this respect, the picturesque scenes combine volatile effects of art with domestic habits and local (not necessarily agricultural) economies as well as with rich references to European cultural heritage (in painting, poetry, music and mythology). These transversal links are vital for imagining a culturally diversified Europe.

---

[38] See, e.g., Richard Payne Knight, *The Landscape: A Didactic Poem...* (1795; Bristol: Thoemmes Press, 2001), 42.

[39] Uvedale Price, *An Essay on the Picturesque...* (1796; Ottley: Woodstock Books, 2000), 263.

[40] John Dixon Hunt, *The Picturesque Garden in Europe* (London and New York: Thames and Hudson, 2003), 76.

JEAN-LUC NANCY, BEING-IN-COMMON AND THE ABSENT SEMANTICS OF MYTH[1]

Erik S. Roraback

> *To write is perhaps to bring to the surface something like absent meaning, to*
> *welcome the passive pressure which is not yet what we call thought, for it is*
> *already the disastrous ruin of thought. Thought's patience. Between the disaster*
> *and the other there would be the contact, the disjunction of absent meaning —*
> *friendship.*[2]
> Maurice Blanchot

> *I shall be speaking [...] of a bond that unbinds by binding, that reunites*
> *through the infinite exposition of an irreducible finitude.*
> *[...] the intensity of the word "revolution" names [...] a word [...] whose*
> *meaning has perhaps still to be revolutionized.*
> *[...] if we do not face up to such questions, the political will soon desert us*
> *completely [...]. It will abandon us to political and technological economies [...].*
> *And this will be the end of our communities [...].*[3]
> Jean-Luc Nancy

---

[1] I take the opportunity to dedicate this article to two first-class teacher-scholars from my student years who continue to be an inspiration and an energy source for me: the late Hebrew Bible scholar J. William Whedbee (1938-2004) of Pomona College in Claremont, California with whom I studied as an undergraduate "The Biblical Heritage" in 1988 and "The New Testament" in 1989, and the late philosopher Jacques Derrida (1930-2004) of the ÉHESS in Paris with whom I studied as a postgraduate "Questions de responsabilité," Martin Heidegger, and Maurice Blanchot in 1995.

[2] Maurice Blanchot, *The Writing of the Disaster*, trans. Ann Smock (Lincoln: University of Nebraska Press, 1995), 41.

[3] Jean-Luc Nancy, "Preface," *The Inoperative Community: Theory and History of Literature, Volume 76*, ed. Peter Connor, trans. Peter Connor, Lisa Garbus, Michael Holland and Simona Sawhney (Minneapolis: University of Minnesota Press, 1991), xl-xli.

The first extract above from Blanchot, who blends literature and philosophy to spawn a new kind of writing, accords with our conception of "absent semantics" embedded in the title of the present essay. The following passage from the quite difficult Strasbourg School thinker Jean-Luc Nancy states unequivocally the exigency of the present task to re-engage the political and the communal, lest we forfeit any positive access to them. It also implies the 'meaning' of our shared lives for any possible movement of community to come and the need to re-think and re-conceptualize the unfashionable concept of revolution in our current, so-called (and weakly self-described) post-revolutionary age. For we are now living in a situation, in which, according to Antonio Negri and Michael Hardt, "[t]he World Bank reports that almost half of the people in the world live on under two dollars a day and a fifth on less than a dollar a day"[4] and in which, I would add, one country among over two hundred sovereign nation-states, the USA, spends more on violence than the rest combined. Moreover, as Negri and Hardt point out,

> [t]he average income of the richest 20 countries is thirty-seven times greater than the average in the poorest twenty – a gap that has doubled in the past forty years. Even when these figures are adjusted for purchasing power – since some basic commodities cost more in rich countries than in poor – the gap is astonishing.
>
> (278)

But the wholesale loss of community is now so ostensible that such data rarely enter into official public discourse. There will be no discussion, for there is as of yet no community or being-in-common to make such a conversation desirable, let alone necessary.

This framing of the problem of myth is in strict opposition to the academic approaches, examining, inter alia, whether myth may still be seen to flourish in present-day Western societies, without acknowledging its complicity with the abuse of some form of ideological, institutional or political power. Moreover, it indicates that in the West myth as such no longer functions effectively, nor can it under current conditions without community.

Our chosen social theorist and philosopher for the present piece, Nancy, remains arguably among the better living French-language

---

[4] Antonio Negri and Michael Hardt, *Multitude: War and Democracy in the Age of Empire* (New York: Penguin, 2004), 278. Further references appear in the text.

thinkers along with his sometime co-author and Strasbourg colleague Philippe Lacoue-Labarthe, Luce Irigaray and Julia Kristeva, to cite but three figures among an increasingly attenuated list of others, now that since 1980, Jean-Paul Sartre (1905-80), Roland Barthes (1915-80), Jacques Lacan (1901-81), Simone de Beauvoir (1908-86), Louis Althusser (1918-90), Michel Foucault (1926-84), Félix Guattari (1930-92), Guy Debord (1931-94), Jean-François Lyotard (1924-98), Gilles Deleuze (1925-95), Emmanuel Lévinas (1906-95), Pierre Bourdieu (1930-2002), Maurice Blanchot (1907-2003), Jacques Derrida (1930-2004) and Paul Ricoeur (1913-2005) have all passed on. It is perhaps not entirely beside the point that the deaths of all these authors constitute a kind of 'thinking world of minds,' which intellectual history may yet come to see as one of the more effervescent in recent Western culture during the period of its very long incubating metamorphosis from a modern to a postmodern world (even while much of the world, including some ideological and existential components of the 'Western civilization,' admittedly, remains pre-modern, of course). For one of the main theses of this essay is based on Nancy's statement inspired by Georges Bataille (1897-1962) that death itself is a key igniter and communal stamp of the conditions of possibility for the existence of any community.

Beyond its polemical aims, the argumentative strategy of this article seeks to think with, through and in Nancy's complicated and path-breaking essays "The Inoperative Community" and "Myth Interrupted" from his work *The Inoperative Community* (La communauté désoeuvré, 1986) and quite cursorily his later work *Being Singular Plural* (Être singulier pluriel, 1996). I will thus attempt to build upon Nancy's investigations as a point of orientation for other meditations and arguments, empirical and speculative. By interrogating Nancy's essays, this article will begin to conceptualize some new ways of thinking of the mythic function and of how it intersects with notions of community and of Being-in-Common and by extension of Being-With; or, even more, how they do not thrive today and what that means for a future myth and community.

In his well-tuned introduction to *The Inoperative Community*, Christopher Fynsk writes: "Nancy is attempting to expose what still speaks in [...] 'community' when we assume the closure of the metaphysics of subjectivity [...]."[5] Hence Nancy is trying to re-semanticize 'community' (or to re-subjectivize its current infantile form of meaning) by interpreting its possible meanings and potentialities as a 'subject' or rather even more a movement in a post-metaphysical, post-

---

5 Christopher Fynsk, "Foreword," in Jean-Luc Nancy, *The Inoperative Community*, xi.

modern, post-representational and post-signifying age. With special clarity, Fynsk also submits that what is fatal for Nancy regarding our contemporary situation, which

> lies in the isolation of the individual in its very death and thus the impoverishment of that which resists any appropriation or objectification. [... W]hen death presents itself as *not ours* [... it] exposes us to our finitude. Nancy argues with Bataille [...] that this exposure is also an opening to community: outside ourselves, we first encounter the other.[6]

Hence, it is the biological fact of death and thus our ontological status as ephemeral biological subjects that might serve as special resources for Nancean and Bataillean social change, and for another community still to be founded. Such a factual basis would function as a special refutation of the notion that our current situation is acceptable with regard to community. According to Nancy, it is a kind of shared abandonment that would resist a fascist form of fusional and immanent power. This abandonment would be required to unleash an actual 'non- or un-community,' to neologize; that is, a community without the evil contours immanent forms of community bring with them, a community open to the innovative and new in a good, positive, and non-coercive way.

For Nancy himself, regarding *The Inoperative Community*,

> community does not consist in the transcendence [...] of a being supposedly immanent to community. It consists on the contrary in the immanence of a 'transcendence' – that of finite existence as such [...] its 'exposition.'[7]

It would require an astonishing imaginative achievement to theorize and to actualize this '*exposition*' of community: a task for some future protagonist of speculative social theory. In the event, however, it is the 'exposition' or 'exposure' of our finitude that constitutes a fact, a happening of sufficient strength, of 'transcendental immanence,' to spawn a so-called community as a process or procedure (instead of as an immanent substance or entity), or, in Deleuze's and Guattari's terms, a

---

6 Fynsk, "Foreword," xv-xvi.
7 Nancy, "Preface," in *The Inoperative Community*, xxxix.

"molecular" (flowing, multiplying, de-territorializing)[8] kind of sharing and of community. Clearly, again the coordinates of the contemporary social and economic situation would need considerable overhaul for the effective realization of such an innovative experience of the communal.

In the essay "The Inoperative Community," which also contains a meditation developing some of Bataille's ideas and arguments on the community concept, Nancy notes that genealogically

> the true consciousness of the loss of community is Christian: the community desired or pined for by Rousseau, Schlegel, Hegel, then Bakounine, Marx, Wagner, or Mallarmé is understood as communion [...]. At the same time as *it is the most ancient myth of the Western world, community might well be the altogether modern thought of humanity's partaking of divine life: the thought of a human being penetrating into pure immanence.*[9]

Here, community is not only the most long-standing myth of occidental culture but today it consists in nothing less than the divine par excellence. Unfortunately, as Nancy reminds us:

> Fascism was the grotesque or abject resurgence of an obsession with communion; it crystallized the motif of its supposed loss and the nostalgia for its images of fusion. In this respect, it was the convulsion of Christianity [...].
>
> (17)

Clearly, the threat of a certain Christian sort of communal fascism remains with us more than ever today, and so it is necessary to improve understanding to this sensitive fact, and at least potentially, reprehensible danger.[10]

---

[8] Gilles Deleuze and Félix Guattari, *A Thousand Plateaus: Capitalism and Schizophrenia*, trans. Brian Massumi (Minneapolis: University of Minnesota Press, 1987), 505-506 and passim.

[9] Nancy, *The Inoperative Community*, 10 (emphasis added). Further references appear in the text.

[10] Usefully for us here, for purposes of historical contextualization, the Frankfurt School social theorist Max Horkheimer writes: "Under National Socialism, the girl's refusal of herself to men in uniform is deemed to be as unbecoming as ready surrender formerly was. In Germany, the image of the Virgin Mary had never quite replaced the archaic cult of the woman. Under the surface of Christian civilization memories of matriarchal conditions were never quite extinguished. These vestiges continued to assert

Nancy, whose later work, *Being Singular Plural*, is pre-eminently a reading of Martin Heidegger, already wrote in "The Inoperative Community:"

> All of Heidegger's research into "being-for (or toward)-death" was nothing other than an attempt to state this: *I* is not – *am* not – a subject. (Although, when it came to the question of community as such, the same Heidegger also went astray with his vision of a people and a destiny conceived at least in part as a subject, which proves no doubt that Dasein's "being-toward-death" was never radically implicated in its being-with – in Mitsein – and that it is this implication that remains to be thought.)
>
> (14)

Hence, the suggestion that while Heidegger is a revolutionary philosopher of Being, he is not one iota of Being-with, which is in fact not posterior to but anterior to the question of Being insofar as for Nancy "ontology itself [is] a 'sacrality' or an 'association' more originary than all 'society,' more originary than 'individuality' and every 'essence of Being.' Being is *with* [...]."[11] It is this lamentable lacuna in Heidegger's thought that Nancy's *Being Singular Plural* seeks to fill in by probing deeper into the nature of the word "with" in Heidegger's incomplete ontology of Being.

---

themselves in the common antipathy to the old spinster as well as in the German *Lied*'s devotion to the deserted mistress, long before National Socialists ostracized prudes and celebrated illegitimate mothers. But the ascetic beatitude of the Christian virgin by far surpassed the pleasure authorized by the National Socialist regime and fed with memories of the buried past. The National Socialist regime rationalizes the mythical past which it pretends to conserve, calling it by name and mobilizing it on behalf of big industry. Where this archaic heritage did not explode the Christian form and assume Teutonic features, it gave to German philosophy and music their specific tone. The mythology in National Socialism is not a mere fake, but the spotlight thrown upon this surviving mythology liquidates it altogether. National Socialism has thus accomplished in a few years what other civilizations took centuries to achieve." Max Horkheimer, "The End of Reason," in Andrew Arato and Eike Gebhardt (eds.), *The Essential Frankfurt School Reader* (New York: Continuum, 1982), 43. A certain vulgarization of the *masses* and 'massing' of the mass mind prevailed with the advent of Nazi power, which went hand in hand with Nazi myth, to quote one outlandish extract.

[11] Jean-Luc Nancy, *Being Singular Plural*, trans. Robert D. Richardson and Anne E. O'Byrne (Stanford, CA: Stanford University Press, 2000), 37-38.

As far as the overwhelmingly important concept of death goes, for Nancy, "[c]ommunity is calibrated on death as on that of which it is precisely impossible to *make a work* [...]." (15) This notion of death's 'surplus value' derives from Bataille's thought discussed by Blanchot in *The Unavowable Community* (published as a direct response to the essay "The Inoperative Community"): "Mortal substitution is what replaces communion [...]. Bataille writes: '[...] it is necessary for communal life to maintain itself at the *height of death*.'"[12] Hence, "communal life" must be a self-sustained quest for blockages and movements of energy, forces continuously registering mortality for a new community dynamics and psychic communal space. Nothing less is needed to forge a certain sort of communal experience.

Similarly, for Nancy, "[a] community is the presentation to its members of their mortal truth (which amounts to saying that there is no community of immortal beings: one can imagine either a society or a communion of immortal beings, but not a community)." (15) Accordingly, it is precisely our shared mortalities that mark a plausible community. Once we expire as organisms, we cease to belong to any Nancean community. However, it seems to me to go against Nancy that one can continue to 'live' in a community if one's own life proves sufficiently powerful as a source of non-organic energies (animating energy forces in one's own locality) for those who are the survivors of the death of the other.

In a pointed provocation, Nancy writes: "Perhaps we should [...] recognize in the thought of community a theoretical excess [...] that would oblige us to adopt another *praxis* of discourse and community." (25-26) Here the inexpressible or the inarticulable wins the day in the intolerable and unbearable disaster: the failed expression of the communal which remains to be thought by human beings who have been eating each other from time immemorial solely for purposes of self-preservation.

For the Padua and Paris-based Italian teacher and scholar Negri (who, while in jail as a political prisoner, wrote a book on Spinoza, translated as *The Savage Anomaly: The Power of Spinoza's Metaphysics and Politics*) and his American colleague Hardt, who authored a volume on Deleuze, "the network struggle of the multitude [...] takes place on the biopolitical terrain [...I]t directly produces new subjectivities and new forms of life. [...C]reativity, communication, and self-organized

---

12 Maurice Blanchot, *The Unavowable Community*, trans. Pierre Joris (Barrytown, NY: Station Hill Press, 1988), 11.

cooperation are its primary values." (83) New subjectivity effects for a new global. The main values of this struggle clearly serve singularities which might thrive in an unmutilated community still to be. Étienne Balibar's felicitous formulation *"expanding subjectivity"*[13] aptly captures what I wish to convey.

The injunction made by Negri and Hardt that "Political action aimed at transformation and liberation today can only be conducted on the basis of the multitude" (99) should not make us think of "the multitude" as something unwieldy that might spin out of control: "The multitude [...] although it remains multiple, is not fragmented, anarchical, or incoherent." (99) In Deleuzian and Guattarian terms, the proof of the pudding is how the multitude effectuates a kind of 'molecularization' (a term inspired by Deleuze and Guattari's usage of "molecular") of the social (and thus of molecularized, or in Guattari and Deleuze parlance "deterritorialized," bodies) for a true social framework open to a more just and free communal encounter and process.

Now, for Negri and Hardt, the crucial concept of the "common" takes the place of at least older notions of community. As they put it,

> [t]he common [...] is based on the *communication* among singularities and emerges through the collaborative social processes of production. Whereas the individual dissolves in the unity of the community, singularities are not diminished but express themselves freely in the common.
>
> (204)

In this paradigm at least, "community" does not function as some sort of transcendent moral or tendential figure that intimidates, if not emotionally, existentially, and temporally appropriates, the other, but rather it operates as an ethically sound becoming or a process of the very living and labor activities of the key concept of the "common." What makes the common such an effective weapon against the oppressive and potent "biopowers"[14] is that

---

[13] Étienne Balibar, *Politics and the Other Scene*, trans. Christine Jones, James Swenson, Chris Turner (London: Verso, 2002), 170.

[14] The term "biopower" comes originally from Michel Foucault's "bio-power" (*The History of Sexuality, vol. I: An Introduction*, trans. Robert Hurley [New York: Vintage, 1980], 140-41, 143-44). By not acknowledging it, Negri and Hardt register the extent to which the notion has now passed into our everyday critical discourse.

it breaks the continuity of modern state sovereignty and attacks biopower at its heart, demystifying its sacred core. [...] This concept of the common not only marks a definitive rupture with the republican tradition of the Jacobin and/or socialist state but also signals a metamorphosis in the law [...].
(206-207)

The common will thus confront head on and diminish, if not negate, various biopowers facilitating an epochal shift or sea-change in history; it will have been a long road, too long for many, and none too early, it is hoped against hope, for the future. As for this paper's political position, it is, moreover, 'post-Jacobin and post-Socialist.' In this sense, it is a third path that goes beyond the two dominant paradigms of Liberalism and Socialism of the twentieth century even while learning from the experiential information, positive and negative they both have to offer us to think with, through, beyond and against them for a new social and economic experience and communication.

To adduce Nancy once more,

[a]s an individual, I am closed off from all community, and [...] the individual – if an absolutely individual being could ever exist – is infinite. [...] However, the *singular being*, which is not the individual, is the finite being. [...] There is no process of 'singularization'[...].
(27)

This accords to the lesson of modern and post-modern art and thought, which teaches us that the docile individual is a kind of ideological ruse used to service the military-industrial-digital complex. Such conceptual fetishes as the individual lay the groundwork for the hegemony of military, financial, state and technological power.

The crucial idea of finitude links up with Nancy's "compearance," a word that signals "*co-appear*" (28) wherein, for instance, "[c]ommunication consists [...] in this compearance (*com-parution*) of finitude [...] constitutive of being-in-common [...] inasmuch as being-in-common is not a common being." (29) Meanwhile, for Negri and Hardt, too, the common "is not a common being" but rather a multitudinous global body, or "global common." As Negri and Hardt claim of the multitude: "The fracturing of modern identities [...] does not prevent the singularities from acting in common." (105) True singularity requires true commonality, and vice versa. This is because they have always been inherently and in practice, if not always in theory hitherto, 'trans-versal' entities. Moreover, as Negri and Hardt point out, "we are a multiplicity of singular forms of life and *at the same time* share a common global existence. The anthropology of the multitude is an anthropology of singularity and commonality." (127) This approach can finally comprehend singularity for the very first time. For

> *[o]nce we recognize singularity, the common begins to emerge. [...] We share bodies with two eyes, ten fingers, ten toes; we share life on this earth; we share capitalist regimes of production and exploitation; we share common dreams of a better future.*
>
> (128)

Thus, there are, in the first instance, *only singularities*. Therefore, if we register singularity, or particularity, then the common will reach its own highly molecular or molecularized and event-oriented form of non-organic being; that is, of true being beyond the totalitarian and hierarchical tendencies of normalizing or naturalizing procedures that usually serve human rapacity. Crucially, if not alarmingly, "[a]ll of the multitude is productive and all of it is poor" (134) because it services the well-heeled more than the other way around. It is noticeable that justice and consequently true wealth remain to be accomplished or experienced for the 'productive multitude' whose own value surpluses are appropriated by a heteronomous current form of barbaric and repressive, immoral society precisely because community as such does not really exist at all yet. Contemporaneously at least, community is a fraudulent concept to invoke. Closer to the heart of real creative power for Negri and Hardt: "Today we create as active singularities, cooperating in the networks of the multitude [...] in the common." (135) This relates to the Kantian ethics of the universal good.

Myth does not allow for singularity for Nancy when he writes in a piece pointedly and agitationally entitled "Literary Communism" from the same collection of essays: "In myth [...] existences are not offered in their singularity [...]." (78) That myth attaches itself to generality causes it to quite barbarically brutalize singular forms, movements, and structures. For myth authoritatively naturalizes, discriminates, normalizes, and thus sets up strictures for what it means to be a human being, to cite only one example, in such cultural practices as reading and writing.

As regards true contemporary power in the economic sphere, for Negri and Hardt "immaterial labor," (which includes knowledge, skills, information, ideas, what they term "affective relationships," and much more) is now ascendant, for "immaterial labor [...] has imposed a tendency on all other forms of labor [...]." (141) It is then partly the well-trodden argument of the information age updated yet again. And

> [j]ust as we must understand the production of value in terms of the common, so too must we try to conceive exploitation as *the expropriation of the common*. The common [...] has become the locus of surplus value. [...] Think, for example, of the profit extracted from affective labor.
>
> (150)

But to go beyond if not against Hardt and Negri, "affective labor," be it education, health care and suchlike, remains subject to not merely exploitation but to what Balibar terms, with reference to the capitalist economy in general, "*super-exploitation*."[15]

In sum for Negri and Hardt: "*For economics to function today it has to be formed around the common, the global, and social cooperation.*" (157) This inter-connective and inter-cooperative state of affairs might then engender a more literate-minded and mature social and economic system which would not truckle down to brute power that keeps the would-be-multitude ignorant, unintelligent and "super-exploited," but instead would assert studied fairness with respect to notions of economic justice and of a plausible true community-moving-in-progress. Also, for Negri and Hardt, "[a] democratic multitude cannot be a political body [...]. The multitude is something like singular flesh that refuses the organic unity of the body." (162) Thus, it accords to the Spinoza-inspired, Artaudian, Guattarian and Deleuzian "body without organs" that unleashes an unfettered body and free life from the constraints of social forms of representation in the world for what the latter two term the "New Earth."[16] A similar line of reflection can be traced in Nancy: "community cannot arise from the domain of *work*. [... O]ne experiences or one is constituted by it as the experience of finitude." (31) This again points out the import of death. And even more, "[c]ommunity [...] takes place in what Blanchot has called 'unworking' [...]. Communication is the unworking of work that is social, economic, technical, and institutional."

---

[15] Balibar, *Politics and the Other Scene*, 142.

[16] For an elucidation of the concept of the "body without organs," see Deleuze and Guattari, *A Thousand Plateaus: Capitalism and Schizophrenia*, 149-66. For a slightly different and more complex explanation, see their *Anti-Oedipus: Capitalism and Schizophrenia*, trans. Robert Hurley, Mark Seem and Helen R. Lane (New York: Viking, 1977), passim.

(31) So "communication" then would be a kind of de-codification or de-territorialization of the dominant straitjackets, codifications and territorialities of the world's mighty "social, economic, technical, ideological, and institutional" powers for other counter-forces, counter-ideologies, counter-institutions, counter-economics, or counter-powers still to be invented for another true communal event or happening. Such counter-logic may seem unpractical at first sight and yet prove one locus after another of true power.

Intriguingly for Nancy, whom I quote here so as not to oversimplify his thought on a peculiar form of the sacral:

> community itself now occupies [...] the sacred stripped of the sacred. [... T]he 'unleashing of passions,' the sharing of singular beings, and the communication of finitude. [... C]ommunity is transcendence [...] which no longer has any 'sacred' meaning, signifying precisely a resistance to immanence [...].
>
> (34-35)

Therefore, a kind of absent or 'interrupted' sacred would be one function of the non-pathological community in the post-modern social: a sort of re-transcendentalization of the transcendent vis-à-vis the concept of community, which would not brutally flesh subjectivities into one immanent dough as did the Nazis, for example, but would instead multiply possible subjectivity effects for our "compearance" in actuality. The injustices and corruptions of that world's vulgar insistence on uniformizations and so-called normative structures for subjectivity might thereby be minimized. All of the discreditable forms of community that have failed in the domain of actuality of the twentieth century might thus be partly chalked up to being mere false starts of what was to come for a more just and desirable community without various communitarianisms. For to look for non-pathological forms of large-scale community without communitarianism in the twentieth century is to look in vain.

As for Nancy's piece "Myth Interrupted," let us highlight a few salient points to increase its appreciation and comprehension. Firstly, we read that

> [w]e shall never return to the mythic humanity of the primal scene, no more than we shall ever recover what was signified by the word 'humanity' before the fire of the Aryan myth. [...] Myth [...] is always 'popular' and 'millenary' [...] according to

our version. [...] In this sense, we no longer have anything to do with myth.

(46)

In this paradigm then, "millenary" and "popular" myth would be an utterly unacceptable area of scholarly inquiry because of the dangers it presents of being an agent of various forms of fascism, super-, micro-, or otherwise: be they ideological, social or technical. In a word, Nancy thus adduces a radical de-Nazification of myth. Moreover, he adds: "Bataille named this state, to which we are doomed, *the absence of myth*. [...] I will substitute for this [...] *the interruption* of myth." (47) Thus, myth would be "interrupted" in our current period which is rather inbetween the modern (indeed, in some regards still pre-modern) and the post-modern era, and in which ostensibly a kind of fraudulent economic myth of global capital serves as a false myth for, partly, the very reason that myth can no longer exist as such. Yet we need myth: this is the paradox. For lack of anything better with which to invest existence, the lowest common denominator of money wins in both right-wing and left-wing capitalist nation-states alike.

To give a greater sense of historical reference for what would be the most recent instances of myth for Nancy: "romanticism, communism, and structuralism, through their [...] precise community, constitute the last tradition of myth [...]." (51) After "structuralism" (and after modernism, one might add), we are left with post-structuralism and post-modernism and now even post-post-structuralism and post-post-modernism in our present age with its futile attempts to re-mythologize the last Nancean myth of structuralism, and I would add here again, of modernism. In actual fact, for Nancy, "all that remains of myth is its fulfillment or its will. We no longer live in mythic life [...]." (52)

Here Nancy is again making the point that buttresses one's sense of myth's very self-same and tautological understanding of itself and hence 'self-presentation' for general popular consumption: "As Schelling put it, myth is '*tautegorical*' (borrowing the word from Coleridge) and not 'allegorical' [...]. Thus, it does not need to be interpreted [...]." (49) Hence, myth's foundational power to which other structures and meanings must adhere. Importantly also, "[m]yth communicates the common, the *being-common*," (50) in which Hardt and Negri's notion of the common fits very neatly. Accordingly, this would seem to open new vistas for myth once the "common" has been much more consolidated as a positive force in actuality. A myth of the planet may be conceived as a certain sort of new non-organic being (beyond large, "molar," or macro powers of representation) with which a non-organic human might identify, for example, thereby allowing a more positive task of the creation of community via myth to come out of Nancy's negative philosophy of myth and of community. Of course, it may take a long time for myth and for community to return in actuality, but that it remains a possibility gives us reason to imagine that such a movement might not repeat the mistakes of the past.

The reason we no longer desire myth in a classical sense is that now, thanks to Nancy, we understand that "[m]ythic will is totalitarian, for its content is [...] of man with nature, of man with God, of man with himself, of men among themselves." (57) Moreover, for Nancy, "the idea of a 'new mythology' is not only dangerous, it is futile [...]." (56) Correspondingly, it would seem that any classical notion of a new community would also be 'dangerous and futile' if "there can be [...] no community outside of myth." (57) Despite all this, it is a form of the inherently immanent transcendence of our co-mortalities whose exposure might spawn a positive form of community. In a movement of extension, Nancy alludes to Blanchot's *The Unavowable Community*: "in the interrupted myth, community turns out to be what Blanchot has named, '*the unavowable community*.'" (58) We need a new sense of myth but cannot ostensibly have it; and, we need a new comportment toward community but cannot avowably experience that either, at least not as classically conceptualized. This is again the current double bind in which we find ourselves.

Nancy's concept of "compearance" fits well with the Negri and Hardt one of "singularity" and by extension of the common and of the multitude. According to Nancy, compearance "is a contact, [...] a contagion: a touching, the transmission of a trembling at the edge of being [...]." (61) This is as close as we get to togetherness, "a touching." Moreover, Derrida entitles one of the longest (and last) productions of his writing career (a three-hundred-and-fifty-page work) which we do not have space to discuss here, *Le toucher, Jean-Luc Nancy*.[17]

Crucially, again, "death as the unworking [...] unites us because it interrupts our communication and our communion" (67) for it disbands us from the great Deleuzian/Guattarian "molar" (large-scale political and "territorial") "machines" of the social, the technical or the organic.[18] Or, as Pierre Joris puts it in regard to Blanchot, "for Blanchot friendship is profoundly linked to the possibility of community. That death, disaster,

---

[17] Jacques Derrida, *Le toucher, Jean-Luc Nancy* (Paris: Galilée, 2000).
[18] Deleuze and Guattari, *A Thousand Plateaus*, 34-35, and passim.

absence are at the core of this possibility of community – mak[es] it always an impossible, absent community [...]."[19] Therefore, it is a kind of absent semantics of myth that will allow for the possibility of a being-in-common, to borrow from the title of this article. And it is "the disjunction of absent meaning" that convokes the concept of "friendship" to allude to the extract from Blanchot that opened this essay, both of which follow the 'disasters' of community of the past and a new respect for the "other" with the conceptual aid of notions of the common, of the multitude and of singularity.

It will, then, be a new regime of affects and of intensities that forge a new human, a new social, and perhaps even a new perspective towards, or a modality of, myth or community. As Negri and Hardt state: "The intensification of the common, finally, brings about an anthropological transformation such that out of the struggle come a new humanity." (213) Such a conceptual schematic seeks to re-conceptualize a new human that would register more true to the reality of things as "molecularized" singularities for a new being-in-common. Or, as Nancy writes in "Literary Communism," "'[c]ommunity' means [...] the presence of a being-together whose immanence is impossible except as its death-work." (80) This in itself suggests that a paradoxical joyful myth of the hard and indefatigable unworking work of death that squarely faces the impossibility of immanence without transcendence within it, namely, a perpetual exposure to our finitude, would be one place to start building a new non-fascist, non-totalitarian, non-organic, and mature event and figure of community; this also is how we are exposed to the very possibility of friendship, to the "New Earth," to being-in-common, to myth and so by extension to a new, developing form of community.

---

[19] Pierre Joris, "Translator's Preface," in Blanchot, *The Unavowable Community*, xiii.

II.

IMAGINING EUROPE

IMAGINING EUROPE – MYTHS, VISIONS, IDENTITIES, MEMORIES

Aleida Assmann

The process of European enlargement is well under way. In Rome at the end of October 2004, the representatives of 25 countries signed the new treaty that will take effect in January 2007, provided that it is ratified by the nations involved. We have watched the rapid expansion of the European Union based on a common currency, economic contracts and complex networks of administration. The lingering question is, however, whether the new political and bureaucratic framework is slowly being filled with some kind of cultural content, whether the *economic expansion* of the EU is accompanied by some process of *cultural integration*. The question of the cultural identity of the Union has been raised continuously, and there are reflections and initiatives evolving at various levels. This problem cannot only be delegated to politicians and professional image designers; as citizens of the member states of this new imagined community, we are all invited and challenged to contribute something to this open process of imagining Europe.

My contribution will investigate the activity of imagining Europe at four levels: myths, visions, identities and memories. The myths date back to antiquity, the visions to the twentieth century, while the construction of identities and the shaping of memories are the open issue of the new millennium.

1. Myths

Much has been written in the last decade on ancient myths that might provide a source of inspiration for forging a common origin and orientation for a new European identity. Anyone who scrutinizes the archive of ancient myths and models that emerged – very roughly speaking – in the area of the Mediterranean Sea, will immediately be puzzled by the paradoxes that he or she is confronted with. The messages to be gathered from this archive of images and traditions are extremely diverse, if not downright contradictory, which means that a message may easily be found for almost every purpose and project. In reassessing some of these myths, I will emphasize this aspect of paradox and tension within the European cultural archive itself.

The mythological prototype of Europe, we learn, was a Phoenician princess, abducted by Zeus in the shape of a bull and carried off to Crete. It is a story not of origin but of divine violence and forced migration; whatever surfaced in the geographical area that we now refer to as Europe had its beginnings elsewhere. This is also true for the great cultural technique of writing, the elaboration of the highly economic because arbitrary script of the alphabet that was invented by the Phoenicians and taken over by the Greeks. In this case, the emphasis is not placed on the *invention* of the alphabet, but on the discovery of its potential in appropriating and elaborating it.[1]

There are two other myths of forced migration that have shaped the European imagination. One is *the story of Moses*, liberating his people from Egyptian oppression and leading them into the promised land. The other

---

[1] For Rémi Brague, the genius of Europe consists exactly in this ability to take over ideas from others and develop them in a new way. For him, Europe is not a 'Vaterland,' but a 'Sohnland:' the identity of Europe is not anchored in the legacy that was bequeathed but in the very process of inheriting: "Für Europa ist das Eigene nichts anderes als die Bewegung einer Aneignung." Peter Koslowski and Rémi Brague, *Vaterland Europa. Europäische und nationale Identität im Konflikt* (Wien: Passagen Verlag, 1997), 28. A second feature that distinguishes Europe from Islam is the return to sources with the possibility to retranslate, reinterpret, reassess them: "Eines hat er [der Islam] aber nicht tun können, und zwar zur Quelle zurückzukehren, um eine frühere Aneignung zu verbessern, gegebenenfalls um sie durch eine andere, neuere, zu ersetzen." Koslowski, Brague, *Vaterland Europa*, 33. Brague comments on this creative retrospection as a creative form of experiencing strangeness and describes the form of European tradition as an "adoption of parents by their sons." ibid., 38. Brague's point is that in Europe, authority and tradition are not transmitted from the past to the present, by a father imposing them on his son, but by reaching back from the present to the past in an act of free choice and volition.

is *the story of Aeneas*, leaving the burning Troy with his father Anchises on his back and his household gods under his arm, escaping from a destroyed kingdom as the destined ruler of a new world somewhere else. Both stories of flight and migration end in new settlements, in taking away the land from those who had lived there before and by legitimizing this colonial move with the authority of a superior God or gods. The story of the exodus focuses on illegitimate rule, the necessity of revolt and the vision of liberation. This myth has captured the experience of the oppressed and given powerful expression to it, serving as a mirror for oppressed minorities ranging from the English (and New England) Puritans to the African slaves in the American South to discover their own very different histories. While in the Jewish tradition, the exodus was until very recently connected to an apolitical philosophy of exile rather than a myth of political subversion (Jewish identity had been religious and diasporic rather than political until the state of Israel was established in 1948), the myth of exodus sparked movements of political liberation all over the world.

The reception history of the story of Aeneas points in the opposite direction. His journey is propelled by a divine mission, while the central focus of his migration is the foundation of Rome as a new kingdom and a second Troy. Unlike Moses', Aeneas' journey is not an escape from oppressive rule, but a refounding of a defeated empire that rises to new grandeur from the ashes of its demise. The emphasis here is on the providential ruler and the legitimacy of the new settlement and empire. This myth became the blueprint for the founding of new empires throughout Europe which, for their legitimation, had to link themselves to this genealogy of empires that passed from Troy through Rome to a new Troy, or a second or third Rome. While the myth of exodus describes the paradigmatic birth of a nation (ethnogenesis), and has fueled not only liberation movements of the oppressed, but also movements of national self-definition, the myth of Aeneas has become the blueprint for empirical rule and a normative model of a transfer (or translation, to use the legal term) of political power and legitimacy from one country to another.

Both of these mythic migrations, that of Moses and that of Aeneas, have become very powerful models of the political imagination with contrasting values: one legitimizing the concept of the self-liberated and self-defined *nation*, the other legitimizing the hierarchical rule of a multi-ethnic *empire*.

If we also take into account here the works of Homer, which continue to shape European imagination, we find a similar polarity expressed in his two epics. One is a story of warfare, presenting heroism in fierce and disillusioned images, the other is another story of forced migration, telling of mythic adventures but focusing on the humane features of its protagonist. In the second decade of the twentieth century, at a time when militant nationalism was disrupting Europe with hatred and unprecedented violence, James Joyce opted for the *Odyssey* as a usable myth for the century, while discarding the military story of the *Iliad*. What once more emphasizes the paradoxical or dual quality of European cultural memory is the fact that the mythic event of the siege and fall of Troy is presented by Homer and Virgil from the opposing perspectives of both winners and losers.

Even the myth of Odysseus is transmitted in two versions, presenting very different kinds of hero. One is the cunning and enduring seafarer whose homeward journey is delayed by the angry God Poseidon, but who finally reaches his home where he restores order and recovers his wife. The other is the Ulysses as elaborated by Dante, a hero who cannot remain in Ithaca because of his restless spirit of adventure and curiosity. He finds new companions and sets out on a second journey beyond the threshold of the closed Mediterranean world where he meets his fate and ends up as a negative exemplar of hybris and unbreakable will in Dante's Christian Hell.

In assessing the European archive of myths, we may summarize that stories of displacement and migration are much more conspicuous than stories of origin. The stories of flight, wandering and forced migration, however, have a clear telos and topographical center, that is, the building of a new nation and the foundation of a new empire. These two myths have lent themselves to illuminate and legitimate historically very different, and even opposite experiences and political claims as the liberation of an oppressed minority and the foundation of new empires. Moses and Aeneas are obviously very different kinds of heroes; they represent a duality and tension that is built into the foundational myths of Europe which incorporate a repertoire of diametrically opposed voices and perspectives.

2. Visions

This part deals with the twentieth-century visions of Europe which arose at the moments of cataclysm, total rupture or sudden change. The three principal historical moments that gave rise to new visions are the aftermaths of the two world wars and the changes in 1989.

Visions around 1918

The Great War was conceived by many Europeans as the catastrophic end of a longer decline and the total disappearance of the world as they had known it. This world had suddenly become the "world of yesterday," as Stefan Zweig put it, a world that was irretrievably lost. While this lost world was recreated by writers such as Hofmannsthal or Proust as a nostalgic literary remembrance, new visions emerged as to what was to follow and replace the world of yesterday.

As an immediate response to the self-destructive unleashing of mutual violence in the Great War, the vision of a federal republic of Europe (*Völkerbund*) was born which was intended to overcome and replace once and for all the malign forces of nationalism. This vision, however, lacked clear political structures and institutions to give it the necessary power. In striking opposition to the mental climate in countries such as France and England, where a strong desire to return to a civil world prevailed, connected with an equally strong aversion towards war and militarism, in Germany there were no similar pacifist trends after the war. On the contrary, radical and militant voices prevailed which had a real chance of being heard and heeded among the majority of the population.

One of these voices was that of Oswald Spengler who had diagnosed the fall of Europe in 1917 even before the end of World War I in his influential bestseller. The old Europe, Spengler confirmed, had irrevocably declined together with its culture that he and many others at the time referred to as the "Abendland."[2] His central question was how to master Europe and maintain its hegemony over the world.[3] The new Europe, according to Spengler, had to overcome the external threats from both East and West. His vision for a new ideology of Europe was a martial "return to Rome."[4] His historical model was Caesar – only

---

[2] When we revisit some of these visions today, we find that various terms were used to shape European destinies. The German translation of "occident" which is "Abendland" (literally "eveningland") became a normative term with great polemical and political potential.

[3] Because of its former legacy as "Heiliges Römisches Reich Deutscher Nation," it was believed by some that Germany held a special claim to represent and reshape Europe.

[4] Richard Faber has pursued this topic in many of his writings with exceptional fervor and diligence. See for instance: *Roma Aeterna. Zur Kritik der konservativen Revolution* (Würzburg: Königshausen & Neumann, 1981); *Das ewige Rom oder die Stadt und der Erdkreis. Zur Archäologie abendländischer Globalisierung* (Würzburg: Königshausen & Neumann, 2000).

another Caesar would be able to deal with the present chaos. The new Caesar would have to wield the power of technical modernism. Europe could once more counter the progressive decline of the West, if it rose from the ashes of the war in the shape of the phoenix of an industrial empire. Such an empire, Spengler argued, could still aspire to the most seminal of European values, which for him was to reclaim its title of a hegemonic world power. Spengler's vision of a technocratic Caesarism that was to re-establish Europe under German hegemony[5] became a seminal inspiration for German Fascism, which came to power a generation later. The claim to imperial European hegemony remained visible in the symbolic framing of the National Socialist state with Roman symbols of military and spiritual power.

Visions around 1945

After World War II, any claim to European hegemony – particularly from the German perspective – had been so monstrously discredited that it had become utterly unthinkable. The millennial German Empire, deemed to be built on terror, aggressive warfare and genocide, had completely collapsed and left traumatic scars all over Europe. But not only had Fascist Germany been extinguished, all grand ideas about Europe were destroyed in World War II. It was generally felt that the demise of the 'Occident' was an accomplished fact. The philosopher Karl Jaspers (who together with his Jewish wife barely escaped pending deportation when the American allies took over in Heidelberg in May 1945) argued that with the end of Europe, history had also come to an end. At an international meeting in Geneva in September 1946, he delivered a lecture entitled "Vom europäischen Geist" (On European Spirit). In this lecture, Jaspers stated blankly: "Passed and gone is that European arrogance which used to think in terms of 'world-history' what was in reality only occidental history."[6] A new era of 'post-histoire' began with the sober recognition that the world had lost its center and central agent of history. In 1947, Jaspers' friend and colleague Alfred Weber published a book with the title *Goodbye to History (Abschied von der bisherigen Geschichte)* which begins with the following sentence:

---

[5] Here we touch upon a fundamental issue: the representative function meaning 'stand for' and 'take over.' According to this political ideology, Germany made a claim to 'represent' Europe, as Europe was to 'represent' the world.

[6] Karl Jaspers, *Vom europäischen Geist* (Munich: Piper, 1947), 7.

In the catastrophe which we have experienced and are still experiencing, we are standing clearly at the end of history as we knew it, that is, at the end of a history determined by the Occident.[7]

From now on, history was de-centered for the Europeans. Its principal centers of action lay east and west of Europe. Or, to put it in Sartre's terms, "up to now we [Europeans] had been the subjects of history, from now on, we are going to be its objects."[8] The superiority complex of Europe was radically crushed at the end of World War II. One of the lessons to be learned after the collapse of 1945 was a new tone of humility. As Germany had been the principal agent of Europe's demise by unleashing unknown potentials of violence culminating in the atrocities of the Holocaust, the first consequence was that it had to renounce once and for all its hypertrophic aspirations towards greatness and political power.

The separation of Germany into two different states that was designed by the allies as a punishment turned out to be a blessing in disguise, however. It opened doors to new alliances with France and to a rapid process of Western integration. While the imperial heritage of old Europe was now 'translated' to the United States, West Germany partook of this aura when it became a satellite of the new imperial power. It indeed became an object of history in the bipolar constellation of the Cold War, but it held the place of a very prominent object.[9]

These political decisions hardened into Cold War reality, in which the topography of Europe was defined by the Iron Curtain, dividing it into a western and an eastern part according to the new bipolar grid. This postwar transformation of Europe extinguished alternative visions of a new Europe that arose as late as the 1940s. In these visions, Rome once more served as a normative model for a new Europe, this time tapping not its military but its religious potential. Rome had been the center of medieval Christendom before the split of the confessions and the rise of nations in early modernity. To go back in time and recover the spirit of Europe in a Christian culture based on Latin classicism was a

---

[7] Alfred Weber, *Abschied von der bisherigen Geschichte. Überwindung des Nihilismus?* (Hamburg: Claaßen und Goverts, 1946), 10.

[8] Jean Paul Sartre, preface to Franz Fanon, *Die Verdammten dieser Erde* (1961), in *Kolonialismus und Neokolonialismus, Sieben Essays* (Reinbek bei Hamburg: Rowohlt, 1968), 76 (my translation).

[9] On the continuity of the European political myth after World War II, see Faber, *Roma Aeterna*, 61ff.

vision cherished by Catholic intellectuals both during and after World War II. Theodor Haecker was one such intellectual who had been persecuted in Nazi Germany. In 1931, before Hitler came to power, he published a book entitled *Vergil – Vater des Abendlands* (Virgil – Father of the Occident), in which he produced an anti-Spenglerian vision of Europe. For him, Rome was not the locus of Caesar wielding military and technological power but of the Classical and the Catholic tradition, which he resurrected as an antidote against secular and liberal trends towards a Westernization of Europe. T.S. Eliot corresponded and collaborated with Haecker when he edited *The Criterion*, a literary journal in which, from 1922-1939, he attempted to mobilize the best minds in Europe and lay the foundations for a new trans-national culture that was to replace the nations. When in a presidential address to the Virgil Society in 1944 T.S. Eliot asked the question "What is a Classic?" his answer was: Virgil, the epic poet of the Aeneid.[10] Eliot designed Virgil as a hero of culture, representing a new center for a European identity. To acknowledge Virgil as *the* paradigmatic classic was to continue the imperial tradition and to claim once more the centrality of Europe. Even after the war, when Europe had changed beyond recognition, when Britain was losing its colonies, when the realm of politics was de-centered, Eliot did not give up this vision of Europe as a central agent. After the political collapse of the nation-states, he saw the chance for a reinvention of Europe as a cultural identity that would maintain its sovereignty against the West and the East in the domain of culture. Eliot was still relying on the rhetoric of the imperial discourse of Europe when he wrote: "Europe is [...] still, in its progressive mutilation and disfigurement, the organism out of which any greater world harmony must develop."[11]

---

[10] The "scarcity of the German Vergil-honoration in 1930" marked for E.R. Curtius the definitive end of German *Bildungskultur*. In his case, there is a similar dialectic of a. a diagnosis of the end of a tradition and b. the reinstallment of an obligatory memory. Curtius' culture therapy took on the form of a scientific work. His encyclopedic book arose "out of a concern for the preservation of occidental culture. It tries to demonstrate the unity of this tradition in space and time. In the spiritual chaos of the present it is necessary but also possible to show this unity. This unity can only be shown from a universal point of view. This is provided by the Latinity. Latin is the cultural idiom of the thirteen centuries between Virgil and Dante." *Europäische Literatur und Lateinisches Mittelalter* (Bern: Francke, 1969), 9.

[11] T.S. Eliot, "What Is a Classic?" in *On Poetry and Poets* (London: Faber and Faber, 1957), 69. It is interesting to note that in his list of fallen and unreal cities in his famous poem *The Waste Land* (1922), Eliot does not include Rome:

Eliot's European Classicism had been designed as a conscious therapy against a notorious modern illness: the illness of being uprooted, of being cut off from the past, of losing traditions, ancestors, heritage, norms and values. According to Eliot, this loss of cultural memory brought about a new kind of provincialism that he called a "provincialism of time." It is the signature of the modern age, Eliot wrote, that

> men seem more than ever prone to confuse wisdom with knowledge, and knowledge with information, and to try to solve problems of life in terms of engineering. [Such a world] is the property solely of the living, a property in which the dead hold no shares.[12]

The opposite of this state is what Eliot called maturity. He defined it as that state of mind or of culture "when men have a critical sense of the past, a confidence in the present, and no conscious doubt of the future." (57) He wanted to overcome the 'time-provincialism' of the postwar era by restoring a memory of old Europe. For this project, he chose Virgil because

> the Roman Empire and the Latin language were not any empire and any language, but an empire and a language with a unique destiny in relation to ourselves; and the poet in whom that Empire and that language came to consciousness and expression is a poet of unique destiny.
>
> (71)

Eliot's reinterpretation of tradition under the specific historical circumstances of World War II arose from a personal commitment to a particular set of values which assumed for him the form of a semi-religious allegiance. After two world wars, in a post-national age, he wanted to restore the unity of Europe by grounding it once more on the

---

> What is the city over the mountains
> Cracks and reforms and bursts in the violet air
> Falling towers
> Jerusalem Athens Alexandria
> Vienna London
> Unreal

T.S. Eliot, *The Waste Land*, in *Selected Poems* (London: Faber and Faber, 1967), 65.

[12] Eliot, "What Is a Classic?" 72. Further references appear in parentheses in the text.

universality of Latin. This 'universality,' of course, only applied to the Western part of Europe, which shows the strong strain of ethnocentrism in his thinking. For Eliot, a common heritage of thought and feeling was the necessary background for cultural excellence. A strong cultural identity, however, was for him also the warrant of a unique imperial destiny.

Visions around 1989

When, four decades after Eliot's essay, new visions of Europe emerged, they no longer came from those who aspired to maintain or re-establish the position of a center. These visions arose in the smaller countries in Eastern Europe. At a time when, for most Germans, the mental map of 'Europe' had shrunk to Western Europe, a new challenge and revision of this concept came from countries beyond the Iron Curtain that had been forgotten or dismissed by many Western Europeans as belonging to another world. The new vision of Europe that emerged under Communist oppression was in every respect the opposite of former visions. It had lost all of its centralizing and hegemonic underpinnings; in this new discourse, the idea of Europe became the very opposite of what it had been: it turned into a subversive category. Instead of hegemony, unity and centrality, it now stood for minority, difference, dissent and plurality.

When Milan Kundera defined Central Europe as "the greatest variety in the smallest space," [13] he had in mind a Europe that was a far cry from Eliot's vision. Eliot had written: "as Europe is whole, so European literature is a whole, the several members of which cannot flourish, if the same blood-stream does not circulate throughout the whole body." (72) While Europe's hallmark had been unity for Eliot, it became diversity for Kundera. The new vision of Europe differed from the older ones in yet another respect: it was generated not from destruction and despair but from hope and resistance; it was not something that had to be saved and recuperated with greatest efforts and at all costs, but something that was found to be in itself 'saving.'

This new counter-vision of Europe emerged from smaller countries in Eastern Europe that had yearned for *perestroika* long before the word became a popular slogan. In countries like Czechoslovakia, Hungary and Poland, to reassess some kind of a European memory was an important

---

[13] Milan Kundera, "The Tragedy of Central Europe," *New York Review of Books*, 26 April 1984, 33.

way to assert autonomy under the enforced political alliance within the Eastern bloc. The claim to a European heritage created a rift between their political and cultural identities. The visions of Europe constructed at the beginning of the twentieth century had been designed to provide legitimacy for political power. Those at the end of the twentieth century were designed to erode the network of power and subvert political ideologies.[14]

The artists and intellectuals who reconstructed European memory clearly differed from traditionalists such as Haecker and Eliot. György Konrad wrested tradition from the traditionalists and reclaimed it for a new liberal orientation, arguing in his phantom description of a new/old Europe: "The conservative and the radical are not to be severed."[15] His vision of Central Europe can be summed up by three features:

1. Diversity vs. unity. Contrary to Eliot who had stressed European unity grounded in the Latin language, Konrad stressed the polyglotism of Europe: "European is what is polyglot, what has many genres and what is multidimensional." His vision is a plea for difference and distinctions, for minorities and mysteries: "A European is (s)he who appreciates a small space in which is crowded a great variety." The virtues in a polyglot and diverse world are the capacities for translation, comparison and curiosity. All of them imply self-distance and a sage relativism.[16]

2. Remembering vs. forgetting. For Konrad, Europe is the continent of little space and much history. It has a long memory. This memory is much too varied to be claimed by any one specific group. It is

---

[14] "The fantasies of intellectuals concerning Central Europe," writes Henning Ritter on 2 July 1988 in the *Frankfurter Allgemeine Zeitung*, "will no doubt also be applauded by German writers, [...] but they will remain without political resonance." Less than four months after this statement, the world witnessed the unexpected breakdown of the totalitarian frame that had held together the Communist Eastern European countries.

[15] György Konrad, "Der verbale Kontinent," *Frankfurter Allgemeine Zeitung*, 2 July1988, supplement "Bilder und Zeiten," n. p. All further quotations come from this article. Many of these ideas can moreover be found in two related books by the same author: *Mitteleuropäische Meditationen an der Bruchlinie zweier Zivilisationen* (Wien: ÖIF, 1989); *Melancholy of Rebirth: Essays from Post-Communist Central Europe, 1989-1994*, selected and trans. Michael Henry Heim (San Diego, New York / London: Harcourt Brace, 1995).

[16] When asked by American philosophers how he would defend his theory against the reproach of relativism, the German philosopher Hans-Georg Gadamer answered: "I don't defend myself. It is only from the point of view of the United States that relativism has a pejorative tone. In Europe, it has not. Here, we live with the fundamental plurality of cultures and languages." Oral contribution to a conference discussion, written down and translated by Aleida Assmann.

the common heritage of different nations and individuals. The European spirit depends on continuity. He wrote: "My utopian view of a culture is one that is able to remember." This memory is codified in literature, in world literature. Konrad calls Europe "a verbal continent" and "a library." In this imaginary library, there is free commerce not only between different nations but also between the living and the dead. The term "world literature" stands for a "temporal and spiritually local reality; it is a sophisticated communication across the millennia."

3. Individualism vs. collectivism. The universe of letters is a spiritual commonwealth of individuals. In this commonwealth, there is no place for a delegation of opinion, for vicarious constructions of world views, for representative thinking and acting, for a usurping and repressive consensus. No institutions are allowed to monopolize a particular position, or to invest it with collective and obligatory norms: "Here, everybody is present in his own right." In the realm of literature as opposed to the realms of politics, religion or science, it is the individual who counts.

Konrad described his vision of Europe as a "fictive metaphor." His vision of a free, pluralistic, and individualistic universe was pitted against a world dominated by censorship and pressure at borders. It was an outcry against a world that ends at the next border, against the pompous celebration of military power and against coercively imposed collective identities. In such a world, the fictive metaphor of Europe bore the power of a subversive vision. A similar vision was articulated against the prosaic reality of a Europe that, from the 1980s, took shape in a growing number of facilities prefixed by 'Euro,' such as Euro Television, Euro trains and Euro cheques. For a critic such as Susan Sontag, these palpable symptoms of a growing economic integration were completely irrelevant to her vision of Europe. In May 1988, she published a statement in the *Frankfurter Allgemeine Zeitung,* entitled "Elegy on Europe." The economic consolidation of Western Europe bore no resemblance to the vision of Europe that Sontag cherished as a New York Jewish intellectual with a Polish background. The supranational economic Europe, Sontag wrote,

> is inexorably reshaping the Europe I love, the polyphonic culture within whose traditions, some of them, I create and

feel and think and grow restless, and to whose best, humbling standards I align my own.[17]

Konrad had outlined his vision of Central Europe as a republic of letters and a civil society in 1988. His vision was a small part of an energy that grew steadily to bring about the fall of the Berlin Wall in November 1989. But it was not the image of a new Europe that became finally visible after the collapse of the Soviet Empire. What became visible in its place was the very opposite: new (or rather old) national myths and memories that had been frozen in the bipolar constellation of the Cold War. The upsurge of this explosive political energy changed the face of Central Europe; hitherto peaceful regions such as the Balkans were torn apart with genocidal wars and new nationalist discourses mobilized suspicion and aggression against neighbors and migrants.

3. Identities

In retrospect, 1989 has been called "the European year." On another level and in other parts of Europe, the consolidation of a new Europe can be told as a success story. After the introduction of the euro and the continuous expansion of the EU, however, there is also a growing feeling that what has been achieved in terms of organization as far as economy, technology and bureaucracy are concerned, still lacks cultural reverberations. Has the achieved reality of Europe obscured the visions of Europe? Will Europe ever become an imagined community? And what could its identity be made of?

Eclectic and Relational Identities

There are at least two possible ways to answer the question of a European identity. I will call the first kind of identity 'eclectic.' It emanates from a list of specific traits, characteristics, features that are defined as genuinely European and therefore confer 'Europeanness' on those who embrace them. The list of these features is long and varied.[18] It comprises inventions, achievements and institutions developed in the

---

[17] Susan Sontag, "The Idea of Europe (One More Eulogy)," *Where the Stress Falls,* (London: Jonathan Cape, 2002), 285. Originally published as "Elegie auf Europa," *Frankfurter Allgemeine Zeitung,* 28 May 1988.

[18] For a comment on what he calls "a spectral-analysis of Europe," see Koslowski, Brague, *Vaterland Europa,* 25-28.

course of European history such as democracy, universities, the free cities, the progress of rational science, the principle of innovation in the arts, the declaration of human rights, professional historiography and the Romantic concept of self-determined nations as the collective subjects of their history.[19] The problem with such lists is that they are always *eclectic*. Athenian democracy, Roman law, Montesquieu's division of power and the ideal of human rights are all very well, but what about the inquisition, slavery, iconoclasm and pogroms that are also European inventions? We want and need to celebrate plurality and diversity, but in doing so, we must not forget the European record of segregations and schisms, of national and religious wars. We want to emphasize the humanist values but we must not forget Auschwitz and Bosnia.[20]

The second kind of identity, which I call 'relational,' emanates from the changing constellations of Europe and its other. For the Greeks, this other was Asia, represented by the Persians against which the Greeks created their first great alliance; in late Antiquity, Western Rome defined itself in contradistinction to Eastern Rome; in the twentieth century, the Occident (*Abendland*) was defined as a middle way between both "West" (American capitalism) and "East" (Russian Communism). In the late eighteenth and nineteenth centuries, Europe was chosen by the United States as its other when it tried to define its own cultural identity.[21] After

---

[19] "The fact that there are nations," writes the historian Hermann Heimpel, "is historically speaking what is European about Europe." See Koslowski and Brague, *Vaterland Europa*, 67.

[20] See the book by the German historian of Graeco-Roman Antiquity Christian Meier, *Von Athen bis Auschwitz. Betrachtungen zur Lage der Geschichte* (Munich: Beck, 2002).

[21] An impressive declaration of American cultural independence from European roots can be found in an essay by R.W. Emerson: "The Greek letters last a little longer, but are already passing under the same sentence, and tumbling into the inevitable pit which the creation of new thought opens for all that is old. The new continents are built out of the ruins of an old planet: the new races fed out of the decomposition of the foregoing. New arts destroy the old. See the investment of capital in aqueducts made useless by hydraulics; fortification, by gunpowder; roads and canals, by railways; sail, by steam; steam, by electricity." "Circles," in *Emerson's Essays*, ed. Sherman Paul (London, New York: Everyman, 1967), 168. On a less spiritual level, the American historian Frederick Jackson Turner saw the "American Frontier" which was continuously moving westward until the end of the nineteenth century as widening the distance from Europe and hence "the really American part of our history." He added: "Thus the advance of the frontier has meant a steady movement away from the influence of Europe, a steady growth of independence on American lines." Frederick Jackson Turner, "The Significance of the Frontier in American History," in *The Frontier in American History* (New York and Chicago: Holt, Rinehart and Winston, 1962), 1-38. When after the end of World War II the aim was no longer to become culturally

World War II, a new alliance was forged between the United States and Western Europe for which the term "West" or "Western" was coined and opposed to the Communist East. Under the impact of September 11, 2001 and the subsequent American war on Islamist terrorism, this unity of the West, which denotes a complex of secularism, modernism, technology and capitalism, is being reinforced. Since the beginning of the war on Iraq in 2003, this Western alliance between the United States and Europe broke up once more, creating (in Donald Rumsfeld's terms) a resilient "Old Europe" and a faithful "New Europe."

It is quite obvious that European identity will continue to shift as political constellations and loyalties vary. This very shifting is itself a sign that Europe is embedded and involved in larger structures of global issues and political conflicts.

Constructing a European Identity

Some of the questions asked with a growing urgency today are: What shall be taught in the European schools of the future? Is there such a thing as a European identity? How should it be defined? Is there some kind of trans-national consensus about common European values? Or about a common history and memory? It is very likely that the only appropriate answer to these questions is a continuous discourse. However, we overlook the fact that a cultural framework for the new Europe is already in the making. Let me mention some of the recent activities that are relevant to establishing this cultural frame.

In October 1999, a conference was held in the European Parliament in Brussels to prepare the founding of a Museum of Europe in 2003. This museum is designed as a supranational historical museum and will serve a similar function as the two German historical museums in Berlin and Bonn established in the era of German Chancellor Helmut Kohl, which was to define and support the historical consciousness of the citizens. The event in Brussels was moderated by Romano Prodi and attended by the former German chancellors Schmidt and Kohl. The discussion at the conference showed the great difficulties of defining Europe in terms of extension in time and space. It was agreed upon that

---

independent but to forge a political alliance with individual European states, the term "West" was coined to obliterate former rivalries and to blur former distinctions. In this tone, Turner already wrote: "The Western spirit must be invoked for new and nobler achievements. Of that matured Western spirit, Tennyson's Ulysses is a symbol." *The Frontier in American History*, 310.

Europe began with Charlemagne and was 'the daughter of Catholicism and the (northern) Barbarians,' as the formula went, which meant that ancient Israel, Greek and Roman Antiquity, as well as Byzantium were excluded from the start.[22]

In March 2000, a number of international scholars met at the Villa Vigoni in Leveno di Menaggio to discuss whether there is or should be such a thing as European *lieux de mémoire*. The background of this workshop was the manifest success of the seven volumes of French *lieux de mémoire* (1984-1992) reconstructed, compiled and edited by Pierre Nora with the help of over a hundred French historians. After Nora's model had been copied by other European countries such as the Netherlands, Spain, Austria and Germany, the question arose whether Europe as a whole cannot also be considered as a continental community with a common memory (*eine kontinentale Erinnerungs-gemeinschaft*), providing a common identity and cultural legitimacy for the supranational institution.[23]

Politicians are looking to historians to construct a common memory of the new Europe. It is not yet clear whether the consolidation of a common European memory can be achieved by creating or identifying common symbols and fixating official dates for public commemoration. It is surely not a task only for politicians and image designers, but one that requires a more inclusive and interactive process.

Double Membership: Connecting National and European Identity

Looking more closely at public debates within individual European countries, we observe a lack of interest in the abstract notion of European identity, while at the same time issues of collective and national identity attract much attention. While the question of European

---

[22] A contrary perspective is taken in an article on "Charlemagne – Karl der Grosse" in a volume on German *lieux de mémoire*. The author of the article surmises that a new Europe that will be extended eastwards beyond its Roman boundaries will no longer have any use for this founding father: "It could be the case of a Europe extended widely beyond the realm of its historical Latinity, a Europe which will no longer be interested in this founding father." Joachim Ehlers, "Charlemagne – Karl der Grosse," in Etienne François, Hagen Schulze (eds.), *Deutsche Erinnerungsorte* (Munich: Beck, 2000-2001), 1:55.

[23] "Schwerpunktthema: Europäische lieux de mémoire?" *Jahrbuch für Europäische Geschichte*, ed. Heinz Duchhardt et al., 3 (2002). In the meantime, another collection of essays on the issue of European *lieux de mémoire* has been published: *Gedenken im Zwiespalt* (Göttingen: Wallstein, 2001).

identity is promoted as a top-down affair by historians and politicians, there are lively debates in both Eastern and Western European countries on national identity. In England, for example, there is currently a growing interest in the concept of "Englishness." In an article with the catching title "The Importance of Being English," Vera Nünning has given a well-informed account of some of the ongoing issues and debates. A wide array of agents such as literary authors, artists, pop stars, journalists and critics are engaging with great interest upon a common search for elements and features that are truly English.[24] In her essay, which comments on some of these features, Nünning notes that the notion of Englishness is gaining in popularity while that of Britishness is obviously declining. Privileging Englishness over Britishness suggests that the English are severing themselves from some unpleasant weight in their historical baggage. While "Britishness" is associated with dominance and political exploitation, "Englishness" as the smaller political and geographical unit celebrates features such as justice and freedom.[25] It is true that the term "Englishness" draws a borderline to exclude anything Welsh, Irish and Scottish, thereby affirming local cultural differences, but it is also true that this smaller unit is one with which non-natives and migrants find it difficult to identify.

The rise of Englishness and the fall of Britishness, I would argue, are intimately tied to the situation in the growing EU, where Britishness as a supranational and encompassing term jars with the European framework. While the European Union as a supranational alliance ousts larger imperial structures, it is wholly compatible with national identities which are highlighted with new emphasis and vigor without calling into question the European framework. Being a commonwealth itself, Europe cannot tolerate a commonwealth within its boundaries.[26] The same dialectic seems to be at work between national and European as between local and global; opting into the European Union triggers a reassertion of a specific national identity to be preserved with its distinguishing features over against the Union and its other members.[27] The European Union, in other words, is a frame and network for nations with their uniqueness and specificity. This European framework, at the

---

[24] Vera Nünning, "The Importance of Being English: European Perspectives on Englishness," *EJES (European Journal of English Studies)*, 8.2 (2004): 145-58.

[25] See Nünning, "The Importance of Being English," 148-50.

[26] On the notion of the EU as a "Reich" or a "commonwealth," see Koslowski and Brague, *Vaterland Europa*, 67-69.

[27] In a dialogue, Pierre Nora made the point that the identification of national *lieux de mémoire* is not a counter-project against the EU but a necessary part of its construction.

same time, helps to guard against aggressive nationalisms of the nineteenth-century kind that were not contained in any political structure but exploded and clashed against each other in two world wars. The dialectic between national and European creates an identity model of dual membership: each nation defining itself both in terms of its unique and distinctive features and in terms of a common European reference.[28]

4. Memories

The question remains, of course, as to what this common European reference could be. Besides founding museums and creating European *lieux de mémoire*, it has been proposed that this common European reference is to be found in the memory of the Holocaust. Dan Diner, for instance, has argued that the Holocaust is the paradigmatic European *lieu de mémoire*, and that any cultural reconstruction of Europe will have to evolve around this memory as its center. And indeed, institutional steps have been taken in this direction. On 27 January 2000, Swedish President Persson invited members of forty European states to Stockholm to attend a conference on commemoration and teaching of the Holocaust. Fifty-five years after the liberation of Auschwitz and in the first year of the new millennium, it was agreed that this traumatic event, which had drawn all of Europe into its lethal vortex, should become a shared memory, grounding a common set of values, such as human rights and the protection of minorities as a common European goal for the future.

The project of reconstructing a transnational memory of the Holocaust, however, has proven somewhat more difficult than had been envisaged by President Persson's initiative. Instead of having become, sixty years later, a unified and homogenous narrative, the events of World War II and the Holocaust are still the object of contested memories and antagonistic perspectives. National and European memory, it turns out, are not yet quite so easily reconciled as the formula of dual membership ('unique national memory plus common European memory') suggests. After a period of highly standardized visions of the

---

[28] This dual membership that brings together national and European elements distinguishes the current construction of identity from cosmopolitan constructions of identity popular at the end of the nineteenth century and presented as an alternative and counter-identity to nationalist identity constructions. An interesting example is the cosmopolitan cultural identity constructed and exhibited in the building of the Dublin National Library which was opened in 1890 and became a favorite space for the cosmopolitan James Joyce who made it the scene of the action in one of his chapters in *Ulysses*.

past that lasted until 1989, many European countries were shaken by the resurgence of contesting memories and compromising historical facts.

Until 1989, a heroic memory of anti-Fascist resistance (GDR) and a memory of guilt, built up slowly but continuously and focusing on Nazi perpetrators and Jewish victims, (FRG) existed side by side in Germany. In this clear-cut antithesis, memory and consciousness were frozen; in the GDR, there was a blackout relating to the uncanny continuity of a repressive authoritarian political framework, and in the FRG, there was a blackout concerning the uncanny continuity in personal careers, big business and institutions. After 1989, a new national memory was forged that takes over active responsibility for Nazi atrocities by transforming the former camps into sites of commemoration and creating a central monument for the murdered European Jews in Berlin. This top-down memory of German guilt that has been established at national and political level has been complemented recently by a bottom-up memory of German suffering relating to events before and after the war, focusing on the experience of area bombings of German cities, of forced expulsion from the eastern countries and of mass rape. Although these facts and memories are not new, they have recently received new forms of expression and much wider attention at a social and public level. New right-wing political activists are now trying to exploit this memory of German suffering in a populist way for a new national identity based upon victimhood and resentment. By speaking of a 'holocaust of bombs,' they are blotting out the consciousness of guilt and fueling hatred against the United States and European neighbors. This, however, is by no means the general drive incorporated into such resurrected memories. When on 13 February 2005 the citizens of Dresden assembled with the mayor and representatives from the UK, France and the United States on the sixtieth anniversary of the firestorm of Dresden, the emphasis of the commemoration ceremonies was on international reconciliation. Another initiative of Dresden citizens emphasized a transnational form of pacifist remembering by creating large posters which placed the victims of Dresden in a list with other attacked or destroyed cities including Nagasaki, New York and Baghdad.

Partly due to newly regained access to Eastern European archives and partly due to the return of 'frozen' memories, other European countries have also experienced the unsettling of official myths and the growing impact of internal strives of conflicting memories. In a 1992 essay on "Myth and Memory in Postwar Europe," Tony Judt has argued that after the demise of the Cold War and the collapse of the Soviet Union, Europe was entering a new phase marked by a profound reshuffling of history and memory. By moving out of the postwar period, the historical reality of the Holocaust and World War II was growing more complex every day. According to Judt, the official version of the past had been that "all responsibility for the war, its sufferings and its crimes lay with the Germans," an account in which the recollection of much that happened during and after the war "conveniently got lost."[29] Not that the general framework of these events has been blurred – there is no debate whatsoever about the centrality of German guilt in this man-made disaster – but the picture has become more complicated and differentiated with the uncovering of ever larger networks of collaboration. The Hungarian writer Péter Esterházy made a similar point in October 2004 when he was awarded the peace prize in St. Paul's Church in Frankfurt: "To cover up one's own crimes by referring to the German crimes is a European habit. The hatred against the Germans is the foundation of Europe in the post-war period." And he went on to reflect on the memories of the new Europe:

> what should be united is torn apart in self-hatred and self-pity. [...] Side by side with the untruth of the exclusive perpetrator there is the untruth of the exclusive victim. And behind both lurks the unresolved 'we' of national memory. [...] A shared European knowledge about ourselves as perpetrators and victims has not yet been developed. [30]

Although these words were spoken in a German context, they must not be misunderstood as a statement to reduce German guilt. The issue that Esterházy deals with does not concern the Germans but is aimed at the internal struggles for memory and history within various European countries that are more or less addressing their share in the monstrous network of murder and extermination. In France, the reality of the Vichy collaboration has exploded De Gaulle's 'myth of the resistance' as an unrivalled official national narrative. In Austria, the master narrative of suffering as 'Hitler's first victim' is only now beginning to be challenged. Poland, a country that suffered so cruelly from German occupation and persecution, is reluctantly looking into its anti-Semitic heritage. Italy is torn between Communist and Fascist memories. And even Switzerland,

---

[29] Tony Judt, "The Past is Another Country: Myth and Memory in Postwar Europe," *Daedalus*, 121 (Fall 1992): 87, 89.

[30] Péter Esterházy, "Alle Hände sind unsere Hände," *Süddeutsche Zeitung*, 236 (11 October 2004): 16.

the paradigmatic neutral state and the haven for so many Jewish refugees, discovered the dark origin of some of the gold in its banks and has made the frontier a site of new inspection and public debates.

All of this has happened only during the last decade, long after the events. It shows that we are still a far cry from what Dan Diner and President Persson had envisaged: the Holocaust as a common historical reference supported by a shared memory and shared values. At this point, memories of the past are not necessarily forging ties but are doing rather the opposite: they are causing considerable turbulences as they clash within nations and along the borders of the member states of the European Union. Memories are not necessarily conducive to the European project: while they can be recalled and contained within a conciliatory European framework, they can also be invoked to refuel ancient hatred in populist media campaigns. Sixty years after the events of World War II, the affects have not cooled but can still be reactivated among the populations. The front page headline of the *Daily Express* of 30 October 2004 read: "The Queen refuses to say sorry for war!" It was issued before her fourth visit to Germany and was a retort to a headline of the German *Bild Zeitung* two days earlier which ran: "Will the Queen finally say sorry?" This is just a trivial example of European memory struggles as carried out at a national and populist level with the support of public media. It seems as though we were still a far cry from Esterházy's notion about "a shared European knowledge about ourselves."

Although this shared European knowledge is not yet a reality, it is certainly a great cultural potential inherent in the process of European unification. It includes the genuine chance to 'face history and ourselves,' to look into our own national memory from a transnational point of view. It may be that what we are experiencing is a transitional period in the process of creating a shared European knowledge of ourselves. The twentieth century left Europe a scarred landscape, and much has already been done to transform this historic space and time into a shared legacy. The camps of exploitation, dehumanization and extermination, the battlefields and graveyards of two world wars and the civic sites of terror and destruction have become European *lieux de mémoire*. To create European sites such as the Marne and Stalingrad, Coventry and Dresden helps to create a transnational framework for national memories. The European borders have become zones of contact in which the neighboring nations are negotiating their memories across generations. As an example, I would like to refer to a case that relates to Czech-German history and memory. A student of mine brought my attention to a book with the title *Zmizelé Sudety* (The Sudetenland that Disappeared) which appeared in a Czech-German edition in 2003.[31] It is the catalogue for an exhibition of a collection of historical photographs taken more than half a century ago in the area, constellating them with new photographs taken on the same spots. In comparing and scrutinizing the pictures, the editors attempt to decipher the unwritten history of their landscape. What these photographs reveal is that the region, which was once quite prosperous and saturated with a rich cultural history, was intentionally destroyed after the expulsion of the Germans by neglect and abandonment. Today, as younger Czech generations are becoming interested in the history of their region, they are meeting with Germans who were its former inhabitants and are visiting their former villages and cities in the spirit of a family memory that is totally devoid of resentments and revisionist claims. It is from these 'memory tourists' that the younger Czech grass root historians learn something about their region and are recovering fragments of a vanished history. The inquiry is part of a civic movement without immediate national and political stakes; it creates an exchange across borders and generations to recover a historical dimension that has been erased after the war. This memory initiative emerged from a younger Czech generation trying to forge a new access to the past, approaching a troubled history with new questions and new interests.

To sum up the final points of my essay: national cultures and memories will certainly not have to disappear; they will form part of the complex and variegated experience of European trauma. What will have to disappear, though, and what will have a real chance of disappearing in a common cultural framework, are national myths, obsessions and resentments that defy integration into the "shared European knowledge about ourselves." In this joint cultural framework, Europeans can learn to face their own memories and listen to each other with empathy. The creation of such a European legacy would not lend itself to political legitimation; it would undermine the reinforcement of auto- and hetero-stereotypes. Without this concept of a common European *Bildung* as an ongoing project for future generations, the cultural notion of Europe will remain hollow. While the EU is rapidly expanding, a process of 'internal colonisation' is needed to keep apace with its interior structure. In a lecture delivered in March 2002 at a celebration of the Goethe-Institut in Weimar, Peter Steinbach described the process of reshaping the idea of

---

[31] Petr Mikšíček et al. (eds.), *Zmizelé Sudety / Das verschwundene Sudetenland* (Domažlice: Český les, 2003).

Europe. "What is necessary at present," he argued, "is not only the extension of Europe but also its perfection." Susan Sontag had already expressed a similar thought in her "Elegy on Europe" sixteen years ago. She wrote: "the new idea of Europe is not of extension but of retrenchment: the Europeanization not of the rest of the world but of Europe."[32]

---

[32] Sontag, "The Idea of Europe," 286. This statement comes close to Rémi Brague's concept of Europe as *de-barbarisation*: "Our chance is still that we feel the need of de-barbarisation and that we engage in such a process of a new formation." Koslowski, Brague, *Vaterland Europa*, 40.

THE DISCOVERY OF EUROPE IN THE SOUTH PACIFIC: TRAVEL WRITING, "BOUNDARY WORK," AND THE CONSTRUCTION OF EUROPEAN IDENTITY

Michael C. Frank

1. Introduction

In his contribution to this volume, Martin Procházka raises the question whether the concept of "imagined communities," introduced by Benedict Anderson in his influential book of the same title, can be applied to Europe. Can we conceive of Europe as an imagined community? If the present paper answers this question in the affirmative, it does so not in a normative, but in a descriptive way. What I am proposing is a discourse-historical approach to the topic at hand. From the point of view of discourse analysis, Procházka's question can be rephrased as follows: *Was* Europe imagined as a collective entity? And, if so, *when* and *where* did this entity emerge? The founding text of discourse analysis, Michel Foucault's methodological study *The Archaeology of Knowledge*, tells us that the reconstruction of discourses necessarily involves an investigation of the "rules of formation" which are the "conditions of existence in a given discursive formation."[1] My analysis, then, will also have to examine the conditions of the possibility of

---

[1] Michel Foucault, *The Archaeology of Knowledge*, trans. A.M. Sheridan Smith (New York: Pantheon Books, 1982), 38.

imagining "Europe." How and under which circumstances *could* Europe be imagined?

Within the confines of this essay, I cannot, of course, do more than give an initial tentative answer to these questions. In order to achieve this, I will combine a theoretical discussion of the process of imagining community with an exemplary analysis of a primary text – I shall call it a fragment of discourse. The first theoretical text I will deal with is Ernest Renan's "What Is a Nation?" Although Renan's lecture has already been extensively discussed over the last two decades, I think it is worthwhile to revisit this well-known text in the present context. As I hope to demonstrate, Renan's main thesis that collective identity is based on a common historical heritage which is only very selectively remembered, can also be applied to the imagination of Europe. This re-reading of Renan will link his lecture to more recent theories of "cultural memory." In a second step, I will argue that the (re-)construction of a common cultural memory is only one process involved in the construction of Europe. The other, equally important process will be described as "boundary work." Authors as diverse as the German sociologist Georg Simmel, the Norwegian anthropologist Fredrik Barth and the cultural theorists Michel Foucault and Edward Said have emphasized the importance of boundary constructions for the constitution, or imagination, of community. Europe is a case in point here because, as I will argue, the imagination of Europe first took place *outside* of Europe, when the geographical and cultural boundaries of "Europe" became tangible.

The subject of my paper is the appearance of the signifier "Europe" in late eighteenth-century travel writing. Whereas sixteenth- and seventeenth-century descriptions of the New World had mostly used the denominators "Christians" and "Indians" to distinguish between "us" and "them," eighteenth-century accounts of South Sea expeditions substituted these older categories with the concepts "Europe" (denoting a geographical entity) and "European" (meaning a particular cultural identity). In this sense, Europe can be said to have been "discovered" in the South Pacific, as will be shown below.

2. Renan Revisited: Cultural Memory and Collective Identity

In a lecture delivered at the Sorbonne in March 1882, the French philosopher and historian Ernest Renan famously addressed the question: "Qu'est-ce qu'une nation?" From a contemporary perspective, Renan's answer to this question seems very much ahead of its time and this is why many recent constructivist approaches to the topic take Renan's lecture as a starting point: Benedict Anderson refers to Renan in his *Imagined Communities* (1983) and Homi Bhabha reproduces the lecture in the volume *Nation and Narration* (1990).[2]

The appeal of Renan's lecture to late twentieth-century cultural theorists is largely due to how Renan dismisses, in a radical way, most current myths of unity, purity, and continuity. Although Renan does not call the nation into question as a concept and an object, he opposes all attempts at *naturalizing* the nation. Nations, he reminds us, are man-made, and, moreover, national unity is "always effected by means of brutality."[3] Thus, the unity of the French nation was forcefully imposed by conquering invaders. This fact, Renan goes on to argue, has to be forgotten by the members of a nation for otherwise it would represent a threat to the nation's precarious unity. "Forgetting," he writes, "I would even go so far as to say historical error, is a crucial factor in the creation of a nation, which is why progress in historical studies often constitutes a danger for [the principle of] nationality."[4]

On the following pages, Renan dismisses all the familiar criteria of national unity. Race, language, or religion, he asserts, cannot supply an adequate basis for the definition of the nation, since they nowhere exist in "pure" or unmixed form. Nor can the nation be explained by a simple "community of interest."[5] Geographical factors, Renan adds, are equally insufficient for a definition of the nation. "No," he writes, summing up his argument,

> it is no more soil than it is race which makes a nation. [...] Man is everything in the formation of this sacred thing which is called a people. Nothing [purely] material suffices for it. A nation is a spiritual principle, the outcome of the profound complications of history; it is a spiritual family, not a group determined by the shape of the earth.[6]

---

[2] See Benedict Anderson, *Imagined Communities. Reflections on the Origin and Spread of Nationalism* (London: Verso, 1983), 15, and Homi K. Bhabha (ed.), *Nation and Narration* (London and New York: Routledge, 1990), 8-22.

[3] Ernest Renan, "What Is a Nation?," in Homi K. Bhabha (ed.), *Nation and Narration* (London and New York: Routledge, 1990), 11.

[4] Renan, "What Is a Nation?," 11.

[5] ibid., 18.

[6] ibid., 18ff.

The nation as a "spiritual principle:" This idea reappears, if in modified form, in Benedict Anderson's *Imagined Communities* published one hundred years after Renan's lecture. In the much quoted title of Anderson's book, the adjective "imagined" replaces Renan's far more ambiguous term "spiritual" with all its religious connotations. For Anderson, the nation is *"imagined* because the members of even the smallest nation will never know most of their fellow-members, meet them, or even hear of them, yet in the minds of each lives the image of their communion."[7] This is an important addition to Renan's lecture: if the individual members of a nation are not naturally *related*, as Renan had argued, it is also true that they are not personally *acquainted* with each other. The same, Anderson goes on to explain, holds for all other communities that are larger than "face-to-face"[8] groups.

As already mentioned, the aim of Renan's lecture is not to dispense with the concept of the nation altogether. Renan's deconstruction of the myth of natural unity is eventually followed by a very emphatic definition of the nation in which the nation's *spiritual* basis is emphasized (a fact frequently overlooked by Renan's recent constructivist readers). Two factors, Renan maintains, unify a nation: the common possession of "a rich legacy of memories" and "the desire to live together."[9] What is striking here is that Renan leaves aside the political and institutional foundations of the nation. Notably absent from his lecture is any mention of states and constitutions. This conspicuous omission indicates that Renan is not primarily interested in the constitutional basis of the nation. Instead, he focuses on what more recent theorists would describe as the "cultural memory" from which a given collective identity is derived.

In his earliest and most condensed definition of the concept of cultural memory, the German Egyptologist and cultural theorist Jan Assmann speaks of a "collectively shared knowledge mainly (but not exclusively) of the past, which constitutes the basis for a group's consciousness of its unity and peculiarity."[10] In his book *Das kulturelle Gedächtnis*, Assmann adds: "What counts for cultural memory is not

---

7 Anderson, *Imagined Communities*, 15.
8 ibid.
9 Renan, "What Is a Nation?," 19.
10 Jan Assmann, "Kollektives Gedächtnis und kulturelle Identität," in Jan Assmann and Tonio Hölscher (eds.), *Kultur und Gedächtnis* (Frankfurt: Suhrkamp, 1988), 15 (my translation).

factual history, but only remembered history."[11] Both Assmann's initial definition of cultural memory and his later elaboration of the concept in his book of the same title are, I think, very much in line with Renan's lecture. Following Assmann's understanding of cultural memory, the nation may be defined as an imagined community based on the (re)construction of a common history in which the nation's inherent ethnic, linguistic, and religious plurality is underemphasized (or, as Renan puts it, forgotten) whereas all evidence of a common, unifying origin is overemphasized (and therefore remembered). It is this emphasis on the dialectics of remembering and forgetting necessarily involved in the construction of collective identities that makes Renan's lecture so useful for an investigation of Europe as an imagined community (more useful, I would argue, than Benedict Anderson's far more recent study).

However, we cannot stop here. For the shared memory of a common origin and history is only *one* basis of collective identity. The anthropologist Fredrik Barth is one of the authors to have pointed this out. Rather than understanding ethnic groups as internally continuous formations that derive their self-image exclusively from their own common origin and history, Barth accentuates the relevance of other, contrasting groups for the construction and maintenance of collective identity. In his preface to the volume *Ethnic Groups and Boundaries. The Social Organization of Culture Difference* (1969), Barth suggests that we shift the focus "from internal constitution and history of separate groups to ethnic boundaries and boundary maintenance."[12] From this perspective, ethnic groups are "categories of ascription and identification"[13] depending "on the maintenance of a boundary."[14] Where Assmann emphasizes the relevance of self-ascriptions that make up the collective self-image of a cultural group, Barth stresses the significance of other-ascriptions that enable the group to define its boundaries. This approach, I think, is not so much an alternative as a supplement to the theories and concepts discussed so far. Much recent writing in the field of cultural theory tends to favor *one* of the two approaches. In order to avoid an excessively one-sided emphasis, the imagination of community should be understood as a process necessarily involving *both*, the drawing of

---

[11] Jan Assmann, *Das kulturelle Gedächtnis. Schrift, Erinnerung und politische Identität in frühen Hochkulturen* (Munich: Beck, 1997), 52 (my translation).

[12] Fredrik Barth, "Introduction," in Fredrik Barth (ed.), *Ethnic Groups and Boundaries. The Social Organization of Culture Difference* (Boston: Little, Brown and Company, 1969), 10.

[13] Barth, "Introduction," 10.

[14] ibid., 14.

cultural boundaries *and* the (re-)construction of a common history. These processes are mutually informing. Every group needs to have some notion of who it is (and where it comes from) in order to define its difference from other, neighboring groups; on the other hand, only after a boundary has been drawn between 'us' and 'them' can a group tell where its own particular history begins – a point I shall return to below.

If the construction of the nation neglects intra-national heterogeneity while simultaneously emphasizing international difference, the same is basically true for the imagination of Europe. In this process, both Europe's common cultural memory and the differences distinguishing Europe from other (supposed) unities, such as the Orient, are accentuated. Starting from the assumption that what has been said so far about nations and ethnic groups must also be true, in a very general sense, for imagined communities larger than individual nations and encompassing more than one ethnic group, I will apply the above theories to the imagination of Europe. In doing so, I do not intend to postulate the existence of a quasi nation-state of Europe, but to reconstruct – through a historical analysis of discourse – a textually constructed, imaginative identity. An identity, I should add, that is best understood "as a 'production' which is never complete, always in process, and always constituted within, not outside, representation."[15] In the following sections of my contribution, I will describe this process of identity construction as "boundary work." Before I begin my theoretical discussion of boundary work, however, let me try to illustrate what has been said so far by an example.

3. The Discovery of Europe in the South Pacific

In his account of Captain Cook's second circumnavigation of the globe, *A Voyage round the World [...] during the Years 1772, 3, 4 and 5*, the German naturalist Georg Forster projects an image of the world as a mosaic consisting of numerous individual "nations" each marked by "national characters" peculiar to them. Although he never explicitly defines the category of "national character," Forster frequently employs the term to describe both non-European peoples and the populations of European colonies. In Forster's broad understanding of the concept, "national character" can apply to a specific mentality – such as the "peculiar

---

[15] Stuart Hall, "Cultural Identity and Diaspora," in Patrick Williams and Laura Chrisman (eds.), *Colonial Discourse and Post-Colonial Theory. A Reader* (New York: Columbia University Press, 1994), 392.

gentleness of disposition"[16] said to characterize the Tahitians – just as well as it can apply to a particular urban topography. Thus, Forster explains that "[t]he national character of the Dutch strongly manifests itself in [one] particular [feature]," namely the canals running in the middle of the principal streets of Cape Town (51). As Forster observes, these canals are perfectly useless and, on top of that, "occasion no very pleasant smell" due to the general shortage of water in the colony which necessitates partial drainage of the canals. If all the Dutch settlements are supplied with canals, Forster argues, "though reason and common sense evidently prove their noxious influence on the health of the inhabitants," (51) this can only be explained by an irrational force behind this and other Dutch idiosyncrasies. The term "national character", then, not only covers cultural and social characteristics, but also psychological propensities.

However, Forster's ethnographic descriptions are not restricted to differences *between* separate nations. Speaking of social hierarchies distinguishing classes and genders, Forster also addresses differences *within* each individual nation, showing that every nation is in turn subdivided into different social groups. All the more surprising is Forster's sudden and rather anti-climactic conclusion to his travelogue, in which he sums up the results of his four year long journey as follows:

> From the contemplation of these different characters, the advantages, the blessings which civilization and revealed religion have diffused over our part of the globe, will become more and more obvious to the impartial enquirer. He will acknowledge, with a thankful heart, that incomprehensible goodness which has given him a distinguished superiority over so many of his fellow-creatures, who follow the impulse of their senses, without knowing the nature or name of virtue; without being able to form that great idea of general order, which could alone convey to them a just perception of the Creator.
>
> (674)

At the end of Forster's travelogue, the world is reduced to two more or less homogeneous collectives: 'us,' the Europeans, and 'them,' the

---

[16] Georg Forster, *A Voyage round the World*, in *Georg Forsters Werke: Sämtliche Schriften, Tagebücher, Briefe* (Berlin: Akademie-Verlag, 1968), 1:157. Further references to this edition appear in parentheses in the text.

inhabitants of other continents. This entails a series of binary oppositions: civilization / savagery, Christianity / disbelief, knowledge / ignorance, virtue / instinct – the oldest criterion for distinguishing Europeans from non-Europeans, Christian religion, thus being supplemented by the more recent Enlightenment ideals of virtue and knowledge.

This unexpected shift from a comparatively complex representation of both inter- and intra-national diversity to a simple dichotomy demonstrates how in spite of all internal European differences there were conceptions of something beyond the boundaries of Europe, the experience of which could make all other boundaries momentarily disappear. It is certainly no coincidence that in Forster's travelogue, the signifier "Europe" occurs most often in the passage describing the expedition's return, after more than two years of travel and hardship in the South Seas, to the Cape of Good Hope. The crews, Forster reports, were euphoric whenever they saw a ship – a fact indicating the "universal longing for an intercourse with Europeans." (641) When encountering Dutch, Swedish, Danish, English, French, Portuguese, and Spanish ships, everyone on board was relieved to be back among "Europeans." At this point, all European nationalities are subsumed under one and the same category. Accordingly, Forster remarks that he and the other men "forg[o]t national characters" (643) when they were generously received by the Dutch governor Mr. Brand. The general feeling of commonness evoked in this passage, however, does not stop Forster from complaining two sentences later that "we dined, according to the Dutch custom, at one o'clock, or during the time of the greatest heat" (643), thus highlighting another habit supposedly characteristic of the Dutch nation.

In Forster's account, the "national characters" distinguishing different European nations never cease to exist. However, the internal European boundaries shift out of focus the moment the external boundaries separating Europe from the rest of the world are put to the forefront. This confirms a general observation made by the historian Jürgen Osterhammel in an article on the significance of cultural boundaries in the European colonial expansion: the experience of cultural *alterity* in the colonies, Osterhammel argues, was the precondition for the realization of European *identity*.[17] In order to

---

[17] Cf. Jürgen Osterhammel, "Kulturelle Grenzen in der Expansion Europas," in *Geschichtswissenschaft jenseits des Nationalstaats. Studien zu Beziehungsgeschichte und Zivilisationsvergleich* (Göttingen: Vandenhoeck & Ruprecht, 2001), 217.

become aware of their "Europeanness," the Europeans paradoxically had to *leave* their continent first. For it was only upon entering the space of the other that the boundaries of Europe became visible and Europe itself gained shape.

4. Boundary Work

As Forster's travelogue illustrates, the imagination of Europe is based not only on the assumption of a common cultural background but also – and perhaps even more importantly – on the awareness of cultural boundaries framing Europe as a cultural entity. What this suggests is that the historical reconstruction of the cultural memory that provides Europe with collective self-images has to be complemented by an investigation of the various distancing strategies used to separate Europe from its Others. This, of course, is not an entirely new finding, since many studies in the tradition of Edward Said's *Orientalism* (1978) do precisely that. Although *Orientalism* is now mainly known for its use of the Foucauldian concept of discourse and its investigation of the power/knowledge nexus tying literature to imperialism, Said's groundbreaking analysis is first and foremost a systematic investigation of the imaginative boundaries that helped Europe to derive a collective identity. As Said demonstrated, "the Orient has helped to define Europe [...] as its contrasting image, idea, personality, experience;"[18] "it is [...] one of its deepest and most recurring images of the Other."[19]

Although *Orientalism* is frequently (and rightly) read as "a pioneering attempt to use Foucault systematically in an extended cultural analysis,"[20] only few critics seem to be aware that parts of Said's critique of Orientalism were anticipated by Michel Foucault in the preface to his first major work, *Folie et déraison. L'histoire de la folie à l'âge classique*

---

[18] Edward Said, *Orientalism*, New Edition (Harmondsworth: Penguin, 1995), 1ff.

[19] Said, *Orientalism*, 1.

[20] James Clifford, "On *Orientalism*," in *The Predicament of Culture. Twentieth-Century Ethnography, Literature and Art* (Cambridge, Mass. and London: Harvard University Press, 1988), 264. For a detailed discussion of Said's use of Foucault's theory of discourse, see also Michael C. Frank, "Kolonialismus und Diskurs: Michel Foucaults 'Archäologie' in der postkolonialen Theorie," in Susanne Kollmann and Kathrin Schödel (eds.), *PostModerne De/Konstruktionen. Ethik, Politik und Kultur am Ende einer Epoche* (Münster: Lit, 2004), 139-55.

(translated, in abridged form, as *Madness and Civilization*).[21] Foucault's preface, which only appeared in the original French 1961 edition of his study, calls attention to the "obscure gestures, necessarily forgotten once they are accomplished"[22] by which a culture rejects something which later comes to represent its other/exterior. Such rejections, Foucault argues, are at the origin of all cultural history: "[i]nterroger une culture sur ses expériences-limites, c'est la questionner, aux confins de l'histoire, sur un déchirement qui est comme la naissance même de son histoire."[23] Thus, the Occident came into existence, as such, only after a boundary had been drawn between 'interior' and 'exterior,' between 'East' and 'West.' The juxtaposition of Occident and Orient was the condition of possibility of European cultural history (and, hence, identity):

> l'Orient est pour lui [l'Occident] tout ce qu'il n'est pas, encore qu'il doive y chercher ce qu'est sa vérité primitive. Il faudra faire une histoire de ce grand partage, tout au long du devenir occidental, le suivre dans sa continuité et ses échanges, mais le laisser aussi apparaître dans son hiératisme tragique.[24]

The history of the "great divide" outlined here by Michel Foucault was supplied seventeen years later by Edward Said. *Orientalism* goes beyond Foucault's exploration of the "limits," though, insofar as it extends the metaphor of the cultural boundary. One of the central concepts developed by Said is that of "imaginative geography." By this term Said understands the "universal practice of designating in one's mind a familiar space which is 'ours' and an unfamiliar space beyond 'ours' which is 'theirs.'"[25] Said himself draws a connection between the concept of imaginative geography and Giovanni Battista Vico's "great observation that men make their own history."[26] Instead of linking imaginative geography to Vico's idea of imaginative history, however, Said could also have referred to the German sociologist Georg Simmel's

---

[21] Michel Foucault, "Préface [à *Folie et déraison. Histoire de la folie à l'âge classique*]," in *Dits et écrits, vol. I: 1954-1969*, ed. Daniel Defert and François Ewald (Paris: Gallimard, 1994), 159-67.

[22] Foucault, "Préface," 161 (my translation).

[23] ibid.

[24] ibid.

[25] Said, *Orientalism*, 54.

[26] Said, *Orientalism*, 4ff.

1903 essay "The Sociology of Space,"[27] which has much in common with Said's own constructivist epistemology of space.

Simmel's essay has only recently been translated into English and is still not very well known to theorists outside of its discipline. I refer to it here because I think that Simmel's discussion of the social imagination of space can serve to supplement Said's brief (and rather fragmentary) excursion into the practice of "imaginative geography." The parallel between both texts becomes most obvious in Simmel's fundamental observation that "space in general is only an activity of the mind."[28] Where Said explains that the mind intensifies "its own sense of itself by dramatizing the distance between what is close and what is far away,"[29] Simmel declares: "It is not the form of spatial proximity or distance that creates the special phenomena of neighbourliness or foreignness [...]. Rather, these [...] are facts caused purely by psychological *content*."[30]

Simmel is concerned with the spatial preconditions of sociation (the word "sociation" being a translation of his original German term "Vergesellschaftung"). Social groups, he argues, always think of the space they occupy as a unity framed in by boundaries, be they geographical or purely imaginative. Only within this clearly defined frame, Simmel goes on to explain, can a society constitute itself as a coherent group. This is an important addition to the theories discussed so far. In order to be able to develop a collective identity, every community needs to have a notion of the space which it, and it alone, occupies; for only by delineating, or collectively imagining, such a common space can it constitute itself as a unity. Simmel's analysis of the interrelationship between the spatial constitution of society and the social constitution of space is summed up in the aphoristic sentence: "The boundary is not a spatial fact with sociological consequences, but a sociological fact that is formed spatially."[31]

The point I would like to emphasize most in Simmel's essay is the idea that *external* boundaries – which, Simmel emphasizes, are always arbitrary with respect to nature[32] – serve to create *internal* unity. This may help to explain why in George Forster's travelogue (as in many other examples that I cannot discuss here) Europe only emerges as a

---

[27] Georg Simmel, "The Sociology of Space," in *Simmel on Culture*, eds. David Frisby and Mike Featherstone (London: Sage, 1997), 137-85.

[28] Simmel, "The Sociology of Space," 138.

[29] Said, *Orientalism*, 55.

[30] Simmel, "The Sociology of Space," 137ff.

[31] ibid., 143.

[32] ibid., 141ff.

transnational unity after its imaginative boundaries have been crossed. The use of the term "European" depends on the respective frame of reference; it is a relational category. Outside Europe, in the realm of the Other, internal European differences are "forgotten" (in Ernest Renan's sense of the term). The concept "European" is as exclusive as it is inclusive. Its signification is produced *ex negativo*: In Forster's book, "European" designates that which is different from the non-European, not a substantial identity that relies on essence. What I would like to suggest, therefore, is that instead of attempting to reconstruct the cultural "substance," or "content" of Europe based on the formation of cultural memory, we should instead focus on the relational definition of Europe on the grounds of − varying and unstable − conceptions of the Other.

Let me conclude with two final observations concerning the process described here as "boundary work." As the above quoted passage from Forster's *Voyage round the World* demonstrates, the common ground of Europe was defined not only in geographical terms, but also in historical or, more precisely, evolutionary terms. In his dichotomous construction of cultural difference, Forster draws both a spatial and a temporal boundary: The superior state, he writes, is to be found *here*, in "our part of the globe" (i.e., the European continent), as well as *now*, in our time (i.e., European modernity). *Beyond* this space and *before* this time, the other, non-European state is to be discovered. This passage shows that apart from the conception of imaginative geographies another distancing strategy was used to delineate Europe: the temporal distancing of the other that the anthropologist Johannes Fabian has described as "the denial of coevalness."[33] From the late eighteenth century onwards, the "relations between the West and its Other, between anthropology and its object, were conceived not only as difference, but as distance in space *and* Time."[34] Cultural difference was equated with both spatial and temporal distance. This double distancing strategy can be traced back to a discursive shift in the history of European knowledge: the emergence of the evolutionist paradigm according to which they (there) are now as we (here) were then (in some former time):

---

[33] Johannes Fabian, *Time and the Other. How Anthropology Makes Its Object* (New York: Columbia University Press, 1983). For a definition of the term "denial of coevalness," see 31ff.

[34] ibid., 147.

> The other is constructed as a system of coordinates (emanating
> [...] from a real center – the Western metropolis) in which
> given societies of all times and places may be plotted in terms
> of relative distance from the present.[35]

In my opinion, Johannes Fabian is right to observe that this form of
boundary work has proved the most enduring. Whereas the spatial
distance separating the West from the rest of the world has been reduced
and overcome by modern technologies of travel and communication as
well as by the processes of economic and cultural expansion known as
"globalization," there is still a very strong notion of an exclusively
western "modernity." We may say that the focus has gradually shifted,
since the late eighteenth century, from primarily geographical
conceptions of Europe to primarily temporal definitions of the
boundaries of Europe:

> The distance between the West and the Rest on which all
> classical anthropological theories have been predicated is by
> now being disputed in regard to almost every conceivable
> aspect (moral, aesthetic, intellectual, political). [...] There
> remains "only" the all-pervading denial of coevalness which
> ultimately is expressive of a cosmological myth of frightening
> magnitude and persistency.[36]

True to Michel Foucault's principle of discontinuity,[37] any enquiry of
European boundary work will have to take into account epistemological
breaks and discursive shifts of this kind. Although there are "ways of
perceiving alterity that remain salient and available, if in varying forms,
over time,"[38] it will necessarily produce a "history of the different
conceptions of difference"[39] employed in travel writings of different
periods. For, as Edward Said rightly points out in his afterword to the
1995 re-edition of *Orientalism* (in which he revises his own earlier concept
of a monolithic and static discourse): "Each age and society re-creates its

---

[35] ibid., 26.

[36] ibid., 35.

[37] See Foucault, *Archaeology of Knowledge*, especially the Introduction and Chapter I.

[38] Nicholas Thomas, *Colonialism's Culture. Anthropology, Travel and Government* (Cambridge: Polity Press, 1994), 68.

[39] Bernard McGrane, *Beyond Anthropology. Society and the Other* (New York: Columbia University Press, 1989), ix.

'Others.' Far from a static thing then, identity of self or of 'other' is a much worked-over historical, social, intellectual, and political process."[40]

The (seeming) persistence and continuity of discursively drawn boundaries really consists in a perpetual process of self- and other-ascription. This incessant boundary work, however, is by no means a sign of stability. On the contrary, it indicates the threatening dissolution of the boundaries that cannot be permanently fixed in discourse. The stereotype, Homi Bhabha reminds us, "is a complex, ambivalent, contradictory mode of representation, as anxious as it is assertive"[41] – and the same, I would like to add, is true for the discursively constructed boundaries separating Europe from its others. Although intended as a distancing strategy, the boundary work in European travel writing keeps on inscribing the other into Europe's own image of itself. As in Forster's travelogue, non-European societies are omnipresent in Europe's cultural memory. So much so, in fact, that "Europe" itself seems to be located somewhere else, beyond the boundaries of Europe, where a (negative) mirror-image is sought.

---

[40] Said, *Orientalism*, 332.
[41] Homi K. Bhabha, *The Location of Culture* (London and New York: Routledge, 1994), 70.

"WHAT HAPPENED TO THE NAMING IN THIS STRANGE PLACE?" REMAPPING THE SPACE OF ONTARIO IN THE (CON)TEXTS OF NATIVE CANADIAN THEATRE

Klára Kolinská

The motto of this essay is a reply from a play by a Native Canadian playwright Drew Hayden Taylor, used by one of the characters, an Indian boy "from the past" to express his consternation at not recognizing the space of the present by its names, which, he assumes, are 'naturally' attributed to places by virtue of their meanings. His comment points as well to the critical influence of linguistic conceptualization upon human perception of space, and to the relation of humans to the inhabited, and also even only temporarily penetrated space in general. Keesic, the character in Taylor's play, is exasperated to learn that today's names do not appear to mean anything at all, and asks: "But what power does a name have if it doesn't have a purpose or meaning?"[1] The loss of language almost amounts to the loss of control over space, and prevents its accurate understanding. This 'loss' implies yielding of one language system to another, and indicates vast cross-cultural differences in the approach to the conceptualization of space. Such cross-cultural contact has a long and intriguing history, which has emerged in a particularly noticeable way since the 'discovery' of the New World, an experience in

---

[1] Drew Hayden Taylor, *Toronto at Dreamer's Rock* (Calgary: Fifth House Publishers, 1990), 22.

itself so strong that Stephen Greenblatt characterizes the Europeans' response to it as that of, simply, "wonder."[2]

In her letter commissioning Captain Martin Frobisher to undergo his second attempt at finding the fabled Northwest Passage across the American continent, Queen Elizabeth I called Canada "a meta incognita of limits unknown."[3] Frobisher's voyage was inspired by a desire for profit, and as such led to disaster, repeated many times in the history of conquering the land. Nonetheless, the European presence set its roots firmly on the American continent, eventually flourished in spite of all difficulty, and fundamentally shaped the character of the continent, as well as the lives of its inhabitants. What was essential for such a success was a rapid realization of the need to know and understand the place, and bring the conceptualization of it to the European culture's own ontological system. Constructing one's own system of mapping was part of this process.

In their *History of Cartography*, J.B. Harley and David Woodward define maps as "graphic representations that facilitate a spatial understanding of things, concepts, conditions, processes or events in the human world."[4] This is a broad enough definition to allow for the fact that there is, pragmatically, no universally agreed idea about what a map should look like, or, even, what purposes it is supposed to serve. What was a "meta incognita" for Queen Elizabeth was very much a 'terra cognita' for the Native people, and the "graphic representations" of it created by them differed from those by the Europeans not only in the actual content, but also in basic methodological approaches. In his profound analysis of historical maps of Canada's West Coast, Ingmar Probst explains:

> Natives usually supplemented solicited maps orally and gesturally with names and descriptions of specific features and conditions and many of these were added to the maps by interrogators or incorporated in the course of transcription. If the names and transcriptions had been both unique and stable over long periods of time, this would have facilitated the

---

2 See Stephen Greenblatt, *Marvelous Possessions: The Wonder of the New World* (Chicago: The University of Chicago Press, 1991).

3 Quoted in *Canada: A People's History*. CBC television and video series.

4 J.B. Harley and David Woodward, *The History of Cartography, Vol. 1.: Cartography in Prehistoric, Ancient and Medieval Europe and the Mediterranean* (Chicago: University of Chicago Press, 1987), xvi.

attribution of representation to referents. Different groups of
Natives, however, used different names and descriptions for
the same feature. Conversely, but equally confusingly, different
features were often named or described by different Indians in
identical or similar ways. Therefore, unless the spatial context
is already fairly clear, the name may not serve to establish the
referent. In addition to this, incorporating a transformed map
into an existing European map of a larger area almost
inevitably introduced new errors as well as perpetuating those
which had already been introduced in the interpreting,
mosaicing, and transforming processes.[5]

Such differences in the philosophy of mapping, resulting in dynamic
cultural misunderstandings, are in line with Benedict Anderson's
observation of "the alignment of map and power,"[6] and with the
description of a map by a Thai historian Thongchai Winichakul, quoted
in Anderson: "A map anticipated spatial reality, not vice versa. In other
words, a map was a model for, rather than a model of, what it purported
to represent [...] It had become a real instrument to concretize
projections on the earth's surface."[7]

The acknowledgement of the existence of the 'New World' within
the reachable sphere of human cartography has resulted in the realization
of the need of re-addressing the investigations of space in new terms, on
both pragmatic and theoretical levels, of an approach referred to by
some as "spatialization" of thought. In a preface to his *Postmodern
Geographies*, Edward Soja announces his intention to

tamper with the familiar modalities of time, to shake up the
normal flow of the linear text to allow other, more 'lateral'
connections to be made. The discipline imprinted in a
sequentially unfolding narrative predisposes the reader to think
historically, making it difficult to see the text as a map, a
geography of simultaneous relations and meanings that are tied
together by a spatial rather than a temporal logic. My aim is to

---

5 Ingmar Probst, "Maps of Cultural Transfer – European and Native Cartographers in
the 18th-Century Canadian West," *Zeitschrift für Kanada-Studien*, 45.2 (2004): 76-98.
6 Benedict Anderson, *Imagined Communities. Reflections on the Origin and Spread of Nationalism*
(London and New York: Verso, 1983), 173.
7 Anderson, *Imagined Communities*, 173-74.

spatialize the historical narrative, to attach to *durée* an enduring critical human geography.[8]

Michel Foucault also expressed the spatialization of modern thought in a very categorical tone:

> The present epoch will perhaps be above all the epoch of space. We are in the epoch of simultaneity: we are in the epoch of juxtaposition, the epoch of the near and far, of the side-by-side, of the dispersed. We are at a moment, I believe, when our experience of the world is less that of a long life developing through time than that of a network that connects points and intersects with its own skein. One could perhaps say that certain ideological conflicts animating present-day polemics oppose the pious descendants of time and the determined inhabitants of space.[9]

It appears, however, that the realization of the importance of the study of space is by no means an exclusively contemporary phenomenon. In his investigation of the social role of geography in the early American republic, Martin Brückner notes that immediately after the Revolution "many Americans self-consciously turned to the discourse of geography to negotiate and transform the representation of personal, regional, and political difference into material figures of national consent,"[10] and proceeds to contend that it was precisely this "discourse of geography," i.e., the newly designed maps and geography textbooks that "introduced the nation as a material and inherently readable form."[11]

This contention can be supported by the views of Noah Webster, who insisted in his essay "On the Education of Youth in America" that "every child in America should be acquainted with his own country,"[12] and that "a tour of the United States ought now to be considered as a necessary part of a liberal education."[13] Webster relied on geography in his plans for a new national education system, since in his view

---

[8] Edward W. Soja, *Postmodern Geographies. The Reassertion of Space in Critical Social Theory* (London and New York: Verso, 1989), 1.

[9] Michel Foucault, "Of Other Spaces," trans. Jay Miskowiec, *Diacritics*, 16 (1986): 23.

[10] Martin Brückner, "Lessons in Geography: Maps, Spellers and Other Grammars of Nationalism in the Early Republic," *American Quarterly*, 51.2 (1999): 311-43.

[11] Brückner, "Lessons in Geography," 315.

[12] Quoted in "Lessons in Geography," 318.

[13] ibid.

geographic competence, which Brückner calls "geo-literacy," promoted a sense of identification for concrete individual citizens and the abstract idea of a nation, then still in the process of inner consolidation. That his view was shared by at least some national administrators is evidenced by the founding of offices such as that of the Geographer General in 1777, and the Topographical Bureau which sponsored national map-making projects.

Part of the larger process of acquiring "geo-literacy" as defined by Brückner was the process of name-giving, of introducing the new space into the inhabitants' own and recognizable referential system. As William F. Ganong noted at the beginning of the nineteenth century:

> Place names form a permanent register or index of the course and events of a country's history; they are fossils exposed in the cross-section of that history, marking its successive periods; and so lasting are they that records in stone or brass are not to be compared with them for endurance.[14]

Choosing appropriate names for the newly recognized spatial realities was prompted by a variety of motivations. Among them – besides the pragmatic ones – was often nostalgia for the old country, desire for success and fulfillment of dreams, as well as acknowledgement, on a certain level, of the pre-existence of American Aboriginal cultures. In his book *The Americans: The National Experience*, Daniel Boorstin sums up:

> In the colonial period, names of new settlements were often retrospective, looking back to England. Some town names, like Boston, Cambridge, Hartford, New London, New York, Plymouth, or Worcester, or county names, like Berkshire, Essex, Hampshire, Middlesex, Norfolk, Suffolk, or colony names like New Jersey, New Hampshire, or New York, were obviously nostalgic. In the South, places like Annapolis, Charleston, Jamestown, or Williamsburg, or Georgia, Maryland, and Virginia, honoured English sovereigns. A few, like Salem (from the Hebrew *shalom*, "peace"), or Providence or Philadelphia, carried a plain message of their own. Some, like Pennsylvania or Baltimore, commemorated proprietors or founders. Others, like Cape Cod, Newport or Long Island,

---

[14] Quoted in William B. Hamilton, *The Macmillan Book of Canadian Place Names* (Toronto: Macmillan, 1978), 1.

were purely descriptive. Still others – like Massachusetts, Merrimack, Connecticut, and Roanoke – came from the Indians.[15]

As for the desire to succeed, and thus to materialize the idea of national and cultural re-creation by defining clearly the connections with the Old World, Boorstin notes that

> [a] surprisingly large number of the names chosen for new communities were intended to foreshadow prosperity, wealth, culture, or glory. Unless the founders were willing to be crudely explicit – like the Kansas boosters who named their town (soon to be extinct) "Wealthy City," or those in Montana who named their town "Paradise" – they inevitably expressed their aspirations by borrowing the names of famous centers of the Old World.[16]

A similar situation to that in the early United States was observed in the neighbouring Canada. While Boorstin describes the early American place names as a "ragbag of reminiscence, nostalgia, aspiration, hyperbole, prefabrication, invention, and whimsy,"[17] Hamilton characterizes a largely identical process in Canada in a slightly more restrained manner:

> During the early years of Canadian history the assigning of place names was largely accidental. Fishermen and mariners, explorers and mapmakers, adventurers, voyageurs, pioneers, and politicians, all took part in haphazard naming. Not surprisingly, wide variations in spelling, in interpretation, and in actual location, were commonplace.[18]

What thus markedly discriminates the overall tradition of European place names from that of the New World ones is that whereas in Europe place names are generally a product of long-term historical developments, and embody certain values or cultural significances, in the North American context place names often express the ambition to

---

[15] Daniel Boorstin, *The Americans: The National Experience* (New York: Random House, 1965), 299.

[16] Boorstin, *The Americans: The National Experience*, 297-98.

[17] *The Americans: The National Experience*, 306.

[18] Hamilton, *The Macmillan Book of Canadian Place Names*, 2.

overcome the Old World's powers, with a telling trace of melancholy after what has been inevitably lost, after the high price that has been paid for national and political independence. As Alan Rayburn declares in his book *Naming Canada: Stories About Canadian Place Names*: "Pride and fond memories of homelands and heroic leaders across the sea have influenced many place names in Canada."[19] Rayburn provides examples of Canadian place names such as London, Ontario, New Glasgow, Nova Scotia, or New Denmark and New Brunswick. This characteristic of New World geographic nomenclature stands, after all, in line with the contention that "[e]very place-name is a challenge to one's natural curiosity, a stimulus to enquiry which merits both commendation and explanation. This instinctive quality of the mind is a vital factor in its education."[20]

Given the central position of the idea of space in relation to that of the nation on the American continent, it is not surprising that it should appear as a theme in the 'national literatures' of that continent as well. Indeed, considering drama as one of the most readily responsive literary genres, and theatre as its – spatial – arena of expression, Alan Filewood finds the issue of 'national drama' and national theatre to remain one of the 'national obsessions' in Canada. The reason for that, in his opinion,

> lies in Canada's complex experience of colonialism, in which the theatre has been identified throughout our history as a site for a debate on the nature of nationhood. What makes this complex is that the evolution of the theatre as an expression of post-colonialism coincides with the historical transformation of the theatre as a cultural industry.[21]

The ongoing search and formulation of Canadian identity has a long history, and marks the development of Canada's early plays, which Filewood condescendingly qualified as "romantic poetic drama that produced the ponderous pseudo-Shakespearean tragedies which plague today's students of CanLit."[22] One such example, Charles Mair's tragedy

---

[19] Alan Rayburn, *Naming Canada: Stories About Canadian Place Names* (Toronto: University of Toronto Press, 2001), 77.

[20] G.H. Armstrong, *The Origin and Meaning of Place Names in Canada* (Toronto: Macmillan, 1930), v.

[21] Alan Filewood, "National Theatre / National Obsession," in Ajay Heble, Donna Palmateer Pennee and J.R. Struthers (eds.), *New Contexts of Canadian Criticism* (Peterborough, Ontario: Broadview Press, 1997), 15-23.

[22] Filewood, "National Theatre / National Obsession," 16.

Tecumseh (1886), which re-tells and dramatizes the nation-making war of 1812 while acknowledging the pivotal role of British Native allies, is prefaced by the author's explicit words on the issue:

> Our romantic Canadian story is a mine of character and incident for the poet and novelist, framed, too, in a matchless environment; and the Canadian author who seeks inspiration there is helping to create for a young people that decisive test of its intellectual faculties, an original and distinctive literature – a literature liberal in its range, but, in its highest forms, springing in a large measure from the soil, and "tasting of the wood."[23]

Symptomatically, the theme of *Tecumseh* is not merely the experience of space as such, but a deadly conflict over its control, and a complex debate over the possibility of peaceful co-inhabitation of land. At the very beginning of the play, one of the Indian characters, named Prophet, utters frighteningly hateful words that point out the fatal, physical bond of the people with land, in which the image of land assumes morally significant symbolism:

> Would that my hands were equal to my hate!
> Then would strange vengeance traffic on the earth;
> For I should treat our foes to what they crave –
> Our fruitful soil – yea, ram it down their throats,
> And choke them with the very dirt they love.[24]

Contrasted to the bloodthirsty Prophet, as well as to the unruly mob of greedy Americans, is the noble Tecumseh, generous, loyal, and outspoken in fluent blank verse, who, together with the no-less-noble General Brock, serves as an exemplary prototype of a new Canadian national.

The development of Canada's 'national' drama of land takes an interesting turn when theatre becomes also a domain of the country's Native people – when these become not only the romanticized heroes of someone else's plays, but at the same time playwrights and actors formulating their own aesthetic. Daniel David Moses, one of Canada's

---

[23] Charles Mair, "Preface," in *Tecumseh: A Drama* (1886; Toronto: University of Toronto Press, 1974), 3.
[24] Mair, *Tecumseh*, 12-13.

leading Native playwrights today, identifies the opening of opportunities for this process to be in 1960, the year in which the Canadian Native people acquired the right to vote, and thus finally became fully recognized citizens of 'their' country. The establishment of Canadian 'national Native' theatre has thus been, understandably, accompanied by a long and uneasy political struggle for the recognition of Canada's genuine and deeply rooted ethnic and cultural diversity.

The year 1986, exactly one hundred years after the staging of Charles Mair's *Tecumseh*, saw the premiere of a play distinctly announcing the fact that Canadian Native theatre was now an aesthetically independent cultural phenomenon which asks to be taken seriously on the mainstream scene: Tomson Highway's *The Rez Sisters*. The story of seven women living on the Wasaychigan Indian reserve on Manitoulin Island in northern Ontario gives dramatic expression to yet another perspective of the issue of geographic space and its inhabitants – that of displacement. The lives of all seven characters evolve around their desire to go to a bingo game in Toronto, which, to them, is "not just any bingo. It is THE BIGGEST BINGO IN THE WORLD and a chance to win a way out of a tortured life."[25] Toronto, to the women, symbolizes a place where real life happens, where it is possible to achieve control over one's destiny. Pelajia Patchnose resolutely announces in the first sentence of the play: "Philomena. I wanna go to Toronto."[26] And she reveals the depth of her frustration accumulated over the years of oppression by poverty, ethnicity and femininity:

> See? If I had binoculars, I could see the superstack in Sudbury. And if I were Superwoman, I could see the CN tower in Toronto. Ah, but I'm just a plain old Pelajia Rosella Patchnose and I'm here in plain, dusty, boring old Wasaychigan Hill... Wasy... waiting... waiting... nailing shining shingles with my trusty silver hammer on the roof of Pelajia Rosella Patchnose's little two-bedroom welfare house. Philomena. I wanna go to Toronto.
>
> (2)

In response to her wish, as yet fantastical, her sister soberly points out: "But you were born here. All your poop's on this reserve." (3) This

---

25 Back cover of Tomson Highway, *The Rez Sisters* (Saskatoon and Calgary: Fifth House Publishers, 1988).

26 Highway, *The Rez Sisters*, 2. Subsequent page references are given in the text.

might sound like an early warning about the fatal and unbreakable bond of people to the land, but, nonetheless, once the rumour spreads – which certainly does not take very long – among the Rez sisters about the Biggest Bingo in the World that is coming to Toronto, nothing can stop them. Toronto is not just the "only place educated Indian boys can find decent jobs these days" (7) but a destination of obsession – the name of Toronto is uttered no less than thirty times in the play – and the scene of a luring hazard promising change. Philomena replies: "Don't give me none of this 'I don't like this place. I'm tired of it.' This place is too much inside your blood. You can't get rid of it. And it can't get rid of you." (4) To which Pelajia promptly counters:

> I'm gonna put that old chief to shame and build me a nice paved road right here in front of my house. Jet black. Shiny. Make my lawn look real nice. [...] And if that old chief don't wanna make paved roads for all my sisters around here I'm packing my bags and moving to Toronto.
>
> (8)

It is deeply ironic that the name of Toronto, a place the women dream about with obsession, but are concurrently distanced from by social, rather than spatial barriers, is among "the most interesting and euphonious Canadian place names [...] attributable to Amerindian and Inuit sources."[27] Although the meaning of the word is the subject of dispute up to this day, it is undoubtedly a word from an Aboriginal language, "which gives us so many of our melodious and strikingly appropriate names descriptive of some physical feature or commemorative of some notable event."[28]

The women's desire to go to Toronto – for them, indeed, a place of promising meetings, and a place of "plenty" – and win at bingo, however

---

[27] Hamilton, *The Macmillan Book of Canadian Place Names*, 6.

[28] Armstrong, *The Origin and Meaning of Place Names in Canada*, vi. It is supposed that linguistically the word "Toronto" originated as the Mohawk phrase *tkaronto*, meaning "where there are trees standing in the water," which was later modified by French explorers and mapmakers. The Mohawks used it to describe the Narrows, the place where today Lake Simcoe empties into Lake Couchiching, where they drove stakes into the water to create fish weirs. Many seventeenth- and eighteenth-century French maps identify Lake Simcoe with variations of *Lac Taronto*. Another meaning given in references is "a place of meetings," derived from the Huron *toronton*. Others suggest that the name means "plenty" or "abundance" or even that it was called after an Italian engineer named Tarento, but such interpretations lack credibility.

obsessive, is motivated by surprisingly humble initial ambitions, which explode into surreal proportions inspired by film and popular culture. Veronique St. Pierre, for example, privately imagines:

> When I win the BIGGEST BINGO IN THE WORLD. NO! After I win the BIGGEST BINGO IN THE WORLD, I will go shopping for a brand-new stove. In Toronto. At the Eaton Centre. A great big stove. The kind Madame Benoit has. The kind that has the three different compartments in the oven alone. I'll have the biggest stove on the reserve. I'll cook for all the children on the reserve. I'll adopt all of Marie-Adèle Starblanket's 14 children and I will cook for them. I'll even cook for Gazelle Nataways' poor starving babies while she is lolling around like a pig in Big Joey's smelly, sweaty bed. And Pierre St. Pierre can drink himself to death for all I care. Because I'll be the best cook on all of Manitoulin Island! I'll enter competitions. I'll go to Paris and meet what's-his-name Gordon Bleu! I'll write a cookbook called 'The Joy of Veronique St. Pierre's Cooking' and it will sell in the millions! And I will become rich and famous! Zhaboonigan Peterson will wear a mink while she eats steak tartare-de-frou-frou! Madame Benoit will be so jealous she'll suicide herself. Oh, when I win the BIGGEST BINGO IN THE WORLD!
>
> (36-37)

Although not all of the women's desires are fulfilled in the way they imagine, the very fact of making the trip to Toronto does change something in their lives, and they leave the audience with an affirmation that the women's unfeigned perseverance, and, no less importantly, sense of humour, guarantees their survival, despite their knowledge of the undeniable truth of "how fuckin' hard it is to be an Indian in this country." (97)

The above-mentioned play by Drew Hayden Taylor, called *Toronto at Dreamer's Rock*, introduces a 'dramatically' different image of Toronto, intended, perhaps, to put the mainstream audience momentarily in the position of experiencing a cultural misunderstanding. Its story, fixed in a single moment of 'contemporary' time, renders a meeting of three Indian youngsters, Rusty "from the present," Keesic, appearing miraculously, and to his own greatest surprise, "from the past," and Michael, visiting likewise "from the future." The place of their meeting is Dreamer's Rock, also on Manitoulin Island, a traditional site of the local Natives' vision quests. When Keesic appears, he and Rusty begin to compare their acculturated ideas about visually representing, i.e., 'mapping' the surrounding space, as is suggested in their exchange:

> KEESIC: Those lines over there cutting through the forest. What do you call them?
> RUSTY: Oh. These are roads.
> KEESIC: Roads. And what do these roads do?
> RUSTY: People drive on them. What else would you do with them?
> KEESIC: I can't tell from here, what do they look like?
> RUSTY: Roads? They are like very wide, hard paths, I guess.
> KEESIC: Paths? That big? Hunting must be good to make people fat enough to need a path that wide. I have this picture in my mind of these roads bringing all these fat young boys here for their dreams.[29]

With the arrival on the scene of Michael, the ghost of the boy from the future, the three protagonists are in for their greatest surprise, and most complicated dispute – namely over the meaning of the word "Toronto." Rusty, not quite coping with the 'outlandishness' of the situation, exasperatedly exclaims:

> RUSTY: I don't believe this. And why am I still talking to you? My mother warned me about people like you but she said they all lived in Toronto.
> KEESIC: Toronto?
> RUSTY: You know about Toronto? Then you aren't real.
> KEESIC: I am as real as you are. My people are great traders. We make trips to the south for goods. And in trade it is better to understand the language of the people you are dealing with. These people to the south have a word for where people gather to trade, but it covers any place where important things happen. It's called 'Toronto.'[30]

Similarly, Keesic has a problem understanding the notion of the mixing of races inhabiting the land, and with the notion of the 'white man's

---

[29] Taylor, *Toronto at Dreamer's Rock*, 26.
[30] *Toronto at Dreamer's Rock*, 37.

coming.' Michael offers his piece of a good schoolboy's informed rhetoric:

> MICHAEL: A lot of nations were displaced by the coming of the white man. And, as a result, traditional migratory patterns were disrupted. Eventually, the Ojibway, Odawa, and Potawatomi reached an agreement whereby they would share Manitoulin Island.
> KEESIC: That's the third time you've mentioned this white man. Why is he white? Is he not well?
> RUSTY: Well, that's a judgment call.
> [...]
> MICHAEL: Well, they are coming. Taking an educated guess, I would estimate you to be from approximately the 1590ies. And Champlain landed in this area around 1615. We're talking a couple of decades at the most.
> RUSTY: Boy, do you have a surprise coming. Guess who's coming to dinner? You better put out an extra 250 million plates, but be sure and check your silverware after.[31]

In spite of the, at times, slightly painful didacticism of the play, it becomes evident that language and, in particular, 'proper' names, also help to construct spatial reality, and the perception of it. Mis-placement of names, originating from mis-conception, sometimes promotes a chain of confusion and inter-textual, inter-cultural language play. In another of his plays, *Only Drunks and Children Tell the Truth*, Taylor has a character named Tonto, which, to the insider, echoes the name of the silent and faithful Indian sidekick from the popular western Lone Ranger series. However, that is not how Taylor's character got his name. When asked, Tonto explains that when he was a child, he would ask about his father, and was always told: '"Your Dad is in Toronto.' Only I couldn't say Toronto, I kept pronouncing it Tonto. The name kinda stuck."[32] Toronto thus becomes a place where fathers disappear, and epitomizes some of the deep social conflicts plaguing Native communities today, such as alcoholism, domestic violence, or disrupted family structures and absent fathers. These social plagues, however, and the discourse of them, consequently amount to stereotypes, to the majority's presumptions

---

[31] ibid., 39-40.
[32] Drew Hayden Taylor, *Only Drunks and Children Tell the Truth* (Burnaby, British Columbia: Talonbooks, 1998), 53.

about what must be, 'inevitably,' attributed to the Native people as a whole, and it is impossible to distinguish which aspects of the meaning Taylor has in mind, and in which proportions they are represented in the place name that operates in his play. What, undoubtedly, remains is the affirmation of creative complexity and ambiguity of language in its 'spatial' applications, which, as has been demonstrated, have historical and cultural implications.

In this context, the increasing number of instances of applying Aboriginal languages themselves to describe, define, and demarcate Canadian spatial, and thus also social realities, can – hopefully – be read as a sign of intention to not only acknowledge the validity of these cultures, but also create a freer and more balanced geo-political space in general. Alan Rayburn contends:

> The varied Aboriginal languages in Canada have given our toponymy a certain distinctiveness and rustic beauty. Increased knowledge of these languages and an appreciation of the nomenclature derived from them are among the elements in the understanding of Canadian geography and history.[33]

The experience of space, its relation to history, and the language in which this experience is embodied, are among the most readily available subject matters of national literatures everywhere in the human world. It has always been recognized by everyday users of national languages, as well as by writers, that "[t]he past of a country is embalmed in its place-names and literature. They are its enduring monuments."[34]

---

[33] Rayburn, *Naming Canada*, 183.
[34] Armstrong, *The Origin and Meaning of Place Names in Canada*, vii.

CURATING PLACE: MAPS, STARCHITECTURE AND MUSEUMS-WITHOUT-BORDERS

Shelley Hornstein

Even if we have never visited the Louvre in Paris, France or the Guggenheim Museum in Bilbao, Spain, the frozen snapshot of each of these architectural monuments is what comes to mind rather than any one of the paintings in the collections housed within their prodigious walls. The image is most likely of the building itself or the place in which it is located: the architecture and architectural place, therefore, and decidedly not the contents. It follows that if architectural buildings of magisterial scale designed by important international architects are increasingly what tourists desire to see, then it behoves us to investigate at close range the narratives and memories that are created by tourists as they chart their cultural itinerary. What the tourist chooses to include, remember and dismiss as worthy of a visit on this performative route is what I want to consider as evidence of the creative touristic intervention of *curating* place.

What is a curatorial act and, moreover, what is a curator? Definitions of the role of curators abound. These range from one who acquires, displays and protects works of art, to one who completely reconsiders critical frameworks for art. Engaging in the process of acquisitions, display and preservation inevitably involves interrogating issues of value, history, cultural identity and museum practice writ large. Because curators are largely invisible to the museum-goer, it is often assumed that it is very simple to assemble and hang paintings, for example, in a gallery space and that, moreover, museums house arbitrary and decorative assortments of important works. This is unconditionally false. Museums are never neutral, much as we might assume their display might have us believe. Daniel J. Sherman and Irit Rogoff summarize this point eloquently:

> museums both sustain and construct cultural master narratives that achieve an internal unity by imposing one cultural tendency as the most prominent manifestation of any historical period. Thus the classification of an object involves the choice of a particular kind of presentation, which then establishes a museological context that provides the object with meaning [...T]he context works to determine the selection of viewing public and the cultural capital that this public gleans from the museum.[1]

While a theorization of collecting and its relationship to curatorial practice informs my project on another level, I would like to limit my arguments here to a consideration of curatorial practice as a need to classify and order within a rubric. While museums have largely been keepers of local and national identity, my point is that the new map of cultural tourism that I wish to suggest is no longer limited to geographic sites. Instead, the new map is formulated by curatorial design *out-of-place* and across nation-state boundaries. That is to say that in so doing, the tourist contributes to the reformulation of a concept of cultural identity, one that politicizes nonetheless, outside the frontiers of political geographies.

Therefore, a *route* of cultural tourism and cultural memory is not necessarily bound geographically to one physical location. We can imagine packaging other *routes* of tourism that construct different kinds of cultural memory across nation-state borders to create new maps, charting a new cartography of place and of memory-making. This empowers subjects to become keepers of international memory. Perhaps Dean MacCannell's suggestions that "sightseeing is a kind of collective striving for a transcendence of the modern totality, a way of attempting to overcome the discontinuity of modernity, or incorporating its fragments into unified experience"[2] still obtains. Yet I propose we

---

[1] Daniel J. Sherman and Irit Rogoff (eds.), *Museum Culture* (Minneapolis: University of Minnesota Press, 1995), xi-xii.

[2] Dean MacCannell, *The Tourist: A New Theory of the Leisure Class* (Berkeley: University of California Press, 1999), 13.

reconsider the action of sightseeing as a curatorial act, a performative and integrated action that situates the *site*-seer as the agent of change, as the mediator of cultural memory and experience, as 'tourist as broker' of a cultural legacy and cultural memory.

Travelers necessarily bring to cities a perspective, or reshape an understanding of a city, its buildings and monuments, and specifically its museums, by such *curatorial* acts. Put another way, travelers select specific places, monuments, architectural buildings or parks they want to visit and come to know, and that selection process – one that enables, even sanctions, tourists to choose by elimination – determines an itinerary, a travel journey, a pathway of visual, haptic and aural knowledge about a place. MacCannell underscores the importance of the "ceremonial ratification of authentic attractions as objects of ultimate value, a ratification at once caused by and resulting in a gathering of tourists around an attraction and measurable to a certain degree by the time and distance the tourists travel to reach it."[3] But he goes on to point out that the "actual act of the communion between tourist and attraction is less important than the *image* or the *idea* of society that the collective act generates."[4] As such, the traveler is an independent curator, carving out a vision from a targeted or random selection of sites to see. And while it is crucial for tourists to recognize the role of the materiality of place and its attendant authenticity, as MacCannell makes clear, I would like to add that it is just as important to validate the experience of the imagination and the power of visual culture in informing desire for a place, even if a tourist never leaves home. The creative curatorial act assumed by the tourist begins with the images of the museums themselves and evolves into an architectural and geographic construction of the mind (and heart). This experience is not necessarily connected to a material place, though making desire material often leads to yet another form of geographic (mental) construction.

Indeed, travel and architecture are entwined in many profound ways. For one, cultural memory, national identity and imagination about places are mediated through represented images that are largely photographic. They extend, reconfigure and curate city space, its architecture (which moulds and defines city space) and – what I hope to demonstrate here – new kinds of tourist maps. We can explore this through two landmark and different European museums: the Louvre and the Guggenheim Bilbao. First, I do this to *situate* the tourist's itinerant

---

3 MacCannell, *The Tourist*, 14.
4 ibid., 14-15.

route within the context of museums-without-borders. Whereas for the local culture museums stood as keepers of other cultures – or keepers of cultures no longer present to educate the local community – contemporary museums, especially those designed by architects of international acclaim, have framed the direction of international art as unbound to nations, and perhaps they even unwittingly contribute to putting the tourist in the position of keeper of a new sort of passport to international travel and memory. Now this necessarily raises the increasingly tangled and thorny issue of what it means to build locally and how this impacts on our perceptions of place and cultural memory through a tourist's nomadic wanderings and "deterritorialization"[5] that I will describe later.

Secondly, not only am I interested in how tourists then create their own geographical and imaginary places, but how this comes to be anchored in memory through photography, in particular, both before and after the travel experience, or even when the travel experience never takes place at all. Visually anchored in photography, an object's history – or in this case, a museum – is subsequently archived for the purposes of preservation, and ultimately, the preservation of national heritage.

Curating Place

The nineteenth century afforded a kaleidoscopic vision of the world mediated by the newest technological inventions: trains, steamships, and cameras. Movement and the new spaces of modernity were measured, recorded and captured. Suddenly the world became two-dimensional, seen through the lens of the camera or panoramic images that framed space through train window panes, portholes and camera view boxes. Travel photography, perhaps the most popular type of photography in its earliest stages, became another form of tourism – a window onto the world – and subsequently piqued enormous interest for unfamiliar places. Yet from the earliest recordings by Westerners of architectural ruins and the triumphs of past cultures – Romans admiring the Greeks; Italian Renaissance masters' reconsiderations of Roman antiquities; the Enlightenment preoccupation with archeological ruins – to the continuing thirst for knowledge of architectural sites today, tourists yearn for a connection to built forms and places.

---

5 Gilles Deleuze and Félix Guattari, *A Thousand Plateaus: Capitalism and Schizophrenia* (Minneapolis: University of Minnesota Press, 1987), 141-45, 381-84, and passim. Further references appear in parentheses in the text.

Travel to places for architectural discovery has been an activity recounted and documented for centuries, accelerating with the democratization of travel when mass tourism developed as a leisure activity during the nineteenth century. Since then, tourists move in greater numbers from a familiar place – such as home – to a faraway place, and then return to the point of departure. The activity of travel is arguably a quest to unearth the foreign and unfamiliar with the possibility of a mild or even a rude cultural awakening. But tourism is accomplished in various ways. Some travel is accomplished by not going anywhere at all. That is, although cities and our navigation of them include the actual experience of our bodily mobility and hence displacement, our imagination and viewing of cities and places is often, as mentioned earlier, exclusively accomplished by way of the imagination spurred by photographs, paintings, postcards, movies, theatre, literature, and the Internet. Yet however fulfilled, the idea of travel is above all to situate oneself imaginatively or experientially in a physical site – an architectural construction – other than the place in which one is located, in order to bring about a redefinition of what is actually familiar in a foreign place or what is new in the adopted culture. Travel is an investigation of place, and almost always of architectonic place, even when it is of a 'natural' setting, such as a rural landscape.

'Starchitecture' and Bilbao

"The word is out that miracles still occur, and that a major one has happened here," announced Herbert Muschamp in the *New York Times* Magazine one month before the October 1997 opening of the Guggenheim Bilbao. With the building hailed as a "masterpiece" and an "instant landmark," its architect, Frank Gehry, continued to lament that he had been "geniused to death."[6] In her terse review of his Guggenheim museum design, critic Joan Ockman suggests it is "[c]entrifugal rather than centripetal, magical rather than machinic" and that it "celebrates the reconsecration of the museum as a space of art."[7] Thomas Krens, the controversial director of the Guggenheim Museum, NY, and the brainchild behind the 'chain' of Guggenheim museums (Berlin, Venice, New York, Las Vegas, and of course Bilbao), is often derided and disdained for his media-driven McGuggenheim concept. Yet as a tourist promoter, there is not much else, save for the Louvre, that comes close

---

6 Herbert Muschamp, "Miracle in Bilbao," *The New York Times* (7 September 1997): 54.
7 Joan Ockman, "Applause and Effect," *ArtForum,* 39 (Summer 2001): 149.

to attracting the cultured or culturally hungry hoards. Ockman proclaims: "In the Gehry universe [...] nothing is sacred but Art. Art, that is, understood as an excessive, impossible, even farcical dream of freedom, imagination, and pleasure."[8]

The critiques of the Guggenheim Bilbao were overwhelmingly adulatory; as a tourist – viewer or public – the idea of being destabilized by architecture, or of what has come to be known in colloquial usage as 'starchitecture' (architecture by rising 'star' architects) in a 'spectaculture' (or a culture of the spectacle) was now palpable. The University of Barcelona's Anna M. Guasch, and the University of Nevada's Joseba Zulaika organized a first-ever conference on the effect of the Guggenheim Bilbao. Entitled *Learning from the Guggenheim,* the organizers' introductory remarks quoted Giorgio Romoli's gushing praise of the museum as follows:

> Its very form, the way it takes root in the environment, is the city's 'first cultural operation.' The building recovers its own history: it laps up the river with confusedly organized 'ship's bow' forms and materials [...] that recall the breadth and grandeur of the Bilbao shipyards, the center of the city's industrial and commercial greatness for five centuries.

They also added Allan Sekula's biting retorts: "In effect, what it imports to Bilbao is an aesthetically controlled, prismatically concentrated version of the high specularity characteristics of the Los Angeles cityscape."[9] While the first statement applauds Gehry's response to the existing town and his ability to know it and integrate his building meaningfully, the second declares that while certainly interesting, it is nothing more than a building that shouts Los Angeles, and perhaps got a bit lost while looking to parachute into California. There is indeed a fine line between the global and the local and this is continually being negotiated so that the opacity of differences between them increases.

Marking the Land: Landmarks

Beyond the Guggenheim as a *tour de force,* Ockman suggests that the Bilbao Guggenheim must be worth considering as an "auratic

---

8 Ockman, "Applause and Effect," 149.
9 Anna M. Guasch and Joseba Zulaika, *Learning from the Guggenheim,* Nevada Museum of Art, 22-24 April 2004, http://basque.unr.edu/Guggenheim/statement1.htm.

artwork,"[10] building on Walter Benjamin's notion of aura, or the stamp of the original. It is not without interest to note that Benjamin's enduring and influential piece began to track the loss of the aura due to technical, namely industrial and assembly-line type, reproduction. Gehry's work relies exclusively on technology and industrially manufactured materials, and in the context of Ockman's remarks, flips the sense of aura to apply to the work of technology and technological reproduction. So indeed, Gehry's oeuvre spins technique on its head resulting in a form that wows and creates "aura," as observed by Ockman, by its monumentality and seemingly effortless reconsideration of the Baroque swirl. While apparently isolated in what Europe and the Western world sees, or at least saw, as a remote tourist location with difficult access, this sensationalism – exacted on the exaggeration of modernist form and technology that preceded it – has become an unlikely and logic-defying site of pilgrimage. Build it and they will come.

'Bilbao as museum' has reconfigured, however unwittingly, the definition of a *landmark*. While dressing in the clothing of a *landmark*, it has moved beyond an identification of site and city. Instead, it is a landmark on the international tourist itinerary of requisite cultural pilgrimage destinations. Further, it might be argued that it no longer plays with its local culture, but rather now enters into a conversation with other international glamorous gallery landmarks, or 'GlamGals' as I will refer to them, to produce a map across the traditional borders of nation-states. This would mean that assumptions about the convention of map-making are necessarily challenged, which is to say that the standard maps we use to guide us to a city or country by car, for example, are guides to nowhere on this performative tourist map. New maps emerge to track cultural pilgrimage routes. More than ever before, these routes are determined by *must-stop, must-sees* of high culture: the splashy 'GlamGal.' They are the one-off designer museums by 'starchitects' (with Gehry leading the pack, and Daniel Libeskind arguably trailing shortly behind). Characterizing Gehry's buildings as "just-add-water," journalist Christopher Hawthorne comments with tongue in cheek on his 'starchitecture' success:

> we've entered an era in which ambitious developers are not just open to the notion of working with architecture's boldest talents but, in certain high-profile cases, are desperate to avoid working without them. So-called 'starchitects' [...] have

---

[10] Ockman, "Applause and Effect," 142.

become too valuable now, as urban alchemists and as marketing vehicles, for developers to ignore.[11]

Rarely, in fact almost never, is a local architect hired to design a museum. The recent building campaign for the Art Gallery of Ontario by Gehry has hitched its publicity to the connections the architect has to Toronto where, fortunately for the Gallery, he was born. (Without a doubt, this has helped cement the project to the city in order to garner support.) As a result of the exposure tourists have to the images published in various media, and the possibility of travel to the sites, images such as architectural landmarks like the Guggenheim Bilbao, designed by internationally recognized architects, are associated one to another in the personal and collective imagination or experience. Eventually for the tourist, this establishes a new thematic map that calls into question local identity and cultural memory and reconfigures by the curatorial process of selection and safeguarding embarked upon by the tourist, a new map of cultural memory.

Let us be clear about what constitutes a landmark. Nineteenth-century urban revisionist, Baron Haussman, used existing monuments in Paris to serve as landmarks: such monuments *mark the land* by creating, identifying or serving as orientation points in that city. One would only need to see a monument to be able to steer a position and guide one's relational abilities to another site. In other words, landmarks guide or act as visual cues. The landmark, according to cultural theorist Brian Massumi, is a vector or a "magnetic pole [...] that vectorizes the space of orientation [...] it is a minimal visual cue functioning to polarize movement's relation to itself in a way that allows us habitually to flow with preferential heading [...and] rise up visibly from a nonvisual sea of self-related movement."[12] The Guggenheim Bilbao is such a landmark. Massumi further suggests that

> each landmark stands alone with its associated coursings. What they mark most directly is a *monad* of relation, a patch of motion referencing its own self-variations [...]. Landmarks and their associated patches of qualitative relation can be pasted

---

[11] Christopher Hawthorne, *Starring Frank Gehry*, http://www.calendarlive.com/ architecture/hawthorne/cl-et-grand25jul22,0,6213588.story?coll=cl-home-more-channels, 22 July 2005.

[12] Brian Massumi, *Parables for the Virtual* (Durham, N.C.: Duke University Press, 2002), 180-81.

together to form a map, but only with an additional effort that must first interrupt the actual course of orientation.[13]

Landmarks arrest movement by interrupting it. What this really means is that unlike two-dimensional geographical maps on paper, landmarks work well as part of cognitive maps or a cognitive understanding of space and place. That is, we move from one landmark to another (unlike on a paper map where we orient ourselves very differently). Landmarks pull us or push us, guide us by design to another landmark or cue.

Gehry's *work-as-landmark* draws on the traditions and history of the grandest museum landmark of all: the Louvre. A magisterial building of dramatic proportions, it was originally a fortress close to the edge of the city, a dungeon, in fact, surrounded by a thick wall mounted with towers, a place of defence which made it possible to shelter the royal treasure or prestigious prisoners. And yet, while constructed to defend Paris during the time King Philippe-Auguste left for the Crusades at the end of the twelfth century, the castle actually went through its first transformation into a Royal Residence in 1360. It housed the most impressive library of manuscripts in the nation. François I built a palace in a new style for his capital during the Renaissance. Entrusted to architect Sebastian Serlio, it was not completed in his lifetime. Next, Pierre Lescot was King Henri II's favourite architect who constructed a new wing and included a large pavilion to house the King's apartments, then another for the Queen. Successively under the reigns of Louis XIII, XIV, Napoleon I and then Napoleon III, through changes in taste and values, construction went through various stages and stretched from 1546 till 1875, until finally the pyramidal addition by I.M. Pei at the end of the twentieth century.[14]

Unlike the passage from a royal collection to a public museum that was taking place in other parts of Europe at the time, the French experience was nothing short of sensational: it marked the birth of a republican France and therefore embodied the principles of Liberty, Equality, and Fraternity. Unlike its other European counterparts such as the Mannheim Electoral Gallery, or the Imperial Galleries in Vienna, the Louvre, as Andrew McClellan has demonstrated, "is best understood as a product of Revolutionary events and strategies to control memory of the

---

[13] Massumi, *Parables for the Virtual*, 181.
[14] Geneviève Bresc-Bautier, "The Louvre: A National Museum in a Royal Palace," *Museum*, 55.217 (2003): 62-63.

past and of the Revolution itself."[15] We might say that the history, fame and power of the Louvre precedes the history of the images of the Louvre to the extent that photography was only invented in the second quarter of the nineteenth century and postdates the opening of the Louvre in 1793. However, its physical grandeur and palatial notoriety (since it was home to the evils of pre-republican France) were known throughout Paris and France, and indeed beyond. The imagination had already been at work for centuries to attempt to create a view of its interior and the treasures it held. And the word was spread by journalists, such as the reporter for *La Décade philosophique* who described what he witnessed when he visited the galleries:

> a young soldier escorting his father, his mother, and his sister, good village people who had never before left their community, and who apparently had never seen paintings other than the sign of the local inn or the smoke-covered daub above the alter [...] but they were all proud to be there; and the son, all the more proud to be leading them, seemed to be saying 'it is I that conquered many of these pictures.'[16]

Hence, the experience of travel is critical to these villagers: you must leave home to travel far from it to witness this great building, this building that embodies the ideals of the new state, this building that houses treasures that will educate the people of France.

Moreover, a century later, Karl Baedeker's *Paris and Environs with Routes from London to Paris*, as part of the twelfth revised edition since 1869, and part of the celebrated series of guidebooks entitled *Handbook for Travellers*, devotes no less than sixty-six pages to the Louvre. Nowhere else in the *Handbook* is a monument afforded so much space: indeed, no other Parisian monument listed therein – or for that matter, excluded (part of that early curatorial process) – merits more than one page at best.

As one of the earliest mass media products, travel guidebooks contributed significantly towards transforming the imaginary and feeding desire for places unknown. Experiencing *in situ* was not as important as conveying a sense of what the experience could evoke. And more than

---

[15] Andrew McClellan, *Inventing the Louvre: Art, Politics, and the Origins of the Modern Museum in Eighteenth-Century Paris* (Berkeley: University of California Press, 1999), 8.

[16] *La Décade philosophique* (10 prairial an VII): 434. Quoted in McClellan, *Inventing the Louvre*, 11.

any other cultural monument of the nineteenth century, the Louvre, and the literature and, subsequently, photographs of it, created a power of place and a mythology surrounding the site.

How did photography contribute to the growing appeal of a place? Barry Bergdoll has suggested that, for example, Félix Duban, a nineteenth-century photographer, was prescient in recognizing that photography "would condition the way architecture was experienced" and that it was "quite a different matter when the photograph was the first image of the three-dimensional reality of a project."[17] Édouard-Denis Baldus, another nineteenth-century photographer, documented the construction of the New Louvre for Napoleon III, producing the largest photographic commission of his career. Initially devised rather humbly, the project expanded to comprise over 2,000 photographs, costing more than 60,000 francs as of 1854. While these were originally intended as a 'stone by stone' documentation of the new construction, Baldus marketed the collection privately in albums sold to the public:

> At the same time that Baldus was producing the Louvre pictures for a very specific purpose and client, he also sold a series of Louvre views to the *Division des Beaux-Arts* as part of his ongoing series of architectural monuments, and exhibited this work widely, both in France and abroad [...]. They were available from print and book dealers across Europe – in Turin, Milan, Florence, Venice, Hamburg, Vienna, London, and Nîmes, as well as from a dozen merchants in Paris.[18]

On a site drenched with memory, this photographic documentary of the Louvre captured all that had been imagined and read for those who had never visited it, and disseminated that visual knowledge in ways that equate our concept of an almost mass distribution of visual images by computer and television today. Suddenly, a vast public was captivated by the widespread and seductive images, pushing the likes of Charles Baudelaire to wax eloquently about photography yet announce its potential demise:

---

17 Barry Bergdoll, "Félix Duban, Early Photography, Architecture, and the Circulation of Images," in Karen Koehler (ed.), *The Built Surface* (Aldershot: Ashgate Publishing Limited, 2002), 23.

18 Malcolm R. Daniel, Édouard-Denis Baldus, Barry Bergdoll and Metropolitan Museum of Art, New York, *The Photographs of Édouard Baldus* (New York: Metropolitan Museum of Art, 1994), 119.

Let photography quickly enrich the traveller's album, and restore to his eyes the precision his memory may lack; let it adorn the library of the naturalist, magnify microscopic insects, even strengthen, with a few facts, the hypotheses of the astronomer [...]. Let it save crumbling ruins from oblivion, books, engravings, and manuscripts, the prey of time, all those precious things, vowed to dissolution, which crave a place in the archives of our memories; in all these things, photography will deserve our thanks and applause. But if once it be allowed to impinge on the sphere of the intangible and the imaginary, on anything that has value solely because man adds something to it from his soul, then woe betide us![19]

After all, photographs of the Louvre not only diffused visual interpretations of the monument, they participated in and indeed generously assisted with the creation of the monument itself. The photographs build on the history and architecture of French national culture and heritage, the sacred bedrock of French identity.

Through that contextualization of 'museum as monument' tied integrally to its geographic site, it can be seen what a different position the Louvre occupies as compared to the detachment of building and site in the Bilbao Guggenheim project. It is not so much that the architect is foreign, or that Gehry's architecture contrasts diametrically with local materials and style. In fact, these are small matters, and perhaps even matters not worthy of debating here. Rather, the contrast only helps to frame the museum's international status and its intellectual, aesthetic, and contemporary connections to the new map of culture, the itinerary of the tourist destined for the exploration of culture and the enduring modernist push to always invent *the new*.

The photographs of the Louvre differ dramatically from those of the Guggenheim. In the former we have overviews of Paris, or the *situatedness* of site, that is, of the ongoing legacy of architectural contributions that add new chapters to the fractious history that shifted with triumph and blood from royalty to the commoner. No matter how unique an object in and of itself, the photograph, as intervening agent

---

[19] Charles Baudelaire, *Selected Writings on Art and Artists*, trans. P.E. Charvet (Cambridge: Cambridge University Press, 1972). Quoted in M. Christine Boyer, "*La Mission Héliographique*: Architectural Photography, Collective Memory and the Patrimony of France, 1851," in Joan M. Schwartz and James R. Ryan (eds.), *Picturing Place: Photography and the Geographical Imagination* (London: I.B. Tauris, 2003), 53.

between object and imagination, between place and memory, mediates between our known place here and now and the imagined place of what occurs or occurred elsewhere. It is no longer our simple physical displacement that creates the image we carry, but rather an image and memory bank that precedes our visit, or sometimes even replaces it. Images plot our performative visual understanding of the world and, through the process of that imagined and real peregrination, create a framework of a manageable quantity of cultural images in a curatorial exhibition of the imagination.

Tourist as Nomad, Architecture and Borders

This brings me to the concept of 'tourist as nomad' in a newly configured cultural landscape, one punctuated with clearly identified cultural landmarks or vectors of *associated coursings,* to hark back to Massumi. I think it is interesting to draw on the concept of nomadic movement in thinking about the wanderings of the tourist both physically and imaginatively and particularly the route itself. Put another way, what are the patterns that chart the action of curating new cultural spaces? And how do we circumvent the endless debate over local and global in a way that becomes useful and where borders melt away to re-emerge elsewhere in different configurations? Deleuze and Guattari point out that

> the nomad can be called the Deterritorialized par excellence [where] [...t]he land ceases to be land, tending to become simply ground [...] or support. The earth does not become deterritorialized in its global and relative movement, but at specific locations, at the spot where the forest recedes, or where the steppe and the desert advance.
>
> (381-82)

They also write that

> [t]he nomads inhabit these places [...]. They are vectors of deterritorialization [...] there is no line separating earth and sky; there is no intermediate distance, no perspective or contour; visibility is limited; and yet there is an extraordinarily fine topology that relies not on points or objects but rather on haecceities, on sets of relations [...] and it alters their

cartography. The nomad, nomad space, is localized and not delimited.

(382)[20]

Unbound by spatial constraints, a nomad, as they suggest, is in a "*local absolute*." By this they mean "an absolute that is manifested locally, and engendered in a series of local operations of varying orientations: desert, steppe, ice, sea." (382)

Discovering places as territorial assemblages of fragments (503-504),[21] 'tourists as nomads' articulate distinct strata of "expression" and "content," and establish a new, reciprocal relation between "a *semiotic system*, a regime of signs" and "a *pragmatic system*, actions and passions." (504)[22] However,

> [t]he assemblage is also divided along another axis. Its territoriality (contents and expression included) is only a first aspect; the other aspect is constituted by *lines of deterritorialization* that cut across it [...and] open the territorial assemblage onto other assemblages [...]. The territoriality of assemblages originates in a certain decoding of milieus, and is just as necessarily extended by lines of deterritorialization.
>
> (504-505)

The 'tourist as a nomad' activates this operation. Moreover, because photography saturates our visual field with images of architectural sites of other places (and specifically these museums), and therefore mediates them (remember that because of images, it is possible to visit these sites without every leaving the comfort of one's home), tourists can then reterritorialize on a being, an object, a book, an apparatus or system. They define the function of deterritorialization as the "movement by which 'one' leaves the territory. It is the line of flight." (508)

---

[20] Deleuze and Guattari define "haecceity" as "[...] a longitude and a latitude, a set of speeds and slownesses between unformed particles, a set of nonsubjectified affects. [...] It should not be thought that a haecceity consists simply of a décor or backdrop that situates subjects, or of appendages that hold things and people to the ground. It is the entire assemblage in its individuated aggregate that is a haecceity [...]." (262)

[21] "Every assemblage is basically territorial. The first concrete rule for assemblages is to discover what territoriality they envelop. [...] The territory is made of decoded fragments of all kinds, which are borrowed from the milieus but then assume the value of 'properties' [...]."

[22] I would like to thank Martin Procházka for his comments on this point.

This is the space and the new map of the *local absolute*. Experience and memory of a place negotiated through the regime of images equip tourists with a geographical nomadic map linking place to place, image to image. Within a realm of visual images that inform the architectural imagination, the new GlamGal-seeking tourist effectively selects from this list and creates a route identical to the construction of a museum exhibition. That is, some sites chosen for the tourists' itinerary become more important destinations. While these choices can be determined by constraints of time, expenses, proximity or levels of cultural comfort, for example, still they reflect similar conditions of constraint that shape any curatorial decision of selection. At the end of the day, a choice is made and an exhibition composed of the works selected takes place. To be guided to these museums is to experience the new cultural and cognitive map that floats parallel and above the physical site of the exhibition galleries, linking one museum to another in a continuum, creating routes of tourism that construct different kinds of cultural memory across nation-state borders. By accepting the notion of the local absolute, the tourist is the new subject of place, self-curated while curating place. Armed with the reterritorialized mental map assembled from guidebooks, films, photographs, or postcards of a place, the cultural tourist calls into play the critical concepts such as national memory, national identity and borders. The new map the tourist obeys is determined by the linkages between GlamGals or other publicized cultural sites. For while the physicality of a museum in a geographical place has limits or borders, the tourist has none.

III.

FUNCTIONS
AND
TRANSFORMATIONS

GERMANS ARE TO GREEKS AS FRENCH ARE TO ROMANS: METAMORPHOSES OF A TOPOS IN GERMAN LITERATURE, 1755-1819

Peter J. Schwartz

"Germans are to Greeks as French are to Romans."

I would like to suggest that this equation expresses a complex of German cultural associations characteristic of the period bracketed by J.J. Winckelmann's seminal essay of 1755 on Greek antiquity and the conservative political reaction of 1819.

Some concrete examples:

The late eighteenth-century commonplace that the German language was in many ways like Attic Greek, and that both German and Greek were superior in their expressiveness to Latin and its derivative, French.

The German passion for Homer, including a German insistence on deep understanding of Homer's original genius – plus a rejection of Virgil as Homer's imitator, and an aesthetic disdain for the French as mere apes of Virgil.

The wishful analogy of Germany to Athens as a pedagogic breeding ground for humanity – *Humanität* – alongside comparisons of Revolutionary France with the Roman Republic at the unstable time of the Gracchine reforms, and then (after 1804) the likening of Napoleonic France to the Roman Empire at its most hegemonic and dissolute.

The task I have set myself is to describe how this set of associations arose as a cultural reflex of German domestic social tensions in the last half of the eighteenth century, and then to show how the associations became truly nationalist only after about 1800, as Napoleon forced the Germans to divide their attention between domestic social issues and the matter of national self-liberation.

Germans and French

The distinction of Germans from French first acquired polemical force around 1770, as part of a strategy of social self-definition, and political self-legitimation, by representatives of a social collective called in German the *Mittelstand*.[1] The word *Mittelstand* – which does not quite mean what the nineteenth century meant by "middle-class" – has best been rendered into English as "non-noble elites," an unwieldy but accurate term that tells us how these people defined themselves. The *Mittelstand*'s project of self-definition relied on its self-distinction from an estate whose power and privilege it both resented and coveted: the German aristocracy. The distinction between German and French arose with the force it did around 1770 because French was the courtly *lingua franca* in this latter phase of German enlightened absolutism; French the German nobility's normative aesthetics and the language of its literature; French its etiquette; French its political self-understanding. It suffices to think of the low opinion that Frederick the Great had of German letters, compared with his high esteem for the French – not to mention the system of taxation Frederick adapted from the French, and contracted to a French minister.[2] French, in short, was the German nobility's *habitus*, in the perception of non-nobles, and it was in contrast to this *habitus* that the *Mittelstand* sought to define and to valorize its own typical forms of behavior.

Such self-definition by contradistinction from others, the legitimation of a non-noble will to power against the dominance of a nobility, involved a revaluation of noble virtues as vices, combined with a definition of *non-noble* qualities as virtues. When these rising elites asked "Was ist deutsch?" they meant not only "Who *are* we?" but also "In what do our typical virtues consist, as compared with what we believe to be the typical vices of nobles?" The question was contrastive,

---

[1] I am thinking here, above all, of the literary movement known as the *Sturm und Drang*, especially Hamann, Herder, Klopstock, and the young Goethe.

[2] Cesare Cases, "I tedeschi e lo spirito francese." in *Saggi e note di letteratura tedesca* (Torino: Einaudi, 1963), 9.

asymmetrically weighted (in Reinhart Koselleck's sense),[3] and polemical. What was *deutsch* was what was not French. What was "French" was the German nobility. What was French was bad. What was *deutsch* was good. What was bad had no right to rule, and what was good, did.

Culture and Civilization

This distinction of Germans from the French often involved another: that of "culture" from "civilization." The French, and the German nobility, were supposed to have "civilization;" non-noble Germans were said to have "culture." It was Kant who first put this distinction down on paper, in his "Idea for a Universal History with Cosmopolitan Intent" of 1784, where he wrote:

> We are *cultivated* to a high degree by art and science. We are *civilized* to the point of excess in all kinds of social courtesies and proprieties. But we are still a long way from the point where we could consider ourselves *morally* mature. For while the idea of morality is indeed present in culture, an application of this idea which only extends to the semblances of morality, as in love of honor and outward propriety, amounts merely to civilization.[4]

Although Kant's "we" means all Europeans, his description of "civilization" sounds very much like the world of the Francophone courtly nobility, viewed through a non-noble's critical eye: a world of "semblance and outward propriety," of over-refinement, dissimulation, artifice and immorality, both personal and political. *Morality*, on the other hand – the ideological core of bourgeois political self-understanding, as Reinhart Koselleck has shown[5] – is found in the contrasting sphere of *culture*, the non-noble sphere.

---

3 Reinhart Koselleck, "Zur historisch-politischen Semantik historischer Gegenbegriffe," in *Vergangene Zukunft. Zur Semantik geschichtlicher Zeiten* (Frankfurt am Main: Suhrkamp, 1989), 211-59.

4 Immanuel Kant, "Idee zu einer allgemeinen Geschichte in weltbürgerlicher Absicht," in *Sämtliche Werke in sechs Bänden. Vermischte Schriften* (Leipzig: Insel, 1912), 1:234; *Kant's Political Writings*, ed. Hans Reiss (Cambridge: Cambridge University Press, 1970), 49. For a further development of this distinction, see §83 of *The Critique of Judgment*.

5 Reinhart Koselleck, *Kritik und Krise. Eine Studie zur Pathogenese der bürgerlichen Welt* (Frankfurt am Main: Suhrkamp, 1973), especially Chapter 2, 41ff.

To Germanists, the distinction of culture from civilization may be most familiar from Thomas Mann's wartime screed *Reflections of an Unpolitical Man* (1915-18), where it is used to distinguish the Germans, as a *Kulturnation*, from the Entente as an "Imperium der Zivilisation."[6] Kant's distinction, however, was not yet nationalist in any modern sense. Norbert Elias was, I believe, the first to notice that

> [Kant's] contraposition [of culture and civilization] [...] relates only vaguely and at best secondarily to a national contrast. Its primary aspect is an internal contrast within the society, a social contrast which nevertheless bears within itself in a significant way the germ of the national contraposition: the contrast between the courtly nobility, predominantly French-speaking and 'civilized' on the French model, on the one hand, and a German-speaking, middle-class stratum of intelligentsia [...] on the other.[7]

Thirty years after Kant (let's say by 1815), what Elias calls the "germ of the national contraposition" was in full bloom, nurtured by war with, occupation by, and liberation from the French – the *real* French. 1789 is the watershed, the French Revolution, the event that turned Frenchness into something more than a brush to tar German aristocrats with. By the time France could concretely inflict on Europe its habit of draping itself "alternately as the Roman Republic and the Roman Empire" – to quote Marx –,[8] the German *Mittelstand* had developed enough sense of its ego as German to think itself representative of a nation, and to cathect its dislike of civilization westward – as the tone of voice changed from speech "with a cosmopolitan purpose" to speech with a German-

---

6 Thomas Mann, *Betrachtungen eines Unpolitischen* (Fischer: Berlin, 1922), 20; see the entire chapter "Der Zivilisationsliterat." The distinction is first developed in Mann's essay "Gedanken im Kriege," in his *Friedrich und die große Koalition* (Berlin: Fischer, 1915), 7-32. As Roger Chickering notes, Mann's formulation of the distinction was the "richest and most perverse exploration" of a theme widespread in wartime Germany from 1914 on. Roger Chickering, *Imperial Germany and the Great War, 1914-1918*, 2nd ed. (Cambridge: Cambridge University Press, 2004), 132-34.

7 Norbert Elias, *Über den Prozeß der Zivilisation* (Frankfurt am Main: Suhrkamp, 1997), 96; *The History of Manners*, trans. Edmund Jephcott (New York: Pantheon, 1978), 8.

8 Karl Marx, "Der achtzehnte Brumaire des Louis Bonaparte," in *Politische Schriften*, ed. Hans-Joachim Lieber (Stuttgart: Cotta, 1960), 3.1:271; *The 18th Brumaire of Louis Bonaparte* (New York: International Publishers, 1963), 15.

national purpose.[9] After the revolutionary wars began (in 1792), and more strongly still with Napoleon's occupation of Germany (begun 1794, completed 1806, over 1814), the German Romantics had real French to reckon with, and rather less animus toward aristocrats. It is as if the anger against the nobility had been turned against the French; and, with that anger, all the stereotypes reapplied.

Greek and Latin

The idea that the German language was somehow like ancient Greek, and that both German and Greek were superior in their expressiveness to Latin and French, depends on a long European tradition of claims to linguistic antiquity.[10] What was the language spoken in paradise? What was the oldest language or languages, from which (it was assumed) all modern languages stemmed?[11] For centuries, Hebrew had held pride of place as the most ancient language, yet from the fifteenth century on, the Humanist challenge to classical languages in favor of European vernaculars had given rise to all sorts of patriotic claims to historical or metaphysical priority, and in the seventeenth century, as the larger European states began to take form (with France foremost among them), theories of *parallel* strands of development began to replace the monogenetic hypotheses of linguistic origins. The world's languages were divided into families supposed to have stemmed from Noah's sons after the flood, and then the nations fought to assert descent from the thickest parts of the family tree.[12]

---

[9] The cultural distinction of German from French did not first *arise* in the late eighteenth century; strictly speaking, it was *revived* then. Since the discovery of the *Germania* of Tacitus in 1455, German writers had espoused an idea of German culture as an entity distinct from Latin cultures. This distinction had been used polemically from the start, as the German Humanists (Celtis, Bebel and Luther) retooled the *Germania*'s implicit critique of Domitian's Rome into a defense of "Germanic" cultural values against Italian cultural hegemony and (in particular) the Papacy. Only in Alsace, where the French were physically present and politically dominant, did the Humanists (Wimpfeling, Murner) think to contrast themselves with them. See Hans Kohn, *The Idea of Nationalism* (New York: Macmillan, 1961), 138-46.

[10] Arno Borst, *Der Turmbau von Babel. Geschichte der Meinungen über Ursprung und Vielfalt der Sprachen und Völker* (Stuttgart: Hiersemann, 1961). See especially vol. 3.2.

[11] Cf. Borst, *Der Turmbau von Babel;* Maurice Olender, *Les langues du paradis* (Paris: Editions du Seuil, 1989); Umberto Eco, *The Search for the Perfect Language*, trans. James Fentress (Oxford: Blackwell, 1995).

[12] Eco, *The Search for the Perfect Language*, 74ff and 102.

In this context, a theory relevant to our theme arose: the Swede Olof Rudbeck's construction, in 1675, of a "Scytho-Gothic" or "Japhetic" language group, descended from Noah's son Japheth, that for the first time included the Nordic languages among the world's most ancient, on a par with Hebrew and Greek. Above all, it is Rudbeck's idea that gave rise to the German tradition of linking the Greek with the German language (while deprecating the French).[13]

Thus, in 1691, one Caspar Stieler, of Erfurt, supposed that the German language had come "as a capital language" (*als eine Hauptsprache*) out of Sinear with Noah's great-grandson Ashkenaz, and that it was related to the Greek of Japheth's fourth son, Javan; he also asserted that it was much older than Latin and the languages derived from it.[14] Eight years later (in 1699), Hiob Ludolf averred that in oldest antiquity Greek, German and Latin had been related as daughters of the *lingua Japetica* of Noah's son Japheth's descendants. He did not forget to add that the Germans had likely belonged to the "European Sanhedrin of the Japhetites" earlier than the French had.[15] Circa 1703, the philosopher Leibniz expressed his conviction "that at the root of the entire Japhetic stock there lay a Celtic language that was common to both the Gauls and the Germans," and that "we may conjecture that this [common stock] derives from the time of the common origin of these peoples, said to be among the Scythians, who, coming from the Black Sea, crossed the Danube and the Vistula, and of whom one part may have gone to Greece, while the other filled Germany and Gaul."[16] Leibniz did not go out of his way to find the French language wanting – after all, he was writing in it – but he did conclude that although "there was nothing that argues either against or for the idea of a single, common origin of all nations, and, in consequence, of one language that is radical and primitive," still it seemed to him "that Teutonic has best preserved its natural and Adamitic aspect."[17] Johann Augustin Egenolff threw the Celts into the mix by suggesting, in 1716, that Japheth and his descendants had spoken Scythian, "that is, the language afterward called

---

[13] Daniel Droixhe, *La Linguistique et l'appel à l'histoire (1600-1800). Rationalisme et révolutions positivistes* (Geneva: Droz, 1978), 118ff; cf., Olender, *Les langues du paradis*, 14ff; Eco, *The Search for the Perfect Language*, 97ff.

[14] Borst, *Der Turmbau von Babel*, 3.2:1473.

[15] ibid., 3.2:1475.

[16] Gottfried Wilhelm Leibniz, *Nouveaux essais sur entendement humain* (Paris: Flammarion, 1990), 218 (quoted in Eco, *The Search for the Perfect Language*, 101).

[17] Leibniz, *Nouveaux essais*, 218.

Celtic or Gothic."[18] And Johann Georg von Eckhardt insisted, in 1723, that Europe's most ancient peoples were the Irish and Scottish, who were related to the Germanic tribes that had spread throughout Europe; he concluded from this that the Franks, a Germanic tribe, were by no means descended from the Trojans.[19]

Now, the timing of Rudbeck's theory explains *how* the German tradition of linking the Greek with the German language *could arise* when it did – but it does not explain *why* it arose at that point with the force that it did, nor why so many German writers insisted on taking the French down a notch in comparison. For this wave of German linguistic nationalism had a political proximate cause: the ongoing challenge of Louis XIV to Habsburg power in Europe, and, in particular, his claims to the Spanish throne after 1700, which would lead to the War of the Spanish Succession (1701-1714).[20] The Baroque German scholars' assertions of the antiquity of their language indirectly challenged a central legitimating myth of the French monarchy, mentioned explicitly by Eckhardt: the medieval idea, revived by Louis XIII and Louis XIV, that the Franks – supposedly the ancestor tribe of the French – were descended from Trojan settlers, and were hence the inheritors of a right to significant parts of the Roman Empire. The Trojan origins of the French were such an article of faith for Louis XIII and Louis XIV that their historiographers deliberately ignored conclusive sixteenth-century proofs (by both German and French scholars) that the Franks were not Trojans, but Germans.[21] And the War of the Spanish Succession came at the end of a long-standing struggle of the Bourbons and the Habsburgs to control parts of the Roman Empire – to which the Habsburgs, as Holy Roman emperors, had their own genealogical claims. This at least partly explains the French predilection for Virgil evident in the aesthetics of the *grand siècle*, as well as the German scholars' choice, around 1700, to dispute the antiquity of the French language. It also explains why in 1714 the scholar Nicolas Fréret could be thrown into the Bastille for showing that the Franks had been Germans.[22] As Fréret's arrest suggests, Louis XIV had a good deal at stake in myths of origin and genealogy – about as much, in fact, as the German nobility would have by the end of the

---

[18] Borst, *Der Turmbau von Babel*, 3.2:1480.

[19] ibid., 3.2:1480.

[20] ibid., 3.2:1473ff.

[21] George Huppert, "The Trojan Franks and their Critics," *Studies in the Renaissance*, 12 (1965): 227.

[22] Huppert, "The Trojan Franks and their Critics," 228.

eighteenth century. At which point the German *Mittelstand* takes a polemic honed against the mythical roots of the Bourbon family tree – and turns it against the Francophone German nobility.

Homer and Virgil

Beginning with Winckelmann, Germany's love for Homer was central to its Hellenism.[23] Besides Winckelmann's essay of 1755 on the imitation of the Greeks in painting and poetry, the strongest motors behind the German preoccupation with Homer were a series of critical texts by British writers: Thomas Blackwell's *Enquiry into the Life and Writings of Homer* (1735, German translation 1776), Edward Young's *Conjectures on Original Composition* (1759, German translation 1760), and Robert Wood's *Essay on the Original Genius and Writings of Homer* (1769, German translation 1773). Winckelmann's portrait of ancient Greece as a land of physical culture and health, of *paideia* and civic democracy, had been among other things a critique of modern Europe. The negative counterparts of these qualities he attached not only to the French, but to all Europeans – perhaps, in fact, to the Germans above all. His utopian (and cosmopolitan) love for Greece thus afforded the Germans with a positive type to aspire to, but not with a negative type to reject. The English writers listed above were the first to provide the Germans with what I will call a formal definition *a priori* of that countertype – in their distinction between originality and derivativeness.

In keeping with this distinction, the Germans' love for Homer as an "original genius" was matched by emphatic disdain for Virgil as a derivative poet.[24] At the same time, aesthetic faults found in Virgil were also found in the French, and Homer's virtues claimed for the Germans.

Thus, in 1766, we find Gotthold Ephraim Lessing comparing Homer's and Virgil's descriptions of shields in the *Iliad*[25] and the *Aeneid*[26] and finding Virgil's description aesthetically inferior – for reasons that

---

[23] See, e.g., Joachim Wohlleben, *Die Sonne Homers. Zehn Kapitel deutscher Homer-Begeisterung* (Göttingen: Vandenhoeck & Rupprecht, 1990). On German Hellenism, see, e.g., the classic study by E.M. Butler, *The Tyranny of Greece over Germany* (Boston: Beacon Press, 1958); or, more recently, Suzanne L. Marchand, *Down From Olympus: Archaeology and Philhellenism in Germany, 1750-1850* (Princeton: Princeton University Press, 1996).

[24] On the precipitous drop in Virgil's popularity in Germany after about 1750, see Werner Taegert, *Vergil 2000 Jahre. Rezeption in Literatur, Musik und Kunst* (Bamberg: Universitätsbibliothek Bamberg, 1982), 14.

[25] Homer, *Iliad*, Book 18, ll. 558-719.

[26] Virgil, *Aeneid*, Book 8, ll. 848-992.

are implicitly socially coded. Virgil is a *Hofmann*, a courtier more interested in flattering Roman rulers by naming them on a Trojan shield than in making an original, organic work of art. Virgil imitates Homer without understanding the inward logic of Homer's poetic art.[27] Lessing uses the soon-to-be-standard non-noble opposition of inwardness and outwardness, originality and derivativeness, honesty and dissimulation, to characterize Virgil as a superficial, dishonest and aesthetically derivative courtly aristocrat (and Homer, conversely, as not being one).[28] Lessing also declares the inadequacy of French as a target language for translations of Homer,[29] while finding German slightly better.[30]

In a similar vein, in 1795, the young Friedrich Schlegel cites J.G. Voss's recent (1793) translation of the *Iliad* as "brilliant proof of how faithfully and with what success the language of the Greek poets can be reproduced in German"[31] – and then he takes Virgil to task for derivativeness.[32]

---

[27] Gotthold Ephraim Lessing, *Laokoon oder Über die Grenzen der Malerei und Poesie* (Stuttgart: Reclam, 1964), 134ff.

[28] "Der witzige Hofmann leuchtet überall durch, der mit allerley schmeichelhaften Anspielungen seine Materie aufstützet, aber nicht das große Genie, das sich auf die eigene innere Stärke seines Werks verläßt, und alle äußere Mittel, interessant zu werden, verachtet." Lessing, *Laokoon*, 137; cf. Taegert, *Vergil 2000 Jahre*, 41.

[29] Echoing Mme Dacier's preface to her 1711 translation of the *Iliad*. Cf. Kirsti Simonsuuri, *Homer's Original Genius: Eighteenth-Century Notions of the Early Greek Epic (1688-1798)* (Cambridge: Cambridge University Press, 1979), 50.

[30] Lessing, *Laokoon*, 132-33.

[31] "Vossens Übersetzung des Homer ist ein glänzender Beweis, wie treu und glücklich die Sprache der griechischen Dichter im Deutschen nachgebildet werden kann." Friedrich Schlegel, "Über das Studium der griechischen Poesie," in *Studien des klassischen Altertums*, ed. Ernst Behler (Paderborn: Schöningh, 1979), 342-43.

[32] "Ich kann sogar die übermäßige Bewunderung des Vergilius zwar nicht rechtfertigen, aber doch entschuldigen. Für den Freund des Schönen mag sein Wert gering sein: aber für das Studium des Kunstkenners und Künstlers, bleibt es äußerst merkwürdig. Dieser gelehrte Künstler hat aus dem reichen Vorrat der griechischen Dichter mit einer eignen Art von Geschmack die einzelnen Stücke und Züge ausgewählt, sie mit Einsicht aneinander gefügt, und mit Fleiß gefeilt, geglättet und geputzt. Das Ganze ist ein Stückwerk ohne lebendige Organisation und schöne Harmonie, aber er kann dennoch für den höchsten Gipfel des gelehrt künstlichen Zeitalters der alten Poesie gelten." Schlegel, "Über das Studium der griechischen Poesie," 349. I should mention that Schlegel suspects the clearly already commonplace idea of a resemblance of German to Greek rhythmic forms: "Man darf der deutschen Sprache zu der, wenngleich entfernten, Ähnlichkeit ihrer rhythmischen Bildung mit dem griechischen Rhythmus Glück wünschen. Nur täusche man sich nicht über die Grenzen dieser Ähnlichkeit!" ibid., 344. August Wilhelm Schlegel agreed with his brother on Virgil's inferiority to Homer, albeit for different reasons: "[Vergils] Sprache hat Feierlichkeit, Hoheit, Pracht,

Finally, Wilhelm von Humboldt measures the likeness of German to Greek by their mutual dissimilarity from Latin.[33] The French, meanwhile, are cast as inheritors of the Latin language and character, indeed as a nation unable to raise itself above imitation of the Romans.[34] Elsewhere Humboldt admits that the Germans, as Moderns, make poor enough Greeks – but still better Greeks than the French do.[35] In the end, he suggests that the Germans are closer in spirit to the Greeks than even the Romans had been.[36]

"Originality" is clearly the prime criterion for Homer's valorization (and Virgil's devaluation).[37] Thus, the question becomes: Why originality? Why did the Germans make such an effort to claim Homer's "original genius" as something to which they could relate, better than the "derivative" French?

I suspect that the German *Mittelstand* focused on originality because origin was how aristocracy legitimated itself: by appeal to heredity, to origins in the past. The *Mittelstand*'s strategy was to counter *origins* with *originality*: in other words, to challenge legitimation by origins in the past with legitimation by originality conceived as immanent, as potentially present in every present, and thus available, in principle, to individual members of any class.

---

womit er selbst gemeine Dinge zu überkleiden sucht; da hingegen Homers Ausdruck kräftig, aber einfältig, niemals prangend und übertreibend und durchaus nur durch Entfaltung veredelnd ist." August Wilhelm Schlegel, "Goethes Hermann und Dorothea" (1798), in *Über Literatur, Kunst und Geist des Zeitalters*, ed. Franz Finke (Stuttgart: Reclam, 1964), 125.

33 Wilhelm von Humboldt, "Über die Verschiedenheit des menschlichen Sprachbaues und ihren Einfluss auf die geistige Entwicklung des Menschengeschlechts" (1830-35), in *Werke in fünf Bänden*, ed. Andreas Flitner and Klaus Giel (Darmstadt: Wissenschaftliche Buchgesellschaft, 1963), 3:574-75

34 Wilhelm von Humboldt, "Latium und Hellas," in *Werke in fünf Bänden*, 2:55.

35 Humboldt, "Latium und Hellas," 2:55: "[B]eide leisten auch am Ende etwas von der Griechischen fast gleich entfernt Liegendes, nur gelangen die Deutschen zu etwas, das dem Sinne des Griechen näher, vielleicht sogar höher, als das von ihm Erreichte, aber eben darum eigentlich unerreichbar ist, da die Franzosen durchaus auf Abwege gerathen und unter dem Erzielten und dem wirklich Erstrebten bleiben."

36 "Für die Römer wurden [die Griechen] nicht ebenso zu etwas Ähnlichem, als sie uns sind." Humboldt, "Über die Verschiedenheit des menschlichen Sprachbaues," 3:407. The Germans are not mentioned here by name, but "uns" seems more likely, in this context, to mean "Germans" than "Moderns."

37 Though there were other criteria, such as Herder's disgust at the bloody power politics of Imperial Rome, of which he thought Virgil a typical apologist. See Taegert, *Vergil 2000 Jahre*, 14.

As a result, Humboldt's argument does not depend on Rudbeck's Scytho-Japhetic hypothesis, or on Biblical genealogy; the same is true of Schlegel's and Lessing's thoughts on translation.[38] By the end of the eighteenth century, the German affinity for the Greeks has become, so to speak, elective.

This shift from legitimation by descent (a principle of the nobility's self-understanding), to legitimation by inner affinity (to which the *Mittelstand* could more easily lay claim) is reflected in the new model of imitation developed by German classicism.

A certain conception of originality already inspires the model of imitation promoted by Winckelmann's paradoxical credo of German Hellenism (1755): "The only way for us to become great, indeed – if it is possible – inimitable, is by imitating the Ancients."[39] As Moderns, we must seek our originality the way the Ancients sought theirs. We are not to *copy* them; and our originality in turn is not to be copied. We are to comprehend and reiterate the *process* by which the Ancients so perfectly realized their particular entelechy, not mimic by rote Ancient expressions of that perfection (as, for example, the *Sturm und Drang* would accuse the French of doing).[40] Our entelechy, as Moderns, must necessarily be different.[41]

---

[38] The same holds for the poet Klopstock. Arno Borst notes that in 1794 Klopstock declared ancient Greek the sister of German without mentioning "die biblische Begründung der barocken Gleichung, daß nämlich Japhet der gemeinsame Vater der Skythen, Griechen und Deutschen sei. Es ging ihm nicht um die Genealogie des Volkes, überhaupt nicht um die Geschichte, sondern um die Heiligkeit seiner Sprache, deren Schöpfungskraft ungeschmälert die Zeiten überdauert." Borst, *Der Turmbau von Babel*, 3.1:1529.

[39] "Der einzige Weg für uns, groß, ja, wenn es möglich ist, unnachahmlich zu werden, ist die Nachahmung der Alten […]." Johann Joachim Winckelmann, *Gedanken über die Nachahmung der griechischen Werke in der Malerei und Bildhauerkunst*, ed. Ludwig Uhlig (Stuttgart: Reclam, 1969), 4.

[40] Cf., e.g., Johann Wolfgang von Goethe, "Von deutscher Baukunst" (1772), *Sämtliche Werke. Jubiläumsausgabe in 40 Bänden*, ed. Eduard von den Hellen (Stuttgart: J.G. Cotta, 1902-1907), 33:5.

[41] Cf. Peter Szondi, "Antike und Moderne in der Ästhetik der Goethezeit," in *Poetik und Geschichtsphilosophie I*, ed. Senta Menz and Hans-Hagen Hildebrandt (Frankfurt am Main: Suhrkamp, 1974), 11-265, especially 21-46 (Winckelmann), 82-98 (Karl Philipp Moritz), 99-148 (Friedrich Schlegel); Hans Robert Jauß, "Ästhetische Normen und geschichtliche Reflexion in der Querelle des Anciens et de Modernes," in Charles Perrault, *Parallèle des anciens et des modernes en ce qui regarde les arts et les sciences* (Munich: Eidos, 1964), 9; Wolf Lepenies, *Das Ende der Naturgeschichte. Wandel kultureller Selbstverständlichkeiten in den Wissenschaften des 18. und 19. Jahrhunderts* (Munich: Hanser, 1976), 106.

Such a model of imitation is connected with Homer not only by Winckelmann, but also by Robert Wood. In his *Essay on the Original Genius and Writings of Homer* (1769), Wood attributes Homer's aesthetic originality (his ability to make a work of art unlike any before it) to the directness of his relation to his subject matter, which Wood calls Nature. To quote Wood: "[H]owever questionable Homer's superiority may be, in some respects, as a perfect model for composition, in the great province of Imitation he is the most original of all Poets, and the most constant and faithful copier after Nature."[42] And Virgil? Wood calls the *Aeneid* "a Roman copy from the Greek original"[43] and a manifestly inferior poem.[44] Homer *imitates Nature*; Virgil *copies Homer*. In the German context, this would become: German writers, like Homer, imitate Nature, and are original (good); French writers copy Virgil, as Virgil did Homer, and are derivative and unnatural (bad).

Although Wood applies two verbs – *copy* and *imitate* – to Homer, still, in Wood's text, the verb *copy* tends overall to adhere to Virgil, and with negative valence. This distinction of two modes of imitation gains full theoretical clarity in Karl Philipp Moritz's essay of 1787 *Über die bildende Nachahmung des Schönen* (a work that reflects conversations with Goethe in Italy) as a distinction between imitation (*Nachahmung*, good) and aping (*Nachäffung*, bad).[45] Moritz does not mention Homer or Virgil, Germans or French. Yet here again, it is Nature that is being imitated, other artists that are being aped. Imitation is, again, a procedural, not a mimetic norm. *Nachäffung* (aping – bad) involves copying the external aspect of objects without understanding the principles of their production; while *Nachahmung* (imitation – good) demands comprehension and replication of the inner principle of the artwork's becoming.[46] What we as Moderns must imitate from the Greeks is thus the way in which they imitated Nature – not their imitations of Nature. Or, to quote Goethe: "Everyone should be Greek in his own way! But he should be Greek!"[47]

---

[42] Robert Wood, *An Essay on the Original Genius and Writings of Homer* (1775), facsimile edition (New York: Garland, 1971), 4-5.

[43] Wood, *An Essay on the Original Genius and Writings of Homer*, 137.

[44] ibid., 139.

[45] Karl Philipp Moritz, "Über die bildende Nachahmung des Schönen," in *Beiträge zur Ästhetik*, ed. Hans Joachim Schrimpf and Hans Adler (Mainz: Dieterich, 1989), 27ff.

[46] Moritz, "Über die bildende Nachahmung des Schönen," 29.

[47] "Jeder sei auf seine Art ein Grieche, aber er seis!" Johann Wolfgang von Goethe, "Antik und Modern" (1818), in *Werke*, ed. Friedmar Apel, Hendrik Birus et al. (Frankfurt am Main: Insel, 1998), 314.

It is clear that unlike their Baroque predecessors, the non-noble Germans of the late eighteenth century were not out to attack the pretensions of Louis XIV by confuting, in Virgil, the myth of the Trojan Franks. Instead, they attacked the pretensions of German nobles by discrediting, in aesthetic objections to Virgil, the type of legitimacy conferred by descent within a tradition. In other words, they devalued descent as derivativeness, and revalued lack of descent as originality or genius, hence as a possible source of new laws – explicitly in their aesthetics, and thus implicitly in the political sphere.[48]

Blutadel and *Adel des Geistes*

This shift from descent to affinity mirrors a radical transformation in the concept of nobility, one first advanced by the *Mittelstand* and later accepted, to their own detriment, by the aristocrats. Thanks in great part to the natural right philosophies of the Enlightenment, "nobility" changes, between 1755 and about 1792, from a quality conferred by birth to a quality of character, and hence implicitly to one in which every class can share.[49] Or to use German shorthand: the concept of *Blutadel* (blood nobility) is challenged by that of *Adel des Geistes* (aristocracy of the spirit).

The text most responsible for the change is doubtless Rousseau's *Discourse on the Origins of Inequality* of 1755, which incarnated natural man

---

[48] The strategy is reflected in a functional shift, circa 1770, in the word field *Ursprung* (origin). Both the adjective *ursprünglich* (original) and the noun *Ursprünglichkeit* (originality) are late eighteenth-century derivates of the much older noun *Ursprung* (origin). Articles "Ur-," "Ursprung," "Ursprünglich" in Jacob and Wilhelm Grimm, *Deutsches Wörterbuch* (Leipzig: Hirzel, 1857-1971), 24:2538-53. The Grimms explain in their dictionary why the new compounds occurred, along with a number of other composita using the prefix *ur-*: "the ever more frequent use of the prefix in the last third of the 18th century is *related to the revolution of intellectual life* that seeks to reach beyond the trivial practical knowledge of Enlightenment learning to the original sources of life" ("der im letzten Drittel des 18. jh. immer häufiger werdende Gebrauch des Präfixes hängt mit dem Umschwung des geistigen Lebens zusammen, das über die Platte Erfahrung der Aufklärungsbildung hinaus zu den ursprünglichen Quellen des Lebens zu gelangen sucht;" my emphasis). Grimm, *Deutsches Wörterbuch* 24:2358. These "original sources of life" are not sites in the past to be revisited, or copied verbatim in the present. They are potential futures to be sought both in the past and in the present as a future past, motors of progress to which history holds the key. The Grimms' comment reflects a fundamental change in European conceptions of history, datable – in Germany – to the last third of the eighteenth century, and linked ideologically to the rise of the non-noble elites.

[49] Cf. Peter J. Schwartz, "Eduard's Egotism: Historical Notes on Goethe's *Elective Affinities*," *The Germanic Review*, 76.1 (Winter 2001): 44ff.

in the unforgettable type of the noble savage; the man most responsible for turning this type to account in the German context is Johann Gottfried Herder. From 1750 on, Rousseau had critiqued "civilization," using that word; only Rousseau did not have Herder's counterterm "culture." He used instead the idea of the "noble savage" – which may have had its prototype in the *Germania* of Tacitus. Herder transforms the Enlightenment type into its pre-Romantic variant by conflating culture and noble savagery – a conflation facilitated, no doubt, by the case of the ancient Greeks. In effect, he endows "culture" (and, by association, the *Mittelstand*) with the spiritual nobility of the "noble savage," while turning the critical edge of that type against nobility by inheritance, blood nobility.

The "noble savage" type has been well defined as "any free and wild being who draws directly from nature virtues which raise doubts as to the value of civilization."[50] It is easy to see here a debt to the polemical strategy of Tacitus's *Germania*, which cloaked its critique of the Roman Empire as an ethnology of the Germanic tribes on its borders.[51]

It is in the *Germania* of Tacitus, in fact, that we find the original prototype of the "noble savage" – and the single most useful key to our topos. Each eighteenth-century instance of the "noble savage" type bears several or all of the virtues that Tacitus applied to the ancient *Germanii* – honesty, loyalty, chastity, and so on, a love for political freedom, a predilection for song, and a disinclination to legalism; while the "civilized" countertypes may be found drowning in the vices of Imperial Rome: decadence, affectation, over-refinement, dissimulation, legalism – and tyranny directed within and without.

Herder combined several eighteenth-century types of the "noble savage" to form his conception of German culture, as distinct from the French. From Winckelmann (who had compared Homer's heroes with the American Indians),[52] he took the Greeks; from Jean de Léry and Pierre de Charlevoix, the natives of the Americas;[53] from the Scot James

---

[50] Hoxie Neale Fairchild, *The Noble Savage: A Study in Romantic Naturalism* (New York: Columbia University Press, 1928), 2.

[51] Cf. Manfred Fuhrmann, "Nachwort. Leben und Werk des Tacitus," in Tacitus, *Germania* (Stuttgart: Reclam, 1972), 102ff.

[52] Winckelmann, *Gedanken über die Nachahmung der griechischen Werke*, 6.

[53] Johann Gottfried Herder, *Abhandlung über den Ursprung der Sprache,* ed. Hans Dietrich Irmscher (Stuttgart: Reclam, 1966), 15.

Macpherson, Ossian's ancient Caledonians;[54] and from the *Germania* of Tacitus, the ancient *Germanii*.[55] These were all "noble savages" with implicit "civilized" countertypes. Winckelmann's Greeks were in part a utopian benchmark for Saxony, whose courtly provincialism disgusted him; the French *philosophes* had often used the North American natives to criticize modern Europe; Macpherson had attacked modern Britain in the guise of virtuous Caledonians fighting Caracalla's Rome; and, before them all, Tacitus had pilloried the moral and political depravity of Domitian's Rome by casting the tribes on the Empire's periphery as natural, honest, lovers of freedom, loyal and chaste. Herder rides the Germans 'piggyback' in each case: the Germanii, the Caledonians, the Greeks and the Indians. Thus, when he asserts: "It is partly because of the Nordic songs that the fate of Europe changed [...], and that we now live where we do;" and that "[w]e have her heroes and bards to thank for the fact that Rome could not win over Germany," he is claiming implicitly as German (and anti-French, that is to say, non-noble) the virtues ascribed by Tacitus to the *Germanii*, by Ossian ascribed to the Scots, by travelers in America to America's native peoples,[56] and by Winckelmann to Homer's Greeks.[57]

Indeed, it was not until Herder welded American Indians, Homer's Greeks, the modern and ancient Scots, the ancient *Germanii*, and modern Germans into one metaphoric chain that our topos really congealed.[58]

---

[54] Cf. Johann Gottfried Herder, "Auszug aus einem Briefwechsel über Ossian und die Lieder alter Völker, 1773," in *Sämtliche Werke*, ed. Bernhard Suphan (Berlin: Weidmann, 1877-1913), 5:162-71; "Ossian und Homer" (1795).

[55] In 1774, he explicitly leans on Tacitus to describe Rome, at its end, as "erschöpft, entnervt, zerrüttet: von Menschen verlaßen, von entnervten Menschen bewohnt, in Üppigkeit, Lastern, Unordnungen, Freiheit und wildem Kriegesstolz untersinkend," as "ein abgematteter, im Blute liegender Leichnam," whereupon he adds: "da ward im Norden neuer Mensch bebohren." Johann Gottfried Herder, "Auch eine Philosophie der Geschichte zur Bildung der Menschheit," in *Sämtliche Werke*, 5:514-15. See also J.G. Herder, "Über die Wirkung der Dichtkunst auf die Sitten den Völker in alten und neuen Zeiten," in *Sämtliche Werke*, 8:399-400.

[56] Cf. Herder, *Abhandlung über den Ursprung der Sprache*, 9ff.

[57] Herder's reference to Germanic bards clearly echoes *Germania* 2, 3: "Celebrant carminis antiquis, quod unum apud illos memoriae et annalium genus est [...]" See Arnaldo Momigliano, "Perizonius, Niebuhr and the Character of Early Roman Tradition," *Essays in Ancient and Modern Historiography* (Middletown, Connecticut: Wesleyan University Press, 1977), 231-51, especially 232.

[58] Herder was not the first to construe such an analogical chain of noble savage types — the Frenchman Joseph François Lafitau first did so in 1724 — but Herder was the first to compare the Germans with all of them. Cf. Hans Robert Jauss, "Mythen des

The German *Mittelstand* may already have seen its counterterm in the French, the French as linguistic descendants of the Romans, and its own potential in Homer's Greeks, but it had not yet explored the Greeks' difference from the Romans – though it is clear that this contrast was waiting to be made. Herder's chain of associations assured that the contrast *would* be made, and that it would be made in the service of German national self-definition. *Once* the contrast was made, the equation "Germans are to Greeks as French are to Romans" was complete, and ready to work as a vehicle for non-noble self-aggrandizement.

From Class Conflict to Nationalism

I would like to complete my argument on the shift from class conflict to nationalism by showing how Herder's statement (quoted above), "We have her heroes and bards to thank for the fact that Rome could not win over Germany,"[59] metamorphosed, after Prussia's defeat by Napoleon at Jena in 1806, from a socially indexed program of cultural liberation from French aesthetics to one of national liberty from French occupation.

I will cite three compositions of the years after Jena: Wilhelm von Humboldt's "History of the Decline and Fall of the Greek Free States"[60] of 1807-08, Barthold Georg Niebuhr's *Roman History* (Volume One) of 1811, and the fourth of J.G. Fichte's *Addresses to the German Nation* (also 1807-08), entitled "Principal Difference Between the Germans and the Other Peoples of Germanic Extraction."

Fichte and Humboldt invest future national hopes in two qualities that they consider typically German, yet archetypically Greek: in an inclination to federalism born of political fragmentation, and in a mutual stress on *paideia*.

Humboldt openly admits to looking for lessons from the Greek past concerning the German present for Germany shows "in language, versatility of endeavor, simplicity of taste, in its federalist constitution, and its most recent destinies an undeniable similarity to Greece."[61] Thus, he compares the loose German federalism just destroyed by Napoleon

---

Anfangs. Eine geheime Sehnsucht der Aufklärung," in *Studien zum Epochenwandel der ästhetischen Moderne* (Frankfurt am Main: Suhrkamp, 1989), 34ff.

[59] Herder, "Über die Wirkung der Dichtkunst," 8:400.

[60] Wilhelm von Humboldt, "Geschichte des Verfalls und Unterganges der griechischen Freistaaten," in *Werke in fünf Bänden*, 2:88-89.

[61] Humboldt, "Geschichte des Verfalls und Unterganges der griechischen Freistaaten," 2:88-89.

with the federalism of the Athenian League, and prefers it to Romanic centralization.[62] Similar concerns move the Roman historian Barthold Georg Niebuhr to research Roman Republican agrarian law in 1803 and 1804, and to open the new University of Berlin with a lecture series on Roman Republican history (in 1810 and 1811). Niebuhr's initial polemical aim had been to disprove the claims of the French revolutionaries, among them "Gracchus" Babeuf, to Roman Republican precedent for the redistribution of noble and ecclesiastical land. By the date of its publication in 1811, his *Roman History* is, among other things, an attempt to clarify the relations of the Roman Republican social orders (patricians and *plebs*), to show by Roman example "that separately existing social ranks are necessary to the continuance of a republic, or of a mixed constitution," and thus to prove illegitimate the Revolution's imitation of Rome – of the Republic until 1804, and then of the Empire.[63]

The stated purpose of Fichte's fourth address, as of the cycle to which it belongs, is to show "what the German in and of himself [*an und für sich*], independently of the fate that has recently befallen him, is in his basic character [*Grundzug*] and has been from time immemorial, since he has been" and to demonstrate "that there lies exclusively in this basic character, before all other European nations, the capacity for and receptiveness to" the development (*Bildung*) of a new race of men *(eines neuen Menschengeschlechts)*.[64] Fichte's aim, at this moment of crisis, is to discover the German nation's entelechy, and thus its potential future, in its past. He means to establish this "character" differentially, by distinguishing modern Germans from other nations of Germanic extraction. No surprise that the French show up fairly quickly. They are not named (not a good idea, under French censorship), but Fichte's

---

[62] ibid., 2:79ff. Humboldt's later assessment of the cultural and political advantages to the Greeks of their several dialects would also seem to imply an analogy to the Germans ("Über die Verschiedenheit des menschlichen Sprachbaues," 3:573ff). For a similar sentiment by an anonymous author of 1819, see Peter J. Schwartz, "An Unpublished Essay by Goethe? 'Staatssachen. Über mündliche deutsche Rechtspflege in Deutschland,'" *The Germanic Review*, 73.2 (Spring 1998): 110.

[63] See Alfred Heuss, *Barthold Georg Niebuhrs wissenschaftliche Anfänge. Untersuchungen und Mitteilungen über die Kopenhagener Manuskripte und zur europäischen Tradition der lex agraria (loi agraire)* (Göttingen: Vandenhoeck & Ruprecht, 1981), 153-188 (on Babeuf, see ibid., 180ff). See also Seppo Rytkönen, *Barthold Georg Niebuhr als Politiker und Historiker. Zeitgeschehen und Zeitgeist in den geschichtlichen Beurteilungen von B.G. Niebuhr* (Helsinki: Suomalainen Tiedeakatemia, 1968), 221ff.

[64] Johann Gottlieb Fichte, *Reden an die deutsche Nation* (Leipzig: Meiner, 1916), 58.

argument points to them. "The [most immediate] difference between the Germans and the other tribes produced from the same root," he writes,

> is that the [Germans] remained in the place where their primitive ancestors originally lived, while the [others] emigrated to other locations, the [Germans] retained and continued to develop the original language of [their ancestors], while the [others] took on a foreign language and gradually transformed it in their own fashion. It is from this earliest difference that the later [differences] must have arisen, e.g., that in the original fatherland, according to Germanic original custom, a confederation of states remained under a chief with limited powers, while in the foreign lands the constitution turned into monarchies, after the prevailing Roman fashion.[65]

The only people this description entirely fits is the French. Settled by the Franks, speaking a Romance language, and until recently (or possibly still) a monarchy, France is implicitly the antithesis of German cultural originality and Tacitean love of political freedom – of the German "basic character."[66] And here again we have German federalism set over against Roman centralization.

Humboldt, like Fichte, hopes for national regeneration through humanistic education.[67] What does this have to do with the Greeks? "The Germans possess the indisputable merit of having been the first to comprehend faithfully, and feel deeply, the Greek *Bildung* [...]. Thus a much stronger bond connects the Germans with the Greeks than with any other nation or era, however much closer it may be."[68] Not that the Germans could ever be like the Greeks; but the Greeks' example could

---

[65] Fichte, *Reden an die deutsche Nation*, 60.

[66] Cf. Borst, *Der Turmbau von Babel*, 3.1:1552.

[67] Humboldt would found the University of Berlin two years later, Fichte would be its rector, and Niebuhr's lectures on Roman history would be the first given there. On Humboldt's and Fichte's role in Prussian educational reform after Jena, see, e.g., Hans-Joachim Schoeps, *Preußen. Geschichte eines Staates* (Frankfurt am Main: Ullstein, 1966), 130-31; for more detail, see Wilhelm Weischedel, *Idee und Wirklichkeit einer Universität. Dokumente zur Geschichte der Friedrich-Wilhelms-Universität zu Berlin* (Berlin: De Gruyter, 1960).

[68] Humboldt, "Geschichte des Verfalls und Unterganges der griechischen Freistaaten," 87.

move the Germans – more than it could other nations – to realize themselves, as the Greeks had once done.[69]

This is where German Hellenism fades into German political messianism. For Fichte, the Germans, above all the nations, hold a new promise for the future of humanity; for Humboldt, they do so by virtue of their cultural affinity with the Greeks. Thanks to their originality, the Greeks had become an origin of Western culture; the Germans could be the new Greeks of a changing Europe. The French and their revolution must thus be discounted, again, as unoriginal. Fichte's distinction of the Germans from other nations of Germanic extraction does as much by recalling the earlier challenge to the myth of the Trojan Franks: the French are Germans, not Trojans, and hence not original settlers; they are Germans, but Romanized ones, and thus not linguistically original.[70] Only a people whose mother tongue stems from its *original* experience of the world (the Germans) can make a viable future out of its past. Here we have the old thrust at French courtly culture transmuted into the kind of Romantic-organic critique of French revolutionary rationalism that would flourish in Germany after 1814 – and emerge as a full-fledged reaction by 1819.

---

[69] Humboldt quoted in Wohlleben, *Die Sonne Homers*, 67.
[70] Cf. Fichte, *Reden an die deutsche Nation*, 61ff, especially 64.

THE MYTH OF THE GAULS IN SIXTEENTH-CENTURY FRENCH HISTORIOGRAPHY: SECRET KNOWLEDGE AND CIRCULAR CONCEPTS

Kirsten Mahlke

In the time of political changes at the end of the Valois era in the 1580s, politics became less self-evident and more attentive to all sorts of new theories and utopias, and King Henry III thus assembled a circle of experts to counsel him in political issues. He was a culturally refined man who loved poetry, dance and masquerades and was obviously interested in a fundamental change of perspective regarding the French monarchy. The cultural values were supposed to define the French monarchy in political and historical terms as an independent, autonomous whole, not a bad copy of Italian and Classical art. The arts were expected to make France the crown of Europe, even the crown of the world. This was the beginning of the glorious times of a newly fashioned original myth: the myth of the Gauls. The aim of my essay is to show how French historiography adopted this myth together with certain views of secret circles, and how secrecy itself became the motor of the culturally renewed nation.

The question as to whether and how an idea or a story suddenly prevails or even eradicates other, older ones, is difficult to resolve. In sixteenth-century France, this was the case with the story of the Gallican ancestry of the French people and the King. It entered national historiography, poetry, and even fashion and customs at the court: between the 1570s and the 1580s, it became fashionable to wear costumes *à la Gauloise* – simple dresses made of undyed cloths instead of purple silk.

I would like to show how important the myth of the Gauls became as a means of national unification, cultural glory and international supremacy, which was – by the end of the sixteenth century – merely imaginary. My article deals with the writings of two major intellectual 'inventors' of the myth who combined the barbarous past of the Gauls with Kabbalistic and neo-Platonic philosophy and thus made a politically influential original myth apt to meet the secular and theological needs of the time. The names of Guillaume Postel,[1] born in 1510, and his disciple Guy Lefèvre de la Boderie,[2] born in 1541, are known for their adherence to occultist circles, their sometimes heterodox views, their language skills, and – most of all – their search for universal harmony under French Christian rule. In the following, I shall present some of the most interesting tendencies in their contribution to what they understood as the healing process of three wounded bodies: France, whose unity was destroyed; religion, which was in constant war due to misunderstandings of the word of God; and the whole world's disharmonic state.

Postel and Lefèvre both aimed for a peaceful unification of all three monotheistic religions under French rule. The elder had been exiled and excommunicated by the time he reached later life, while the younger went on to become one of the most influential counselors of the French King.

Until the end of the twentieth century, Guy Lefèvre de la Boderie was largely neglected. No one seemed interested either in his stylistic refinement or in his various translations, for instance, of the Syrian

---

[1] Two out of three books by Postel discussed in this paper had remained unpublished until the twentieth century, when they were edited by François Secret, a sixteenth-century scholar whose publications are vital for further research. Guillaume Postel, *Le Thresor des propheties de l'univers. Manuscrit publié avec une introduction et des notes par François Secret* (La Haye: Martinus Nijhoff, 1969) and Postel, *De ce qui est premier pour reformer le monde,* édition critique d'après le manuscrit autographe conservé à la Bibliothèque Nationale, avec introduction et notes, in Claude-Gilbert Dubois, *Celtes et Gaulois au XVIᵉ siècle. Le développement d'un mythe nationaliste* (Paris: Vrin, 1972). The volume published during Postel's lifetime was *Le Prime Nove del altro mondo* (Venice, 1555). For a complete bibliography, see François Secret, *Les Kabbalistes Chrétiens de la Renaissance* (Paris: Dunod, 1964).

[2] Major scholarly research on Lefèvre was done in the 1990s by François Roudaut, *Le Point centrique. Contribution à l'étude de Guy Lefèvre de la Boderie (1541-1598)* (Paris: Klincksieck, 1992). It resulted in a critical edition of Lefèvre's major work: Guy Lefèvre de la Boderie, *La Galliade. De la Révolution des Arts et des Sciences* (1582), ed. François Roudaut (Paris: Klincksieck, 1994).

Bible.[3] In one of the few books referring to him – a nineteenth-century historical dictionary – his poetry is mentioned as a bad example: "florid style, incomprehensible phrases, forced comparisons, low expressions, childish allusions, ridiculous puns, and cold pleasantries."[4] Even in the twentieth century, hardly anyone was familiar with his work except for a few specialists, whose books are now mostly unavailable. One precious and very detailed study[5] of Lefèvre's Hebrew and Kabbalistic sources has never found its way to a publishing house. It exists as a single copy in the archives of the Hebrew University Library.

Despite all this, the mere fact that Lefèvre's books were owned by the French King and that Lefèvre became personal counselor to the Duc d'Alençon in 1568, during a period when politicians would have been interested in anything but poetry, seems worthy of closer examination. My question regarding the works of Lefèvre is: Why would the King be interested in it? And the question that follows: Is Lefèvre's work an example of poetry used as an instrument of political change? My further intention is to show how significantly the groups around Postel and Lefèvre contributed to the making of the foundation myth of the French nation.

To clarify my points, I will begin with some historical data: sixteenth-century France is geographically, politically and religiously highly tumultuous. The reign of the French kings is still jeopardized in the southeast and the southwest of today's territory. The neighboring countries in the north and south are governed by the Spanish enemy. Five kings in a row die of unnatural causes. And the civil or religious wars have weakened the monarchy morally and economically.

In the area of culture, which flourished surprisingly throughout the thirty-eight years of civil war, the highly debated question remained as to whether vulgar French was able to become a poetic language like Greek

---

[3] Except for the libraries of King Henry III, Auguste du Thou and Marguerite de Valois, his books could hardly be found on the shelves of his contemporaries. Cf. Roudaut, *Le point centrique*, 15.

[4] "[...] style empoulé, phrases inintelligibles, comparaisons forcées, expressions basses, allusions puériles, jeux de mots ridicules, plaisanteries froides." L.M. Chaudon et F.A. Delandine, *Nouveau dictionnaire historique ou histoire abrégée de tous les hommes qui se sont fait un nom par des talents, des vertus, des forfaits, des erreurs etc., depuis le commencement du monde jusqu'à nos jours* [...] (Lyon: Bryset, An XII, 1804), 95-96.

[5] Gabriel Sivan, *Guy Le Fèvre de la Boderie and his Epic 'History of Gaul:' The Biblical, Rabbinic and Kabbalistic Foundations of a French Renaissance Legend*, an unpublished PhD dissertation, Jerusalem, Hebrew University, 1974. I am thankful to the Hebrew University Library for lending me this unique work.

and Latin, or the highly elaborated Italian tongue of Petrarch and Dante. As always with definitions of language, this question was a political one: it was important to show the Italian neighbors that the French language and style were no bad copies of the purer and more subtle Italian or Latin ones and that poetic and political influence did not emanate from Rome alone. The argument for a newly refined poetic language was won in the famous debate between Du Bellay and the conservative defenders of exclusive Greek and Roman style in the middle of the sixteenth century.

At the same time and linked to the inferiority complex as far as culture was concerned, there was the effort of the French moderate Catholics (not the Ligue), who became famous as the Gallicans emancipating themselves from Rome in terms of direct papal influence. Therefore, there were quite fundamental problems to resolve in the second half of the sixteenth century at various interconnected levels:

1. The strife for political unity: the King seeks to centralize his dominion;
2. The strife for religious unity: to put an end to the post-reformation struggle between Huguenots and Protestants;
3. The strife for cultural autonomy and independence from Italy.

Lefèvre was neither the first nor the last to contribute to a narrative of the beginning of the cultural glory of France. The history of the Gauls as the ancestors of the French is as old as Greek philosophy. But given Cesar's embarrassing contribution (*De bello gallico*) to their fame as barbarous, ferocious, and treacherous people, it was clear that a redefinition and new foundation of the whole story was necessary.

The myth of the Gauls had, by that time, become one of the two major myths of origin in France, the other being the myth of the Franks and their famous ancestor in Troy, King *Francus*, who had made the long way from Asia Minor to France.[6] This myth was normally used when political claims of the aristocracy were to be vindicated or when noble heritage had to be proven. The myth of the Gauls was predominantly one of the rural population, the peasants, and, if necessary, the valiant soldiers against Romans or those of Roman-Italian ancestry. The co-existence of the two myths mirrored and affirmed social differences of power and subjection, while the subjects were depicted as victorious and strong enough to fight the numerous Roman foes. It may have been this ironic and less serious view of the Gauls that made their tradition so

---

[6] For a comparative approach, see R.E. Asher, *National Myths in Renaissance France: Francus, Samothes and the Druids* (Edinburgh: Edinburgh University Press, 1993).

long-lasting and influential, as can be seen from the world-famous
Asterix stories. Returning to the initial question concerning the King's library: How
did Lefèvre handle the problem of French ancestry? How could the
Gauls become poets after centuries of barbarism? The slowly emerging
solution to the political/religious unification problem turns out to be the
abolition of the twofold ancestry, that is, one for the royals and nobles,
another for the population – in favor of a myth combining the exigencies
of governance with the politico-religious unification of all classes of the
population. The king became one with his people through common
ancestors, and this was a real revolutionary feature of the myth of the
Gauls rewritten in the 1560s. After Lemaire de Belges'[7] first steps
towards a French genealogy starting with Noah's grandson and Etienne
Pasquier's reformulation of this thesis in his great book on French
history *Recherche de la France* (1560),[8] it was Lefèvre's teacher Guillaume
Postel, a mathematician, orientalist and universal philosopher who based
the Gauls' myth on a particularly elaborate and mystical interpretation of
the French people. Postel's relevance for French sixteenth-century
attitudes and actions must not be underestimated, even if many of his
works remained in manuscript. There was at least one important secret
circle connected to the Antwerp publisher Plantin[9] consisting of exiled
Jews, heretics, and Guy Lefèvre de la Boderie and his brothers which
distributed copies of Postel's books throughout Europe. Inspired by his
Pythagorean search for harmony through geometry and his idiomatic
capacity – Postel mastered twelve languages, mostly oriental, and
developed a symmetrical system with a circle combining various
philosophical elements like Platonism and Kabbala on a temporal circuit:
the French King, as a sacred institution, is arranged on the same circuit
as Adam, Moses and David. Postel explained this genealogy by means of
the idea of figuration, based on metempsychosis, which allows ideas to
pass through the ages. The transformation is understood to be necessary
to keep these ideas alive.

Apart from the concept of figuration, Postel was also fascinated by
the archeological capacity of language. He believed that truth could be

---

7 Jean Lemaire des Belges was the first to write the 'Gaulish' history of France, filling the
historical gap between the Trojan War and the Great Flood. See Lemaire des Belges,
Les Illustrations de Gaulle et singularitez de Troye (Paris, 1533).

8 Etienne Pasquier, *Recherches de la France* (Paris: Jean Longis et Robert Magnier, 1560).

9 Cf. Jean-François, Maillard, "Christoph Plantin et la Famille de la Charité en France:
documents et hypothèses," in *Mélanges à la mémoire de Verdun-Louis Saulnier* (Geneva:
Société Française des Seiziémistes, 1984), 235-49.

found in the letters of words. In this respect, he adhered to the strict and exclusive scriptural theory of the Kabbalists. Every single letter bears the divine truth. As God is eager to protect the truth from the pagans and the heterodox, the Scripture is a system of hidden truth. This is concealed so well that only wise men can get close to it, and even they can grasp only the lowest level of the ten divine emanations or *sephiroth*. Postel believed that the French language bears the divine truth and he developed a method called "emithology,"[10] derived from the Hebrew word אמת for "truth" in order to reveal this truth. Secrecy as a divine tool is mentioned in the epitaph of Lefèvre's own work, a poem in hexameters called *La Galliade*, a hermetic piece of literature reflecting all the neo-Platonic, Pythagorean and Kabbalistic structures of the secret circle. It is, like an underlying latent structure, the ineffable, with every other element arranged around it like metal pieces on a magnetic plate. The epigraph is written in Hebrew, the divine and original language. It says: "It is the glory of God to conceal the Word / It is the glory of the Kings to search the Word."[11] Celestial and secular dominions enter a complementary relationship, where one side strives to hide and the other to reveal.

Lefèvre wrote his *Galliade* in 1578. It is a national poem telling the story of the Gauls from Biblical times to the present. He pointed out that he did not want to imitate the famous, but fictitious *Iliad* or *Aeneid*, which he despised for their lies.[12] His effort to unveil the Greek tradition as treachery can be seen on the margins where he diligently replaced the Greek etymologies of proper names by Hebrew ones. Over two thousand years of Greek and Roman history had to be penetrated in order to reveal the truth. Every word was believed to be a cover for another, the 'real one.' Historiography in this sense became a deeply suspicious project that did not believe in stories, phrases or words, but in letters alone. Kabbalistic devices like the Notaricon, Gematria and

---

[10] It was François Secret who coined the term "emithology" for this method. See "L'Émithologie de Guillaume Postel," in Enrico Castelli (ed.), *Umanesimo e Esoterismo* (Padua: Cedam, 1960).

[11] The Hebrew epitaph was translated by Postel as follows: "C'est la gloire de Dieu la parole cacher / C'est la gloire des Rois la parole chercher." Postel commented on this Biblical phrase: "Ce fut toujours jusqu'ici, où il faut que toutes choses soient restaurées, la gloire de Dieu de cacher sa parole, pour qu'en chacun des temps il y eut toujours progrès." Postel, *Thresor*, 106.

[12] "Or l'ay-je nommé Galliade, non pour imiter Iliades, Eneides, ny autres tels Poëmes et inventions empruntees des fables moisies des Grecs, ou des vieux Romains." Guy Lefèvre de la Boderie, "Avertissement aux lecteurs," in *La Galliade*, 153.

Temurah were used in order to reconstruct and purify the tarnished testimony of God's truth.

The title of Lefèvre's *La Galliade* misleads the reader: Lefèvre explains the Hebrew roots of the word *galal*[13] which means "to turn around," "to go back," a word more accurately translated with the Latin word *revolutio*. The subtitle underlines this meaning: "De la Revolution des Arts et des Sciences." It points to the philosophical concept of time underlying the whole poem: a circular time, which, like the Greek serpent Ouroboros bites its own tail. Revolution, in this sense, means the encounter of the past and the future at a single point. But instead of infinity, the completion of the circle marks the end of history. The Kabbalistic concept underlying the Revolution or *galal* is the contraction of God within himself, the creative process of *Zimzum*, the return to simplicity and unity.[14] The search for unity has to be seen in the millenarist context of the sixteenth century. As the end of time was expected to occur soon, order had to be re-established on Earth. But this apocalypse was not reduced to a moral and theological problem. It was a frequent theme of political debates which kingdom should lead the Christian Church to Christ and which king could reign the post-apocalyptic world, imagined as the celestial Jerusalem. Secular needs and expectations were freely combined with theological prophesy. It was Lefèvre who developed an integral poetical system of worldly and heavenly aspirations of the French kings in this context.

In relation to the circular time concept, it was important to link one's national roots as far back in time as possible in order to merit the last reign. *Galal* was one of the favorite proofs that the Gauls carried the divine truth in their proper name: *gal* means "flood" or "survivor of the flood." Noah himself is the ancestor of the Gauls. They were the ones to return to power after they had survived the great flood.

Lefèvre gives the emithological, truth-bearing revelation of the Hebrew word Noah: Repose.[15] It is not only the Platonic concept of the *movens immotus*, the principle of movement, but also a historical paradox

---

[13] "J'emprunte l'etymologie, et deduction de Galliade du verbe Hebrieu גלל galal, qui signifie Reployer et retourner." Lefèvre de la Boderie, "Avertissement aux lecteurs," 153.

[14] Boderie also refers to Ficino's comment on Plato: "Momentum autem temporis, praeteritum quidem terminat futurum inchoat, praesens ostendit & sui replicatione totum efficit tempus, quemadmodum **punctum replicatione sui** totam corporis molem adaequat aeternitas omnium temporum momentorum." Quoted in Roudaut, *Le Point centrique*, 65.

[15] Noah means *repos*. Comment on the margin of *La Galliade*, 163.

hidden in the name of the famous Biblical ancestor. Referring to an explanation of Nicholas of Cusa, movement and quietness entertain a subtle relationship. If you look at the movement attentively, it is a serially arranged quietness and in this aspect history (temporal movement) is the unfolding of quietness.[16] Noah becomes the principle of history. As the Hebrew word for history is synonymous to "generation,"[17] the beginning of genealogical development and history as a whole are combined in Noah's person.

Following the logic of secrecy, Noah is the outspoken name that hides another one: Lefèvre reveals his secret name Janus, the double-headed one, which symbolizes the two aspects of his singular position: he is the only one to remember the times before the Great Flood and the first to bring forth a New World:

> Janus
> A deux visages peints, auxquels furent connus
> Les temps du premier monde, & qui vit le repaire
> De ce monde fécond duquel il est le Pere.[18]

Lefèvre was convinced that he could heal the war-ridden world through poetic creation and geometric harmony.[19] In order to effect political concord, he aimed at unifying all the ambivalences, to reconcile oppositions, to speak out the ineffable, to remember the forgotten. And as there are two principles, one and two, male and female, East and West, he evokes the hidden names of women who remain anonymous, for example, the wife of Noah, Arethia. Her name is derived from the

---

[16] "Ita quidem quies est unitas motum complicans, qui est quies seriatim ordinata, si subtiliter advertis, motus igitur est explicatio quietis [...]." Nicolas Cusanus, *Doct. Ignor.* II.3; quoted in Roudaut, *Le point centrique,* 63.

[17] In Biblical Hebrew, the same word was used to express "generation" and "history." See Howard Bloch, *Etymologie et généalogie. Une anthropologie littéraire du Moyen-Age français* (1983; Paris: Le Seuil, 1989), 51.

[18] "Janus / has two faces / to which were known / the times of the first world / and who saw the upcoming / of the fertile world whose father he is." Lefèvre, *La Galliade,* Cercle II, vv. 885-888, 86.

[19] The reference to the Platonic concept of the healing capacity of the poet through the *furor poeticus* probably stems from the Ficinian translation of Plato's writings: "Donques il nous est besoing principalement de la fureur Poëtique, laquelle par tons musicaux esveille les parties qui dorment: par la douceur harmonique adoucisse celles qui sont troublees: et finalement par la consonance de choses diverses chasse la dissonante discorde, et tempere les variables parties de l'âme." Marsilio Ficino, *Disc. Honn. Am.,* vii, quoted in Lefèvre, *La Galliade,* 97.

Hebrew word for land *arets*, and thus unites Noah's function as the founder of history and genealogy with the idea of colonizing the earth. The idea of autochthony is inherent in Noah's marriage with Arethia.

In the context of healing and union, it is worth examining the gender concept that underlies the vision of history and eternity: in Kabbalistic terms,[20] secular and divine power are female and male, occidental and oriental, political and divine. The philosophical elaboration on the gender issue in Postel's thinking is not to be transferred to any social reality. When he speaks of the female soul, he does not refer to women but the feminine principle in Kabbalistic and neo-Platonic understanding.[21] This idea reflects the arrangement of the ten *sephiroth*: the first, *Qeter*, the Crown, is a masculine concept, pertaining to the East, while the last, *Malkhuth*, is feminine, pertaining to the West. The last principle is also known as the incarnation of God in the world, or the *Shekhina*.[22] The Zoharic role of the *Shekhina* is not at all powerless: thanks to her capacity to transform herself from masculine to feminine she is the most powerful principle of the *sephiroth*: dominion itself.[23]

---

[20] He refers to Kabbalistic books as follows: "secreti interpreti Hebrei se ne troua testimonij, come nel libro Diuinissimo & Rarissimo del Zohar, cosi nelli Rabboth, Midrass, Ialcut, Hagadoth Bariathoth, Ilanoth, & principalmente nelli interpreti delli 10 Sefiroth & della Mercava & di tutti li libri di Cabala, doue si mostrano che nella sacra scrittura Hebrea sono luoghi senza numero li quali douendo secondo il senso esser masculini sono à posta scritti Feminili per mostrare il colmo delli Diuini Mysterij nella detta Maternita & nel suo figliuolo Restitutore di tutte le Primogeniture [...]." Guillaume Postel, *Le Prime Nove del altro mondo* (Venice, 1555), Chapter 10, n. p.

[21] Cf. Secret, *Les Kabbalistes Chrétiens de la Renaissance*, passim.

[22] "*Shekhina*, heb. שכינה; lit. 'dwelling,' 'resting' or 'Divine Presence,' refers in rabbinic literature most often to the numinous immanence of God in the world. The *Shekhina* is God in spatio-temporal terms as a presence, particularly in a this-worldly context: when he sanctifies a place, an object, an individual, or a whole people – a revelation of the holy in the midst of the profane." *Encyclopedia Judaica*, vol. 14 (Jerusalem: Keter, 1971). The identification of *Malkhuth* and *Shekhina* is explicit in the *Bahir*. "C'est dans le *Sefer-ha-Bahir* que la *Shekinah* est identifiée avec *Malkut*, la dixième Sefira, et devient 'fille,' 'princesse,' le principe féminin dans le monde des Sefirot divines." Geneviève Javary, *Recherches sur l'utilisation du thème de la "Sekina" dans l'apologétique chrétienne du XV ème et XVIIIème siècle* (Lille: Atelier reproduction des thèses, Université Lille 3, Champion, 1977), 4.

[23] Geneviève Javary explains the Zoharic *Shekhina* as follows: "elle se présente sous l'aspect 'd'une femme passive, qui reçoit et transmet l'émanation qui coule des puissances actives du mâle.' N'ayant pas de lumière propre, elle sert de miroir et réfléchit 'toutes les lumières et toutes les couleurs.' C'est parce qu'elle peut prendre toutes les couleurs, qu'elle est capable de diriger le monde entier." Javary, *Sekina*, 10 ff.

Following this scheme, Lefèvre's teacher Postel divided every structure – geographical, historical, or political – into masculine and feminine. Identification of *Malkhuth*, *Shekhina* and the French kingdom only makes sense according to Postel's interpretation of the *Zohar* as the prophesy of the final unification. One of Postel's initial and theologically relevant concepts was that the original sin was caused by cutting into Adam's body in order to create woman. The wound is the never-healing sign that the formerly androgynous soul of Adam lost its female part, and that Jesus' death, repeating the sign of Adam's wound, only redeemed the male part of the human souls.

In the book of *Zohar*, which Postel had translated from Hebrew to Latin, the mystical interpretation of the original sin is that the *Shekhina* was cut off from the rest of the *sephiroth*. Cutting off the female principle is represented in several allegorical ways: on one occasion, woman is created from the male rib, and, on another occasion, the apple is plucked from the tree by Eve.

As the ten *sephiroth* can be represented in the form of a tree,[24] the Zoharic mystical interpretation takes the Biblical passages of the Genesis as various aspects of the same structure. The separation of the lowest of the *sephiroth* from the rest of the divine emanations means a struggle and a loss of harmony, a structure Postel identifies as the illness of history. In his ongoing search for healing devices for the wounded body of the French kingdom and the whole world, it was necessary to repossess the female part of Biblical history, which can be seen in Lefèvre's retrieval of Noah's bride Arethia.

This framework then explains the references to the masculine Jerusalem and the feminine French kingdom, the oriental, Adamitic masculine world in opposition to the occidental feminine world of Eve. The apocalyptic visions were, in Lefèvre's as well as in Postel's terms, part of a newly formed unity of the most fundamental philosophical

---

[24] Postel describes the human being as a tree: "Pero noi hauemo il capo & le mani con le sue radici uerso il Cielo per la Oratione tanto dell'animo, quanto della bocca & delle mani gionte, ouer ministre delli sacramenti, & della Charita, li piedi con la parte conseruatiua della specie, & con il fegato uanno ouero stanno da basso uerso la terra. Il core sta nel mezzo doue tutti gli altri principii si congiungono, come li Nerui dal ceruello, le Arterie dal pulmone, & le Vene dal fegato, & cosi dipoi come tre arbori con il quarto che è il corpo, uanno la metá in su & l'altra metá in giu, tutto per l'ordine Imagine, & similitudine delli duoi detti arbori, liquali s'acquetano nel Terzo accioche indi nel quarto luoco cioe nella Chiesa Santa facino frutti con il seme immortale simil à se." Postel, *Le Prime Noue*, E ij.

opposites of the time: universal harmony through unification in sexual analogies.

By the marriage of Noah and Arethia, two perfectly complementary parts became one in their sons: Sem, Ham and Japhet were known as the founders of the three main genealogical lines in the three areas of the world – Asia, Africa and Europe. Their dwelling place was on Mount Ianiculum in Rome. As experienced emithologists, we can easily recognize that Noah-Ianus was its patron.

In fact, this genealogical method of reading and recombining letters instead of words is revolutionary in a fundamental point. If the Gauls had been the first lawful colonizers of Rome, the conventional idea of the *translatio imperii*[25] as a transposition of political power from the East to the West, from Assyria, Persia, and Greece to Rome, was entirely subverted. Lefèvre made his readers believe that there was a direct line between the first empire, Noah's and Arethia's, and their son Japhet who settled down on the French territory. According to Lefèvre's writings, time had to go along the same line, but in the opposite direction, in order to restore the ancient state.

It was only natural in this context to define the planned conquest of Jerusalem by the French king, which Postel had prepared in secret negotiations with Soliman, the Turkish Emperor, as the holy marriage of woman and man, of Lily and Rose, the respective symbols of the two reigns, again politically elaborating on a Zoharic picture: the lily, *Shoshanna*, is the symbol of earthly kingdom, that is the *Shekhina*. Her vulnerable role as a holy principle amidst profane matter is illustrated in the Zohar: the lily must fight the evil forces like a lily has to fight the thorns of the roses.[26]

What Postel interprets on a theologico-political level, Lefèvre takes as the starting point for his insistence on French supremacy: the original truth that God had communicated to the survivors of the Flood was clothed in the human words of the Druids, the successors of Japhet and inventors of magical cures and the arts. As a French poet, communicating the secrets, pronouncing the vowels between the quiet

---

[25] This idea is explicitly connected to the circular concept in the following verse: "En Grece les Romains les allerent apprendre / Tirant la monarchie, & les lettres chez eus / Qu'ils ornerent si bien qu'égaus ils peurent rendre/Leur empire à la terre, & leur courage aux cieus / Et ores nous deuons des Romains les reprendre / Et poβeder le bien qui est de noz ayeus / Afun que le sçavoir, de l'Empire couuercle / Viene en Gaule auec vous finir le rond du Cercle." Lefèvre, *La Galliade,* 24.

[26] "Elle doit lutter contre les 'Ecorces,' les forces d'impureté; elle est au milieu d'elles comme 'un lis entre les épines.'" Javary, *Sekina,* 11.

consonants, he sees himself as their direct successor. His primary role is to use the magic force of words – combining them in a poem – in order to restore the final harmony of the world.

The myth of the Gauls as unfolded in the *Galliade* cannot be reduced to a mere foundation text of a political entity. Although the radical separation of classical Antiquity can be seen as a motor for political separation within Europe, the unifying power of the concept – a Gaulish rule encompassing the generation of all nations, countries, and religions – has not so much a national but more a global tendency in its apocalyptic dimensions.

THE MYTH OF MEDEA AND THE FEMINIST IMAGINATION IN VICTORIAN AND EDWARDIAN BRITAIN

Ann Heilmann

Medea, as Edith Hall notes, has "murdered her way into a privileged place in the history of the imagination of the West."[1] At least 2,500 years old, the myth takes many different forms. The most well-known version is Euripides' fifth-century BC play in which Medea, sorceress and princess of Colchis, helps Jason, the leader of the Argonauts, steal the golden fleece in exchange for his sworn love. In the course of their travels, she commits gruesome murders to further his claim to power, only to see herself and her sons abandoned in middle age when Jason decides to marry Glauce, the daughter of Corinth's ruler Creon. Medea dispatches her rival by means of poisoned wedding gifts, and takes further horrific revenge on Jason by killing their sons, after which she exits triumphantly in a chariot of winged dragons.[2]

The figure of the infanticidal mother has galvanised artists throughout the centuries, from Classical authors like Ovid and Seneca to seventeenth- and eighteenth-century playwrights like Pierre Corneille (*Médée*, 1635) and Charles Johnson (*Tragedy of Medea*, 1730), nineteenth-century dramatists like Franz Grillparzer (*Medea*, third part of *Das goldene*

---

[1] Edith Hall, "Medea and British Legislation Before the First World War," *Greece & Rome*, 46.1 (April 1999): 42.

[2] *The Medea of Euripides*, trans. and with explanatory notes by Gilbert Murray (London: George Allen & Unwin, 1910).

Vlies, 1819), and twentieth-century novelists like Hans Henny Jahnn (*Medea*, 1926). Medea has been represented in the visual and fine arts (see the Pre-Raphaelite paintings of "Medea" by Anthony Frederick Sandys and Evelyn de Morgan, 1889),[3] and her story has inspired ballet (Jean-Georges Noverre's *Médée*, 1761), opera (Simone Meyer's *Medea in Corinto*, 1826), and film (Pier-Paolo Pasolini's *Medea*, 1969). Our own time is particularly rich in treatments of the subject; Duarte Mimoso-Ruiz and Lillian Corti note that close to a hundred new versions of the myth have appeared in the twentieth century alone in countries all over the world.[4] Modern adaptations in particular tend to invoke Medea as a "symbol of the freedom fighter."[5] Thus, Toni Morrison's fugitive slave mother in *Beloved* (1987) commits murder to save her children from capture, and Brendan Kennelly's 1988 version of Euripides' play is set within the context of a divided Ireland.

The Medea myth has had an extraordinary resonance among European women writers and artists, who, across the centuries, have sought to reclaim Medea from her "lurid" reputation as the most "seductive, sinister and transgressive" woman haunting the male cultural imagination of the West.[6] As early as the fifteenth century the French writer Christine de Pizan celebrated Medea in her *Book of the City of Ladies* (1405) as a figure of outstanding wisdom, artistic brilliance, and beauty who, significantly, does not harbour any aggressive impulses. The wrongs of Medea have continued to capture the attention of European feminists. Like Pizan, the contemporary German writer Christa Wolf clears Medea of the charge of violence, instead turning her into a figure of resistance in her novel *Medea: Stimmen* (1998). Anything but a callous infanticide, Wolf's Medea uncovers chilling evidence of paternal child murder and sees her children killed as a punishment.

My essay focuses on the female and feminist dimensions of the cultural 'memory' of Medea at a particular moment in time and in a

---

3 For late-twentieth-century visual representations, see Marianne Hochgeschurz (ed.), *Christa Wolfs Medea: Voraussetzungen zu einem Text; Mythos und Bild* (Berlin: Gerhard Wolf Janus Press, 1998), 129-84.

4 Quoted in Lillian Corti, *The Myth of Medea and the Murder of Children* (Westport, Conn.: Greenwood Press, 1998), 177.

5 Marianne McDonald, "Medea as Politician and Diva: Riding the Dragon into the Future," in James J. Clauss and Sarah Iles Johnston (eds.), *Medea: Essays on Medea in Myth, Literature, Philosophy, and Art* (Princeton: Princeton University Press, 1997), 301-302.

6 Margaret Atwood, "Introduction," in Christa Wolf, *Medea: A Novel* (London: Virago, 1999), ix.

particular location: Victorian and Edwardian Britain. This choice of temporal and geographical setting is not accidental, as the 1850s to 1910s experienced a momentous social transformation in gender relations. The emergence of the cultural trope of the monstrous mother reflected contemporary anxieties prompted by an alarming rise in infanticide statistics[7] exacerbated by fears about the impact of the burgeoning women's movement on the family and society, generating an 'epidemic' of Medea productions on the British stage that coincided with legislation on women's right to child custody, divorce, higher education, professional careers, property, and suffrage.[8] The preponderance of plays inspired by the Medea myth testifies to its perceived topicality to contemporary debates about women's rights in marriage. Many of these plays – such as James Robinson Planché's *The Golden Fleece; or, Jason in Colchis and Medea in Corinth* (1845), Mark Lemon's *Medea; or, a Libel on the Lady of Colchis* (1856), and Robert Brough's *Medea; or, the Best of Mothers, with a Brute of a Husband* (1856)[9] – offered sympathetic, albeit conservative treatments of the subject, reaffirming the sanctity of marriage and its benefits for women by exploring the plight of the abandoned and abused wife, and exculpating Medea by circumventing her violence, redirecting the responsibility for it to others, or mitigating it by presenting it as the product of momentary madness or as an act of mercy.[10]

Victorian women writers and artists responded to this 'Medeification' of feminist concerns in a number of ways. Endeavouring to shift the emphasis of Medea's tragedy firmly on to the social conditions which drove working-class women to commit acts of desperation, realist writers like George Eliot and George Egerton sought to generate sympathy for the single and deserted mother. Others such as Augusta Webster, Amy Levy and Vernon Lee reconceptualised the figure of Medea as the *femme fatale* and avenger, dramatising the rage of the (proto)feminist about women's position in marriage and the family. New

---

7 Hall, "Medea and British Legislation," 67; Josephine McDonagh, *Child Murder and British Culture, 1720-1900* (Cambridge: Cambridge University Press, 2003), 123.

8 "Medea and British Legislation," 56, 50. For women's rights legislation, see Mary Lyndon Shanley, *Feminism, Marriage and the Law in Victorian England, 1850-1895* (Princeton: Princeton University Press, 1989).

9 Hall, "Medea and British Legislation," 58-60, and Fiona Macintosh, "Medea Transposed: Burlesque and Gender on the Mid-Victorian Stage," in Edith Hall, Fiona Macintosh and Oliver Taplin (eds.), *Medea in Performance 1500-2000* (Oxford: Legenda, 2000), 83.

10 "Medea and British Legislation," 53-61; Macintosh, "Medea Transposed," 79-82.

Woman writers like Mona Caird adapted the Classical myth in order to repossess and "re-member" the paradigm of the wronged artist overwritten by the cultural trope of the infanticide. More problematically, *fin-de-siècle* writers such as Emma Frances Brooke, Elizabeth Robins and Victoria Cross promoted infanticide as a means of feminist eugenics. After the turn of the century, female-authored representations of Medea assumed more positive dimensions in suffragette drama.

Medea as Victim: The Single Mother

The most famous maternal infanticide in Victorian fiction is arguably Hetty Sorel, the fallen girl of George Eliot's first novel *Adam Bede* (1859). Here the trope of the seduced and abandoned working-class girl, brought to prominence in Elizabeth Gaskell's *Ruth* (1853) and sensationalised at the close of the century in Thomas Hardy's *Tess of the d'Urbervilles* (1891), is transposed into a more ambiguous narrative which exonerates even as it inculpates the infanticidal mother: "it's *his* doing", Adam Bede, Hetty's fiancé, rails against her seducer, Captain Arthur Donnithorpe; "if there's been any crime, it's at his door, not at hers. [...] Let them put *him* on his trial – let him stand in court beside her [...] Is *he* to go free, while they lay all the punishment on her [...]?"[11] Hetty, however, is a victim also of her own foolishness, vanity, and self-indulgence. In this she bears a greater resemblance to Gustave Flaubert's Madame Bovary than to either Ruth or Tess, both of whom are unequivocally vindicated by their authors, while Hetty is continually censored for her emotional shallowness. Worse than her superficiality is her consummate dislike of children:

> Hetty would have been glad to hear that she should never see a child again: they were worse than the nasty little lambs that the shepherd was always bringing in to be taken special care of in lambing time – for the lambs were got rid of sooner or later. [...] The round, downy chicks peeping out from under their mother's wing never touched Hetty with any pleasure [...]
>
> (168)

---

[11] George Eliot, *Adam Bede* (London: T. Nelson & Sons, n.d.), 447-48. Subsequent references appear in the text.

Her lack of a mothering instinct signals her 'unnaturalness' to the reader, setting the scene for her later crime: "I seemed to hate it," she says of her baby, "it was like a heavy weight round my neck; [...] the thought came into my mind that I might get rid of it, and go home again." (495) Eliot nevertheless takes pains to stress the excruciating severity of Hetty's condition as a deserted mother, diminishing her responsibility by stating that "if she were to take any violent measure, she must be urged to it by the desperation of terror." (267) More interestingly still, Classical myth blends with the European fairytale when Hetty wanders through the woods "in her red cloak and warm bonnet, with her basket in her hand." (398) A cross between Little Red Riding Hood and Hawthorne's "scarlet" woman,[12] Hetty also integrates within herself the figures of Medea and Glauce, murderess and victim. Thus, the poisonous garment which in Euripides engulfs Glauce in flames and Medea's prior spinning of this garment are conjoined in the narrator's comment that

> it is too painful to think that she is a woman, with a woman's destiny before her – a woman spinning in young innocence a light web of folly and vain hopes which may one day close round her and press upon her, a rancorous poisonous garment, changing all at once her fluttering, trivial butterfly sensations into a life of deep human anguish.
>
> (274)

Like Medea, Hetty is banished from a civilisation which considers her a barbarian; like Glauce's, her death haunts the ending of the text. For, as Josephine McDonagh has noted, Hetty's live burial of her child in a wood pile is mirrored in her own textual 'burial' after her transportation to the colonies, her sole titular appearance coinciding with the consummation of her transmuted death sentence at the point of her threatened return to Victorian society. Through the expulsion of Hetty, McDonagh argues, "the new society of George Eliot's modern England accrues the veneer of [...] civilisation [...C]hild murder is at once the marker of cultural alterity; but also the redemptive sacrifice."[13] Not only does Eliot associate her version of Medea with Glauce, at the close of the novel she turns her into the murdered child, the blood sacrifice exacted by the new society.

---

[12] Lucie Armitt (ed.), *George Eliot: Adam Bede / The Mill on the Floss / Middlemarch* (Cambridge: Icon Books, 2000), 23.

[13] McDonagh, *Child Murder and British Culture*, 128.

Blood sacrifice is also central to George Egerton's short story "Wedlock" (*Discords*, 1894). "Wedlock" narrates the tragic disintegration of a cook whose husband promises to provide a home for her illegitimate daughter, but then fails to stick to the deal. Married, she is more divided from her daughter than ever, as her husband appropriates her savings and beats her for visiting the daughter. In her despair and rage, she takes to drinking and physically abusing her stepchildren. When she discovers that her husband has withheld a telegram summoning her to her daughter's deathbed, she kills his children to avenge hers:

> Upstairs in a back room in the silent house a pale strip of moonlight flickers over a dark streak on the floor, that trickles slowly from the pool at the bedside out under the door, making a second ghastly pool on the top step of the stairs – a thick sorghum red, blackening as it thickens, with a sickly serous border. Downstairs the woman sits in her chair with her arms hanging down. Her hands are crimson as if she dipped them in dye. A string of blue beads [a reminder of her daughter] lies in her lap, and she is fast asleep; and she smiles as she sleeps, for Susie is playing in a meadow, a great meadow crimson with poppies, and her blue eyes smile with glee, and her golden curls are poppy-crowned, and her little white feet twinkle as they dance, and her pinked-out grave frock flutters, and her tiny waxen hands scatter poppies, blood-red poppies, in handfuls over three open graves.[14]

A striking piece of late-Victorian Naturalism, the story attributes the plight of the single mother and her desperate act of child murder to the failure of society to take responsibility for those on the edge. The two individuals who witness the unfolding tragedy fail to intervene at the crucial moment: the middle-class woman writer is too preoccupied with her writer's block to devote more than fleeting attention to her landlady; the gentle bricklayer engaged in building a wall between neighbouring properties – an apt symbol for the story's theme of alienation – is the only person sympathetic to the alcoholic mother because his own wife developed a drinking disorder after the loss of their child. He observes the woman's extreme distress on her return from her daughter's funeral and conjectures the worst, but is prevented from averting the tragedy by

---

[14] George Egerton, "Wedlock," in *Discords* (1894); reprinted in *Keynotes and Discords*, introduction by Sally Ledger (Birmingham: Birmingham University Press, 2003), 126.

a neighbour urging him to call a doctor for her ailing baby. The lawful child and mother poignantly overrule the single mother's desperate claims to attention, a fact already signalled by the protagonist's marked lack of a name as opposed to the married mother's instant legitimation as "Mrs Rogers." Medea, the playwright Brendan Kennelly has observed, is about a woman's rage, not jealousy, [15] and this rage of the silenced and dispossessed is explored to its fullest in the conclusion to Egerton's story.

Medea as Avenger: Rage and the (Proto)Feminist Rebel

It was Medea's rage that made her into such a potent symbol of Victorian feminism. If Victorian stage productions depicted Medea in her despondency and subjection and strategically underplayed her violence, feminist poets and writers like Augusta Webster, Amy Levy, and Vernon Lee were drawn to the mythical theme precisely for its transgressive potential. Thus, in her dramatic monologue "Medea in Athens" (*Portraits*, 1868) Augusta Webster explores Medea's exultation at the news of Jason's death. Filled with "the virulent hate / that should be mine against mine enemy," she rejoices at the extinction of his line even as she mourns her sons, and imagines the dying man lamenting that "My house is perished with me – ruined, ruined!"[16].

Like Webster's Medea, Emma Frances Brooke's heroine in *A Superfluous Woman* (1894) avenges herself by inverting the maternal role, obliterating the paternal line and, with it, its legacy of vice and venereal disease. After bearing two children afflicted with hereditary syphilis, she wills herself to kill the third one in her womb. Here child murder is performed "from within," by sheer willpower and concentration of mind, and is invoked as a quasi-divine act of purification:

> I will cancel it – from *within*. I will repudiate it – reject it – from *within*. [...] I will throw myself on the side against it. I myself will annul it. I shall *will* – and *will* – and *will*. [...] I beat with my willing against the very door of heaven. I will tear my wish out of the centre of things [...]. Who has a right to his will, if not I? And I shall win it! There is nothing [...] stronger than a mother.[17]

[15] Brendan Kennelly, *Euripides' Medea: A New Version* (Newcastle: Bloodaxe, 1991), 6.

[16] Augusta Webster, *Portraits* (London: Macmillan and Co., 1870), 2, 6.

[17] Emma Frances Brooke, *A Superfluous Woman* (London: Heinemann, 1894), 261.

Jessamine Heriot duly miscarries, and the rest of the family perishes, Bertha Rochester like, in a fire started by her disabled daughter: the House of Heriot, its name an ironic reminder of the infanticidal Herod, becomes extinct.

A more complex version of the theme is presented by the Jewish writer Amy Levy, the protagonist of whose "Medea" (*Cameo Series*, 1891) proudly affirms the primacy of her origins:

> You never knew Medea. [...]
> She was not born to serfdom.
> I have knelt
> Too long before you. I have stood too long
> Suppliant before this people. You forget
> A redder stream flows in my Colchian veins
> Than the slow flood which courses round your hearts,
> O cold Corinthians, with whom I long have dwelt
> And never ere this day have known myself.
> Nor have ye known me. Now behold me free,
> Ungyved by any chains of this man wrought;
> Nothing desiring at your hands nor his.
> Free, freer than the air or wingèd birds;
> Strong, stronger than the blast of wintry storms;
> And lifted up into an awful realm
> Where is nor love, nor pity, nor remorse,
> Nor dread, but only purpose.[18]

Victorious and triumphant as a woman and foreigner, Medea is, however, also depicted as a tragic figure who suffers social rejection precisely because of her racial alterity. "From natural fellowship cut off," she feels herself "grown / No woman, but a monster" (43-44): monstrosity is thus a response to the condition of exile. Here the myth of Medea is fused with Mary Shelley's Frankenstein paradigm.

Social isolation and exile are fates that Vernon Lee's Medea is unlikely to suffer. In her 1890 short story "Amour Dure: Passages from the Diary of Spiridion Trepka," Lee unravels, through a male narrative consciousness, the story of Medea da Carpi, a sixteenth-century Lucrezia Borgia. In his longing for romance, Spiridion Trepka, a young Polish academic working on the history of Urbania, explores the life of the

---

[18] Amy Levy, "Medea (A Fragment in Drama Form, After Euripides)," *Cameo Series* (London: T. Fisher Unwin, 1891), 49-50. Subsequent references appear in the text.

former Duchess of Urbania, Medea da Carpi, reputed to have killed her five husbands and lovers. Captivated and soon enthralled by what quickly assumes the dimensions of a love object, Trepka aims to recover the "real" woman beneath the myth of the evil seductress, and empathises with the rage of an exceptional woman who from childhood was used as a pawn in men's power games. Ultimately, however, Trepka fails to move beyond the paradigms which have kept Medea confined to the narrow spaces of male-constructed desires and cultural memories: "a bogey for naughty little boys,"[19] she embodies the *femme fatale par excellence* to young men like him, and is constructed as a deadly witch by patriarchal figures like Duke Robert. It is only in the gaps of her officially documented and mythically constructed story that the learned woman, the scholar, emerges, as when Trepka discovers hitherto unknown letters in her hand and remarks on her "round, scholarly" handwriting, befitting "a learned princess who can read Plato as well as Petrarch." (103) But at the very point at which Medea's voice might come to be heard, she is relegated to a subordinate position: "The letters are of little importance" (103), Trepka decides, and her version of the story is instantly overwritten by that of her arch enemy Robert, whose letters cast her in the light of "'la pessima Medea' – worse than her namesake of Colchis." (103) Robert contrived to have her strangled by two convicts; significantly, Medea's executioners were female infanticides. (95) Read in metaphorical terms, Medea is 'killed' into a permanent association with child murder: a symbolic rendering of the workings of the Classical myth. The Duke's flawed attempt to protect his afterlife from Medea's dreaded revenge provides another encoding of the myth. Thus, Robert arranged for his portrait (an emblem of his soul) to be buried deep within his statue, where, presumably, Medea would not be able to get at it. Overcome by progressive madness, Trepka believes himself to be under the spell of Medea and follows her instructions to destroy the statue. The Medea-inspired destruction of the patriarchal statue signals the feminist breaking asunder of a myth with which patriarchal men have sought to protect themselves, with the death of the narrator releasing the woman from its stranglehold.

If, as Christa Zorn argues, Lee "exposes the cultural construction of historical myths" through the figure of "a male historian whose imagination she saw conditioned by the suppressed fears of individual

---

[19] Vernon Lee, "Amour Dure: Passages from the Diary of Spiridion Trepka," in *Hauntings* (1890); reprinted in Vernon Lee, *Supernatural Tales: Excursions into Fantasy* (London: Arena, 1988), 104. Subsequent references appear in the text.

and collective male history," the New Woman writer Mona Caird engaged on a similar project of "female aesthetic historicism"[20] in her representation of Medea as a tragic artist.

Medea and Pro/Creativity: Mother Versus Artist

As literary and dramatic representations of Medea gained in cultural currency throughout the Victorian period and "Medea bec[ame] the prototype for the 1890s New Woman,"[21] *fin-de-siècle* feminist writers adapted the myth of the extraordinary and learned woman with a tragic fate in order to explore questions of female artistic agency in a society which valued women only as mothers but then debarred mothers from cultural, social, and political authority. In the myth, Medea establishes her power as a sorceress by defying and fracturing the father's rule; later, betrayed by her lover, the only way for her to repossess herself and reclaim her identity is to obliterate the mother and kill the children who, alive, will always represent her subject status within patriarchal society, her biological function, and her ties to Jason. Medea the priestess of magical arts is thus constructed as the binary opposite of the mother. This dichotomy between artist and mother was one that greatly exercised late-Victorian feminist writers such as Mona Caird, whose *Daughters of Danaus* explores the Medea myth not on its literal level of infanticide but in its metaphorical ramifications. Caird's modern-day tragedy unfolds against the backdrop of rich mythological associations: the titular invocation of the Danaid myth, textual references to Euripides' Medea and other tragic hero/ines of Classical drama and myth, a replica Greek temple adorning the Scottish countryside, magic rituals and dances which unearth buried memories of a forgotten collective past, frequent narrative dislocations between modern and primitive time[22] – all relate the protagonist's experiences to a mythic framework.

Medea's plight and rage is figured not through the paradigm of child murder, but through the conflict between mother and daughter and the consequent 'murder' of the heroine's creative aspirations. A gifted

---

[20] Christa Zorn, *Vernon Lee: Aesthetics, History, & the Victorian Female Intellectual* (Athens: Ohio University Press, 2003), 167.

[21] Macintosh, "Medea Transposed," 77.

[22] See Lisa Surridge, "Narrative Time, History, and Feminism in Mona Caird's *The Daughters of Danaus*," in Mark Llewellyn and Ann Heilmann (eds.), *Women Writing History*, special issue of *Women's Writing*, 12.1 (2005). For a detailed discussion of the Medea myth in Caird's novel, see my *New Woman Strategies: Sarah Grand, Olive Schreiner, Mona Caird* (Manchester: Manchester University Press, 2004), 222-30.

pianist, Hadria Temperley fails to distinguish herself as a professional musician due to the interventions of her querulous and demanding mother, who monopolises the time required for study and practice with trivial tasks, propels her into an unhappy marriage, and, at the very point of Hadria's breakthrough as a composer, contrives through hysterical illness to coerce her to abandon her career and return home. Here and in Caird's Edwardian novel *The Stones of Sacrifice* (1915), mother and daughter are locked into a grim fight for survival, represented graphically in the later text's juxtaposition of two mother-daughter pairs, each of which suffers a casualty. Infanticide is here transmuted into the stark choice between (figurative, psychological, even literal) matricide and suicide: as one of the characters remarks in *The Stones of Sacrifice,* "The mother drives one daughter to suicide by chaining her to her Sphere, and the other kills the mother by refusing to be so driven."[23]

While Hubert Temperley is anything but a congenial partner, the central conflict in *The Daughters of Danaus* is not between an abused wife and her deceitful husband – for here it is the wife who absconds from marriage and later takes a lover – but, rather, it is a deadly contest between mother and daughter about the nature and quality of the daughter's life. The mother-child relationship in the Medea myth is thus inverted in Caird's novel in that the focus of narrative attention is placed on the injured child. The text also depicts Hadria's lack of rapport with her own children, two sons who, to her, represent nothing but coercive marital relations. Indeed, the failure of Hadria's marriage and her dysfunctional relationship with her mother are mirrored in her indifference to her biological progeny, a want of affection that is implied in her sons' de-individualised and nameless condition, and which is further reflected in the ease with which she leaves them behind when she removes herself to Paris. A 'bad' mother in the conventional sense, Hadria is, however, not so much the aggressor as the victim in the Medean conflict dramatised in the text; for here Medea directs the knife against herself:

> Knowing [...] that if her mother lived, her own dreams were ended for ever, she wrestled with desperate strength for the life that was at stake. [...] She realized now [...] the sadness of her mother's life [...]: the injury from without, and then the self-injury, its direct offspring; [...] the unconscious thirst for the sacrifice of others, the hungry claims of a nature unfulfilled,

23 Mona Caird, *The Stones of Sacrifice* (London: Simpkin, Marshall, 1915), 325-26.

the groping instinct to bring the balance of renunciation to the level, and indemnify oneself for the loss suffered and the spirit offered up. And that propitiation had to be made. It was as inevitable as that the doom of Orestes should follow the original crime of the house of Atreus. Hadria's whole thought and strength were now centred on the effort to bring about that propitiation, in her own person. She prepared the altar and sharpened the knife.[24]

The novel ends with Hadria's resigned acceptance of her failed life and her determination to act as a deterrent to other female artists.

If Caird's Hadria concludes her narrative existence as a scarecrow, the anti-heroine of Elizabeth Robins' *George Mandeville's Husband* (published under the pseudonym of C.E. Raimond in 1894) is introduced as a figure of abjection, her physically repellent body swelling in size as her poor husband grows "greyer and thinner" under the impact of the role reversal enacted in their marriage.[25] In this artistic coupling, the wife is the dominant force, while the husband assumes the domestic function of childcarer, suffers alienation in being known only by virtue of his wife's name, experiences sexual coercion, and in his artistic capacity is pushed to the margins when his painters' studio is converted into a feminist salon. The husband here constitutes a satirical inversion of the Victorian Angel of the House sacrificed on the altar of marriage. The woman artist, on the other hand, is constructed as a deadly, devouring monster, without even the compensations offered by Lee's exquisite if fatal Medea da Carpi.

Whereas Caird adapts the Medea myth from the point of view of the adult daughter, Robins assumes the narrative perspective of the husband, exploring a downtrodden Jason's impotent rage and venom in the face of his consummate subjection. The text was (and is) read as an attack on the woman writer,[26] but Robins, who was soon to become a prominent spokeswoman for the Edwardian suffragette movement, may

---

[24] Mona Caird, *The Daughters of Danaus* (1894; New York: Feminist Press, 1989), 363.

[25] C.E. Raimond [Elizabeth Robins], *George Mandeville's Husband* (London: Heinemann, 1894), repr. in Ann Heilmann (ed.), *Anti-Feminism in the Victorian Novel*, 6 vols. (Bristol: Thoemmes Continuum and Edition Synapse, 2004), 6:29. Subsequent references appear in the text.

[26] Elaine Showalter, *A Literature of Their Own* (1978; London: Virago, 1984), 108. For the novel's contemporary reception, see my "Introduction," in *Anti-Feminism in the Victorian Novel*, 1:xxxvii-xxxviii.

have intended her first novel as an object lesson in how to read (and write) against the grain. As she later noted in "Woman's Secret,"

> In print, even more than elsewhere [...a woman] must wear the aspect that shall have the best chance of pleasing her brothers. [...] What she is really doing is her level best to play the man's game, and seeing how nearly like him she can do it. So conscious is she it *is* his game she is trying her hand at, that she is prone to borrow his very name to set upon her title-page.[27]

This is of course the narrative strategy on which both George Mandeville and her creator had embarked. In the clash of the novel's conflicting perspectives, it is the daughter, Rosina, who is the ultimate victim, violated as she is by both parents alike: by her caring but deeply misogynist father, who seeks to stamp out any desire for independent agency in her; by her overbearing mother, whose insensitivity and probing over-familiarity cause her to take flight. Trapped between her father's insistence that "nothing on earth would be so disappointing to me as to see you trying to paint – nothing, that is, except seeing you try to write" (56) and her mother's dreaded woman-to-woman intimacies, poor Rosina is left no room for manoeuvre and eventually dies from a cold contracted while being obliged to watch one of her mother's plays. Unaffected by lasting guilt about her involuntary child murder, George speedily proceeds to cannibalise her daughter's memory for her novels.

Medea as Eugenist: Child Murder and Turn-of-the-Century Feminism

George Mandeville's Husband appeared a year after Robins performed the lead role in the pro-eugenist play she had co-authored with Florence Bell, *Alan's Wife*. Based on a short story by the Swedish writer Elin Ameen,[28] the play responds to the dilemma posited at the end of Ibsen's *Ghosts* (1881, first performed in Britain in 1891) by promoting the murder of a disabled child as an act of love and social responsibility:

---

27 Elizabeth Robins, "Woman's Secret," in *Way Stations* (London: Hodder and Stoughton, 1913), 6.

28 Linda Fitzsimmons and Viv Gardner (eds.), *New Woman Plays* (London: Methuen, 1991), 4.

Oh, I seem to see you in some far-off time, your face distorted like your body, but with bitterness and loathing, saying, "Mother, how could you be so cruel as to let me live and suffer? You could have eased my pain; you could have saved me this long martyrdom; when I was little and lay in your arms. Why didn't you save me. You were a coward – a coward!" [...] Are your lips moving, dear? [...] Are you asking for life? No, you don't want to live, do you? No, no, you cannot![29]

Jean Creyke's conclusion that it is morally more reprehensible to let her child live than to end its (presumed) suffering are indebted to the Nietzschean Superman idea; earlier in the play, she had exulted in her husband Alan's Herculean physique and expressed her pride in having chosen for a mate a man "who is my master as well as other folks'." (12) When Alan is killed in an accident and their child is born disabled, Jean is unable to reconcile its condition with her eugenic ideals and smothers the baby. The ending sees her calmly awaiting her execution.

While *Alan's Wife* has been read as emblematic of the "New Woman's critique of motherhood,"[30] the chilling implications of Robins' and other *fin-de-siècle* feminists' espousal of eugenic social planning makes for difficult reading. Ironically, the Medea myth, which had been co-opted to liberate women from patriarchal structures in marriage and society, found its most problematic expression in turn-of-the-century feminist eugenics. Eugenic thought held potent appeal for many feminists, not least because the conservative faction within the Victorian social purity movement had long subscribed to the belief that the regeneration of society could be achieved only by means of suppressing the biologically and racially inferior. Thus, social purity feminists like Sarah Grand and Charlotte Perkins Gilman advocated a marriage bar for morally substandard males, and Gilman additionally promoted the implementation of strict moral and physical health screens for immigrants to the United States.[31] As Angelique Richardson has noted, many women felt attracted to eugenic ideas "*because* rather than *in spite of*

---

[29] Florence Bell and Elizabeth Robins, *Alan's Wife* (1893), in Fitzsimmons and Gardner, *New Woman Plays*, 21. Subsequent references appear in the text.

[30] Catherine Wiley, "Staging Infanticide: The Refusal of Representation in Elizabeth Robins's *Alan's Wife*," *Theatre Journal*, 42.4 (1990): 442.

[31] Janet Beer and Ann Heilmann, "'If I Were a Man:' Charlotte Perkins Gilman, Sarah Grand and the Education of Girls," in Janet Beer and Bridget Bennett (eds.), *Special Relationships* (Manchester: Manchester University Press, 2002), 178-201.

the fact that they served racialist ends."[32] The determination of Brooke's heroine to eliminate the corrupt dynasty of the Heriots reflects late-Victorian middle-class concerns about the eugenic viability of a decaying aristocracy, moral and physical contagion here being equated with racial degeneration. In *Anna Lombard* (1901) by Victoria Cross, these fears are projected onto interracial sexual relations within the context of the British Empire.

The narrator, Gerald Ethridge, a lieutenant stationed in India, instantly falls in love with Anna Lombard, the university-educated, beautiful, and unconventional daughter of his colonel. His plan to propose to her is delayed by a year's summons to a dangerous Burmese outpost. This serves to establish Gerald as a New Man of outstanding moral stature and virtue: though urged to do so by his colleagues, he refuses to take a native child-"wife" (he is offered a choice of eleven to thirteen-year-olds who would be contracted out to him for the duration of his stay, subsequently to be returned to their families with any ensuing children), rescues an eleven-year-old widow from a violent relative, and rejects all her sexual advances. Released from his post, he hastens back to Anna, but their engagement is followed by Anna's disclosure of her secret marriage to her Pathan servant, Gaida Khan. Professing deep love for Gerald but an uncontrollable sexual passion for Gaida, Anna refuses to leave her lover, and pleads with Gerald to accept the current arrangement: "He is a beautiful toy to me. He is like some pet [...]. He is a possession that I value. [...] Let me keep him [...] for a little while – at first."[33] As the contemporary critic W.T. Stead remarked, the novel enacts a powerful role reversal.[34] Virginal, heroically self-restrained and self-abnegating, gentle, patient, and forbearing, Gerald "mimics the conduct of ideal Victorian womanhood,"[35] whereas with her simultaneous love for two men, carnal experience, erotic objectification and consumption of the sexual and racial Other, Anna is thoroughly masculinised. This sexual role reversal is accompanied by an inversion of racial categories, for the dark-skinned Gerald looks Asiatic, while Gaida has the appearance of a Greek Hercules.

---

[32] Angelique Richardson, "The Birth of National Hygiene and Efficiency: Women and Eugenics in Britain and America 1865-1915," in Ann Heilmann and Margaret Beetham (eds.), *New Woman Hybridities* (London: Routledge, 2004), 245.

[33] Victoria Cross, *Anna Lombard* (1901; Birmingham: University of Birmingham Press, 2003), 56-57. Subsequent references appear in the text.

[34] W.T. Stead, "*Anna Lombard*: A Novel of the Ethics of Sex," *Review of Reviews*, 23 (1901): 597.

[35] Gail Cunningham, "Introduction," in Cross, *Anna Lombard*, xvi.

Gaida's death from cholera appears to resolve the crisis caused by Anna's radical disregard for racial boundaries, enabling her, after her convalescence from purifying illness, to assume her rightful place within white imperial society as the wife of Gerald. The birth of Gaida's child, however, and Anna's overpowering love for it, threatens to carry the germ of miscegenation into the very heart of empire: "the child was hideous, horrible in its suggestion of mixed blood." (128) The resolution offered by the novel is maternal infanticide. The child must die so that the confused moral, sexual and racial order can be reinstated; the child must die by his mother's hand to ensure her complicity with and reintegration into this order. As Melisa Britain argues, "Anna is *not* a white man" (who by fathering a mixed-raced child would merely add to the imperial "stock," as Gerald's colleagues do in Burma), but as an English woman "must [...] violently extricate herself from the racial ties that prohibit her full commitment to Gerald, who has the power to include or exclude both her and her baby from proper English society."[36] And although it is Anna's decision to smother the child, her prior declaration of her absolute subordination to Gerald's will implicates him in the act. The novel thus projects facets of the mythical Medea onto all three central actors: Gaida represents Medea's racial Otherness, Gerald suffers her sexual jealousy, and Anna carries out the blood sacrifice that Gerald obliquely desires.

The geographical location of the novel's infanticide – the Indian subcontinent – is significant and furnishes an otherwise unlikely link with the first text examined here, *Adam Bede*. In her discussion of Eliot's novel, Josephine McDonagh draws attention to contemporary Victorian concerns about the rising incidence of infanticide in Britain coinciding with racial anxieties prompted by the influx of foreign (especially Oriental) populations into Britain and the fear that barbaric native customs might spread moral infection across the nation. As the *Pall Mall Gazette* warned in 1866, Britain was already at risk of becoming a "nation of [home-grown] infanticides;"[37] what was to happen if it were exposed to what in the *Parliamentary Papers* was called a "race of infanticides?"[38] In *Adam Bede*, the threat of a contagious foreign element, invoked in the narrator's reference to "the Egyptian sorcerer" in the novel's first

---

[36] Melisa Britain, "Erasing Race in the New Woman Review: Victoria Cross' *Anna Lombard*," in Ann Heilmann (ed.), *Masculinities, Maternities, Motherlands*, special issue of *Nineteenth-Century Feminisms*, 4 (2001): 89.

[37] Quoted in McDonagh, *Child Murder and British Culture*, 124.

[38] Quoted in *Child Murder and British Culture*, 143.

sentence (1), is exorcised by means of Hetty Sorel's (the Other's) exile and death. "[T]he child murder in *Adam Bede,*" McDonagh writes, is

> crucial to the novel's attempt to define and locate the new society as civilised and child-loving, inhabited by healthy, reproductive families, rather than the wild child-killers who are expelled beyond its borders. But it is also the event around which the new society bonds, and in that sense is something like a founding sacrifice.[39]

In *Anna Lombard*, published in the final year of Victoria's reign, it is not the child murderess, but her child who becomes the "founding sacrifice" of the new (Edwardian), racially purified society.

Suffragette Medea: The Feminist as Mother of the Nation

The cruelty of this new Edwardian society towards women and children was at the heart of suffrage literature's drive for wholesale social and political renovation through female enfranchisement. And while Euripides' *Medea* assumed a central place in the suffragette imagination,[40] it was the woman warrior rather than the child murderess who came to represent the suffrage movement. In Elizabeth Robins' founding suffrage play, *Votes for Women!* (1907), and its companion novel, *The Convert* (1907), child murder via abortion functions as the crucial initiatory experience propelling the protagonist, Vida Levering, into social reformism and suffrage militancy. Far from endorsing Jean Creyke's biologist standpoint, the play and novel place social culpability on male shoulders, as Vida, vulnerable after the death of her father, is first seduced and then pressurised into an abortion by a friend of the family. This experience becomes a turning point in her life, making her aware of women's sexual exploitation, and transforming her into both an avenger and a socially responsible 'mother' figure engaged in practical solutions to social problems caused by men (at the opening of the play Vida is working on plans for a women's shelter). Robins takes pains to introduce her heroine as a child lover adored by her friends' offspring with "rapturous devotion"[41] who has never quite recovered from her loss. If women like Vida, the text implies, turn into modern-day Medeas

---

[39] *Child Murder and British Culture*, 128.
[40] Hall, "Medea and British Legislation," 42-46.
[41] Elizabeth Robins, *The Convert* (1907; London: Women's Press, 1980), 5.

and suffragette iconoclasts, the responsibility – as well as the remedy – lies with men; with their assistance, the mother who killed can assume her role as mother of the nation; the play ends with Vida's former lover, now a conservative MP, pledging his party political support for woman suffrage.

In conclusion, if the figure of Medea, as Josephine McDonagh argues, constitutes "an important icon of both female potency and women's oppression [...], a figure through which to explore both their exclusion from patriarchal power and their means of redress,"[42] this duality of purpose is addressed through five central narrative paradigms in Victorian and Edwardian feminist literature. Constructing her as a distraught victim of adverse circumstances and male exploitation who commits a violent crime in a state of mental irresponsibility, Victorian novelists aimed to direct sympathetic attention to the predicament of the single and working-class mother. At the same time, in exploring the rage of the wronged woman, they turned Medea into a powerful emblem of Victorian women's dissatisfaction with contemporary gender relations. Towards the close of the century, New Woman writers reinvented Medea as a tragic artist and fused the figure of the child murderess with that of the ill-treated child in their analysis of mother-daughter relations. The turn-of-the-century rise of eugenic feminism was reflected in a narrative shift towards 'rational' (eugenic or racially motivated) infanticide. In the new century, Edwardian suffrage literature sought to exculpate Medea from the taint of child murder and embraced her as a heroic woman warrior. Each of these configurations sustains the words of the Greek scholar and Euripides translator Gilbert Murray that Medea "might have been written for the women's movement."[43]

---

[42] McDonagh, *Child Murder and British Culture*, 164.

[43] Sibyl Thorndike, "Gilbert Murray and Some Actors," in J.A.K. Thomson and A.J. Toynbee (eds.), *Essays in Honour of Gilbert Murray* (London, 1936), 74, quoted in Hall, "Medea and British Legislation," 43.

IN SEARCH OF THE NATIONAL REVOLUTION: FRENCH NATIONALIST NARRATIVES OF THE SPANISH CIVIL WAR[1]

Martin Hurcombe

The impact of the Spanish Civil War upon French culture, society and politics is forever overshadowed by that of the Second World War. Yet, it nevertheless left a mark on French literature, giving us André Malraux's *L'Espoir* (translated into English as *Man's Hope*) and Georges Bernanos's celebrated essay *Les Grands Cimetières sous la lune*. As is the case with English-language responses to the Civil War, those works which opposed Franco's military rebellion have stood the test of time, and of critics, far better than the works of those writers, artists and intellectuals, no less numerous, who gave their support to the Nationalist movement. Whilst, in France, little attention was given to Franco in the early days following the *pronunciamiento*, the protracted warfare that followed the initial military uprising drew the attention of a French far Right increasingly and vociferously opposed to French republicanism to events unfolding beyond the Pyrenees. From September 1936 onwards, a number of French intellectuals of the far Right sought to travel to Nationalist Spain to witness the birth of this new society for themselves and to report back on it to the French public. The result was, between the autumn of 1936 and Franco's eventual victory in May 1939, a series

---

[1] The present study expands upon some arguments I have already advanced in "Touring the Spanish Labyrinth: The French Far Right and the Spanish Civil War, 1936-1939," *Forum of Modern Language Studies*, forthcoming special edition "War and Literature."

of travel journals and histories of the Civil War and Nationalist Spanish society. It is these and their use of pre-existing mythical paradigms that will form the basis of this study.

Yet, whilst it is perhaps usual to think of French nationalism today as a single entity in the form of Jean-Marie Le Pen's National Front party, the French far Right of the 1930s was a far more ideologically diverse body. In the late nineteenth century, the forces of French reaction had undergone a series of changes; what had once seemed a single movement dedicated to the restoration of the monarchy had fractured, in the course of the Boulanger and Dreyfus Affairs, into a variety of reactionary stances to the Republic and the French Left. When civil war broke out in Spain in July 1936, French nationalism was divided between monarchists, Republican conservatives, Catholic traditionalists, Fascists and neo-Fascists. Before studying the representations of Nationalist Spain produced by these travellers, it is worth identifying some of the dominant groups of the French far Right in the late 1930s.

Although an ideological relic of the nineteenth century, Charles Maurras' Action Française remained one of the most dominant nationalist groups in France. Maurras, and followers such as Henri Massis and the sculptor Maxime Réal del Sarte, sought nothing less than a return to the absolute monarchy of pre-Revolutionary France, a France where aristocratic and Catholic values would supplant those of a Republic sponsored by the vast international Judeo-Masonic conspiracy that they perceived behind the Revolution of 1789 and behind the Republic that now invoked its legacy and drew on its iconography.

From the shadows of Action Française's primarily intellectual and aesthetic opposition to the Republic, a number of more radical and energetic monarchist groups emerged in the 1930s, such as the Camelots du roi and the terrorist organisation known as La Cagoule. Moreover, the influence of Italian and German Fascism could be perceived in nationalist war-veteran movements, such as Colonel de la Rocque's anti-Communist strikebreakers, Les Croix de Feu. In French far Right intellectual circles, younger writers who had been nurtured by Action Française, such as the novelist Robert Brasillach, were beginning to turn towards more overtly Fascist doctrines. Brasillach was to declare himself a Fascist writer in 1938. By then his fellow novelist Pierre Drieu la Rochelle had already aligned himself with what was to become the only avowedly Fascist political party in France, the Parti Populaire Français. Drieu went on to become the party's ideological spokesman and resident intellectual until finally becoming disillusioned with its transition from a pseudo-revolutionary movement, which drew inspiration from the Italian *squadristi* of the 1920s, to a pale imitation of German National Socialism. Both Drieu and Brasillach went on to collaborate during the German occupation of France, however.

The far Right therefore offered no effective unified front in opposition to that of the Left which swept to victory in France in the spring of 1936. Increasingly in the early 1930s, it had become divided between those who looked back towards the long-forgotten France of the Bourbons and those who were beginning to look to foreign regimes for domestic inspiration. Unlike Germany and Italy, however, France had gained from the Treaty of Versailles and had suffered less economically than Germany after the Wall Street Crash.[2] The far Right therefore lacked appeal for the vast majority of French voters. It also lacked its own common political praxis. It was united only by the rhetoric underlying its various factions: nationalism and opposition to Communism, democracy, modernity, political and economic corruption, and to that non-French Other said to lurk behind these, the Muscovite or the Jew.

However, it was this opposition to the Other that was to offer the potential for far Right unity, a unity which it immediately perceived in the Spanish Nationalists; here old-style conservatism, militarism, Catholicism, monarchism (both Carlist and Alfonsine) along with the Fascist Falange had come together in order to overthrow the newly united Left and Spanish democracy. Unlike Germany and Italy, the Spanish Nationalist regime offered no direct threat to France; theirs was primarily a domestic crisis, a battle against an allegedly Soviet-sponsored regime that threatened the very fabric of Spanish civilisation, but one which illustrated the real perils awaiting France under its left-wing Popular Front. The Spanish Nationalists were therefore engaged in a battle against the Eastern other in the form of Communism which sought, in its support of Spanish Republicanism, to undermine not only Spanish but Western civilisation as a whole. Such an interpretation of the Spanish Civil War, I shall argue, is possible because it is predicated upon an existing and well-established myth in the minds of those writers and thinkers of the far Right who were drawn to travel to Nationalist Spain to witness this struggle for themselves. It is this myth that underpins the writings of both monarchists, such as Maurras and Réal del Sarte, and Fascists, such as Brasillach, when they write of the war they witness.

---

[2] Eugen Weber, *The Hollow Years: France in the 1930s* (London: Sinclair-Stevenson, 1995), 120.

As several commentators have observed, before 1936 France had paid Spanish cultural and political life little attention. French intellectuals of the 1930s would have been familiar with certain classics of Spanish literature, principally *Don Quixote*, but even here this appears to be through reputation rather than detailed study. Prior to 1936 French cultural representations of Spain, when Spain was represented at all, tended to highlight what Nick Hewitt refers to as a "generalised Spanish exoticism" rather than a subtle understanding of France's neighbour across the Pyrenees.[3] From Corneille's *Le Cid* to the novels of Montherlant, Hewitt argues, Spain is portrayed as the locus of a constant battleground between the forces of passion and abandon on one side, and reason, duty and honour on the other. This opposition between chaos and order, deemed by pre-war French literature essentially Spanish, supplies the writers of the far Right with not only an understanding of why the Civil War broke out, but an established narrative structure and source of metaphor for the war they were to represent.

Yet, whilst grounding the Civil War in a supposedly essentially Spanish battle between competing, eternal national values, these writers also perceive in the Spanish Civil War a Europe-wide struggle for ideological and moral supremacy. Maurice Bardèche and Robert Brasillach, in their early history of the conflict, were eager to internationalize this modern conflict between the Left and Right, arguing that this international conflict is rendered all the more pertinent precisely because it takes place in Spain:

> In the grey smoke of shellfire, under a sky crisscrossed by Russian and Italian fighter planes, through blood, pain, and death, ideological contradictions were being resolved in this ancient land of conquerors and acts of faith. Spain was conferring its blessing and its nobility of the war of ideas.[4]

Spain renders the immediate, present-day conflict eternal. Yet such an understanding is only possible through the cultural inheritance that the French observer perceives not in a conflict he in fact rarely witnesses, due to the restrictions placed on his tour, but which is ever-

---

3 Nicholas Hewitt, "Partir pour quelque part: French Novelists of the Right and the Spanish Metaphor, 1936-39," *Romance Studies*, 3 (Winter 1983-84): 117.

4 Maurice Bardèche and Robert Brasillach, *Histoire de la guerre d'Espagne* (1939; Paris: Godefroy de Bouillon, 1995), 406. All translations are my own except where indicated.

present in his own understanding of the war and of Spain itself. This war may well be "modern warfare where chemistry plays its role [...]," but it is also, for Massis and Brasillach, "eternal Spain's war, that of the *reconquista* and that of the Cid, where battle is above all personal combat and where disdain for death and honour take pride of place."[5] As this suggests, it is Corneille's play *Le Cid* and the Cid legend more generally which form the myth through which the French far Right begins to interpret the Spanish Civil War.

According to both narratives, that of the legend (promoted through Spanish epic poetry and ballads) and that of Corneille's play, the Cid is a faithful defender of Catholicism and of the Spanish monarchy, preserving Spain from the Eastern other in the form of the Moors who threatened it in the eleventh century. What Corneille adds to the historical legend in his seventeenth-century tragi-comedy is the conflict between duty and honour, on the one hand, and love, passion and personal happiness, on the other. The Cid must choose between his love of Chimène and obeying his father's command that he avenge an affront suffered at the hands of Chimène's father, Don Gomès, by killing the latter in a duel. The Cid obeys his father. Chimène then asks the King to sentence him to death, but the situation is resolved by the Cid successfully repulsing a surprise attack by the Moors and saving the monarchy. In the light of this, neither the King nor Chimène want to pursue Don Gomès's vengeance and Chimène is ordered to marry the Cid, an order she is now only too happy to obey.

The Cid legend and Corneille's rewriting of it prove a particularly useful narrative for understanding the 1936 siege of the Toledo Alcazar and magnifying it so that it achieves the status of icon for the French far Right. The Alcazar immediately recalls in the mind of the French far Right traveller half-remembered histories of the fortress turned imperial palace and provides a link with the legendary Cid, who was its first governor. Between July and September 1936, a handful of Nationalist army cadets, their officers and local Civil Guards held off the Republican militia until they were relieved by Franco's defeat of the loyalist forces. The Nationalist victory at Toledo henceforth enabled the French far Right to equate the Nationalist cause with an ongoing and eternal battle with the East. Thus, for enthusiastic far Right historians of the siege, such as Massis and Brasillach, the liberation of the Alcazar constitutes another chapter in this history and can be read in such terms:

---

5 Henri Massis and Robert Brasillach, *Les Cadets de l'Alcazar* (Paris: Plon, 1936), 72.

The resistance of the cadets of the Alcazar is the most recent in a series of violently contrasting, colourful images, all blood and gold; it encapsulates the Spanish soul in a powerful symbol which transfigured these combatants from the first day of the war.[6]

There is, in many French far Right narratives of the Alcazar siege, a sense that this site was destined to become the locus of just such a symbolic struggle. Thus, the Tharaud brothers assert that "There are people that destiny has singled out for the most sinister of adventures. Similarly, destiny singles out certain monuments; the Alcazar is one of these."[7] Such an understanding is, of course, the result of hindsight: all of the writers featured here were only able to visit the site long after the battle had been won. It is also a result of the conflation of the Cid legend and of Corneille's work on the subject. This conflation can be seen to be at work again in the narration of the events of late July 1936, which features in all of the travel writings and histories of far Right travellers to Nationalist Spain. On 23 July the Republican militia are alleged to have telephoned General Moscardó, the Nationalist officer in command of the Alcazar, ordering him to surrender. In the course of the call, they informed the besieged General that, if he failed to obey their order, one of his sons, a prisoner of the Republicans, would be executed. The Republicans then allowed Moscardó to talk to his son. The ensuing conversation, reproduced with slight variants in each of the texts studied here, is referred to explicitly in terms of "a Corneillian dialogue [...]" by the travel writer Georges Oudard where national duty and paternal love vie.[8] Moscardó, in response to his son's assurances that he will do as his father bids, is alleged to have replied: "Confide your soul to God, my child, and let His will be done."[9] In Charles Maurras's version this becomes: "I command you to cry 'Long live Spain, Long live Christ the King' and then to die as a hero."[10] The story then tells of how Moscardó hears his son's execution down the telephone line, despite this not taking place until 23 August.[11] Regardless of the story's authenticity, it is clear that the tension reproduced in these exchanges recalls and echoes the

[6] Massis and Brasillach, *Les Cadets de l'Alcazar*, 3. Italicised in the original.

[7] Jérôme and Jules Tharaud, *Cruelle Espagne* (Paris: Plon, 1937), 186.

[8] Georges Oudard, *Chemises noires, brunes et vertes en Espagne* (Paris: Plon, 1938), 122.

[9] Massis and Brasillach, *Les Cadets de l'Alcazar*, 2.

[10] Charles Maurras, *Vers l'Espagne de Franco* (Paris: Editions du Livre Moderne, 1943), 130.

[11] Paul Preston, *A Concise History of the Spanish Civil War* (London: Fontana, 1996), 94.

antithetical tension already known to these French writers and felt by the characters of Corneille's *Le Cid* as they negotiate between what their hearts desire and what their honour dictates.

The trope of the expulsion of the Eastern other from Spanish, and therefore from Western soil, is a further extrapolation from the Cid narratives. Both the play and the legend tell of how the Cid rids Spain, and therefore the European continent, of the Moors. The Civil War is just such a struggle and a further example of Spain's role in this eternal struggle against the Eastern other. The ranks of the Republican army and the International Brigades are therefore alleged by Maurras to be filled with "Communist Jews and German Marxist immigrants [who] come from the four corners of Russia and Poland" and who, for Maurras, and also Maxime Réal del Sarte, threaten Latin civilisation.[12] This assault on *latinité* constitutes the real aim of Spanish Republicanism, as Réal del Sarte asserts: "I've recently come to understand all the more why the red hordes of Madrid clamour in their hate 'Down with Latin civilisation!' This is their real agenda."[13] The internationally, racially and ideologically diverse forces of Republican Spain are nothing other than another barbarous Eastern horde knocking at the door of Western civilisation.

Moreover, as much as the Spanish Civil War is a conflict between the West and the East, between chivalry and barbarity, it is also for the French far Right a battle between believer and non-believer, between the upholder of Catholicism and the infidel. Once more, the echoes of the Cid legend can be heard in these far Right narratives. The real presence of Moors in the ranks of Franco's army, however, is rarely acknowledged in these works. When it is, it is simply neutralised through the claim that Islam too is threatened by the Judeo-Marxist conspiracy that comes from the East. In this, far Right narratives of the war use a process of "inoculation," as Roland Barthes terms it; the reader is "inoculated" against the historic complexities of the war through the partial admission of the truth in order to make greater claims on the myth promoted.[14] Thus, the Tharaud brothers quote one Moorish officer who has just helped to defeat the Republicans at Toledo in order to reassure their readers as to the nobility of the Moors in their common cause with the

---

[12] Maurras, *Vers l'Espagne de Franco*, 49

[13] Maxime Réal del Sarte, *Au pays de Franco, notre frère latin* (Paris: Collection la Caravelle, 1937), 42.

[14] Roland Barthes, *Mythologies* (1957; Paris: Seuil, 2000), 225. Cf. *Mythologies*, trans. Anette Lavers (New York: Hill and Wang, 1973), 145.

Nationalists and to make greater claims for the truthfulness of their pro-Nationalist account.[15]

The Spanish Civil War is therefore narrated in the works of the French far Right through a binary system that opposes West to East, chivalry to barbarity and Catholicism to faithlessness. The purpose of this recourse to a pre-existing and larger cultural narrative as a way of understanding a contemporary conflict was, as Peter Montreath writes, "to transform the war [...] from a contest between rival political ideologies into a contest between moral, metaphysical or even mythical elements, the less tangible the better."[16] The use of existing narratives built on the binary system described above ensures that the war becomes, as Christopher Flood argues, a battle between abstract values that, allegedly, transcend politics.[17] The result is that the Spanish Civil War in these writings appears to be both de-politicised and de-historicised, ever receding in terms of its real, historical tangibility as it retreats into the realm of myth.

Let us now examine more closely how this process of mythification operates through Barthes' explanatory model proposed in *Mythologies*. According to Barthes, a sign in language results from the conjunction of signified and signifier; thus, the rose becomes the sign of my love for another through the conjunction of the rose as signifier and the concept of my passion as signified.[18] Myth, according to Barthes, adopts a similar tripartite system. A myth is thus formed from the conjunction of a signifier and a signified. The signifier of myth, and myth's very foundation, however, adopts the meaning of an earlier system of signs. It is potentially rich in meaning, possessing a history and a past full of ideas, but these are held in reserve by myth in order to exploit the form these supply.[19] The signified of myth is the concept and the motive behind the myth; it is historically specific and exists in order to be appropriated by the reader through the adoption of the myth.

As regards French far Right travel narratives, we can take the Cid legend as the source of the signifier of the myth that these seek to

---

[15] "If Franco's troops hadn't been victorious [here], it would have been the end for Western civilization." Tharaud and Tharaud, *Cruelle Espagne*, 205-6.

[16] Peter Montreath, *Writing the Good Fight: Political Commitment in the International Literature of the Spanish Civil War* (Westport, Conn.: Greenwood Press, 1994), 43.

[17] Christopher Flood, "Crusade or Genocide? French Catholic Discourse on the Spanish Civil War," in J. Pérez and W. Aycock (eds.), *The Spanish Civil War in Literature* (Lubbock, Texas: Texas Technical University Press, 1990), 55-56.

[18] Barthes, *Mythologies*, 185-86.

[19] *Mythologies*, 190-91.

circulate. The Cid legend, principally understood through Corneille's representation of it in *Le Cid*, supplies, through its opposition of passion to duty, abandon to honour and self-containment and, more generally, of East to West, the formal structure of the far Right myth of the war and of Nationalist Spain. Any complexity, historicity and wealth pertaining to the original narrative that now constitutes the signifier of the myth is held in abeyance, impoverished in order to bring forth its primarily formal quality which is then called forth to support the concept behind the myth. We sense, however, that this complexity lurks in the background and that it may even support the veracity of the myth.

The signified of the far Right myth, the concept that conjoins the form, is thus the overarching theme that the present conflict is a conflict between duty, honour, and dignity, on the one hand, and passion, abandon, and indignity, on the other. This historically specific conflict is de-historicised, however, by the impoverishing of the signifier designed to highlight a certain timeless formal state of affairs. The historicity of the concept, its ideological allegiances in the historically and ideologically unresolved present, is translated into "un considérant éternel [...]" (an eternal justification) allowing the signification, the myth itself, to appear, as if by magic, detached from historical conditions.[20] The myth that emerges from these travel narratives of Nationalist Spain and of the Spanish Civil War is consequently removed from the specificity of the war itself; in fact, it is not even concerned with Nationalist Spain. It is that of a generalised far Right to which the French far Right belongs, and whose glory it shall henceforth reflect in the eyes of the reader, which, like that of Nationalist Spain, with its alliance of bourgeois conservatives, monarchists, military and Falangists, stands for eternal, immutable order and the victory of the West over the East. Thus, the very real and continued divisions of the French far Right are masked by the myth of an international alliance of nationalist parties no longer riven by internal differences in their domestic politics and by national rivalries at international level.

Barthes' model of the structuring of myth might therefore be adapted to supply a model for understanding the mythical representation of the Spanish Civil War and Nationalist Spain in French far Right travel narratives as follows:

---

[20] ibid., 198.

SIGNIFIER	SIGNIFIED
(Form)	(Historically-specific concept)
Cid Legend	Spanish Civil War as a battle between order/disorder, duty/abandon, honour/passion etc. Nationalist Spain as a bastion of social harmony and discipline.
SIGNIFICATION	
The far Right are to be equated with eternal order, dignity, harmony etc.	

The war evoked in these works is therefore a myth that functions in order to promote the belief in an eternal and immutable state of affairs and values.

Yet, I would like to conclude by turning my attention to an alternative, yet not, I think, incompatible mythical understanding of the conflict; that explicitly proposed principally by the young French Fascist writer, Robert Brasillach, but which underpins the far Right's mythologisation of the Spanish Civil War more generally. For the most part, Massis and Brasillach's *Les Cadets de l'Alcazar* reflects the mythical model already discussed. Like the Cid and those who fought alongside him, the Alcazar's cadets have fought on behalf of "the Catholic West."[21] Here, as in all other narratives of the Alcazar, the siege is subsumed into the larger established narrative of the Cid legend. Yet, in the conclusion to *Les Cadets de l'Alcazar*, Brasillach, the disciple of Mussolini and Georges Sorel, openly discusses the potential for the Alcazar to become a mythical counterpoint to the myths of Soviet Communism. According to Brasillach (and one senses that it is Brasillach writing here, and not the faithful acolyte of the monarchist Action Française, Massis): "Only Russian Bolshevism has understood the value of images. [In Soviet images] a whole series of symbols is raised up before the eyes of the masses in order to magnify the work behind it, to spread its mystique."[22]

The echoes of the anarcho-syndicalist Georges Sorel's thinking are evident here. Sorel's political myth establishes an event in the future towards which the people of the present work. It does this through the use of images representing action and the active process of change, Sorel's preferred myth being that of a general strike which would bring about the conditions necessary for proletarian revolution. Thus,

---

[21] Massis and Brasillach, *Les Cadets de l'Alcazar*, 92.
[22] *Les Cadets de l'Alcazar*, 91.

according to Zeev Sternhell, the Sorelian myth "was thought and action; it was a creation of legend, and it enabled the individual to live that legend instead of living out history. It enabled one to pass beyond a detestable present."[23] For Sorel, therefore, "the myth must be judged as a means of acting on the present [...]."[24] According to Brasillach, therefore, the Alcazar episode supplies "Western man" with an exemplary image that should be magnified and mystified so that we too, Brasillach's readers, might rise up to confront "another threat emerging from a perhaps more insidious East."[25]

Brasillach's use of the Spanish Civil War as a political myth, in the Sorelian sense of the term, reflects the French far Right's more general use of the Spanish Civil War as an image, duly magnified, mythologised and mystified, held up to its French readership as a goal to which it should aspire. Like the Spanish Nationalists, Brasillach argues, the French far Right are already engaged in this eternal conflict against the Eastern other on behalf of Western civilisation. However, the mythologisation of the Spanish Civil War in these narratives does not simply serve to remind their readers of this apparently immutable state of affairs; it also serves as a call to arms, as a promise of action after relative passivity in the form of a national revolution, the goal of which would be a united national front, comprising of traditionalists, Catholics, monarchists and Fascists, which would overthrow the Soviet-inspired French Popular Front. French far Right representations of the Spanish Civil War therefore operate through two different, but affiliated types of myth; on the one hand, the echoing of the Cid legend, with its binary opposition of values, appeals to traditionalists through its evocation of the eternal and the immutable. On the other, the use of the political myth, based on the Sorelian model, is designed to appeal to modernists and those who crave action after the passivity of recent years.

Yet, the myth upon which both understandings of the conflict are founded is that of a narrative with little grounding in concrete, historic reality. Unlike Sorel's general strike, grounded in the social reality of the worker's ability to withdraw labour, the foundation myth of these narratives is a largely fictional character located in a series of legendary

---

23 Zeev Sternhell (with Mario Sznajder and Maia Asheri), *The Birth of Fascist Ideology: From Cultural Rebellion to Political Revolution*, trans. David Maisel (Princeton: Princeton University Press, 1994), 59.

24 Georges Sorel, *Reflections on Violence*, trans. T.E. Hulme (London: George Allen & Unwin, 1925), 135-36.

25 Massis and Brasillach, *Les Cadets de l'Alcazar*, 91.

events; the Cid of historic reality was not always the steadfast defender of the West that these writers would have him be, but a mercenary who fought for both Catholic and Moor depending on his allegiance of the moment. The myth of Spain evoked in these works is therefore one that, as Barthes argues of myth more generally, reduces complexities and denies historicity. The Spanish Civil War for these writers is a narrative and not an historical event. Ironically, in their efforts to see in the war and their own domestic conflict the chivalry of the Cid's world, these writers share not so much the dilemmas, decisions and values of Corneille's hero, but reveal rather the misjudgements and deceptions of Cervantes's; like Don Quixote, they forever believe themselves engaged in a battle of absolutes only to be found in the pages of myths and legends.

REPRESENTATIONS OF "BOHEMIA" IN THE WORKS OF LIBUŠE MONÍKOVÁ (1945-1998)[1]

Brigid Haines

The work of Libuše Moníková fits extraordinarily well into a volume on myths, foundation texts and imagined communities, especially one published in Prague. The Czech-born Moníková, who wrote in German by choice, crosses borders between languages, cultures, political regimes, literary genres, and media, while constantly foregrounding the omnipresence of the past in the present. My research project aims to read her not as a woman writer or a marginal figure on the German literary scene, but within the appropriate Czech contexts that continued to influence her work after she left Czechoslovakia in 1971. I will confine my remarks here to two aspects of her Czechness, namely her acceptance of the Shakespearean topos "Bohemia by the sea," and the representation of Czech history in her works.

Bohemia by the Sea

Shakespeare commentators differ on whether his ascription of a sea coast to Bohemia in *The Winter's Tale* resulted from ignorance or

---

[1] This paper contains extracts from Brigid Haines, "'Liegt Böhmen noch am Meer,' or, When Writers Redraw Maps," in Juliet Wigmore and Ian Foster (eds.), *Neighbours and Strangers: Literary and Cultural Relations in Germany, Austria and Central Europe since 1989* (Amsterdam: Rodopi, 2004), 7-25, and Brigid Haines, "Barren Territory for Grand Narratives? Czech History in the Works of Libuše Moníková," in Brigid Haines and Lyn Marven (eds.), *Libuše Moníková: In Memoriam* (Amsterdam: Rodopi, 2005), 179-200.

represented a wilful appeal to fantasy for perhaps political reasons. It has been argued that he turned to romance after the accession of the authoritarian James I because it allowed him to continue to write about political themes without appearing to do so: Lear and Othello had been punished for their human failings, while the history plays had allowed for reflection on the traits of the ideal king; King Leontes, by contrast, is forgiven for his tyrannical behaviour as husband and king because the genre of romance allows for a reconciliatory ending. In untying Bohemia from its geographical location in order to explore political themes, Shakespeare created a trend which was continued in the twentieth century by Franz Fühmann, Volker Braun, Ingeborg Bachmann and Libuše Moníková, among others. They all work intertextually with Shakespeare, playing with the utopian or dystopian potential of his topos in order to comment on contemporary political developments. They do not, in other words, simply invoke the Bohemia associated with the German phrase, "Das sind mir böhmische Dörfer" (which roughly translates as "it's all Greek to me").

Fühmann's story "Bohemia by the Sea" (1962), for example, uses the topos to justify the controversial expulsion of the Sudeten Germans from Czechoslovakia after the war and to praise the German Democratic Republic as the incarnation of a really existing socialism where those expellees who were innocent find security.[2] Volker Braun's play of the same name (1992), "a merry tragedy,"[3] deals with the crisis of ideology following the collapse of the Eastern bloc states. His Bohemia by the sea is a dystopia in which the old values are no longer valid and chaos dominates in the sexual, political and environmental spheres. There is "nothing to hold on to"[4] in this play. But the references to Bohemia should be read in the context of Braun's longstanding preoccupation with the Prague Spring, in the expression of which he had already used the phrase "Böhmen am Meer" some years before. As a GDR author, he was not allowed to criticise the Soviet invasion of 1968, but his poem "Prag" nevertheless expressed his shock. "Bohemia by the sea" became:

---

2 Franz Fühmann, "Böhmen am Meer," in *Erzählungen 1955-1975* (Rostock: Hinstorff, 1993), 285-318.

3 Volker Braun, *Böhmen am Meer*, in *Texte in zeitlicher Folge 10* (Halle: Mitteldeutscher Verlag, 1993), 61-116. This is how it is described in the blurb to the first edition. English translations of titles and quotations are my own.

4 Theodore Fiedler, "Apocalypse Now? Reading Volker Braun's *Böhmen am Meer*," in Margy Gerber and Roger Woods (eds.), *Changing Identities in East Germany: Selected Papers from the Nineteenth and Twentieth New Hampshire Symposia. Studies in GDR Culture and Society 14/15* (Lanham: University Press of America, 1996), 100.

"Bohemia / By the sea / Of blood?"[5] implying that the ideals of "Böhmen am Meer" had been betrayed. Bachmann, by contrast, called her complex and ambiguous poem "Bohemia *Lies* by the Sea", thus stressing the positive in Shakespeare's "mistake."[6] It is about a crisis of faith, a search for identity in a post-Holocaust world of collapsing certainties; it gives a positive value to rootlessness, to "bohemianism" and asserts the power of the imagination: the loss of "Heimat" can mean being at home everywhere.

It might be expected that Czech Bohemians (as opposed to German Bohemians like Fühmann, or would-be "Bohemians" like Bachmann) would object to the use of their country as an image of utopian longing or dystopian gloom. But clearly this is not the case for Moníková. In her essay on Bachmann, she affirmed Bohemia by the sea, as "the unreachable empire of poetry on the horizon."[7] This is because her most enduring concern was the trauma occasioned by Czech history, and in particular the great betrayals of the twentieth century: 1938 and 1968. A defining moment for her was when "the burning youth" in Braun's poem about the Prague Spring, Jan Palach, set himself alight in protest against his countrymen's passive response to the Soviet invasion: Moníková cannot forget that she was yards away at the time, in a cinema.[8] She identifies with the feeling of helplessness in Bachmann, "the feeling after a catastrophe has occurred,"[9] and approves of the use of "bohemian" as a synonym for "set free, unprotected, unanchored."[10]

Therefore, just as for Shakespeare, for Fühmann, Braun, Bachmann and Moníková, Bohemia by the sea does not so much signal an escape from politics as a way to reflect indirectly on it. They show that mapmaking is too important to be left to the cartographers, the politicians and (in the era of global capital) the business interests they serve. Moníková in particular places her faith in an imaginary cartography – she allows Bohemia to be placed by the sea – because the maps on which Bohemia has been and still is represented, are "cadasters

---

[5] Volker Braun, "Prag," in *Texte in zeitlicher Folge 4* (Halle: Mitteldeutscher Verlag, 1990), 99-101.

[6] Ingeborg Bachmann, "Böhmen liegt am Meer," in *Werke I: Gedichte, Hörspiele, Libretti, Übersetzungen*, 2nd ed. (Munich: Piper, 1982), 167-68.

[7] Libuše Moníková, *Prager Fenster* (Munich: Hanser, 1994), 62.

[8] Moníková, *Prager Fenster*, 113.

[9] *Prager Fenster*, 59.

[10] ibid., 60.

of power"[11] where Bohemia is dominated and marginalised. She lays claim to a share in Europe's coastline (which, the historian Norman Davies points out, was established long before any land frontiers)[12] because for her national borders are associated with anxiety. They may not protect: they can be breached and redrawn, which is what has happened in living memory. This causes trauma. Moníková writes that after 1968, she experienced "a country, a Bohemia, which no longer lay by the sea – the armies came and moved it where it was to belong, on the edge of the steppes."[13]

Czech History

Moníková s protagonists are shown wrestling with this trauma, often by rehearsing historical data in conversation in an effort to understand it, while at the same time, at the macro level, each work also foregrounds Czech history by means of a central allegory, metaphor or symbol which encapsulates something of the fate of the Czechs. Her first novel, *Damage* (*Eine Schädigung*, 1981), opens with the rape of a woman and invites the reader to understand this violent act as an allegory of the "rape" of Czechoslovakia in 1968. The protagonist of *Pavane for a Dead Infanta* (*Pavane für eine verstorbene Infantin*, 1983) takes to her wheelchair although there is nothing physically wrong with her. Moníková's third, longest and most highly acclaimed novel, the picaresque, Švejkian *The Façade* (*Die Fassade*, 1987), is organised around an equally striking metaphor, namely the endless, Sisyphean task of restoring the sgraffiti on a Bohemian castle, a task which represents the ongoing, subversive memory work of Czech history at a time (the period of "normalisation" of the 1970s) when official discourses of history allowed no space for organised resistance or personal expression.

Drift Ice (Treibeis, 1992) employs the metaphor of drift ice to explore the twentieth-century condition of wandering exile. *Transfigured Night* (*Verklärte Nacht*, 1996), the last completed novel, set in Prague in the last days of Czechoslovakia (late 1992), seeks a resolution of historical tensions between Czechs and Germans and strives towards closure. A work of homecoming and reconciliation, its central metaphor is a love affair between a returning Czech exile and a Sudeten German.

---

[11] Derek Sayer, *The Coasts of Bohemia: A Czech History* (Princeton: Princeton University Press, 1998), 16.

[12] Norman Davies, *Europe: A History* (London: Pimlico, 1997), 16.

[13] Moníková, *Prager Fenster*, 57.

Moníková's final word, however, was not to be "transfiguration" but the more negative and disorientating "falling:" the unfinished, posthumously published novel *Giddiness* (Der Taumel, 2000) uses the metaphor of epilepsy, the falling sickness, to explore life under normalisation. Here the historical discussions which have been a feature of all her novels are taken up again by Brandl and Halina; the latter speaks for another significant group of the absent in postwar Czechoslovakia, the Jews, for Halina is a survivor whose family was exterminated in Treblinka. Moníková's essays and speeches, written for the large part just after the Velvet Revolution, are also published under a title strong in both old and new symbolism: *Prague Windows (Prager Fenster*, 1994). This alludes to the act of defenestration which has occurred three times in the nation's history at times of crisis,[14] but now it takes on a new, personal gloss: Moníková interprets it as a cause of optimism that on her last visit, the people of Prague had all cleaned their windows.[15] Like the fiction, these essays explore traces of Czech history in the continuously evolving present and are very much concerned with the place of Prague within Europe.

A rape, a wheelchair, the restoration of a castle façade, drift ice, Prague windows, transfiguration, falling: the peculiarity and inventiveness of the images show the complexity and resistance to representation of the history Moníková is trying to convey and also her persistence in returning to the problem from different angles. The chronological and emotional trajectory implied above – from profound shock at the crushing of the Prague Spring via the depression of normalisation and the memory work of exile to the hopefulness and confusions of post-Velvet Revolution homecoming – betrays the author's closeness to her material and its autobiographical base. The events of 1968, which reinforced her sense of Czechness,[16] are, however, seen as secondary to

---

[14] On 30 July 1419, a crowd stormed the Town Hall of the New Town and threw its councillors from the windows, marking a new stage in the Hussite revolution. On 23 May 1618, a mob threw the Catholic imperial officials from the window of Prague Castle; they survived, but the Thirty Years War was unleashed. On 10 March 1948, Jan Masaryk, Foreign Minister and son of Tomáš Masaryk, died after jumping or being pushed out of a window of the Foreign Ministry building.

[15] Moníková, *Prager Fenster*, 5.

[16] She was not alone in this; Milan Kundera writes: "In August 1968 the Russian army had invaded the country; for a week the streets in all the cities howled with rage. The country had never been so thoroughly a homeland, or the Czechs so Czech." Milan Kundera, *Ignorance*, trans. (from the French) Linda Asher (London: Faber and Faber, 2002), 67.

the primary trauma of the Munich Agreement: "Munich is for a Czech a national trauma, synonym for betrayal and ignominy."[17]

The tension between didacticism and powerlessness, between emotional engagement and detachment – indeed between allegory and symbol – lies at the heart of Moníková's project, which is powered by a political desire to counter the official, closed histories of the Communist era and also to enlighten her German readership. Writing in German gave her access to the audience whose blind spots about their small and apparently inconsequential neighbour she hoped to address. In acting as a mediator of and an advocate for Czech history and identity in a court perceived as hostile, Moníková proposes a concept of national identity which is composed of loyalty to the state founded by Tomáš Masaryk in 1918 as well as to a much older cultural entity based on language which stretches back to the mythological beginnings of Bohemia.[18]

Moníková is by no means unique in this dual loyalty to a state and a cultural tradition. It is my contention that the two broad impulses in her work – the clearly visible poststructuralist and political desire to counter official histories by allowing space within her literary text for memory, subjective experience and the most diverse material, however confusing and uncontrollable the effect of this, and also the underlying, modernist, patriotic desire to assert continuities in and state the case for Czech history – create a productive tension that reflects current debates in Czech historiography.

Barren Territory for Grand Narratives

Like Moníková, the Canadian historian and sociologist Derek Sayer highlights the instability and the continual reinvention of Czech history, as well as the constant "call to history."[19] Seen from the outside, he argues, Czech history is "barren territory for grand narratives" because it appears to consist of little more than "an incoherent series of lurching discontinuities" with no clear trajectory and no

> unambiguous and unified subject. Bohemia slips into a narrative no-man's-land, where it becomes a passive victim of its unfortunate situation between opposed political and cultural

---

[17] Moníková, *Prager Fenster*, 81.
[18] Helga G. Braunbeck, "The Body of the Nation: The Texts of Libuše Moníková," *Monatshefte*, 89.4 (1997): 489-506, 490.
[19] Maria Dowling, *Czechoslovakia* (Oxford: Arnold, 2002), 68.

worlds: Catholic and Protestant, German and Slav, capitalist and communist, democratic and totalitarian.[20]

Although periodically at the centre of international action, the Czech lands recede from view in the meantime. This of course says more about the blindness of the Western onlooker and of grand narrative history than it does about the reality of Bohemia, and Sayer suggests that a "Copernican turn" is needed so that Bohemia is taken as the vantage point.[21]

Sayer's title, *The Coasts of Bohemia: A Czech History*, plays on the fluidity of real and imagined Bohemias. He stresses that, whatever the historical evidence may reveal about outstanding figures and events from the past – typically the Přemysl dynasty, Charles IV, the Hussites and the Battle of the White Mountain – what is significant in the creation and cultivation of a collective Czech identity is the way these become "materials of memory,"[22] to be continually reinvented and ascribed new meanings to suit, in turn, the National Revivalists of the nineteenth century who were retrospectively creating a sense of Czech nationhood, Tomáš Masaryk who sought to justify the new independent creation, "Czechoslovakia," in 1918, the Nazi regime, the Communists who were in power from 1948 until the Velvet Revolution, and also Václav Havel and others since. The palimpsest, in other words, takes precedence over any originary meaning.

Moníková's eponymous façade, with its ludic quality and in-built irreverence for all totalising systems, conceived as her anti-ideological riposte to the prescriptive and closed historiography of the Communist era, is precisely such a palimpsest as Sayer describes. Reinvention, and the porous boundary between history and fiction are invoked in the very location of the castle that the façade adorns, referred to as Friedland-Litomyšl. It is based on two real castles which have been deliberately combined to create a half-fictional, half-factual place. Friedland is a German castle in northern Bohemia, with historical links to Wallenstein, and visited occasionally by Kafka on business. It has been subject to speculation as the source of Kafka's castle. Litomyšl is a Renaissance

---

[20] Sayer, *The Coasts of Bohemia*, 15. Though Sayer does not quote him, the concept of grand narratives, or metanarratives, is taken from Lyotard; see Jean-François Lyotard, *The Postmodern Condition: A Report on Knowledge* (Manchester: Manchester University Press, 1984).

[21] Sayer, *The Coasts of Bohemia*, 13.

[22] *The Coasts of Bohemia*, 29-52.

castle in eastern Bohemia with strong links to the National Revival.[23] It is Litomyšl which has a sgrafitti façade; it was restored by four artists between 1974 and 1992.[24] The eight thousand non-repeating panels were recreated, partly from original designs but also with the use of the artists' imaginations. The metaphorical potential of this appealed to Moníková.

Her four artists are working in a medium, plaster, which has a very limited life, mainly because of its constant exposure to the weather. The task is thus potentially infinite in duration. The artists feel free to take enormous liberties, adjusting existing figures as they see fit, and creating new ones from whatever takes their fancy. History is thus continually effaced and reinvented from below, with injections of subjective meaning. The spectator on the ground has an invidious choice between focusing on one of the individual panels and losing the big picture, or standing back and obtaining only a serial impression of the relevant wall in which details are lost and an artificial three-dimensional effect resulting from the shading of the panels is accepted as true. This dichotomy mimics the incompatibility of narratives of history that perforce simplify and falsify, and individual experience that resists the big picture.

The façade, which has been described as "a striking metaphor for work on the myth of history,"[25] illustrates the paradox, also inherent in Sayer, that in writing about what is most intimately Czech, Moníková was also enabling her foreign readers to see history through new eyes, for it indicates also the wider applicability of the topos for history writing *tout court*. The reader is invited to revel in the fact that the raw material of history – facts, evidence, testimony, casts of characters, all traces of the past in the present – can be emplotted in different ways, officially and unofficially, or may escape emplotment altogether, an insight which renders all historical narratives partial.[26]

Moníková addresses the created nature of Czech identity directly when her four artists act out a spontaneous comic drama between four

---

[23] For an elaboration of these links, see Braunbeck, "The Body of the Nation," 495-6.

[24] Two sculptors, Zdeněk Palcr (a personal friend of Moníková) and Olbram Zoubek, and two painters, Stanislav Podhrázský and Václav Boštík.

[25] Jürgen Eder, "Die Jahre mit Acht – 1918, 1938, 1948, 1968... Zum Historischen bei Libuše Moníková," in Delf Schmidt and Michael Schwidtal (eds.), *Prag – Berlin: Libuše Moníková* (Reinbek: Rowohlt, 1999), 87.

[26] For an elaboration of the relationship between history and narrative form, see Hayden White, *Metahistory: The Historical Imagination in Nineteenth-Century Europe* (Baltimore: Johns Hopkins University Press, 1973), and Hayden White, *Tropics of Discourse: Essays in Cultural Criticism* (Baltimore: Johns Hopkins University Press, 1978).

of the National Revivalists, Magdalena Dobromila Rettigová, Bedřich Smetana, the scientist Jan Evangelista Purkyně and the writer Alois Jirásek, poking fun at their pretensions as they do so. For example, Rettigová's "Czech" recipes are shown to be borrowed from Hungarian sources,[27] and Smetana, the composer of the romantic, nationalist anthem "My Country," has a shaky command of Czech[28] and uses a police informer as his librettist.[29] What is lampooned here is the reification of history that results in the exclusion from accepted narratives of complicating detail.

It is possible to see the reinvention of history in *Die Fassade* positively: liberated from constraints, this playfulness functions as a counter to the disempowering lack of comprehension which is a symptom of trauma. By showing the relativism of "victors' history,"[30] and insisting on alternative, sometimes only partially transmitted images, Moníková's work shows an optimism that history can be recreated with aesthetic means and points the way towards an open national history. Yet *Die Fassade*, which ends as it began with the work on the façade, is anti-teleological, implying no future in which the work of the artists will serve as anything other than private resistance. As such it can be also read, despite its humour, as a pessimistic monument to the leaden time of normalisation when the grand narrative of the onward march of the proletariat seemed a hollow jest, but the iron grip of the Soviet empire made any other kind of historical progress impossible.

Grand Narratives and Small Histories

Moníková's writing thus reflects and expresses both the trauma arising from events which springs apart any explanatory frameworks, and the peculiarly fractured and malleable nature of Czech history in particular, which is not only a twentieth-century phenomenon. Yet the Copernican turn which Moníková's works effect does not only reveal fragmentation, individual acts of resistance, recycling and discontinuity. It also, as Sayer implied, reveals different continuities which might be more visible to Czech readers. As we have seen, Moníková is well aware of the constructed nature of Czechs' sense of identity and history and is sceptical of myth building and the petrifaction of values. Yet, like many

---

[27] Libuše Moníková, *Die Fassade: M.N.O.P.Q.* (Munich: dtv, 1990), 122.
[28] Moníková, *Die Fassade*, 121-22.
[29] *Die Fassade*, 129.
[30] Eder, "Die Jahre mit Acht," 93.

Czechs, she inherits and reproduces, in her essays and interviews, and frequently through the mouthpiece of her characters, certain concerns which date from the National Revival, namely a patriotic attachment to the continuity of the Czech nation, and in particular to its expression in the First Czechoslovak Republic, a tendency to define Czech identity in relation to Germans rather than, for example, Slovaks, an underlying warmth towards the Russians and fellow Slavs, and an ambivalence towards her fellow Czechs. These are not personal idiosyncrasies but can be traced to what one might call the Czechs' own grand narratives, or rather, to borrow a term from the philosopher Jan Patočka (1907-1977), from their "small history." Patočka saw the late Middle Ages as the time when the Czechs had had their own "great history" within Europe, and argued that greatness had been retained for as long as Czechness was not an issue. The chance of greatness was lost with the Battle of the White Mountain in 1620 and the Czechs' "small history," with its concern with nationhood and survival, sealed with the National Revival in the nineteenth century.[31] The most influential text here was František Palacký's *History of the Czech Nation in Bohemia and Moravia* (1836-1867), which acquired the status of a national epic:

> For Palacký, the very beginning of Czech recorded history is characterised by the "old-Slavonic democratic spirit," standing in sharp contrast to German feudalism. What later came to be seen as his "philosophy of Czech history" is his view of that history as the continuous realisation of the nation's libertarian, egalitarian, and democratic spirit in the constant struggle against German autocracy.[32]

A key component of the National Revival in the nineteenth century was thus the new self-definition of the Czechs as an emerging nation in relation to their perceived oppressors, the Germans, and in friendship with other Slav nations.

In mourning the lost democracy of the First Republic,[33] Moníková joins other Czech patriots who, the anthropologist Ladislav Holy tells us, tend to view its founding as one of only two glorious victories in the

---

[31] Robert Pynsent, *Questions of Identity: Czech and Slovak Ideas of Nationality and Personality* (Budapest: Central European University Press, 1994), 184.

[32] Ladislav Holy, *The Little Czech and the Great Czech Nation: National Identity and the Post-Communist Social Transformation* (Cambridge: Cambridge University Press, 1996), 81.

[33] Libuše Moníková, *Prager Fenster: Essays* (Munich: Hanser, 1994), 83.

modern period (the other being 1989),[34] despite the fact that it was an artificial creation which effaced differences between Czechs and Slovaks, creating a spurious "Czechoslovak" language and nationality, and relegated the German and Hungarian populations to the status of minorities. Though undoubtedly democratic in comparison with its immediate neighbours, historians now point out that it had major flaws, for example, "severe political censorship of the press" and widespread police violence.[35] In fieldwork conducted in 1992, Holy established, however, that a majority of living Czechs had no personal experience of democracy, yet it lived on in their social memory.[36] Moreover, Czechs "conceptualise their nation as a natural entity that has existed for at least a millennium."[37] At various times, there has been a political need to do this; for example, Maria Dowling points out that the "call to history" was needed in 1945 because Edvard Beneš and others feared that Czechoslovakia might not be revived at all as it was widely viewed in the West as an experiment which had failed,[38] and Braunbeck reminds us that loyalty to the Republic held its citizens together during the Communist era.[39] Holy shows how a strong awareness of cultural continuity pervaded the events of the Velvet Revolution. This powerful sense of cultural continuity (and statues of the legendary Duchess Libuše are commonplace in Prague) can be traced back to Palacký, who, in his later years, rejected the hope of a future within a federalised Austria that he had entertained in 1848, declaring instead, "We were here before Austria and we shall be here after it."[40] Sayer and Moníková use the same striking illustration of how this popular sense of national continuity was maintained under Communist rule: in 1970 the Communists banned the singer Marta Kubišová for a song with the lyrics "Now, that the government of your affairs / Returns to you, people." These words originated with Jan Amos Komenský, the philosopher exiled after the Battle of the White Mountain in 1620, were inscribed on Jan Hus's memorial (unveiled 6 July 1915), and repeated by both Tomáš Masaryk and Václav Havel.[41]

---

[34] Holy, *The Little Czech and the Great Czech Nation*, 130.

[35] Pynsent, *Questions of Identity*, 179.

[36] Holy, *The Little Czech and the Great Czech Nation*, 79.

[37] *The Little Czech and the Great Czech Nation*, 38.

[38] Maria Dowling, *Czechoslovakia* (Oxford: Arnold, 2002), 68.

[39] Braunbeck, "The Body of the Nation," 502.

[40] Quoted in Holy, *The Little Czech and the Great Czech Nation*, 38.

[41] Sayer, *The Coasts of Bohemia*, 270. Kubišová remained banned until the Velvet Revolution – see Dowling, *Czechoslovakia*, 123. Moníková refers to Havel's speech in

Moníková's ambivalence about her fellow Czechs – celebrating martyrs and unsung heroes, such as Palach,[42] the writer Božena Němcová,[43] the assassins of Reinhard Heydrich[44] and those citizens who boycotted German cinema newsreels during the Nazi occupation,[45] while regretting Czech cowardice and passivity, for example[46] – is also not a personal idiosyncrasy but has deep cultural roots. Holy demonstrates that such ambivalence is typical of Czechs, who are, as a nation, extremely self-critical but also take huge pride in the image of the Czech nation as democratic, well-educated and highly cultured.[47] It is worth noting in this respect that all Moníková's major protagonists are artists or intellectuals, in keeping with the high regard in which culture is held by the Czechs, seen in the cemetery at Vyšehrad in Prague, where artists and writers since the National Revival are buried and which Leonora Marty, the returning exile in *Verklärte Nacht*, visits as part of her reintegration into Czech culture.[48] Indeed Brandl, Moníková's final literary creation, is an artist of inner emigration: he will not allow his work to be shown at home or exported to the West; all he can do is pass on his humanist values to his students.

A House of Mirrors

Insofar as it is characterised by rupture, reinvention and, in the twentieth century in particular, by trauma, Moníková does demonstrate that Czech history is barren territory for grand narratives. Her fractured and non-teleological presentation of history is curiously appropriate for an age where the twin Enlightenment-derived paradigms of history as progress and the onward march of the proletariat have lost their currency, and

---

her essay, "Semiaride Landschaft mit Küste: Neues Verhältnis Ost – West?," *Prager Fenster*, 18. Another example of the recycling of materials of memory is that Havel's philosophy of "life in truth" is a deliberate recycling of Hus's "the truth prevails," which is now part of the new republic's coat of arms. Holy, *The Little Czech and the Great Czech Nation*, 40.

[42] Moníková, *Prager Fenster*, 104-13.

[43] Moníková, *Die Fassade*, 23-24.

[44] Moníková, *Prager Fenster*, 16.

[45] Moníková, *Verklärte Nacht* (Munich: Hanser, 1996), 116.

[46] Moníková, *Treibeis* (Munich: Hanser, 1992), 227.

[47] Holy, *The Little Czech and the Great Czech Nation*, 74-77.

[48] Holy points out that the Velvet Revolution was led by artists and intellectuals. Holy, *The Little Czech and the Great Czech Nation*, 140. This marks a significant difference from the "Wende" in the GDR where intellectuals were quickly outmanoeuvred by popular feeling.

reminds us that history now must accommodate the subjective and allow space for the forgotten, what is not yet and perhaps never to be emplotted.

When Peter Filkins described *The Façade* in the *New York Times* as a "house of mirrors"[49] he unwittingly refashioned a central metaphor from Palacký for the latter half of the twentieth century. Palacký intended his work to be a mirror in which the Czech nation would recognise itself and feel an enhanced sense of oneness and pride. Moníková retains a little of his didacticism and a lot of the patriotism. But despite her desire to inform her German readership and to make them undergo just such a Copernican turn as Sayer advocates by questioning the grand narratives which have declared Bohemia marginal (not only Western imperialist narratives but also, particularly in *The Façade*, the Marxist-Leninist one which subjugated many peoples, including the Czechs), her mirrors are kaleidoscopic, reflecting and refracting a plural and dynamic reality. On the other hand, Moníková's deep attachment to the continuity of the Czech nation and the possibility of endlessly redefining it in relation to a changing Europe and her continual search for symbols appropriate to conveying this are a reminder that there is a place for patriotism in modern conceptions of subjectivity.

Moníková disliked the maps and historical narratives on and in which Bohemia was represented because Czechs had little part in their making. This changed in 1918 when Czechoslovakia as a political entity was created. That she should be outraged by its forced interruption in 1939 and its repression in 1968, and mourn its passing in 1993 is hardly surprising. Neither is it surprising that she should endorse Bohemias of the mind and the imagination, claim a share in what is most essentially European – its coast – and have frequent recourse to the same store of myths, facts and stories used by generations of others to reinvent a sense of Czechness.

---

[49] Peter Filkins, "Fractured By Reality," *The New York Times,* 5 January 1992, section 7, 10.

QUOTING EUROPE: MOTTOMANIA IN THE ROMANTIC AGE[1]

Rainier Grutman

In 1832, the Spanish columnist Mariano José de Larra chastised his countrymen for their overabundant use of quotes and mottoes. Questioning the purpose of these adornments, he claimed "pedantry has always been, in every nation, the forerunner of periods of literary decadence."[2] According to Larra, Spain's literature was in a sorry enough state and had no need for such derivative practices. When one's own ideas are sound and truthful, he went on to say, relying on someone else's authority is superfluous; when they are not, neither Horace nor Aristotle will compensate for one's stupidities. He took further exception to the tendency to quote in Latin and French, adding that there was no need "to look for water in foreign rivers:" *"almost everything has been said and written in Castilian* [Spanish]."[3]

---

[1] The research leading up to this paper was funded by a grant from the Social Sciences and Humanities Research Council of Canada for the project "Intertextualité et idéologie: usages de la citation à l'époque romantique."

[2] "[E]l pedantismo ha sido siempre en todas las naciones el precursor de las épocas de decadencia de las letras." Juan Pérez de Munguía (pseudonym of Mariano José de Larra), "Manía de citas y epígrafes," *El pobrecito hablador. Revista satírica de costumbres*, 6 (Nov. 1832): 20. See also Mariano José de Larra, *Artículos completos*, ed. Melchor de Almagro San Martín (Madrid: Aguilar, 1968), 909. Unless otherwise indicated, all translations are mine.

[3] "Nosotros [...] desearíamos que, más celosos de nuestro orgullo nacional, no fuésemos por agua a los ríos extranjeros, teniéndolos caudalosos en nuestra casa. [...] *Creemos que*

Larra, it should be pointed out, was a satirical writer. In his many contributions to (often short-lived) periodicals, he examined Spanish society with a very critical eye, repeatedly mocking its closed-mindedness and its lack of refined culture. We would therefore be well-advised not to take his article on what he calls a "manía de citas y epígrafes," a *mottomania* in other words, at face value. How, for instance, could Larra, himself the son of an *afrancesado* – the nickname routinely given to Spaniards who had embraced the French way of life a little too eagerly, especially during the rule of Joseph Bonaparte – disapprove of anyone well-read in the language of Molière? And what are we to think of the fact that Larra had himself practiced some of the excesses he would later criticize, using for instance the very quotes that had, in his view, been turned into clichés.[4] These and other details seem to point to the supremely ironic nature of his 1832 article.

However oblique and tongue-in-cheek Larra's observations may be, they do raise some legitimate questions about the Romantic infatuation with mottoes. Considering their sheer number, his choice of words seems justified. For more than a century, solemn Latin quotes had been adorning title pages of books,[5] but by the 1820s, all kinds of textual fragments had become fashionable as headers of individual poems, chapters, or even newspaper articles. Larra is also right in pointing out their multilingual dimension: when quoting foreign writers, mottoes often did so in the original language, without providing a translation. For the Spanish satirist, this was the ultimate proof of pedantry on the part of his fellow writers, and at the same time of "puerile vanity"[6] on the

---

casi todo está dicho y escrito en castellano." Larra, "Manía de citas y epígrafes," 22-23 (1832); 910-11 (1968).

[4] In 1828, Larra begins a scathing review of *Trente ans ou la vie d'un joueur*, a play by Victor Ducange, with the very quote from Boileau's *Art poétique* ("C'est un droit qu'à la porte, on achète en entrant") that he will be poking fun at four years later. Larra, *Artículos completos*, 461 (1832); 910 (1968). Larra seems to have been wrought with contradictions. Himself a translator of contemporary French playwrights like Scribe, Delavigne and Ducange, he nonetheless criticized the stifling influence of French literature. His long review of Alexandre Dumas' *Antony*, for instance, bears the significant subtitle "Consideraciones acerca de la moderna escuela francesa. Estado de la España. Inoportunidad de estos dramas entre nosotros." ibid., 574-86.

[5] Famous eighteenth-century examples include Montesquieu's *Esprit des lois* (*Prolem sine matre creatam*), Rousseau's *Confessions* (*Intus et in cute*), Buffon's *Histoire naturelle* (*Naturam amplectimur omnem*), and Fielding's *Tom Jones* (*Mores hominum multorum vidit*).

[6] "Verdad es que el vulgo, que ignora la lengua en que se le trae la cita, suele quedar deslumbrado. [...] Cada cual se apresura a reírse, para que no piense el que tiene al lado

part of the average reader, who would rather die than admit to his ignorance of the foreign language, and therefore of the supposedly "deep" meaning of the quote.

In short, Larra confines mottomania to the realm of pedantry and criticizes its perpetrators for their lack of originality: like an oft-repeated dish, he says, "that old litany of worn-out sayings has lost its novelty and seems flavourless to our palate."[7] There is indeed reasonable ground to believe that the unbridled multiplication of mottoes in the early nineteenth century diminished their hermeneutic impact. Originally meant to provide the discriminating reader with interpretive keys to the texts, they had become so common that they could seem gratuitous or even frivolous, a device devoid of any real meaning.

This, however, is exactly the kind of conclusion literary theory warns us not to draw too quickly. Classic structuralism – as it developed in Prague during the 1930s – considered a literary work of art as a structured whole whose parts are interdependent and derive their meaning from their position relative to other parts. As Jan Mukařovský put it in a 1941 essay:

> As a unity of meaning, a structure is more than a mere additive whole, arising through a mere aggregation of parts. The structural whole signifies each of its parts, and each of these parts in turn signifies the whole. Another essential feature of the structure is its dynamic nature, a result of the fact that every individual component has a particular function in the common unity which incorporates it and binds it into the structural whole. The dynamism of the structural whole is created by the energetic nature of these individual functions and their interrelations, which are prone to constant change.[8]

---

que no ha entendido toda la picardía de aquella palabra. *Tal es la candición de nuestra pueril vanidad.*" Larra, "Manía de citas y epígrafes", 20-21 (1832); 910 (1968). Emphasis added.

[7] "[T]oda esta retahila de viejísimos proverbios literarios [...] han perdido ya para nuestro paladar, como manjar repitido, toda su antigua novedad y su picante sainete." ibid., 22 (1832); 910-11 (1968).

[8] Jan Mukařovský, "Structuralism in Aesthetics and in Literary Studies," in *The Prague School: Selected Writings, 1929-1946*, ed. Peter Steiner (Austin: University of Texas Press, 1982), 69-70. After the Communist takeover in 1948, Mukařovský attempted to reconcile structuralism with Marxism but ended up rejecting his former views. He did consent to a collection of his *Studies in Aesthetics*, where we can read: "The concept of structure is based on an inner unification of the whole by the mutual relations of its parts: and that not only by positive relations, agreements and harmonies – but also by contradictions and conflicts." *Studie z estetiky* (Prague: Odeon, 1966), 117, translated by

The presence vs. absence of an element therefore modifies the entire text. In the case of the motto, its mere presence can be one if its more powerful effects. The motto sends a signal by just being there, or to put it in more technical terms, it always connotes, even without denoting anything. Whatever its actual message, it is a sign in and of itself. A sign of a particular kind, as Gérard Genette correctly points out, using the terminology of Peircean semiotics: much like smoke indicates fire (i.e. is an *index* of fire), an epigraph signals culture. In Genette's words: "elle [l'épigraphe] est un peu, déjà, le sacre de l'écrivain, qui par elle choisit ses pairs, et donc sa place au Panthéon."[9]

This was unmistakably true in the early 1800s, when mottomania had become one of the hallmarks of a new way of writing, reading, and conceiving literature, known as Romanticism. A keen observer of the international literary scene, Larra could hardly have ignored this fact; yet he chose not to pay attention to the implications of what he saw as an eccentric mannerism, an annoying tic. If I were not afraid of incurring his wrath for using hackneyed cultural references, I would even venture to use the words of Polonius: "Though this be madness, yet there is method in't."

These implications, it is my contention, concern both the poetics and the politics of literature. From the very outset, Romanticism was thought of by its main proponents in terms of discontinuity and rupture, of breaches and breakthroughs, of *Sturm und Drang*. Breaking with the past was the order of the day. Rejecting the neoclassical tastes of the ruling classes was part of the new deal: "European Romanticism discovered the past as past and completed the transition from a received heritage to a conscious, reflective confrontation with tradition."[10] In France this change in mentality had been translated into political terms at a relatively early stage; elsewhere it was to remain within the confines of what was increasingly being called "aesthetics." Age-old literary pedestals were dismantled and replaced by new ones. A different, European canon quickly emerged. Shakespeare and Dante were most obviously heralded as geniuses, but more recent writers also made it into the pantheon:

René Wellek in *The Literary Theory and Aesthetics of the Prague School* (Ann Arbor: Department of Slavic Languages and Literatures, University of Michigan, 1969), 5.

[9] Gérard Genette, *Seuils* (Paris: Seuil, 1987), 149. The entire part devoted to the motto ("Les épigraphes," 134-49) should be required reading for anyone interested in the subject.

[10] Peter Uwe Hohendahl, *Building a National Literature. The Case of Germany, 1830-1870*, trans. Renate Baron Franciscono (Ithaca and London: Cornell University Press, 1989), 141.

among them, Scott and Byron, Schiller and Goethe, Calderón and Lope de Vega.

Mottomania provides us with a case study for the analysis of such processes of re-canonization. What did the literary map of Europe, as drawn from epigraphs, look like? What were its hot spots, its main crossroads, its best-travelled circuits? What kind of intercultural dialogue was fostered, if any, by the Romantics' repeated appeal to certain authors? I should emphasize that the actual "sources" of individual texts will be deemed less important than their interconnectivity and selection criteria, which reveal the underpinnings of literature in the Romantic Age.

Let us first remember that there was some sort of social *etiquette* of the motto, famously denounced by Henri de Latouche in his 1829 pamphlet against "la camaraderie littéraire."[11] In quoting, Latouche realized, one did not only negotiate with the dead,[12] one could also flatter (or irk) the living. Mottoes brought particular literary works into circulation, and as such were good publicity for their authors, who could return the favour by quoting the writers that had previously quoted them... In addition to weaving a web of intertextual references by means of poetry, novels, and articles in journals, mottoes succeeded in establishing a social network of people who could and did in fact meet in the literary salons of the day: the conversion of cultural currency into social recognition was complete.

Contemporary documents leave little doubt as to the deliberate and systematic nature of mottomania. In the late 1820s, an obscure poet by the name of Adolphe Mathieu published a parody of the new school with the telling title *Les derniers instants. Élégie, ode ou dithyrambe.* It was dedicated *À tous les singes du romantisme, passés, présents et futurs* and contained almost sixty mottoes spread over six pages, with a note at the

---

[11] It first appeared in the Revue de Paris of October 1829. See Vincent Laisney's analysis in *L'Arsenal romantique. Le salon de Charles Nodier 1824-1834* (Paris: Honoré Champion, 2002), 643-51.

[12] To use the title of Margaret Atwood's Empson Lectures, delivered at the University of Cambridge in 2000: *Negotiating with the Dead. A Writer on Writing* (Toronto: Anchor Canada, 2003). Incidentally, the two-hundred-page volume that resulted from this exercise contains no less than 38 epigraphs, an extravaganza Atwood briefly alludes to in her Prologue: "The grab-bag nature of the citations is [...] a feature of the inside of my head, and despite all efforts to make this locale tidier, nothing much could be done about it." (xxv) The following statement, coming from a writer so openly indulging in mottomania, thus becomes revealing: "I assume that we are still living in the shadow cast by the Romantic movement, or in the fragments of that shadow." (xxvi)

very end promising to explain the significance of each quote in two volumes with notes and commentaries, portraits, facsimiles, and obituaries of the quotees.[13] Most significantly, these companion volumes were supposed to be published by Urbain Canel, the Paris librarian who had made a name for himself with some of the greatest Romantic authors: Alphonse de Lamartine (*Nouvelles Méditations poétiques*, 1823), Victor Hugo (*Bug-Jargal*, 1826), Alfred de Vigny (*Cinq-Mars*, 1826; *Poèmes antiques et modernes*, 1826) Alfred de Musset (*Contes d'Espagne et d'Italie*, 1829), and, in particular, his friend Honoré de Balzac. Canel had published them all by the time Adolphe Mathieu wrote his biting parody.

Regarding Balzac, one recalls his own changing attitude towards mottoes. Like Larra, but for altogether different reasons, he would become allergic to them after an "overdose." Several of Balzac's early novels – all of the "gothic" kind and published under outrageous pseudonyms – bear witness to his mottomania: every single chapter of *L'héritière de Birague*, *Jean-Louis*, and *Clotilde de Lusignan* (all published in 1822) is preceded by at least one quote or purported quote. By the end of the 1820s, however, Balzac would change strategies and come into his own. When *Le Dernier Chouan* (the first of a long series of novels that would eventually make up the vast *Comédie humaine*) appeared in book form in 1829, it was strangely devoid of mottoes. Yet its previous incarnation, published serially in daily newspapers, still had had more than its share of them, which suggests that their elimination must have been a conscious step on Balzac's behalf, part of his tinkering with and rethinking of the novelistic formula.[14]

Balzac was to give considerable credibility to a genre thus far considered as an upstart, and therefore shunned, by France's leading literary institutions. His systematic adaptation of Walter Scott's historical

---

13 "Le complément de ces épigraphes, formant deux volumes grand in-8o, avec portraits, fac-simile, articles nécrologiques, notes et commentaires, paraîtra incessamment chez Urbain Canel, libraire, rue Saint-Germain-des-Prés, no 9, à Paris." Adolphe Mathieu, *Œuvres en vers, t. 1er, Juvenilia (passe-temps poétiques)* (Brussels: Devroye, 1830?), 74. The poem was first published in 1826 according to Gustave Charlier, "Le mouvement romantique en Belgique," *Bulletin de l'Académie Royale de Langue et Littérature françaises de Belgique*, 5.5 (1927): 135.

14 Lucienne Frappier-Mazur, "Parodie, imitation et circularité: les épigraphes dans les romans de Balzac," in Roland Le Huenen and Paul Perron (eds.), *Le roman de Balzac* (Montreal: Didier, 1980), 79-88. In a discarded preface to *Le Gars* (as the Chouan project was still known in 1828), Balzac has his alter ego Victor Morillon say: "J'abhorre les épigraphes. [...] tout en ayant soin de ne leur rien faire annoncer au lecteur, j'en ai poussé le luxe jusqu'au ridicule, elles sont les premières et les dernières dont j'embarrasserai mes narrations." Quoted in Genette, *Seuils*, 138.

romance to the observation and analysis of present-day mores, as opposed to a stylised picture of the past, signalled the advent of the realist *novel*.[15] Within the framework of this new aesthetic, mottoes came to be viewed as distracting devices: they put up barriers between the words on the page and the world outside by constantly reminding readers that they were reading fiction instead of encouraging them to temporarily suspend their disbelief. That is not to say that realist novels stood by themselves, without interference from other texts, but there was no longer any need to highlight these references in the ostentatious manner reminiscent of Ann Radcliffe, Matthew "Monk" Lewis, Charles Maturin, and Walter Scott. The great realist fiction for which the nineteenth century would become famous did very well without mottoes: Gustave Flaubert, Émile Zola, and Henry James had no use for them.[16]

By placing texts in a chain of other texts, quotes tend to isolate them from the outside world (an effect that would lead to their abandonment by more mimetically inclined novelists). Yet by the same token, they also effectively enshrine them within the realm of fiction, since the quoted authority's prestige reflects favourably on the quoting text, thus lending it the coveted status of a work of art. I agree with Donatella Montalto Cessi when she points out the major difference between the motto as epigraph (*l'epigrafe*) and its medieval ancestor, the phrase accompanying a coat of arms or crest (*la divisa*): while they both reveal the values held dear by those that chose them, only the modern version is obtained by means of literature and by "the precise conscience and will to produce literature."[17]

---

[15] My use of italics here is meant to indicate that the terms "novel" and "romance" are taken in the oppositional sense they have in the Anglo-American tradition, from Hawthorne's preface to *The House of Seven Gables* all the way to Northrop Frye's *Anatomy of Criticism* (Princeton: Princeton University Press, 1957), 303-14.

[16] Genette, *Seuils*, 138. George Eliot is an important exception – see J.R. Tye, "George Eliot's Unascribed Mottoes," *Nineteenth-Century Fiction*, 22.3 (1967): 235-49. Further testimony to the negative link between mottoes and realist aesthetics is the fact that French writers who see their fin de siècle projects as a reaction to Émile Zola's naturalism, such as Proust (*Les plaisirs et les jours*), Gide (*Paludes*) and Villiers de l'Isle-Adam (*Contes cruels*), happen to 'rediscover' mottoes.

[17] "[...] l'impiego di una epigrafe fa conoscere le predilezioni, l'amore per una tradizione artistica di chi adotta quella frase o quei versi; questo ora avviene in modo più riflesso rispetto a cuanto accadeva nel lontano passato con [la divisa] perché mediato dalla letteratura e dalla precisa coscienza e volontà di produrre letteratura." Donatella Montalto Cessi, "Uno specchio per i testi: l'epigrafe letteraria nel romanticismo spagnolo," *Culture: Annali dell'Istituto di Lingue della Facolta di Scienze Politiche dell'Università degli studi di Milano* (1989): 21.

Witness Rudolf Böhm's doctoral dissertation on mottoes in British literature between 1820 and 1920.[18] Based on the analysis of 128 writers – a startling 108 of whom used some 3 600 mottoes[19] – his findings provide us with precious insights. He discovered the vast proportion of quotes (2 536 out of a total of 3 595 to be precise, or roughly 70%) to be taken from literature. Biblical and religious sources together accounted for slightly more than 10% (404/3 595), while quotes from historians, philosophers, and the like represented an even smaller portion (159/3 595, or 4.4%). Within his main category of literary sources, Böhm distinguishes between "native" (*einheimisch*) mottoes and "foreign" (*ausländisch*) ones. This is where it becomes really interesting, because no less than one out of three literary quotes[20] is borrowed from a foreign author, most often, it appears, from French writers. Among foreign literatures, France's (10%) clearly comes out ahead of the pack, providing twice as many mottoes as Latin (6.3%), Greek (5%) or Italian (4.9%) authors do, who in turn score better than their German (3.1%), American (1.8%) and Spanish (0.5%) counterparts. The presence of most modern literatures is limited to a handful of writers, however, who become figureheads (or even synecdoches) of their respective traditions: Schiller and Goethe thus represent Germany (51/79 quotes), Dante, Petrarch, and Tasso Italy (92/125 quotes), and Cervantes Spain (7/14 quotes). The image of French literature, as it can be gathered from the analysis of mottoes, shows a slightly greater diversity. A large number of French sources (97) are spread over several centuries, with quotes ranging from Marie de France's medieval *lais* all the way to Mallarmé and Villiers de l'Isle-Adam. That is not to say that nineteenth-century British mottomaniacs did not have their favourites: in that regard, the conspicuous absence of Flaubert and Zola, the undisputed masters of French realism, is as revealing of a hidden agenda as the more than 90 quotes taken from a wide array of Romantic writers (with a marked preference for Hugo, Musset, and George Sand).[21] At the same time, and not surprisingly, France's "grand siècle," the neoclassical tradition to which Romanticism chiefly reacted, is also being downplayed. Of the names normally associated with the seventeenth century, only Molière –

---

[18] Rudolf Böhm, *Das Motto in der englischen Literatur des 19. Jahrhunderts* (München: Wilhelm Fink Verlag, 1975).

[19] Böhm, *Das Motto*, 15. The following numbers were calculated from the tables at the end of his book.

[20] 813/2 536; one out of five or 813/3 595, when looking at the overall number of mottoes.

[21] Böhm, *Das Motto*, 60-61.

hardly a classicist in the narrow sense of the word – seems to have been favoured (14 mottoes); Racine appears but twice in Böhm's corpus of 256 French mottoes, Boileau only once, Corneille and Bossuet not at all.[22]

Based on such a large number of texts, Rudolf Böhm's research on nineteenth-century England allows us to reconstruct the 'hit parade' of motto-providing writers. What follows is a list of those quoted more than twenty times:[23]

Shakespeare	386 mottoes
Wordsworth	70
Beaumont & Fletcher	61
Tennyson	52
Byron; Scott	51
Dante	43
Horace	41
Milton	37
Hugo; Jonson; Schiller; Virgil	32
Spenser; Tasso	28
Crabbe; Euripides	25
Chaucer	23
Aeschylus	22
Cowper; Petrarch	21

Compiling such lists would be superficial, were it not for a strong tendency among Romantic writers to indulge in what we now call name-dropping. The actual text of mottoes can prove to be less important than the identity, reputation, and prestige of the quotee.[24] In *Le Rouge et le Noir* (1831), for instance, perhaps the most playful and ironic example of

---

22 ibid., 59.
23 ibid., 249-50.
24 Genette, *Seuils*, 147; Montalto Cessi, "Uno specchio per i testi," 26.

mottomania in French literature, Stendhal uses epigraphs in much the same way eighteenth-century novelists (Fielding, Sterne and Diderot) used long-winded titles, i.e. to comment on the action that is about to unfold.[25] He does not hesitate to attribute what are sometimes mundane lines of his own invention to other writers: Schiller's name thus appears under half a dozen quotes which turn out to be fakes.

More exceptionally, several mottoes are borrowed from the same author, which has the effect of conjuring up the latter's image behind his quoted work. In *Smarra* (1822), Charles Nodier – the translator of Maturin's *Bertram* and, to my knowledge, the first French writer to use chapter mottoes – systematically matches a Latin quote with a passage from Shakespeare, thereby symbolically putting the English playwright on an equal footing with the great Romans of Antiquity. A later example of a such pairing is Christina Rossetti's *Monna Innominata* (1881), a wreath of fourteen sonnets, each preceded by two quotes: one from Dante and one from Petrarch. Now, if in Rossetti's case Italian mottoes seem to have been chosen for aesthetic reasons, it does not follow that foreign mottoes in general are to be taken as a sure sign of openness to other countries and their literatures.

A second look at the list I distilled from Böhm's research will hopefully make this last point clear. Granted, nearly half of our 21 writers hail from countries other than Britain, so much so that this list almost provides us with a Top 10 of foreign quotees as well: Dante, Horace, Hugo, Schiller, Virgil, Tasso, Euripides, Aeschylus and Petrarch (Number 10, Goethe, was only quoted 19 times and therefore did not make the initial list). Together, these highly respectable members of what looks like an international academy, a list of Nobel prize winners *avant la lettre*, account for more than 10% (295/2 536) of all literary mottoes, which is certainly not negligible. Yet none of them make it into the British Top 5, and Shakespeare appears more often than all of them put together. Even allowing for the Bard's exceptional status as the undisputed ruler of 'quotationland,' this situation points to a paradox that I will briefly address before concluding.

How are we to interpret the apparent contradiction between the unprecedented recourse to modern foreign material – unprecedented because seventeenth- and even early eighteenth-century use of the motto

---

[25] I.D. McFarlane, "L'épigraphe dans le roman romantique en France et en Angleterre (1790-1840)," in Georges Jacques and José Lambert (eds.), *Itinéraires et plaisirs textuels. Mélanges [...] Raymond Pouilliart* (Brussels and Louvain-la-Neuve: Nauwelaerts and L'Université Catholique de Louvain, 1987), 77.

was restricted to Roman and Greek classics and, as such, did not entail any real international preoccupations – and the national agenda of these same Romantic writers who held their own literary tradition in high esteem? How, in other words, did the discovery of European literature as an intertextual whole complement or contradict other Romantic endeavours, like the reinterpretation of the past and the redefinition of literature along national lines?

This contradiction is by no means limited to British Romanticism. Similar paradoxes can, for example, be found in Goethe's musings on the advent of *Weltliteratur*, a concept intended to reflect the growing mutual understanding between nations but that somehow ends up promoting local German culture. In a famous January 1827 conversation with Eckermann, Goethe is quoted as having said: "I study foreign nations and advise everybody else to do the same. National literature does not mean much at present, it is time for an era of world literature, and everybody must endeavour to accelerate this epoch." [26] Yet later that same year, in a review of Alexandre Duval's historical drama *Le Tasse*, which he considered to be a mere imitation of his own *Torquato Tasso*, Goethe is "convinced that a world literature is taking shape in which an honourable role is set aside for us Germans. All nations look to us, praise or reprove us, assimilate and reject us, imitate and deform us, understand or misunderstand us, open or close their hearts to us." [27]

I am not sure whether this intermingling of cultural nationalism and global literary traffic should be thought of in conflictual terms, but propose to see it instead as an instance of overlapping between the international and national dimensions of literary systems in the Romantic age. Whereas the intertextual repertoire of these literatures had become

---

[26] "Ich sehe mich daher gern bei fremden Nationen um und rate jedem, es auch seinerseits zu tun. Nationalliteratur will jetzt nicht viel sagen, die Epoche der Weltliteratur ist an der Zeit, und jeder muß jetzt dazu wirken, diese Epoche zu beschleunigen" (31 Jan. 1827). Quoted and translated by Hendrik Birus, "The Goethean Concept of World Literature and Comparative Literature," *CLCWeb: Comparative Literature and Culture*, 2.4 (December 2004), http://clcwebjournal. lib.purdue.edu/clcweb00-4/birus00.html.

[27] "[Ich will] doch von meiner Seite meine Freunde aufmerksam machen, daß ich überzeugt sei, es bilde sich eine *Weltliteratur*, worin uns Deutschen eine ehrenvolle Rolle vorbehalten ist. Alle Nationen schauen sich nach uns um, sie loben, sie tadeln, nehmen auf und verwerfen, ahmen nach und entstellen, verstehen oder mißverstehen uns, eröffnen oder verschließen ihre Herzen." Johann Wolfgang von Goethe, *Kunsttheoretische Schriften und Übersetzungen. Schriften zur Literatur, II: Aufsätze zur Weltliteratur. Maximen und Reflexionen* (Berlin: Aufbau, 1972), 326. My translation.

increasingly cosmopolitan, their everyday functioning as "institutions"[28] very much remained a national affair. Writers vying for the attention of readers fought their battles locally, not internationally. Victor Hugo put it perhaps most blatantly when he purportedly said as a fourteen-year old: "Je veux être Chateaubriand ou rien."[29] Other examples also come to mind: one thinks of Walter Scott's decision to turn to writing novels after feeling outdone as a narrative poet by Byron, or of the latter's fierce competition with Poet Laureate Robert Southey. The Elysian Fields of international literary glory might be fictional, but the national playing field, with its allies and opponents, its official policies and unwritten rules, its subtle and not so subtle ways of excluding or co-opting individuals, is a much more concrete reality for writers in search of recognition.

This might explain why so many foreign references in Romantic mottoes seem oddly out of sync. Returning to the Top 10 of foreign writers quoted in nineteenth-century England, one is struck by the fact that British authors rarely engage in an intertextual dialogue with living writers of other nationalities: such a dialogue, it seems, can only take place between fellow citizens. Putting aside the Greek and Roman classics, we are left with: two medieval and one Renaissance Italian poet (Dante, Petrarch, and Tasso); two eighteenth-century German playwrights often classified as Romantics outside of Germany even though they themselves refused to be associated with that label (Schiller and Goethe), and one prolific French writer whose aesthetic evolution had come to a standstill by mid-century but who was able to reinvent himself as a political prophet (Hugo). European literature as represented in this 'hit parade,' is not avant-garde by any stretch of the imagination, but conjures up images of staleness and petrifaction. We should therefore question the idea that the mere fact of quoting foreign writers guarantees knowledge of or even familiarity with foreign literatures. It might well be a self-serving gesture, used to delineate national spaces and thereby reaffirm borders rather than abolish them.

In the light of these findings, simply dismissing mottomania as a pedantic tic, as Larra pretended to do, and as many modern editors of Romantic texts have actually done, completely misses the mark by

---

[28] As Harry Levin used to say. See his *Gates of Horn. A Study of Five French Realists* (New York: Oxford University Press, 1963), 21-23 and Hohendahl, *Building a National Literature*, 1-43.

[29] "Cette proclamation du jeune homme [...], dont l'authenticité est douteuse, daterait du 10 juillet 1816." Hubert Juin, *Victor Hugo* (Paris: Flammarion, 1980), 1:264.

underestimating the potential, both strategic and ideological, of this highly intertextual device. Bearing in mind its profoundly semiotic nature – the motto is a sign in the strictest sense of the word – it can be said to have played a triple role in the Romantic age.

First, mottoes were clearly a symptom of increased textual traffic between budding nation-states: the works of medieval and Renaissance Europe had become a reservoir of themes and topics, plots and storylines, a fact that has already been given extensive attention by the pioneers of comparative literature before World War II, albeit within a very different framework. Today we no longer view comparative literature as a competition of sorts between national traditions but tend to see interliterary contacts as a welcome addition to the discovery of "national genius" and the subsequent "invention of tradition" (Hobsbawm) that were no less typical of the nineteenth century. As mentioned above, there is, however, a risk of overemphasizing the horizon-widening potential of such border crossings, be they real (involving people) or metaphorical (involving texts). Unfortunately, increased contact with different cultures does not *ipse facto* breed tolerance.

There is no denying the intertextual thrust of mottoes either. They were part of a sophisticated, if elitist, game played between writers and readers, the ideal audience whom Stendhal liked to refer to, in English, as "the happy few."[30] In his novel, *Le Rouge et le Noir*, a string of quotes from Byron's *Don Juan* effectively act as a parallel story to, and a commentary of, the main character's sentimental education.[31] In the same covert manner, Stendhal was able to convey a political message. Many of his mottoes are actual or false quotes from some of the French Revolution's greatest orators: Danton, Mirabeau, Antoine Barnave and Emmanuel Sieyès. Because they are by definition incomplete and allusive, quotes are indeed ideal vehicles for ideological messages. This third function is doubly revealing of the way literature worked in the Romantic era: in addition to blurring the boundaries between fiction and non-fiction, it points to the dialectical nature of an opposition such as "local" vs. "universal." On the stage of Goethe's *Weltliteratur*, behind the curtains, so to speak, local battles were being fought.

---

[30] A slogan which, it turns out, is itself an indirect quote from Shakespeare's *Henry V*, by way of Oliver Goldsmith's *Vicar of Wakefield*. Genette, *Seuils*, 119 n1.

[31] See George M. Rosa, "The Presence of Byron in the Novels of Stendhal, with Special Reference to *Armance* and *Le Rouge et le Noir*" (D. Phil. thesis), Oxford University, Balliol College, 1980, 238-39.

Take the master of quotations himself, Walter Scott. In *Waverley* we are introduced to the Baron of Bradwardine, a nobleman of Jacobite allegiance who is given to sprucing up his discourse with phrases from the Classics. Looking at the blackened walls of his residence, the victim of English marauders, he turns to Edward Waverley and says: "To be sure, we may say with Virgilius Maro: *Fuimus Troes* [We were Trojans once],"[32] thus establishing a connection between Caledonians and Trojans. The quote is taken from the part of Virgil's *Aeneid* (2.325) where Aeneas, himself a survivor of the fatal battle of Troy, tells the story of his city's downfall at Dido's request. This tale within a tale has thus been lifted from its context by Bradwardine (and hence, by Scott) to lend it exemplary value. The defeat of the Highlanders at Culloden (1746) becomes the stuff legends are made of. No longer the story of a lost cause, intertextuality turns its retelling into a compensatory process whose narrative mould was handed down from Antiquity.

The same holds true for that special kind of quotes known as mottoes. When Stendhal chose to adorn *La Chartreuse de Parme* with a line from Ludovico Ariosto's fourth Satire (*"Gia mi fur dolci inviti a empir le carte / I luoghi ameni"*), he most obviously did so for the same reasons that would later lead him to have inscribed on his tombstone *Arrigo Beyle, Milanese*, namely, a fondness of all things Italian. The novel itself, on the other hand, contains many passages[33] that explicitly develop the motto's implicit themes. We also know, from a passage in Stendhal's *Vie de Henry Brulard*[34] (a thinly veiled Henri Beyle), that Ariosto's *Orlando furioso* shaped his character as much as Cervantes' *Don Quixote* or Rousseau's *Nouvelle Héloïse* did. Considering the ideological nature of epigraphs, however, nothing seems to be more telling than Stendhal's decision to place under the aegis of Ariosto a *Bildungsroman* about a young boy who becomes a man after enrolling in Napoleon's troops and witnessing the battle of Waterloo. This was his way of paying tribute to the man whose armies had allowed himself as a young man to discover Italy, during the very campaign of 1796 that is described in all its glory in the opening pages of *La Chartreuse*. For Ariosto, we are told by none less than Chateaubriand, was one of the Emperor's favourite poets: "Napoléon

---

[32] Walter Scott, *Waverley*, ed. Andrew Hook (Harmondsworth: Penguin, 1985), 443.

[33] As when countess Pietranera sighs: "Au milieu de ces collines aux formes admirables et se précipitant vers le lac par des pentes si singulières, je puis garder toutes les illusions des descriptions du Tasse et de l'Arioste. Tout est noble et tendre, tout parle d'amour, rien ne rappelle les laideurs de la civilisation." Stendhal, *La Chartreuse de Parme*, ed. Béatrice Didier (Paris: Gallimard, 1972), 44.

[34] Quoted in Levin, *The Gates of Horn*, 100.

était poète aussi, comme le furent César et Frédéric: il préférait Arioste au Tasse; il y trouvait les portraits de ses capitaines futurs, et un cheval tout bridé pour son voyage aux astres."[35] The viscount, on the other hand, liked to portray himself as a noble victim, an aristocratic martyr. As such, he felt closer to the unfortunate Torquato Tasso, locked up by the jealous Duke of Ferrara. On his visit to the Holy Land in 1806, Chateaubriand used Tasso's *Gerulasemme liberata* as a guidebook. Many years later, while passing through Ferrara, he would insist on seeing his idol's cell in the Sant'Anna hospital, and after a pilgrimage to the poet's tomb in Rome's Sant'Onofrio convent, he famously commented, not without envy, on the Italian's immortality: "Le Tasse remporte dans ces lieux une victoire plus mémorable: il fait oublier l'Arioste."[36]

Here we touch upon what is perhaps the most surprising characteristic of the motto. In its Romantic incarnation at least, it has a transitive quality: its text often becomes a pretext, its direct reference an indirect allusion, an indexical sign of an aesthetic programme or a political tendency. Which is why mottoes should not be taken at face value, as Mariano José de Larra knew quite well, having been a fervent mottomaniac before declaring war on those who indulged in such extravagant behaviour. So entrenched was the habit that even Larra, at the end of his 1832 article, reserves himself the right to list the epigraphs and quotes he could have used more or less appropriately, in case the reading public had any doubts about his own knowledge of Latin or French.[37] Isn't that what they call "having your cake and eating it too?"

---

[35] Chateaubriand, *Mémoires d'outre-tombe*, ed. Jean-Paul Clément (Paris: Gallimard, 1997), 1099 (Book XIX, Ch. 5).

[36] Chateaubriand, *Mémoires d'outre-tombe*, 2811 (Book XLI, Ch. 2).

[37] My paraphrasing of: "Sin embargo, por si el público curioso dudase de nuestra mucha latinidad y de nuestros adelantamientos en la lengua francesa, nos reservamos el derecho de darle [...] una listita de los epígrafes y citas más o menos oportunas, que hubiéramos podido usar." Larra, "Manía de citas y epígrafes," 23-24 (1832); 911 (1968).

"MOVING TIMES – NEW WORDS:" THE SIXTIES ON BOTH SIDES OF THE CHANNEL

Mara Cambiaghi

> *What do you remember of 1968? Snakes and snooker and a set white face, with a frown, and tears brimming in proud eyes.*[1]

This is how Frederica Potter, the protagonist of A.S. Byatt's series of novels portraying life in England during two decades, looks back on her past, musing on the legacy of a significant historical date. In an authorial aside providing a temporary suspension in the unfolding of the plot, Frederica considers how few and fragmentary her precise memories of this time are. She wonders if this is "the case with all thirty-year old memories, whether you were thirty in 1868 or 1968" (50), and ponders that

> [f]or one thing, historically, it takes a few decades to learn that younger generations than 'the young' sprout like mushrooms, that if the young of the 60s could not remember the War they were followed rapidly by generations who could not remember Vietnam, who were followed by generations who could not remember the Falklands.
>
> (49)

---

[1] A.S. Byatt, *A Whistling Woman* (London: Chatto & Windus, 2002), 51. Subsequent references are given in the text.

With considerable insight, Byatt captures the dynamic workings of memory alternating between awareness and oblivion as generations follow one another, echoing what Eric Hobsbawm has expressed more succinctly, albeit from an entirely different standpoint and in a different form: "Most human beings operate like historians: they only recognize the nature of their experience in retrospect."[2]

Although the time and events around 1968 have been the object of historical investigation,[3] literature has devoted considerably less attention to this period and only rarely has the student protest been portrayed in fiction. Even wishing to limit this observation to a mere historical frame, an authoritative scholar like Donald Sassoon remarks that the student protest "remains a much under-researched area," adding that "it is difficult to provide an adequate analysis of the phenomenon of student and youth protest,"[4] The ingrained paradox of this statement is remarkable considering that many of the protagonists of the rebellion were active in schools and universities, as Sassoon also observes.

In the light of these premises, A.S. Byatt's exploration of the period in her recent novel proves all the more significant, even though her particular rendering of the student protest is not sympathetic. I should also like to point out by way of introduction that the subject of the depiction of 1968 in fiction might not have crossed my mind if the author's own fictional portrayal of this time had not led me to focus on it, and if a proliferation of courses on cultural and generational memory held at the University of Constance had not provided further food for thought. In 2002, the novelist published the concluding part of her *roman fleuve* in four volumes, which ends fatally when a rebellious group of

---

[2] Eric Hobsbawm, *The Age of Extremes* (London: Abacus, 1995), 257.

[3] See Arthur Marwick, *The Sixties. Cultural Revolution in Britain, France, Italy and the United States, c. 1958-c. 1974* (Oxford: Oxford University Press, 1998), 533-675; James J. Farrell, *The Spirit of the Sixties* (New York and London: Routledge, 1997); Luisa Passerini, *Autobiography of a Generation. Italy, 1968* (Hanover: Wesleyan University Press, 1996); Robert Lumley, *States of Emergency* (London: Verso, 1990); David Caute, *Sixty-Eight. The Year of the Barricades* (London: Hamish Hamilton, 1988); Ronald Fraser, *1968. A Student Generation in Revolt* (London: Chatto & Windus, 1988); Gerd Langguth, *Mythos '68* (Munich: Olzog Verlag, 2001). For a literary overview of the period see Patricia Waugh, *Harvest of the Sixties* (Oxford: Oxford University Press, 1995); Robert Hewison, *Art and Society in the Sixties 1960-75* (London: Methuen, 1986); Heinz Bude, *Das Altern einer Generation* (Frankfurt a. M.: Suhrkamp, 1995); Mirella Billi and Nicholas Brownlees, *In and Around the Sixties* (Viterbo: Sette Città, 2003).

[4] Donald Sassoon, *One Hundred Years of Socialism. The West European Left in the Twentieth Century* (London: I.B. Tauris, 1996), 388. I thank Ilaria Favretto for drawing my attention to this volume.

students, hippies and dropouts who are part of anti-university movement based in a commune just outside the college campus disrupt an interdisciplinary academic conference. The conference focuses on the problematic question of the body-mind relationship and takes place in 1969 at the fictional University of North Yorkshire. This is ideal timing if we consider that it was in the sixties that sexuality entered the realm of social and cultural politics, pervading much of the intellectual debate that was to be sparked off from French universities. Indeed, *A Whistling Woman* portrays both the scientific enquiry that engaged the learned profession, as well as the very tangible aspirations of women struggling to achieve an identity of their own outside their private homes.

Wishing to assess A.S. Byatt's own picture of this time in England, I began to focus on the legacy of 1968 in other countries as well, realising what most social historians have long recognised, namely that 1968 is one of the archetypal myths which inform our Western consciousness. While contradictory views prevail as to the actual social and political significance of the events which make 1968 a memorable date, most scholars agree that what happened then had profound implications for the future development of the century. Umberto Eco is among those who acknowledge its beneficial effects. In 1986, he remarked:

> Even though all visible traces of 1968 are gone, it profoundly changed the way all of us, at least in Europe, behave and relate to one another. Relations between bosses and workers, students and teachers, even children and parents, have opened up. They'll never be the same again.[5]

Considering the significance of this social and cultural turning point, we hardly need to mention that Michel Foucault had already commented on the changed role of the intellectuals a decade earlier. In his conversation with Gilles Deleuze on "Intellectuals and Power" dating from 1977, he openly referred to the May events in Paris as "the most recent upheaval," attributing to this moment a new awareness in the shifting relations of the so-called system of power. He claimed that

> [t]he intellectual's role is no longer to place himself 'somewhat ahead and to the side' in order to express the stifled truth of

---

[5] Scott Sullivan, "Master of the Signs," *Newsweek*, 22 December 1986: 49. Quoted in Robert Lumley, *States of Emergency. Cultures of Revolt in Italy from 1968 to 1978* (London and New York: Verso, 1990), 2.

the collectivity; rather, it is to struggle against the forms of power that transform him into its object and instrument in the sphere of 'knowledge,' 'truth,' 'consciousness,' and 'discourse.'[6]

Foucault's views, characterising a time of social and cultural change, described well a widespread mood which, at the turn of the new millennium with its new scenario of global threats, may appear inadequate. However, these views survive as consciousness of our European past, even though no unified picture of the period can prevail today in a transnational assessment of the time. While, for some, 1968 remains a myth about origins, "a Genesis recounting epical deeds in the past," for others, it is a "myth manqué" marked by mere nostalgia, "an exhausted narrative" with no actual relevance for the present or the future,[7] or else it is remembered only in connection with its most regressive developments, such as radical social conflict and terrorism as it developed in Italy and Germany.

It is not my intention to ascertain the historical weight of these remarks in the present context. I intend to focus in what follows solely on fiction dealing with the era. My hope is that a transnational picture of a tumultuous period fraught with utopian promises and radical criticism may finally emerge, also from a literary angle. For this purpose, I have ventured into a comparative analysis, taking into account some European novels with stylistic, imaginative or historical features that show some affinity which forms a useful basis for comparison.

I shall juxtapose Byatt's work, discussed in the central part of my paper, with Maria Corti's *Le pietre verbali* (2001), a short novel which portrays a similar scene of generational change and student unrest against the silent and immemorial background of the ancient monuments of Pavia. In my exploration of authors dealing with the sixties in their novels, I have touched upon the work of Christine Brooke-Rose who portrays the May events of 1968 in Paris in her experimental autobiographical novel *Remake* (1996), and of Milan Kundera who wrote unforgettable accounts of the tragic end of the Prague Spring.

---

[6] Michel Foucault, *Language, Counter-Memory, Practice*, ed. Donald F. Bouchard, (1977; Ithaca, New York: Cornell University Press, 1980), 207-208.

[7] Sheldon Wolin, "The Destructive Sixties and Postmodern Conservatism," in Stephen Macedo (ed.), *Reassessing the Sixties. Debating the Political and Cultural Legacy* (New York and London: W.W. Norton & Co., 1997), 142. Wolin speaks of a "myth of the Sixties" in a conservative version, namely as countermyth. When referring to the defenders of the sixties, he speaks of a "myth manqué."

Among the many German authors who have dealt with the generational conflict characterising this crucial time, I shall consider the case of Uwe Johnson, albeit in a rather oblique and fragmentary fashion. This is because the large scale of his *Heimat* novel in four volumes, *Jahrestage* (1970-1983), only allows me to make a fleeting reference to his astonishing work in this context. Yet, within the general issue of a conference held in Prague, Johnson appears to me to be of interest, since he is really the narrator of the separation of Europe in its middle, with all its surrounding myths.

As we shall see, his long novel connects the region of Mecklenburg, in East Germany, with New York and Prague because the protagonist – an East German who lives in New York – has her heart in Europe while being confronted by her young daughter Marie with persistent questions about the past. The novel ends on the eve of the Soviet invasion of Czechoslovakia on August 20, 1968 – a date that, in retrospect, can be said to have ended the hopes of all 'sixty-eighters' of a New Left and non-Stalinist future for the East which might also bring an end to the Cold War.

Having to limit the scope of my tentative transnational analysis, I shall restrict my task to only three of these authors – A.S. Byatt, Maria Corti and Uwe Johnson – because in their fiction I recognise some distinct imagery which recurs in the current discourse on memory.

Maria Corti's novel portrays the climate of a grammar school in Milan through the eyes of Berto Casati, a teacher of Italian and Latin who registers the vibrant mood and inclinations of a generation of students prior to the emergence of riot and disorder that affected schools and universities in the following year. In the second half of the novel, the setting shifts to Pavia, a provincial but renowned and ancient university town in Northern Italy, near Milan, where the unfolding of the plot is registered by a discreetly observant university lecturer named Marta Torci. The author's alter-ego is clearly suggested by the anagram of her name, since in Pavia Maria Corti taught and continued to pursue her scholarly activity until 2002, when she died aged 86. It should be noted that Corti ranks among the most distinguished names in Italian scholarship, having devoted her interest to both the early period of Italian literature, Dante and the *Dolce Stil Novo*, and to contemporary authors such as Fenoglio, Montale and Calvino. It is even reported that Calvino wrote his *Il castello dei destini incrociati* (1969) in order to please Maria Corti, who was not only a fine semiotician, but also a novelist in her own right.

Aside from these significant biographical parallels – both Byatt and Corti have travelled along the paths of academic and creative writing – it is their particular attitude towards both everyday and literary language that has struck me as worthy of comparison. In their portrayal of youth culture and student unrest, these two writers reveal the same scrupulous attention to slogans and slang expressions which they either submit to an almost philological enquiry or else analyse in their social and historical specificity. Cast on the literary page as fictional invention or verbal fossils that have left an indelible imprint on later usage, these slogans are often combined with a jocular tone or comic comments. However, while comic and ironic effects prevail in Byatt's case, the linguistic and social enquiry is sharper, more focused, even rigorous in its philological enquiry in Maria Corti, who presents an altogether more sympathetic picture of the students' motives for causing all that social turmoil. A brief example will illustrate my point:

> The Italian language of the Sixties was restless, something was happening in it [...] The students' slang revealed a side escape, with ironic-allusive and polemical hints towards a certain kind of literary language which held sway in our schools and on that average standard language, oscillating between autonomism and conformism due to a cultural fixity of a conformist nature – "gaoled" language, as the young called it. [...] All came to an end eventually, the language of sixty-eighters survived in the memory, a verbal fossil. And yet an ongoing repetition of languages may occur in different ways. Is it not the case that the typical sixty-eight expression 'the system must be changed' works perfectly well even nowadays? It has not become unfashionable, it is still at the centre of the world.[8]

---

[8] My translation from the original paperback edition: "La lingua italiana degli anni Sessanta era irrequieta, in essa succedeva qualcosa [...] Il gergo studentesco rivelava un'evasione laterale, con sfumature ironico-allusive e polemiche nei riguardi di una certa lingua letteraria su cui si reggeva da noi la scuola e su quella lingua media standardizzata, oscillante tra l'autonomismo e il conformismo, lingua 'carcerata' come la definivano i giovani, dovuta a una fissità culturale di natura conformista. [...] Tutto è poi finito, il linguaggio sessantottesco è rimasto nella memoria, fossile verbale. Ma c'è un ripetersi continuo dei linguaggi in modo diverso. Forse che la frase tipicamente sessantottina 'il sistema va cambiato' non funziona ancora oggi benissimo? Essa non è andata giù di moda, è ancora al centro del mondo." Maria Corti, *Le pietre verbali* (Torino: Einaudi, 2002), 67-68.

The narrator hints at the specificity of a certain kind of speech derived from a new 'mental set,' and one can easily detect Foucauldian overtones suggesting the impact of discourse as the product of ideology. Wandering through the secluded cloisters of the university and the old streets of Pavia, she reflects on the genealogical function of the city and its ancient architecture, while also perceiving the influence of a new language: *industria della conoscenza, multiversità, disobbedienza civile, controcorso autogestito, docentecentrismo.*[9] Frequently, these expressions are both memorable and hilarious. For example, she wittily selects *affumicatoio dello spirito* ("smoke-house of the spirit") to describe an institution experienced as a mere "mechanism" rather than "organism:"

> *Smoke-house of the spirit* or compulsory indoctrination, which was thought to derive from a protester from Pavia in love with Musil, floated in the air. [...] Words wandered around as if borne by the wind, sprouting in one university town or the other, yielding flowers and fruit.[10]

Corti's characterisation of Italian 'sixty-eighters' is humorous but benevolent; it captures the linguistic idiosyncrasies of a generation in the midst of a collective dream that is about to explode. The narrator knows that its naive utopianism has limited scope. Indeed, she registers both the language produced during the early creative moment of the protest and its subsequent sedimentation into the bureaucratic jargon of student assemblies.

Corti's comments are validated by historical insight. Robert Lumley, an English historian who has devoted an entire study to this period, reminds us that the Italian student movement created its own slang, "a strange mixture of swear words and political jargon, which was later dubbed *sinistrese* (left-talk)" bearing "the imprint of the institutions in which it was formed, especially in its more verbose and sententious manifestations."[11] Luisa Passerini raises similar points in her extraordinary survey of 1968, *Autobiography of a Generation: Italy 1968* (1996), a highly original work combining chapters of self-examination

---

[9] Corti, *Le pietre verbali*, 66: "industry of knowledge," "multiversity," "civil disobedience," "self-taught counter-course," "lecture-centrism." (My translation.)

[10] "Vagò anche nell'aria *affumicatoio dello spirito* o indottrinatura obbligata, che si diceva risalisse a un contestatore pavese innamorato di Musil [...] I vocaboli vagavano come portati dal vento, attecchivano ora in una sede ora in un'altra, producevano fiori e frutti." *Le pietre verbali*, 67. (My translation.)

[11] Robert Lumley, *States of Emergency* (London: Verso, 1990), 90.

based on her diaries with documentary testimonies and historiographic commentary highlighting the unresolved tensions from the Fascist and postwar years.[12]

Corti's novel also captures the heavy burden of this historical legacy when describing the discussion of students planning a new school magazine, only too aware of the importance of carefully selecting the most suitable collaborators on the basis of a common mind-set: "La Resistenza, per esempio. Prova a dividere la gente in base a come giudica la Resistenza. Vedrai che la divisione va bene anche per il resto."[13]

Alternating a lyrical and philological glance, the narrator of *Le pietre verbali* also acts as a faithful observer when documenting the general lack of attention given by the newspapers to the first episodes of unrest. In a rapid survey of the media, she remarks "fu strano: dei giornali che non riflettevano la vita" ("strange reading newspapers which did not reflect life").[14]

By contrast, Byatt's picture takes up much more space in a volume covering well over 400 pages that is much less sympathetic towards the student movement and the counterculture. I should also point out here that Corti's picture does not venture outside educational institutions, whereas Byatt's includes much more of the world of the sixties – television, therapy groups, scientific language and the communes of the counterculture. What struck me in both authors, however, is their distinct sense of their respective language as a plastic, incisive tool inscribing their subject matter on a mental space – a *locus* of the mind - and on the blank page. This idea reflects very much a monumental understanding of language and cultural memory. We find it virtually translated into a visual image on the cover of Corti's novel, showing three stones on an open book. Byatt has a similar image translated into the prologue of *Babel Tower*, the third novel in her series, where a stone bears the inscription of a few letters from a broken alphabet. The implied imagery is suggestive of the very process by which life experience may turn into stone-like memory: stones are best preserved in time and provide the best *locus* for a repository of memory, even though they may be the verbal stones of the protest.

---

[12] Luisa Passerini, *Autoritratto di gruppo* (Firenze: Giunti, 1988); trans. as *Autobiography of a Generation* (Hanover and London: Wesleyan University Press, 1996).

[13] "Take the Resistance, for example. Try and split people according to how they think about the Resistance. You'll see that the split fits everything else, too." Corti, *Le pietre verbali*, 29. (My translation.)

[14] *Le pietre verbali*, 92.

Unwillingly perhaps, Corti and Byatt translate what Foucault named the archaeological discourse of knowledge into the language of fiction. In doing so, they are helped by their distinct sense of humour that dispels the heavy weight of philosophical thought into imaginative narrative – for Byatt, after all, "language is the dress of thought."[15] This operation is more substantial in Byatt's long series of novels about the sixties, overarched by her concern with memory both in its rhetorical and dialectical concepts of retrieving and ordering, inspired by ancient practices of memorisation and Renaissance forms of systematising thought, and in its more scientific aspects relating to the physiology of the mind. While the art of memory derived from Antiquity and resurrected in the early sixties by scholars such as Frances Yates and Paolo Rossi informs the narrative structure of the opening novel of Byatt's quartet (*The Virgin in the Garden*), the scientific discussion on the mnemonic operations of the brain in humans and animals characterises the interdisciplinary conference at the end of *A Whistling Woman* and the conversation of various protagonists throughout the novel.

In *A Whistling Woman*, the author addresses a number of subjects, including the physiology of psychological experiences and the impact of visual culture. Her characters become transformed into vehicles for some of the ideas current at the time the novel is set. In fact, Byatt's fictional microcosm of the sixties seems to claim the status of a community of ideas rather than one of individuals. At the opening of the novel, we find the main character, Frederica, walking into a new profession. Having survived marriage to an uncongenial and violent husband and worked part-time as a teacher of English and a reader of manuscripts for a small publisher, she now enters the world of simulacra and becomes a TV journalist. She conducts a new television programme entitled *Through the Looking Glass*. Frequently throughout the novel, Frederica will be referred to as "an adult Alice." Clearly, the novel addresses the issue of gender and the transformation required of the individual, and of women in particular, when taking on a public role, since Frederica is also a single mother. But in her new glittering role, she also embodies the move of British television in the sixties from the margin into the centre of culture. As Frederica's old friend Edmund Wilkie – now producer of a new BBC cultural programme – makes clear to her in his instructions, television will change everyone's consciousness. He says:

---

[15] A.S. Byatt, *Passions of the Mind* (London: Vintage, 1993), 10.

Rhetoric would go, must go, was going. If you were going to sway the masses you must be able to do it one by one 'sight unseen' as the lovely phrase has it. It will look more honest and *be* more insidious and dishonest.

(47)

For this TV editor, all products of creativity should mirror even the most trivial facets of reality and be conceived to be seen on TV in coloured images: "and all this can be woven together, as the technology advances, into one great living tapestry." (48)

Important here is the metaphor of a woven tapestry which may be said to represent both a single artistic object and the dynamic process of culture. This leads me to one of the key principles underlying Byatt's leaning towards constructivist theories of memory and the discussion among scientists in the fictional academic conference. Byatt is fascinated by metaphors derived from scientific discourse and resembling those used by George Eliot in her fiction, such as the image of a woven cloth symbolising the social structure of the provincial world of *Middlemarch* or that of a pier-glass with random scratches on the surface which a radiant and powerful eye must order and give shape to in its vision. Transposing these images into her fictional world of the sixties, Byatt superimposes them on the general scientific discussion on the physiological activity of the brain engaged in visual perception. In Chapter 5, for example, Jacqueline Winwar, a young woman scientist conducting research on the memory of snails, explains her interest in neurotransmitters as she refers to a real-life scientist (Hebb) who had "seen the brain as a system of flashing lights, building electric links." (53) During the fictional interdisciplinary conference, an American cognitive psycholinguist with left-wing ideas reminiscent of Chomsky speaks of metaphors ingrained in the language of neurology and psychology, such as dendrite "derived from the Greek word for tree" (353) and "the 'entry' of a sense impression into the brain." (354)

For Byatt, the creative process is best described as the activation of synaptic connections in the brain in their unceasingly reconstructive labour, while this image is also a powerful analogy for the larger implications binding memory to its social and historical context. However, since Frederica's memory of the sixties is rather imprecise, her woven carpet turns into

a fishing net woven horribly loose and slack with only the odd very bright plastic object caught in its meshes, whilst everything else had rushed and flowed through, back into the undifferentiated ocean.

(50)

This brings me finally to the author's portrayal of the student protest and of the counterculture as a dangerous and destructive force. In Chapter 6, the narrator lists all the communes and historical hotbeds of student activism in 1968: Nanterre, Kommune I in Berlin, Copenhagen, Essex and the LSE in England. Her description of Jonty Surtees, the young anarchist emerging from these dark venues makes for a rather comic figure; ultimately, he is portrayed as a mere caricature. In turn, Nick Tewfell, the legitimately elected leader of the student union, gradually moves into the cult located outside the college campus and controlled by the forces of chaos and unreason. In fact, when the protesters eventually disrupt the academic conference, this character is confronted by the vice-chancellor as he is about to break some precious glassware in a cabinet inside the university. At this point, the narrator tells us in an authorial aside that years later, "when Tewfell became minister in Tony Blair's government, he would still wake at night and remember that moment, the broken box, the splinters of glass." (372) We also learn that the vice-chancellor does not report him to the police: "And for a few years, he had hated him for that. And then, as he grew older, he had almost loved him. He had, he saw, come in a way to resemble him." (373) The implication of this gesture is best revealed in a quotation from Konrad Lorenz inserted earlier in the novel: "It takes only two generations to kill a culture that has taken generations to evolve." (30)

Space limitations do not allow me to highlight all the many incidents that partake of the rebellious climate in and outside the university. Byatt's narrative is, as always, populated by a wealth of characters and ideas arranged into a very complicated plot. We have, for example, the correspondence between a psychiatrist, Dr Kieran Quarrell, and Dr Elvet Gander, a psychoanalyst loosely modelled on the real-life author of *The Divided Self* and the leader of the anti-psychiatry movement, Ronald D. Laing. Further expert characters include the sociologist Brenda Pincher and her colleague and lover Avram Snitkin. These figures appear initially as external observers who exchange comments on the life of the commune and, in particular, on those characters affected by heavy personal traumas. Byatt immerses her fictional student community into a climate of social malaise, showing signs of spiritual and mental crises. Individual traumatic memory, coupled with allusions to the collective traumas of twentieth-century European history, becomes enacted in the novel through the character of Joshua Ramsden, a visionary figure with Manichean convictions and a charismatic leader of the cult whose members he sets on fire.

Byatt's portrayal of the period is accurate in so far as creativity and introspection were focal aspects of the counterculture of the sixties. But, ultimately, Frederica seems to belong to a generation grown up "politically placid," as J.M. Coetzee reminds us in his review of *Babel Tower* (1996), the novel preceding *A Whistling Woman*.[16] Coetzee's judgement may sound harsh. Although Byatt provides an imaginative reconstruction of the era, she cannot help feeling distrust towards the radical culture of the sixties, rejecting in particular its moments of fusion and collective excitement and fearing the authoritarian aspects of utopianism with its desire for total solutions. In an interview, she stated that she sees "a dangerous lack of thought" in certain expressions of that time, such as cults and religious or political communes.[17]

One might judge Byatt's rendering of the period as conservative or lacking authentic insight. Yet, in her fictional reconstruction – largely based on David Caute's historical study of 1968 and Charles Lindholm's anthropological investigation of cultic milieus and charisma as mental illness[18] – she does refer to those aspects of the counterculture or gregarious student lifestyle which even individuals with undoubtedly non-conservative views have recognised as potentially regressive manifestations of group culture. One of the oral testimonies of the Italian '68 movement collected by Luisa Passerini in her *Autobiography of a Generation*, for example, offers the following retrospective view of her former life style:

> We never lost sight of each other, that's the thing. We were always together in one way or another, whether it was in the occupied university or in the Camera del Lavoro or in the

---

[16] J.M. Coetzee, "En Route to the Catastrophe," *New York Review of Books*, 6 June 1997: 19.

[17] Shelagh Rogers, "Interview with A.S. Byatt," *Morningside*, CBC Radio, 3 June 1996. Quoted in Jane Campbell, *A.S. Byatt and the Heliotropic Imagination* (Waterloo, Ontario: Wilfried Laurier University Press, 2004), 245.

[18] Caute, *Sixty-Eight*. It is interesting to note that the historian Donald Sassoon judges this study as lacking "depth and analysis:" Sassoon, *One Hundred Years of Socialism*, 827 n15. Joshua Ramsden loosely resembles the figure of Charles Manson, the leader of one of the most destructive cults in America, described by Charles Lindholm in *Charisma* (Oxford: Basil Blackwell, 1990), 117-36.

biology building or in the architecture building or at the trattoria [...] We went around in herds. The individual had disappeared, I didn't have an individual life, I no longer did anything by myself, I didn't read a book, I lived in this herd.[19]

Comments of this kind uncannily echo Byatt's strong dislike for such moments of self-loss and crowd behaviour, often evoked in her writing.

The most dogmatic aspects emerging from the protest also call to mind a well-known poem by Pier Paolo Pasolini, "L'ortodossia," in which the poet hints at the inherent perils of a new orthodoxy contained in every form of heresy aspiring to dogmatic truth:

> E pensare che la ribalda e superba gioia giovanile
> di possedere una verità eretica
> non contiene (nè altro può essere) che nuova ortodossia;
> [...]
> L'ortodossia covava in fondo alla rivolta
> opponendosi agli accoliti che avevano ceduto alla storia
> e alle sue necessità.[20]

However, Byatt seems to have been concerned not so much with a genuine social or political reading of those events, but chiefly with the workings of the individual psyche and collective behaviour in a situation when a charismatic figure takes on a leading role in a group formation, as her detailed description of various members of the therapy groups in her novel show. While this particular perspective is entirely plausible, it does not seem to do full justice to a time which many have thought remarkable in determining trends and social values which still inform our Western world.[21]

An altogether different reconstruction of the political climate of those years is to be found in Uwe Johnson's novel *Jahrestage* (1970-1983), an entirely different work, of course, which chronicles the life of several generations of Germans, in particular East Germans, from the

---

[19] Passerini, *Autobiography of a Generation*, 89.

[20] Pier Paolo Pasolini, "L'ortodossia," in *Trasumanar e organizzar* (Milano: Garzanti, 1971), 148. "And to think that the reckless and proud youthful joy of possessing a heretical truth / contains (neither can it be otherwise) nothing but new orthodoxy [...] Orthodoxy lay hidden beneath the revolt / opposing the acolytes who had yielded to history and to its necessities." (My translation.)

[21] Cf., e.g., Marwick, *The Sixties*. In his extensive and transnational study of the period, Marwick repeatedly stresses the unique significance of the decade.

perspective of a female protagonist, Gesine Cresspahl, who emigrates to New York in the early sixties together with her daughter, Marie. Since the latter demands a narrative of her mother's life from her childhood in Nazi Germany to her youth in the socialist GDR, Gesine Cresspahl cannot help confronting her life history and the traumas enacted in it. Like Byatt's, this is also a massive work in four volumes, chronicling with meticulous, obsessive precision two periods, the years 1967-1968 in Gesine's diary, and her childhood and youth in the Third Reich and in the GDR respectively prior to her move to the West. It is clearly impossible for me to give an adequate summary of this astonishing work which has its *dénouement* during a journey to Prague, where Gesine is sent by the New York bank which employs her, in order to negotiate a loan to the socialist country just at the time of the Prague Spring, dramatically ended by the Soviet invasion. Here, I merely wish to draw attention to some aspects that made me think of Uwe Johnson in connection with Byatt and Corti. All of their novels are very much works of memory, sharing a concern with the social climate of the sixties and making use of some distinct imagery which recurs in the contemporary discourse of memory. Unlike Byatt and Corti, however, who employ spatial metaphors to suggest the idea of a monumental culture defeating the erosion of time, Uwe Johnson draws attention to the difficulty of reconstructing the past and uses episodic forms of memory. Although Gesine Cresspahl has excellent semantic memory which sustains her in school exams and in her everyday work, she is not interested in recouping the past as mere repetition of what has been. She is much more interested in the function of remembering as opposed to archival retrieval or mechanical repetition:

> Ihr kam es an auf eine Funktion des Gedächtnisses, die Erinnerung, nicht auf den Speicher, auf die Wiedergabe, auf das Zurückgehen in die Vergangenheit, die Wiederholung des Gewesenen: darinnen noch einmal zu sein, dort noch einmal einzutreten. Das gibt es nicht.[22]

> [What mattered to her was the function of memory, remembrance, not the storage, the reproduction, the return of the past, the repetition of what has been: to be there once more, to enter there once more. This is impossible.]

---

[22] Uwe Johnson, *Jahrestage. Aus dem Leben von Gesine Cresspahl* (Frankfurt: Suhrkamp, 1970), 1:63.

Johnson's conception of memory may well be informed by an entirely different reading of history, suggestive of Walter Benjamin, who rejected both the monumental conceptualisation of history and the historicism current in his lifetime. In *Über den Begriff der Geschichte*, Benjamin opposes these ways of thinking about history precisely because they ignore the perspective of the teller in the process of reconstructing the past. Therefore, Johnson juxtaposes two temporal lines in his long novel, allowing Gesine Cresspahl to ask questions about the past in order to confront the future. In doing so, he adds a significant development in ethical and political consciousness and, ultimately, in the construction of community.[23]

In conclusion let me quote from the first volume of Uwe Johnson's novel which contains the memorable metaphor of the past seen as a huge grey cat through the naive eyes of a child:

> Daß das Gedächtnis das Vergangene doch fassen könnte in die Formen, mit denen wir die Wirklichkeit einteilen! [...] Das Depot des Gedächtnisses ist gerade auf Reproduktion nicht angelegt. Eben dem Abruf eines Vorgangs widersetzt es sich. Auf Anstoß, auf bloß partielle Kongruenz, aus dem blauen Absurden liefert es freiwillig Fakten, Zahlen, Fremdsprache, abgetrennte Gesten; halte ihm hin einen teerigen, fauligen, dennoch windfrischen Geruch, den Nebenhauch aus Gustafssons berühmten Fischsalat, und bitte um Inhalt für die Leere, die einmal Wirklichkeit, Lebensgefühl, Handlung war; es wird die Ausfüllung verweigern. Die Blockade lässt Fetzen, Splitter, Scherben, Späne durchsickern, damit sie das ausgeraubte und raumlose Bild sinnlos überstreuen, die Spur der gesuchten Szene zertreten, so daß wir blind sind mit offenen Augen. Das Stück Vergangenheit, Eigentum durch Anwesenheit, bleibt versteckt in einem Geheimnis, verschlossen gegen Ali Babas Parole, abweisend, unnahbar, stumm und verlockend wie eine mächtige graue Katze hinter Fensterscheiben, sehr tief von unten gesehen wie mit Kinderaugen.[24]

---

[23] For a detailed discussion of the episodic form of Johnson's novel, see D.G. Bond, *German History and German Identity: Uwe Johnson's Jahrestage* (Amsterdam: Rodopi, 1993), 87-128.

[24] Johnson. *Jahrestage*, 1:63-64. I thank Neal O'Donoghue for his help with translating both passages quoted from the original German.

[If only the memory of what has been could take hold of those forms into which we organize reality! [...] The storehouse of memory is simply not meant for reproduction. The retrieval of the event alone is something that works against itself. On inducement, on mere partial congruence, out of the blue absurd it voluntarily delivers facts, numbers, foreign languages, sequestered gestures; hold out a tar-like, putrefying, yet wind-fresh odour, the half-waft of Gustafsson's famous fish salad, and ask for substance on behalf of the emptiness that was once reality, an awareness of and a feeling for life, action; it will refuse all flesh. The blockade lets shreds, splinters, shards, shavings seep through so that they senselessly scatter the raided and spaceless image, crush the sought-after scene underfoot, so that we are left blind with open eyes. The piece of the past, acquired through our having being-there, remains tucked away in a secret, deaf to Ali Baba's password, cold, unapproachable, dumb and full of temptation like a mighty grey cat behind window panes, seen from way below as if with the eyes of a child.]

This highly charged excerpt signals the anguish of those young Germans who, like the protagonist of Johnson's novel, became conscious of the need to confront the memories of the past in the sixties, both to mark a radical distance from it and to secure a new beginning. Endowed with many of the biographical traits of the author, Gesine Cresspahl still carries hopes of a democratic form of socialism with her. Only a few years older than the protagonists of the '68 movement, she also seeks to understand her relationship with her father, her family and her *Vaterland*, though her geographical displacement has rendered her perception of time complex and disruptive.

Johnson's novel can thus be said to address the historical roots of the movement. Extracts from the *New York Times* are incorporated into the narrative and read avidly by Gesine. They chronicle the main events of 1968 in various countries, including references to the Nazi trials taking place in Stuttgart while French students parade the streets of Paris on May 1, and clashes between students and police occur at Columbia University in New York.

The grand theme of the sixties, namely the gap between old forms of authority and the new generation, acquired in Germany a highly poignant note which continues to be acknowledged to date. A protagonist of the Italian feminist movement of those years, for example, relates her participation in the student protest in Amsterdam, Bonn and Paris and describes the German "sixty-eighters" as "the diamond point" of the student movement in Europe.[25] According to the historian Ronald Fraser, what distinguished them was "a long training and theoretical preparation,"[26] while the British student leaders faced an entirely different political reality in a country with a comparatively stronger liberal tradition which had never given rise to major confrontations with the state. Therefore, Byatt's *A Whistling Woman* captures the student protest and the counter-culture in the UK as a mass phenomenon that produced fashionable trends and the conformism of cultic milieus. Nonetheless, the novel as a whole is a celebration of the life of the mind, including the minds of women, and of the possibility that new forms of thought can make a difference in the world. Indeed, the novel addresses the issue of gender most emphatically.

In turn, Maria Corti paints a different picture of the initial stage of the student protest in a country where, unlike in Germany and England, students were later to succeed in becoming allied with the working class and, for a while, seriously challenged the established order. Here, the student protest entailed a revival of the old values associated with the Italian Resistance. What Corti shows in her novel are the early attempts of a movement to democratise fossilised forms of institutional power, while hinting at the embedded social implications of this change. As is frequently observed, each culture presupposes a certain way of looking at the world, "like a distinct mindset or glance."[27] In a note reminiscent of Bloch, she finally delivers her hopeful message for posterity that the '68 movement may not be entirely forgotten because:

> Ne riparleranno i poeti, lo studieranno i filosofi. Appartiene alle cose che restano, anche se non ci saranno più quei giovani che anelavano al nuovo e a cui la realtà non bastava.[28]

---

25 Laura Lombardo Radice, Chiara Ingrao, *Soltanto una vita* (Milan: Baldini & Castoldi, 2005), 256.

26 Fraser, *1968. A Student Generation in Revolt*, 234.

27 Chantal Millon-Delsol, "Irriverenza," in *Identità culturale europea*, ed. Luisa Passerini (Scandicci/Florence: La Nuova Italia Editrice, 1998), 107.

28 Corti, *Le pietre verbali*, 125. "Poets will speak of it again, philosophers will study it. It belongs to things that live on, even though those youths who longed for the new and were not content with reality will no longer be there." (My translation.)

IV.

MEDIATION AND ORIGINALITY

LOOKING FOR RICCARDO: TWO ITALIAN VERSIONS OF *RICHARD III*

Mariangela Tempera

Any survey of the popularity of foreign authors in continental Europe places Shakespeare very near the top. His plays are regularly translated, performed and rewritten in every European language. Understandably, the author's 'greatest hits' keep resurfacing all over the continent. Not only are they appreciated as examples of English writing at its best; they also influence the formation of national canons in ways that are undergoing closer and closer scrutiny. A prime example is the role of *Hamlet* in German culture. With their emphasis on English nationalism and their intricate plots, the Histories do not travel across continental borders quite so easily as the Tragedies, with the notable exception of *Richard III*, which critics and spectators alike tend to consider an honorary Tragedy.

Richard III is the only History play regularly performed on the Italian stage. Its larger-than-life protagonist appeals to the *mattatori*, the star actors who continue the nineteenth-century tradition of Ernesto Rossi and Tommaso Salvini. Its emphasis on conflicts and violence among family members makes *Richard III* easy to follow even for spectators unfamiliar with the intricacies of the Lancaster-York genealogy. Its ruthless portrayal of political power games encourages stagings that use the play to comment on Italian politics. In 1950, for example, Giorgio Strehler chose *Richard III* to start exploring the evils of the civil war that had ravaged the country at the end of World War II. His Richard was modelled on a Fascist chief notorious for his vicious cruelty.[1] At the time, it was a very topical, almost too topical, reading. Decades of peace and prosperity later, directors have to find different ways of luring their audiences into the world of the play.

I will examine two versions of *Riccardo III* which were created twenty years apart and that, in totally different ways, successfully inscribe Shakespeare's tragedy within Italian culture. One is a very faithful, highly sophisticated translation by Patrizia Valduga that commands the kind of attention seldom given to those who are faced with the daunting task of rendering Shakespeare in a foreign language. The other is a very unfaithful adaptation by Carmelo Bene that was highly controversial when it was first staged but has now become a classic.

Patrizia Valduga's Translation

A few years ago, Susan Bassnett created quite a stir in the UK by pointing out that nowadays the wit of a play like *A Midsummer Night's Dream* is lost on young Britons because they have become unfamiliar with the intricacies of Elizabethan wordplay. She suggested that the leading poets and playwrights of modern Britain could be asked to 'translate' Shakespeare into modern English.[2] The proposal met with almost general disapproval, but she did have a point.

The spectators of foreign productions of Shakespeare combine the enormous disadvantage of not hearing his original verse with the advantage of actually being able to understand every word spoken by the characters. However, not all foreign languages are equally suited to do justice to Shakespeare's plays. Written Italian, for example, is far from ideal. It does not lend itself to verbal punning, its formality cannot convey a variety of registers, its lengthy, Latinate words make a line-by-line translation virtually impossible. As Agostino Lombardo, one of the most prolific and successful Italian translators, insisted: "the translation is always of a time, the text is timeless."[3] Barring a few masterpieces, he said, translations have a life span of fifty years at the most. After that,

---

1 On Strehler's early stagings of the Histories, see Mariangela Tempera, "Rent-A-Past: Italian Responses to Shakespeare's Histories (1800-1950)," in Ton Hoenselaars (ed.), *Shakespeare's History Plays* (Cambridge: Cambridge University Press, 2004), 128-29.
2 See Susan Bassnett, "Should Shakespeare Be Made Modern?" *The Washington Post*, 21 June 2001.
3 Maddalena Pennacchia, "Tradurre *Amleto*: Intervista ad Agostino Lombardo," in Maria Del Sapio Garbero (ed.), *La traduzione di Amleto nella cultura europea* (Venice: Marsilio, 2002), 166: "la traduzione è sempre nel tempo, mentre il testo è fuori del tempo."

they become unstageable. And stageability was of the utmost importance for Lombardo, who did his best work in collaboration with leading directors. When he died in 2005, he was well advanced in his ambitious project of providing Italian readers and spectators with a new translation of the Complete Works by a single hand.

This version of *Tutto il teatro* by Agostino Lombardo would have been particularly important for a country that has no canonical translation of Shakespeare's plays, no standard against which all new translators feel they should measure their work, no single rendering of the major monologues that, though too old-fashioned for the stage, still survives as part of the collective memory of generations of educated readers. When Shakespeare speaks the same Italian words for all Italians, they are the words of Giuseppe Verdi's librettists. Othello, Macbeth, Falstaff are ill served by the quaint language of second-rate nineteenth-century poets. Such lines as "Niun mi tema," "Due vaticini compiuti or sono," "Bocca baciata non teme ventura," would have been long forgotten if Verdi's music had not given them the status of immortal arias. The vast majority of Shakespeare's heroes, however, only exist in translations that were not meant to be set to music. In recent years, the translators appear to have gone too far in adopting Lombardo's concern with stageability. Oversensitive to the needs of the actors, they bend over backwards to avoid any awkwardness in performance. Translations are usually in prose and in plain everyday language. The need to reduce the text to a maximum of two, two and a half hours encourages cuts that dispense with the most arduous passages. As Guido Almansi observes, "in Italian translations, Shakespeare appears as a great creator of plots, but not much of a writer."[4]

A notable exception to the wealth of run-of-the-mill translations, commissioned by theatre directors who cannot wait for very long to have their chosen play on stage, is Patrizia Valduga's *Riccardo III*. An accomplished poet in her own right, Valduga had no specific staging in mind when she began work on the play, and she took as long as she deemed necessary – three years – to complete the translation. She saw herself as a go-between, whose task it was to make highly educated readers experience the rich poetic texture of Shakespeare's original lines. She also proposed to pay homage to Shakespeare by offering him "verse

---

[4] Guido Almansi, "Re Riccardo? In Italia è nudo," *Panorama*, 8 August 1996: "nelle versioni italiane un grande facitore di trame, ma come scrittore non un gran che."

for verse, alliteration for alliteration, metaphor for metaphor."[5] In order to do so, she chose the Italian equivalent of blank verse, the hendecasyllable, and aimed for a line-by-line correspondence between the original and her translation, an admittedly impossible task given the difference in length between words in the two languages. To ascertain the meaning of rare or technical English words, she used only one bilingual dictionary, Ferdinando Altieri's, published in the eighteenth century, thus giving internal coherence to the old-fashioned words that she often selects to enrich her thoroughly modern sentence structure. The impressive result of her 'labour of love' was published by Einaudi in the prestigious "Writers Translated by Writers" series in 1998. It reads beautifully, but it seemed highly unlikely that a director would be so daring as to try and stage it. And yet, it was in fact performed before it was published because Antonio Calenda used it for his *Riccardo III* in 1997.

To convey the quality of Shakespeare's verse, Valduga calls upon her remarkable poetic skills and her familiarity with Italian poets. Sometimes she weaves phrases from Italian classics into her lines. To translate "Thy bruising irons of wrath," for example, she borrows Torquato Tasso's "ferri acuti" (383),[6] a borrowing she feels the need to acknowledge in her notes, since very few of her readers would identify it. More often, she evokes the style of major Italian poets. By rendering "But yet you see how soon the day o'ercast" with "guardate come in breve il giorno inombra" (211), she gives Shakespeare's line the quality of Dante's hendecasyllables. She is particularly sensitive to the rhythm of the verse – "grave's due by life usurp'd" becomes "spettanza di tomba che vita usurpa" (305) – and acknowledges the importance of Shakespearean alliterations by providing an Italian equivalent: "He is not lulling on a lewd love bed" has the same quality as "Non sta a languire su lascive alcove" (251), "ripe revenue" has the same aural effect as "pronto provento." (259) Sometimes she settles for the modern Italian equivalent of an obsolete English word, but she then compensates by selecting rare and old-fashioned Italian words for plain English ones: "pale" becomes "cereo" (135), "atro," an adjective that no longer exists outside the opera

---

5   Patrizia Valduga, "Note del traduttore," in William Shakespeare, *Riccardo III*, trans. Patrizia Valduga (Turin: Einaudi, 1998), 417: "verso con verso, allitterazione con allitterazione, metafora con metafora." All quotations are from this edition.

6   All quotations from *Richard III* are from *The Norton Shakespeare*, gen. ed. Stephen Greenblatt (New York: W.W. Norton & Co., 1997). The page numbers in brackets following the Italian quotes refer to the Einaudi edition of Valduga's translation (see Note 5).

house, is used for both "black despair," "atro sconforto" (145), and "stern murder," "atro delitto." (391)

   Valduga meets with evident relish the challenge of the curses that are so important in *Richard III*. She goes for the comic effect of an unusual word – "o'erworn widow" becomes "vizza vedova" (17), or for the alliterative insult by rendering "lump of foul deformity" with "raccozzata / sozza deformità." (31) She is at her Baroque best when she takes

> Windy attorney's to their client's woes,
> Airy recorders of intestate joys,
> Poor breathing orators of miseries,
> Let them have scope.

and turns it into:

> Causidici sfiatanti ai guai dei clienti,
> tutori enfiati di gioie intestate,
> alenanti oratori di miserie,
> che abbiano campo.

(313)

The passage makes severe demands on the linguistic competence of the Italian readers/spectators who, like Susan Bassnett's young Britons, could probably make use of a translation into everyday language.

   It was quite bold of Antonio Calenda to choose such a sophisticated and literary translation for his *Riccardo III*. It premiered in Verona in the summer of 1997 at the Teatro Romano, an open-air Roman amphitheatre that provides a wonderful setting for a Summer Shakespeare Festival. On a minimalist setting, the characters moved in costumes that were the combination of army fatigues and period accessories Italian directors seem to love for their Shakespearean stagings. The company too was typical: an audience-pulling star (Franco Branciaroli) was surrounded by mediocre or barely adequate supporting actors, a recipe for disaster for most Shakespeare plays. Only about half of them knew how to intone Italian hendecasyllables properly, and yet the spectators welcomed the unusual challenge of Valduga's translation and the reviewers raved about verses that flow smoothly "to strike, enmesh, astonish, fascinate the spectators."[7]

Carmelo Bene's Adaptation

The life span of a theatrical production is usually very short. Valduga's translation is still in print, whereas Franco Branciaroli's interpretation of the evil king has been quickly forgotten. To acquire some sort of immortality, a stage performance must be recorded, or rather reinvented in another medium. This is the case with Carmelo Bene's *Riccardo III*. First performed in 1977, it was immediately recorded for television, in a shorter and much revised version which cuts most of the nudity and sexual innuendoes that had thrilled and shocked the spectators. First broadcast in 1981, this adaptation of *Richard III* is occasionally repeated (most recently, in 2005) as a late night or satellite treat for discerning viewers.

Vilified by some critics and idolised by others, Carmelo Bene (1937-2002) was a protagonist of Italian avant-garde theatre in the 1970s and 1980s. A gifted actor, he tailored his shows around his own charismatic figure. In his hands, the words of the classics (which he himself translated) were transformed into a sort of musical score with results that could be both fascinating and infuriating. His devoted followers saw him in many different versions of *Hamlet,* as well as in *Othello* and *Romeo and Juliet* (where he played a Mercutio who refuses to die and completely takes over the play). His meeting with Shakespeare's evil king was almost inevitable because in an actor's life, he noted, "the general collapse of *Macbeth* is almost always preceded by deformity in *Richard III*."[8] And *Macbeth* did in fact follow *Richard III* in his exploration of the Shakespeare canon.

Bene's *Riccardo III* was first published in 1978, together with an essay by Gilles Deleuze and the actor's response to the essay, in a book aptly entitled *Sovrapposizioni* (Superimpositions). Bene's prose translation superimposes on Shakespeare's tragedy his visionary approach to the role of the director/performer. Unlike Valduga, Bene makes no demands on the linguistic competence of his spectators because he renders the English verse into simple and colloquial Italian. He does not, however,

---

[7] Magda Poli, "Un seduttore in nero chiamato Riccardo III," *Corriere della Sera*, 10 March 1999: "a colpire, irretire, sgomentare, affascinare lo spettatore."

[8] Carmelo Bene, "*Riccardo III* o del delitto mondano," in Carmelo Bene, *Opere* (Milan: Bompiani, 1995), 1185.

share her reverence for the original, and makes serious demands on the culture of the spectators by occasionally grafting onto Shakespeare's lines excerpts from other literary texts. His first graft is typical of his mischievous wit. Immediately before the seduction scene with Lady Anne, Bene's Riccardo is given a non-Shakespearean monologue:

Perch'io non spero più di ritornare
perch'io non spero
perch'io non spero più di ritornare
perché dovrei rimpiangere
l'abusata potenza del mio regno? [...]
E prego di poter dimenticare
queste cose che troppo
discuto con me stesso e troppo spiego
poi che non spero più di ritornare [...][9]

(Because I do not hope to turn again / Because I do not hope / Because I do not hope to turn / Why should I mourn / The vanished power of the usual reign? [...] / And pray that I may forget / These matters that with myself I too much discuss / Too much explain / Because I do not hope to turn again [...])

It is a metatheatrical moment well suited to a staging that never allows the spectators to forget they are watching actors performing a story they know very well. Before his most famous scene, Bene/Riccardo takes a moment to brood upon his fate in words that are not Shakespeare's. Whose words are they? Most spectators would recognise the first line as a slight variation on one of the most famous openings of Italian poetry, "Perch'io non spero di tornar giammai, ballatetta, in Toscana [...]," by Guido Cavalcanti (1260?-1301). Far fewer would realise that what Bene has grafted onto Shakespeare's text is an Italian version of lines from T.S. Eliot's "Ash Wednesday," which opens with an English translation of Cavalcanti's best-known line. By connecting Shakespeare with a thirteenth- and a twentieth-century poet, Bene's "sovrapposizione" is perfectly inscribed within the boundaries of the Western canon. His approach to performance may be outrageously unconventional, but for his raw material he favours the most hallowed among Dead White Men. By allowing the "Perch'io non spero" line to

---

[9] Carmelo Bene, "*Riccardo III*" in Carmelo Bene and Gilles Deleuze, *Sovrapposizioni* (1978; Macerata: Quodlibet, 2002), 30. All quotations from Bene's text are from this edition.

ricochet from Cavalcanti's original to Eliot's English to the translator's Italian, Bene reveals that, the plainness of his own version of *Richard III* notwithstanding, he is well aware of the cultural complexities of translation. In all of Bene's adaptations, more important than what he superimposes on the texts is what he subtracts from them. In his essays, Gilles Deleuze describes how this strategy works for *Richard III*:

> What is being subtracted, amputated here is the entire royal and princely system. Only Richard III and the women are left intact. [...] *Richard III* is perhaps the only Shakespearean tragedy in which women autonomously deal with war matters. As for Richard III, he covets not so much power as the new invention or introduction of a war machine [...]. The man of war has always been considered in all mythologies different in origin from the man of State or the king: deformed and murky, he always comes from elsewhere. Bene puts him on stage [...] Richard III [...] will put himself together with artificial limbs which he fishes out of a drawer.[10]

"La nottataccia di un uomo di guerra" (The Rough Night of a Man of War) is Bene's subtitle for his version of Shakespeare's play. Not only does it isolate the key to his reading of Richard's character as a war machine, it also announces the time frame into which the five acts will be fitted. As Gianfranco Bartalotta observes, Bene's compression of time brings together on stage "private memories and Shakespearean references, the construction of the play and its actual staging."[11]

Bene sets his *Riccardo III* in a nineteenth-century bedroom, cluttered with furniture, faded roses, coffins for dead kings and princes. The stage

---

[10] Gilles Deleuze, "Un manifesto di meno," in *Sovrapposizioni*, 87: "Ciò che qui si amputa, si sottrae, è tutto il sistema regale e principesco. Restano intatti solo Riccardo III e le donne. [...] *Riccardo III* è forse la sola tragedia di Shakespeare in cui le donne hanno rapporti di guerra in proprio. E Riccardo III, da parte sua, ambisce non tanto al potere quanto alla nuova invenzione o introduzione di una macchina da guerra [...]. L'uomo di guerra è sempre stato considerato in tutte le mitologie di origine diversa dall'uomo di Stato o dal re: difforme e torbido, viene sempre da altrove. Bene lo fa arrivare sulla scena [...] Riccardo III [...] si comporrà con protesi secondo gli oggetti che trae a caso da un cassetto."

[11] Gianfranco Bartalotta, *Carmelo Bene e Shakespeare* (Rome: Bulzoni, 2000), 94: "i ricordi privati e i riferimenti shakespeariani, l'ideazione dello spettacolo con la sua realizzazione."

is dominated by an all important "comò" (chest of drawers). The word Bene uses in his stage directions to refer to this piece of furniture is old-fashioned and slightly out of place in the context of a tragedy. And yet it keeps reappearing. In combination with repeated references to Richard, the man of war, as in turn wanting and not wanting to become a *civetta* (an owlet, but also a coquette), it eventually triggers the memory of a very popular Italian nursery rhyme about three owlets on a chest of drawers: "Ambarabà ciccì cocò / Tre civette sul comò..." The deliberate reference to the rhyme gives an extra layer of meaning to some elements of the production: the sudden incursions of Bene/Richard into the world of female vanity and mannerisms and the wayward behaviour of the Queens who, in the stage version, throw tantrums, take off their clothes and are sexually aroused. They are his coquettish owlets and he yearns to join them on the magical "comò" of his childhood where fantasies can be played out. Only readers who share the same cultural background can fully appreciate that he will adapt Shakespeare's tragedy by applying to it the lopsided logic of a nursery rhyme for adults.

Through the stage directions, Bene encourages his Italian readers to see his work on Shakespeare's play from yet another angle. As the women mourn Edward, Richard unsuccessfully tries to attract their attention with fragments of words "balbuzie, come in un prologo di *Eduardo* e nulla più [...] (16; "a stutter, like a prologue by *Eduardo* and nothing else"). Eduardo is, of course, Eduardo De Filippo, the Neapolitan actor and playwright who wrote some of the best twentieth-century Italian plays in his dialect. The brief reference to Neapolitan culture is taken up again in the same scene: "Cresce da fuori la serenata napoletana a tutto scapito dell'interno [...] Ricorda ristoranti e 'gusci d'ostrica' [...] e le prime idee su di un eventuale *Riccardo III*" (27; "a Neapolitan serenade off-stage swells and distracts from the interior [...] It evokes restaurants and 'oyster shells' [...] and the first ideas for a possible *Richard III*"). The adaptation of Shakespeare's gruesome tragedy must have been first discussed by actors mellowed by wine and food at the end of an open-air meal by the sea. Not only does the serenade disrupt the solemn atmosphere of the wake. It also combines with the name of Eduardo to foreground a culture, which, with its emphasis on family ties and motherhood, can generate the most moving theatrical moments and the most embarrassingly maudlin songs. Eduardo's famous line "I figli so' piezz 'e core" (Our children are pieces of our heart) becomes surprisingly relevant to Bene's otherwise iconoclastic reading of *Richard III*. His strange ladies cannot be faulted as mothers. They rush off whenever they hear the voices of crying babies, they are fiercely protective of their offspring, they mourn the dead princes with deepest sorrow.

On a set reminiscent of a nursery rhyme, a dandified Richard, all in black except for a white jabot, moves among ladies in crinoline. He is the only male character on stage. Margaret, the Duchess, Elizabeth and Lady Anne are given strong supporting roles. Mrs Shore huddled in bed, and a young servant girl called Buckingham complete the cast. This Richard starts the play as an ordinary-looking, able-bodied man who soon catches on to the arousing effect male physical weakness and infirmity have on women. One after the other, he dons a hump, a monstrous hand, a cloven foot – and the women find him irresistible. When confronted with him and with each other, the nurturing mothers turn into scheming, conniving, overpowering politicians. They silence Richard when he attempts to give his famous monologue at the beginning of the play, although they allow him to complete it once he has begun to cast his spell over them, feigning deformity in the scene with Lady Anne. They dress and undress as if uncertain about their roles on the stage. The grotesque is always on the verge of overcoming the pathos, but it never does. The scenes in which Richard bends each of them in turn to his will are not played for laughs. They belong to that twilight zone of sexual power games where "fair is foul, foul is fair," a dimension Bene will fully explore in his *Macbeth Horror Suite* (1996).

The nineteenth century evoked by Bene in his staging is the age when melodrama superseded tragedy as the artists' favourite means of expressing great passions. Therefore, opera music by Verdi and Donizetti, among others, plays a very important role in this production. Bene is well aware that Italians were introduced to Shakespeare's plays by Verdi's operas. In almost all his adaptations, he inserts famous arias which throw a different light on familiar Shakespearean passages. Towards the end of his adaptation, in keeping with his view of *Richard III* as a stepping stone towards *Macbeth*, he chooses a mandolin version of "Pietà, rispetto, onore" as a comment on Richard's early morning musings and his plans for battle. It starts as a very moving scene, with Macbeth's desperate acknowledgment of his isolation enriching Richard's insight into his own predicament: "Non c'è creatura al mondo che mi ami e se muoio nessuno avrà pietà di me [...]" (79-80: "There is no creature loves me / And if I die no soul will pity me."). But Bene pushes the music to the point where melancholy gives way to the maudlin. The piece is badly played, almost reminiscent of the facile rhythms of the organ grinder. It does not encourage self-discovery but self-delusion. It steers Richard from the tragic towards the farcical. His tone becomes more and more strident as he, supported by the mandolins, masterminds his impossible battle from the cosy interior of his bedroom: "Tutta in lunghezza stesa l'avanguardia! [...] I nostri arcieri al centro" (111: "My forward shall be drawn out all in length! [...] Our archers placèd strongly in the midst").

By selecting a musical theme from Gaetano Donizetti's *Anna Bolena* to comment on another key scene of his *Riccardo III*, Bene reminds his spectators that nineteenth-century Italian opera plundered not only Shakespeare but the whole of sixteenth-century English history in its relentless search for new plots. After the death of the Princes, the Queens rummage in Richard's chest of drawers. They find "un bel 'Riccardo' fatto a pezzi: i suoi arti difformi, [...], e mani e piedi tronchi e braccia orrende, i suoi trucchi infiniti, ma nient' altro" (66: " a handsome 'Richard' dismembered: his deformed limbs, [...], amputated hands and feet, his infinite tricks, but nothing else"). In the version for television, Richard's mother sits inconsolable on the floor and tries to put him back together. Momentarily off-stage, the leading actor leaves behind a dismembered dummy that resists the Duchess's attempts to breathe life into it. As she cradles the components of the war machine that her son has become, in a deposition scene, the orchestra plays a fragment from "Al dolce guidami castel natio...," Anne Boleyn's aria of remembrance before her beheading.

Dismembered bodies are quite prominent in the fragments from Early Modern English history, which fall into the hands of continental artists, who appropriate them to create stories that will appeal to their audiences. In Italy, the borrowings were especially frequent in the age of melodrama and did not necessarily imply familiarity with Shakespeare. In 1834, for example, Felice Romani was greatly surprised when the censors rejected his libretto *La gioventù di Enrico V*. There could be nothing objectionable in a story that was "about the age-old feud between Lancaster and York which has provided material for innumerable stories, novels, and tragedies in all countries and in all times."[12] In the twentieth century, Shakespeare became the inevitable mediator between the episodes from English history he has treated in his work and European culture. To make the story of Gloucester his own, Bene had to take apart

---

[12] Felice Romani, "Letter to C. Visconti di Modrone" (15 October 1934), reprinted in Alessandro Roccatagliati, *Felice Romani librettista* (Lucca: Libreria Musicale Italiana, 1996), 384: "poiché trattasi in esso degli antichi dissidii fra le case di Lancastro e d' Yorck di cui sono piene tutte le storie, tutti i Romanzi, e tutte le tragedie d' ogni tempo, e d' ogni nazione."

Shakespeare's text. Unlike his Duchess, however, he proved capable of breathing new life into its scattered fragments and created a *Riccardo III* that throws an interesting light on *Richard III*.

"THE GLOBE:" ROMANIAN POETRY AND SHAKESPEARE'S HISTORIES

Monica Matei-Chesnoiu

> *If the character of existence should be false – which would be possible – what*
> *would truth, all our truth, be then? – An unconscionable falsification*
> *of the false? The false raised to a higher power?*
> Friedrich Nietzsche[1]

If Shakespeare had not existed, would we have invented him or another like him? Are historical, social and institutional circumstances constitutive of specific dictates regarding national literary and theatrical traditions? To what extent do the shifts in interpretation and historicising the past influence the frames of value in a given present? In the case of Romanian culture, as in many others, these questions have only putative answers because the relationship between life and its representation is at its best volatile, and in most cases, the ineffable cannot be captured at all. Only by means of forgetfulness can we ever arrive at imagining that we possess truth to a certain degree,[2] Nietzsche thinks, and he enlarges on the harmfulness of the study of history as a substitute for living culture in the second of the *Untimely Meditations*.[3] In order to determine the

---

[1] Friedrich Nietzsche, "The Will to Power," in Julie Rivkin and Michael Ryan (eds.), *Literary Theory: An Anthology* (Oxford: Basil Blackwell, 1998), 362.

[2] Friedrich Nietzsche, "On Truth and Lying in an Extra-Moral Sense," in Rivkin and Ryan (eds.), *Literary Theory: An Anthology*, 358.

[3] Friedrich Nietzsche, "On the Use and Abuse of History for Life," in *Untimely Meditations*, trans. Jan C. Johnston, September 1998, http://www.publicappeal.org/

borderline at which the past must be forgotten if it is not to become the gravedigger of the present, Nietzsche adds, we have to know precisely how great the "plastic force" of a culture is. This is the force of reshaping and incorporating the past and the foreign, compensating for what has been lost and rebuilding out of traumatised structures.

Considering the specific case of the absorption of English history as dramatised by Shakespeare into the Romanian culture, it is apparent that the process shows a certain plasticity but also a form of resistance. The plasticity is shown in the complex and often quite sophisticated forms of integration of Shakespeare, through translations, productions, and adaptations, into the national cultural fabric. The resistance, however, is generated by the volatility of meaning at the level of multifaceted readings and concerns particularly the assimilation of the histories.

While Romania was aligned to the other European countries that displayed a variegated history of appropriation and dissemination of the Shakespeare myth along the centuries, the absorption of the histories into the Romanian culture, through translations and productions, was a more 'troublesome' phenomenon in point of frequency and rate of interest. It is only fair to admit, together with the editors of *Four Hundred Years of Shakespeare in Europe*, "the excessive degree to which, in later centuries, the ideology of European nations was associated with the image of Shakespeare, as, together, they achieved their politico-cultural expansion."[4] However, English history as dramatised by Shakespeare, though apparently more apt to offer sufficient opportunities for social and political commentary on current issues, did not enjoy as much popularity as plays on other subjects, probably because English medieval history seemed more alien to Romanian readers and audiences, and the presentation of plays, in print or theatre, required lengthy introductions explaining the historical background and the intricacies of the plot, involving extensive genealogical tables and dreary historical surveys. *Richard III*, naturally, was popular in Romanian theatres, because of the acting potential of the leading role and the haunting power of the hunchback body on stage, and the "Henriad" dominated the later production choices, with a notable exception: *Henry V*. Since this play is

---

library/nietzsche/Nietzsche_untimely_meditations/on_the_use_and_abuse_of_History.htm (accessed December 6, 2004).

4 Ton Hoenselaars and A. Luis Pujante, "Shakespeare and Europe: An Introduction," in A. Luis Pujante and Ton Hoenselaars (eds.), *Four Hundred Years of Shakespeare in Europe* (Newark: University of Delaware Press / London: Associated University Presses, 2003), 19.

concerned with the exploration of the responsibilities of royal power and the diversity of the people in Britain, thus offering distinctive English flavour, it seemed less adaptable to the Romanian context.

A brief survey of the reception of Shakespeare's histories in Romania is necessary to substantiate the insertion of allusions to English historical past, via Shakespeare's plays, into the self-evaluation and specific requirements of culture at a certain time. In the nineteenth century, when Shakespeare's canonised status emerged along with attempts to shape national identity throughout Europe, Romania entered the grand gate of modernity also by appropriating Shakespeare successfully in translations and productions. However, compared to other plays, the histories are placed in a subsidiary position, being directed to specific purposes regarding the political situation at that time. In the introduction to the 1892 translation of *King John* by Scarlat Ioan Ghica,[5] for instance, the importance of the Magna Carta in shaping British democracy is emphasised, although we know that Shakespeare did not dwell on this episode; the allusion to democratic organisation was however necessary in the context of Romania's recent emergence from the Ottoman rule and the national aspiration to autonomy and self-governing values. The first translation of *Richard III* appears in the same edition and the translator dutifully explains in the "Historical Notes" the dire consequences of the Wars of the Roses on English social and political life, practically alluding to the recent Russian-Turkish war, which resulted in Romania's independence. Few productions of these two history plays were mounted in Romanian theatres of Iaşi and Bucharest in this period.

The twentieth century was more liberal with the appropriation of Shakespeare's histories. While by the 1960s all the plays had been translated in various versions, the popularity in the theatres of plays dealing with the English past was still limited when compared to the other Shakespeare plays, particularly the great tragedies and the comedies. In analysing how theatrical meanings are encoded and circulated in this period and, in particular, how theatre criticism negotiates between the present of the performance and the historical past encoded in the plays, in the interests of keeping alive the traditions of the national theatre, but also for circumstantial reasons, it is safe to conclude that the histories have been used only as occasional triggers for social or political meaning. There was a distinct fissure in the theatre of

---

[5] Scarlat Ioan Ghica (trans.), *Regele Ioan. Regele Richard III. Neguţătorul din Veneţia de William Shakespeare* (Bucharest: Tipografia Gutenberg, 1892), v.

the 1960s and 1970s in Romania related to the marriage between critical practice and the reality of the performance. For instance, Brecht's non-Aristotelian epic theatre exercised a remarkable influence on Romanian Shakespeare productions, in the sense that directors observed the potential of illustrating Brecht's concepts of "distancing"[6] and historicising certain events in the actual representation of Shakespeare's histories. In so far as foreign productions of these plays could yield Brechtian readings, some directors tried to incorporate the German dramatist's social and political theories into their theatrical practice. Certain audiences could discern visible political approaches to these plays, and their relevance to contemporary public issues was transparent in almost every performance.

Theatre critics, however, tended to overemphasise the Marxist side of Brecht's theory, in an attempt to cope with the ideological requirements of the period.[7] The socialist-oriented rhetoric used by theatre criticism at that time was eventually coined as "wooden language," an ideologically adjusted interpretation of all authors so as to suit the conceptual requirements of the Communist rulers of the time. Gertrude's demand for more matter with less art could have been a suitable description of the socialising commentaries that theatre critics used in Communist Romania in order to conform to the dictates of power at the time. Occasionally, certain theatre reviewers cloaked their personal resentment of the political regime under the guise of oversized Marxist critical assumptions. This dramatic split between thought and practice, at both institutional and individual level, created an inherent – though not admitted – rejection of ideological critical interpretations. While professing to promote social-materialist criticism in an allegedly Marxist-oriented society, a form of subversive resistance towards these ideas could be discerned with regard to personal options. A direct example of such a disruptive intellectual impediment in the late sixties and seventies is the reception of the otherwise popular Shakespeare scholar Jan Kott. While his *Shakespeare Our Contemporary* was translated

---

[6] According to Brecht, the "distancing" effect of the epic theatre corresponds to a mode of placing the events in historical perspective. This technique is actualised through songs, sets, film selections, epic commentary. The consideration of people as a variable of the environment and the environment as a variable of the people, in other words, the fusion of the environment with inter-human relations springs from this mode of thinking, historical thought. Bertold Brecht, "Efectul de distanţare în arta teatrală chineză," in *Scrieri despre teatru*, trans. Corina Jiva (Bucharest: Univers, 1977), 148. Translated from *Schriften zum Theater* (Aufbau-Verlag: Berlin and Weimar, 1964).

[7] Bertold Brecht, *Teatru*, trans. V. Moglescu (Bucharest: E.S.P.L.A., 1958).

into Romanian with utmost promptitude,[8] the book had only a superficial and contingent influence on directors and theatre critics. Criticism acknowledged the Polish author's importance in the field of Shakespeare studies,[9] but the effect of his ideas on theatre directors was barely perceptible.

Considering the "resistance" of Shakespeare's text to being bridled (*imbrigliarlo*) to a single interpretative hypothesis, according to Mariangela Tempera,[10] or admitting to its "foreignness" (*estraneità*) and lack of complete "translatability" (*traductibilità*) as Maria del Sapio Garbero[11] puts it, building a coherent image of the incorporation of Shakespeare's histories into Romanian culture through translation, performance, or adaptation seems to be a hopeless project. Moreover, when integrated with a difference from drama into poetry, historical fact suffers a triple process of cultural transfiguration: once in Shakespeare's drama, then the Romanian translations of the histories, and finally the poetic significance derived from interpreting the past through the political and cultural present. However, since literature, and especially poetry, is able to express the quintessential involvement of a national culture with the particular sources of its self-definition and transformation, I have chosen this specific form of assimilation of the Shakespeare text, or its conversion into something of great constancy, namely the poem entitled "The Globe" by Ion Stratan.[12] The poem appeared in a literature weekly journal in 1997. Therefore, its audience, though not very large, is expected to be well informed and appreciate cultural allusions. For that reason, the meaning of Shakespeare as a symbol and his emblematic Globe is well driven home. Romanian readers are aware of, to use Dirk Delabastita's words, "the undisputed and indisputable canonized status of Shakespeare as the ultimate icon of literary art, a status that bestows

---

8 Jan Kott, *Shakespeare contemporanul nostru*, trans. Anca Livescu and Teofil Roll (Bucharest: Editura pentru literatură universală, 1969).

9 Dan Grigorescu, *Shakespeare în cultura română modernă* [Shakespeare in Modern Romanian Culture] (Bucharest: Minerva, 1971); Dan Lăzărescu, *Introducere în shakespeareologie* [Introduction to Shakespeare Studies] (Bucharest: Univers, 1974); Leon Levițchi, *Studii shakespeariene* [Shakespearean Studies] (Cluj-Napoca: Dacia, 1976); Aureliu Manea, *Comentarii pe marginea teatrului lui Shakespeare și confesiuni* [Commentary on Shakespeare's Theatre and Confessions] (Cluj-Napoca: Dacia, 1986).

10 Mariangela Tempera (ed.), *The Merchant of Venice dal testo alla scena* (Bologna: Editrice CLUEB, 1994), 7.

11 Maria Del Sapio Garbero (ed.), *La traduzione di Amleto nella cultura europea* (Venice: Marsilio Editori, 2002), 8.

12 Ion Stratan, "The Globe," *Luceafărul*, 41 (1997): 6. For an English translation of the poem, see the appendix to this essay.

on him a wisdom and authority of almost metaphysical depth and therefore a universal, transcendental quality."[13] However, when reading the poem's six sections, entitled "The Taming of the Shrew," "The Comedy of Errors," "King John," "The Life and Death of King Richard II," "King Henry IV and King Henry V," and "The First and Second Part of King Henry VI," it is difficult to derive affirmative themes, because only anger, confusion, deceit, murder and injury emerge from the text.

Ion Stratan is considered a representative poet of the 1980s generation, and the essential themes of his writing are, in his own acceptance, the sacred and the word. In an interview with the critic Bogdan Stoicescu, Stratan says about "The Globe" that it is meant to illuminate the "mechanistic" way of reading in parallel the plays' text, the theatrical script, and the actors' movement. This parallelism seems to Stratan suggestive of the intellectual dilemmas of the generic playwright, the actor, and the director.[14] Therefore, Stratan attempts to demolish traditional interpretations of the Shakespeare text in performance based on attributing meanings to the authorial or directorial intention, or the meanings construed in the actors' interpretation, pleading for the reality of performance that, like life, has nothing superfluous or externally attributable because it just *is*. Highlighting the slipperiness of transmission, Stratan's statement reminds us that values are relative, but can, nonetheless, be defined quite precisely in context, once paradigm shifts have been recognised. As W.B. Worthen has pointed out, "performance criticism tends to assimilate 'Shakespeare' to a universalised sense of theatrical practice, practice which is founded on modern notions of identity and the subject."[15] However, Stratan's term "mechanistic" adduces the reference to Jan Kott's "Grand Mechanism" of history seen as a destructive cycle in which the end is the beginning, and one villain replaces another. This theatrical de-romanticisation of Shakespeare grew out of the traditions of Brecht and Beckett and lay at

---

[13] Dirk Delabastita, "More Alternative Shakespeares," in A. Luis Pujante and Ton Hoenselaars (eds.), *Four Hundred Years of Shakespeare*, 126.

[14] Bogdan Stoicescu, "Poetul este un fel de asistent social: Convorbire cu poetul Ion Stratan, realizată de Bogdan Stoicescu" [The poet is a kind of social assistant: Discussion between the poet Ion Stratan and Bogdan Stoicescu], *Teatrul Equinox Ploiești*, 17 (February 2004), http://www.ploiesti.ro/equinox/Romana/Atelier%2021. %20Februarie.htm (accessed December 6, 2004).

[15] W.B. Worthen, *Shakespeare and the Authority of Performance* (New York: Cambridge University Press, 1997), 40.

the basis of most Romanian interpretations of Shakespeare's histories in the seventies and eighties, under the Communist regime.

In a 1970 essay on Shakespeare's histories, entitled "Shakespeare's Modern Realism," the critic Ion Manolescu uses Jan Kott's metaphor of the inexorable mechanism of power when he writes:

> With Shakespeare, history is not rational, like, for example, with Hegel, who considers that only individuals in history have the tragic flaw; history is tragic and meaningless because it represents an absurd Mechanism, a reiteration of the same fatal circle of events. Order in history is as indifferent to people as universal order is; there is no freedom, only monstrous necessity, there are no causes and purposes, only an endless sequence of power cycles.[16]

This might seem a statement in accordance with the Marxist rules. The generalised form of expression and the impersonal tone, however, leads to a subversive interpretation of Manolescu's commentary, which is inscribed in the academic spirit of resistance to the Communist ideology. This critical consideration of the Romanian productions of Shakespeare's histories could be deciphered as an accurate, though clandestine, description of the dictatorial regime in Romania. The socialist political system tried to impose an alien Marxist-Leninist materialistic ideology and practice on a nation whose history had shown very few moments of freedom from different world powers. Under the guise of materialist criticism, Manolescu's message about Shakespeare's histories tells readers covertly that communism is inhuman, acting like an "absurd mechanism" on individual consciousness. It has no regard for the human being, and all the political rulers of the day care for is to obtain power at all costs and enjoy its benefits for as long as possible. Irrationality and insensitive cyclical movement, the sense of waste and impossibility of significant action were only a few of the people's general emotions in Romania during the seventies and later. Ion Stratan lived in these historical circumstances and it is reasonable, therefore, to suppose that he would take these feelings with him to the theatre to watch how the productions of Shakespeare's histories matched different expectations.

Despite all assumptions of authorial intentionality, Stratan's "The Globe" is published in 1997, in a period when Romania is seen as a

---

[16] Nicolae Manolescu, "Realismul modern al lui Shakespeare" [Shakespeare's modern realism], *Teatrul*, 3 (1970): 33 (my translation).

democratic country, and the suspicion of using allusions to English history as a subversive attack on the present regime is no longer viable. Moreover, to use Stephen Greenblatt's words when referring to Shakespeare's absorption of the fundamental energies of the political power in his time, "the crucial point is less that he *represented* the paradoxical practices of an authority deeply complicit in undermining its own legitimacy than that he *appropriated* for the theatre the compelling energies at once released and organized by these practices."[17] Similarly, Stratan integrates in the poetic fabric both the interpretative expectations related to Shakespeare's histories as assimilated by Romanian culture at a particular moment in time (i.e., the notion of history as a great mechanism versus the Communist authority) and the subversive energies released by this historical reality with an impact on later times. This suggests, to me at least, that historical culture can turn into infirmity and defect when improperly negotiated, and that the cultural evaluation of any interpretation of Shakespeare's histories works as *pharmakon*,[18] acting as both remedy and poison. This criticism does not address Ion Stratan's poetry, or his vision of the Romanian theatrical versions of Shakespeare's histories, but it refers to the special duplicity we were all forced to experience for so many years in the Communist past, which made us sever thought from action, feeling from word.

The poem has six parts, and the first two focus on the comedies *The Taming of the Shrew* and *The Comedy of Errors*. Although these plays were most popular in Romanian theatrical practice during the Communist period, mainly because comedies could be bent towards social and at times political commentary, Stratan disregards the cheerful ingredients infusing each of them and concentrates on the theme of "taming" in the former, and "confusion" in the latter. The two stanzas in blank verse are composed of lists of characters, in the manner of the dramatis personae on the front page of the play's text, and in "The Taming of the Shrew" each character "is taming" another, while in "The Comedy of Errors" characters "confound" each other. The repetition imparts a sense of mechanical downbeat, and the comedies' characters are mere stepping stones against which this automatic device measures its rhythm. There is no comic relief in the inexorable reiteration of names taming names, or characters confounding characters. While the Communist regime used

---

[17] Stephen Greenblatt, "Invisible Bullets," in Rivkin and Ryan (eds.), *Literary Theory: An Anthology*, 791-92.

[18] See Jacques Derrida, "Plato's Pharmacy," in Rivkin and Ryan (eds.), *Literary Theory: An Anthology*, 429.

productions of Shakespeare's comedies to create a make-believe world of fantasy that would take people's minds off the grim realities of their oppressed existence, or sometimes directors used them to promote social and political allusions cloaked in laughter, Stratan offers a monotonous list of names, meant to be recited in tedious sequence, thus probably showing that when real people become words on a page, or sounds articulated *ad infinitum*, all stability is lost and the theatre's vitality dissolves into meaningless vocables.

In the stanza entitled "King John," however, everyone is someone's son or daughter. As if dwelling on the theme connected with the question of legitimacy and fitness to rule, which is the real focus of Shakespeare's play, Stratan highlights family relationships, legitimate or spurious, by beginning his list with King John, Prince Henry, his son, and then all the subsequent characters are "his son" or "his daughter." It is true that a certain confusion arises because it is not clear to the reader whether all the names are supposed to be King John's sons or daughters, or whether each character is the son or daughter of the previous one, starting with the head of the list, the king, and his princely son. In fact, the exact elucidation of the family sequence is irrelevant, as long as the mechanical repetition of the list of names is allowed to impose its tedious pace. In Shakespeare's play, events in the plot disrupt the connection between intention and outcome – the characters are thwarted by historical accident and adversity, and thus *King John* is more a pragmatic representation of political events than a story shaped according to aesthetic ends. Shakespeare treats history as an unpredictable unfolding of events, in which seemingly decisive moments become insignificant episodes in a haphazard universe. As Paola Pugliatti remarks about *Shakespeare the Historian*, the plays are neither jingoistic nor pessimistic, but politically ambivalent, characterised by a *"polyphony"* which signals the dialogic and conflictual nature of historical issues."[19] Similarly, by emphasising the family relationships (real or preposterous) connecting various characters, in the manner of an interminable genealogical list, Stratan displaces the reader's attention from the grand issue of "monumental history,"[20] as Nietzsche ironically calls it, towards an understanding of the past as a continuum in which people live, love, and die, connected by family ties and existing in the shade of trivial events. Moreover, this live version of history is achieved through mind-numbing

---

[19] Paola Pugliatti, *Shakespeare the Historian* (New York: St. Martin's Press, 1996), 45.
[20] Nietzsche, "On the Use and Abuse of History for Life."

repetition because any artificial attempt to pin down the vitality of life, or the theatre as life, must give us pause.

Another interesting example of poetic licence with a key in the same stanza on *King John* is the character of the Bastard. Hereditary legitimacy – the validity of the passage of land, title, or position to children from their deceased parents, according to an elaborate code of social rules – is a main concern in *King John*. Unlike many of the characters in the play, the Bastard is not an actual historical figure, and in many ways he is less a coherent character than a set of theatrical functions. Shakespeare based him in part upon the vice figure, which combined a commitment to evil with an intimacy with the audience and an alluring sense of fun. In asides and soliloquies, the Bastard denounces the failings of the royals while he gleefully announces his subscription to their self-interested schemes. However, later in the play, the Bastard becomes one of the more responsible figures, proving himself an ethical centre in a play largely without the rhetoric of positive values. The Bastard becomes a vital and interesting character. This is probably why Stratan eliminates him altogether from his family list, because the unproductive enumeration is intended to highlight the mechanical transition from the real life of historical fact (where we are not sure if this person existed), through its dilution or distortion by various records of this past (like, for example, Holinshed's chronicles, where the Bastard is referred to in passing), to the interpretation in Shakespeare's fictionalisation of history, and then the multiple appropriations of this character in various translations, productions or adaptations in many languages. It is no wonder that, subjected to so many alterations, a personage who did not even really exist should be obliterated from a random family list that means nothing when set against the play's world.

The stanza entitled "The Life and Death of King Richard II" is divided into two parts: "The people King Richard II met during his life" and "The people King Richard II met during his death." Stratan perceives Richard's two differently graded hypostases represented by him as king in power, and the psychological "death" after the loss of power. Therefore, Richard's death is not the process of dying, or a spiritualistic life after physical death, but a crucial period, an expanse of time probably more meaningful than his life. In Shakespeare's drama, Richard's poetry becomes increasingly exalted, and his wordplay obviously superior to that of anyone around him as the play progresses towards his end. At the same time, however, he becomes increasingly self-absorbed and abstracted from the realities around him. Stratan's monotonous character list in this stanza has no connection with the antagonist parties, Richard's and Bolingbroke's, and all the characters belonging to the two sections, before and after Richard's death, or loss of power, are listed apparently at random, in a sequence that does not speak so much of the play's plot as suggest a casting of characters in the script. The effect is of mechanical repetition, also pointing out the amalgamated nature of Shakespeare's drama, which since the nineteenth century has created ongoing debates in the separate fields of performance and text. For two centuries, Shakespeare has been evoked to authorise the director, or the critic, or received notions of theatrical practice. What is left in the end, Stratan suggests, is but a lifeless catalogue of characters who, taken out of their live theatrical contexts, become merely part of meaningless lists of names on a page, some of them unpronounceable for Romanians, but certainly appealing because they bear Shakespeare's and the Globe's brand name in visible signs.

"King Henry IV and King Henry V" records most characters in *1 Henry IV* and in *Henry V*, without discrimination as to their royal or low-life status, and the main theme is "killing." Starting with King Henry IV who kills King Henry V, everybody seems seized with murderous frenzy, killing character names at random. Sometimes the killing rage is taken to ludicrous extremes, as when "Prince John of Lancaster kills the Duke of Bedford" while a reader conversant with the genealogy of English kings would know that they are the same person, the third son of Henry IV, only mentioned by different names in *1 Henry IV* (John of Lancaster) and in *Henry V* (Duke of Bedford). Though an apparently hilarious confusion, the suggestion of a character in a play killing himself as a character in another play suggests the distinction that must be made between characters in fiction and real people in history. Just as Michael D. Bristol instructs us to differentiate between "real people and make-believe people,"[21] Stratan teaches us to negotiate successfully between beliefs and make-beliefs, triggering in the background the more troubling question of why Shakespeare had to become a banner to legitimise cultural debate at various points in time. In fact, this stanza is patterned on a mechanical parallel of characters, according to which one character from *1 Henry IV* kills another character from *Henry V*. The interchange is confusing at first, but when the pattern is observed, we see that characters are treated as having life only within the circumscribed world of their respective plays, and they become the antagonists of *any* character from the rival parallel play. Thus, Stratan opposes antithetically

---

[21] Michael D. Bristol, "How many children did she have?" in John J. Joughin (ed.), *Philosophical Shakespeares* (London: Routledge, 2000), 26.

1 Henry IV and *Henry V*, making no reference to *2 Henry IV*, probably because he considers it just a sequel to the former. The juxtaposition of these tensions between the realistic and the theatrical provides however an alternative model of approaching cultural investigations of Shakespeare which resists any authoritative practice.

The antagonism between characters in different plays is emphasised in the poem's last stanza, "The First and Second Part of *Henry VI*," when King Henry from the second part "wounds" King Henry from the first part, and other characters do the same. This time, the characters' names from the first and second part of *Henry VI* (with no reference to *3 Henry VI*) are identical. However, the identity of the names is sometimes real, sometimes assumed, but it never supports the idea of symmetrical distinctiveness except in name. For instance, the statement "DUKE OF BEDFORD from the first part wounds DUKE OF BEDFORD from the second part" is symmetrical only in form. In Shakespeare's *Henry VI, Part 1*, the Duke of Bedford, uncle to the King, rushes off to France to help Talbot, is brought in sick in a chair, though urged to seek safety witnesses his enemies vanquished, and dies. In *2 Henry VI*, this character no longer exists, although his policy is commemorated. The DUKE OF GLOUCESTER appears under the same name in *Henry VI, Parts 1* and *2*, but the character from the first part is capable of wounding the one from the second part. THOMAS BEAUFORT from the first part appears under the name of Exeter and becomes a kind of commentator, remaining behind at the end of scenes after everyone else has exited and remarking on the problems caused by internal dissention and strife in England and abroad. However, he does not appear in *Henry VI, Part 2*, though Stratan has him wounded here. The confusion is increased by the use of different characters named Beaufort, each with their own importance in either *Part 1* or *Part 2* of *Henry VI*, though they act under different names, or do not appear at all in one of these plays. Stratan's theme of injury and murder, emphasised so much in this poem, takes the characters and their relationships to the bitter end in two of the *Henry VI* plays, while dismantling any preconceptions about the identity of characters in the two plays, or authorial intention, or even interpretative practices attributed to these Shakespearean figures.

Exploring the changing identity of *1 Henry IV* onstage, David Scott Kastan traces the steps by which Falstaff's play came, by the beginning of the nineteenth century, to be seen as Hotspur's and then, in the twentieth, as Hal's, showing how these changing perceptions of the play resulted from various pressures, as political and theatrical circumstances affected the play's reception. No particular model, however, as Kastan acknowledges, can fully account for the range of meanings that the play can "provoke" for "specific readers and spectators at specific historical moments."[22] Therefore, the plays we now call the "histories" are shifting entities that both give shape to history and are constantly reshaped within it. In tracing how a Romanian poet remodelled his understanding of the English past through Shakespeare's plays, my argument does not rest on an understanding of authorial intentionality. In no way would I presume that Stratan intended his poem to be a pessimistic commentary targeted at the cyclical and recurrent murder episodes that marred English history as dramatised by Shakespeare. It is not clear whether he looked at the English past and its Shakespearean representations with the critical eye of the King of Brobdingnag, who told Gulliver, after listening to his narrative regarding the social and political life in his England, that his native people emerge from his description as "the most pernicious race of little odious vermin that nature ever suffered to crawl upon the surface of the earth."[23] Yet Stratan rewrote English history dramatised by Shakespeare according to this vision as a series of harmful actions and repetitive power cycles.

Each culture and each individual in that culture sees in Shakespeare what the past centuries have conditioned them to see, and Stratan is the product of an age when the grinding machine of Communist ideology turned history into an inhuman instrument of individual or mass oppression. Stratan's chronicle of the past has emerged from the poet's infirmity because he was the product of a period of oppressive compulsion, in which Shakespeare, and indeed any representative figure of universal culture, was used as a double-edged instrument: to legitimise current political practices by the authorities, and as a subversive weapon against these practices by the directors and critics. Stratan brought this load of hurtful history with him in the present, when the current system of democratic values is supposed to act as a buffer zone against which any traumatising experience from the past should find its healing safe haven. Moreover, Stratan's fractured and antagonistic image of English history is not consistent with the traditional aura of our Shakespeare as a cultural icon, whose dramatic representations of times past are expected to be placed on a pedestal of cultural accomplishment and authenticity. However, Stratan's fractured view of Shakespeare's English history, a result of detrimental cultural memory, has the force to work on the

---

[22] David Scott Kastan (ed.), *King Henry IV, Part 1, The Arden Shakespeare* (London: Thompson Learning, 2002), 40.

[23] Jonathan Swift, *Gulliver's Travels* (London: Penguin, 1994), 140.

times, with the effect of changing the present through the re-evaluation of past cultures through corrosive action.

Appendix

THE GLOBE
by Ion Stratan

The Taming of the Shrew

CHRISTOPHER SLY is taming
BAPTISTA, a gentleman of Padua
BAPTISTA, a gentleman of Padua
is taming VICENTIO of Pisa
VICENTIO of Pisa is taming
LUCENTIO, in love with Bianca
LUCENTIO, in love with Bianca
Is taming PETRUCHIO of Verona
PETRUCHIO of Verona is taming GREMIO
GREMIO is taming HORTENSIO
HORTENSIO is taming TRANIO
TRANIO is taming BIONDELLO
BIONDELLO is taming GRUMIO
GRUMIO is taming CURTIS
CURTIS is taming KATHARINA
KATHARINA is taming BIANCA

The Comedy of Errors

SOLINUS, Duke of Ephesus, confounds EGEON with ANTIPHOLUS
EGEON, a merchant of Syracuse, confounds ANTIPHOLUS of EPHESUS with
    ANTIPHOLUS of SYRACUSE
ANTIPHOLUS of EPHESUS confounds ANTIPHOLUS of SYRACUSE with
    DROMIO of EPHESUS
ANTIPHOLUS of SYRACUSE confounds DROMIO of EPHESUS with DROMIO of
    SYRACUSE
DROMIO of EPHESUS confounds DROMIO of SYRACUSE with BALTHAZAR
DROMIO of SYRACUSE confounds BALTHAZAR with ANGELO
BALTHAZAR confounds ANGELO with PINCH

ANGELO confounds PINCH with EMILIA
PINCH confounds EMILIA with ADRIANA
EMILIA confounds ADRIANA with LUCIANA
ADRIANA confounds LUCIANA with LUCE

King John

KING JOHN
PRINCE HENRY, his son
ARTHUR, DUKE OF BRITTANY, his son
WILLIAM MARECHALL, his son
GEFFREEY FITZ PETER, his son
WILLIAM LONGSWORD, his son
ROBERT BIGOT, his son
HUBERT DE BURGH, his son
ROBERT FALCONBRIDGE, his son
JAMES GURNEY, his son
PHILIP, his son
LOUIS, his son
ARCHDUKE OF AUSTRIA, his son
CARDINAL PANDULPH, his son
MELUN, his son
CHATILLON, his son
ELEANOR, his daughter
CONSTANCE, his daughter
BLANCHE, his daughter
LADY FALCONBRIDGE, his daughter

The Life and Death of King Richard II

The People King Richard II Met During his Life

EDMUND OF LANGLEY
JOHN OF GAUNT
BOLINGBROKE
DUKE OF AUMERLE
THOMAS MOWBRAY
DUKE OF SURREY
BUSHY
BAGOT
GREEN
HENRY PERCY

The People King Richard II Met During his Death

LORD ROSS
LORD WILLOUGHBY
LORD FITZWALTER
LORD MARSHALL
SIR PIERCE OF EXTON
SIR STEPHEN SCROOP
DUCHESS OF GLOUCESTER
DUCHESS OF YORK

King Henry IV and King Henry V

KING HENRY IV kills KING HENRY V
HENRY PRINCE OF WALES kills the DUKE OF GLOUCESTER, the king's brother
PRINCE JOHN OF LANCASTER kills the DUKE OF BEDFORD
SIR WALTER BLUNT kills the DUKE OF EXETER
THOMAS PERCY kills the DUKE OF YORK
EDMUND MORTIMER kills LORD SCROOP
SIR MICHAEL kills SIR THOMAS GREY
OWEN GLENDOWER kills SIR THOMAS ERPINGHAM
SIR RICHARD VERNON kills GOWER
SIR JOHN FALSTAFF kills FLUELLEN
POINS kills MACMORRIS
GADSHILL kills JAMY
PETO kills BATES
BARDOLPH kills COURT
LADY PERCY kills WILLIAMS
LADY MORTIMER kills NYM
MRS QUICKLY kills PISTOL, former servant to SIR JOHN FALSTAFF

The First and the Second Part of King Henry VI

KING HENRY VI from the first part wounds KING HENRY VI from the second part
DUKE OF BEDFORD from the first part wounds DUKE OF BEDFORD from the
        second part
DUKE OF GLOUCESTER from the first part wounds DUKE OF GLOUCESTER
        from the second part
THOMAS BEAUFORT from the first part wounds THOMAS BEAUFORT from the
        second part
HENRY BEAUFORT from the first part wounds HENRY BEAUFORT from the
        second part

JOHN BEAUFORT from the first part wounds JOHN BEAUFORT from the second
part
RICHARD PLANTAGENET from the first part wounds RICHARD
PLANTAGENET from the second part
LORD TALBOT from the first part wounds LORD TALBOT from the second part
JOHN TALBOT from the first part wounds JOHN TALBOT from the second part
EDMUND MORTIMER from the first part wounds EDMUND MORTIMER from the
second part

Luceafărul, 41 (1997): 6.
Translated by Monica Matei-Chesnoiu

WRESTLING WITH HIS FORM: THE GENESIS OF MACPHERSON'S *FRAGMENTS*

Mícheál Mac Craith

The conception of the Ossianic phenomenon can be traced back to a fateful encounter between James Macpherson and the dramatist John Home at the Spa town of Moffat in September 1759. This encounter, perhaps, was not as fortuitous as appeared at first sight. Home's burgeoning interest in the Gaelic culture of the Scottish Highlands had been whetted some years before by the philosopher Adam Ferguson. Macpherson himself, already a gatherer of Gaelic poems "for his own amusement,"[1] had previously met Ferguson when he visited his father's house early in 1759 and there is reason to believe that he came to the encounter with Home armed with an introduction from Ferguson.[2] The child conceived at Moffat came to birth with the publication in Edinburgh of *Fragments of Ancient Poetry, collected in the Highlands of Scotland, and translated from the Galic or Erse Langua*ge on 14 June 1760.[3] What exactly happened during the nine months gestation is difficult to fathom, but the correspondence of certain eminent literary figures during this

---

[1] Howard Gaskill (ed.), with an introduction by Fiona Stafford, *The Poems of Ossian and Related Works* (Edinburgh: Edinburgh University Press, 1996), 50. Henceforth referred to as *PO*.

[2] Thomas Bailey Saunders, *The Life and Letters of James Macpherson* (London: Swan Sonnenschein & Co., 1894; reprinted New York: Haskell House, 1968), 64

[3] Robert Morell Schmitz argues that 14 June 1760 as the date of publication for the *Fragments* can be deduced from the *Edinburgh Evening Courant* of that date. See *Hugh Blair* (New York: King's Crown Press, 1948), 46.

period concerning these poetic discoveries sheds considerable light on the subject. This correspondence centres on three important *literati*: George Lawrie (1727-1799),[4] Church of Scotland minister and patron of Scottish letters and the main intermediary between Macpherson and Hugh Blair; the poet Thomas Gray (1716-1771); and William Shenstone (1714-1763), a poet highly regarded by his contemporaries but whose star has dimmed in recent times.

I will start with George Lawrie who received four letters from Macpherson between 27 February and 11 April 1760. These letters, as yet unpublished, are held in the Beinecke Rare Book and Manuscript Library of Yale University (Yale, Boswell Papers, C 1869-72) and I would like to thank Beth Rogers-Ho, assistant librarian, for her help in procuring copies of these letters for me and for permission to cite them.

The first letter, dated 27 February, was accompanied by a translation which unfortunately has not survived. Countering the doubts raised by an unnamed acquaintance of Lawrie, Macpherson is at pains to point out that his fragments are Scottish and not Irish. Furthermore, those writers who see Scotland as colonised by the Irish are wrong. It is the other way round. The Scots in fact have been in Albion "anterior to the highest antiquity the Irish can avouch with certainty." Although the languages of the two countries are similar, there was no need for the Scottish bards to borrow their literary heroes from the Irish who "have never been famous for their prowess of mighty exploits." The ancient place names in the poems are not only located in Scotland but are still in use. As regards dating, "I mistake them much if we have not some more than a thousand years old."

One of the most contentious features of Macpherson's later dissertations concerning the poems of Ossian is his complete rewriting and distortion of the facts of Irish and Scottish history. This letter is highly significant, however, in demonstrating that Macpherson had already conceived his historical scheme prior to any of his Ossianic publications.[5] The next three letters, dated 18 March, 24 March and 11

---

[4] As the *Oxford Dictionary of National Biography* (Oxford: Oxford University Press, 2004) uses Lawrie instead of Laurie, I have decided to adhere to the former spelling.

[5] While historians such as Lloyd, Stillingfleet and Innes had endorsed the view that Scotland was colonised from Ireland rather than the other way round, the debate on this issue still prevailed among the general public in both countries. In his comedy *Love à la Mode* (1759), Macklin offers a fine example of this rivalry in the following altercation between the Scotsman, Sir Archibald MacSarcasm, and the Irishman, Sir Callaghan O'Brallaghan:

April respectively, I will deal with as a group. Some very important conclusions emerge from them:

1. Ossian is not once mentioned by name in this correspondence.
2. Neither is there any reference at all to a Scottish epic.
3. The original plan was to publish a small book of twelve fragments. When the *Fragments* were eventually published, they actually contained fifteen translations, the final three being extracts from *Fingal*. This is a further indication that the idea of a Scottish epic emerged quite late in the day.
4. By 18 March Macpherson had supplied Lawrie with five or six fragments but had not kept any copies of them for himself. He wanted Lawrie to return these poems, the very subject of some of which he claimed to have forgotten. The fragments in Lawrie's possession, plus another six Macpherson had already translated, would make up the dozen required. Macpherson's negligence in keeping copies for himself seems to indicate a certain diffidence and lack of confidence in the credibility of the project.
5. Lawrie replied on 20 March but only enclosed four poems. Macpherson found that he had seven in his own possession, meaning that he was still one short of the required number. He remembered sending another poem to Home in October or November, but again had neglected to keep a copy. Perhaps Lawrie could procure one for him, especially if Home had given a copy to Adam Ferguson or some of his friends. It is interesting that the latter's name crops up again in the proceedings.
6. Macpherson remembered another fragment which would make up thirteen, one he had sent to "a certain noble person." I suspect that the person in question was Sir David Dalrymple, Lord Hailes and that the poem in question is the one later known as "The Six Bards." This

---

Sir Archy: Hut, hut, awa, mon, hut awa, ye mun na say that; what the deevil, conseeder our faimilies i'th' North; why ye of Ireland, sir, are but a colony frae us, an oot cast! a mere oot cast, and as sic ye remain till this 'oor.

Sir Callaghan: I beg your pardon, Sir Archy, that is the Scotch account, which, you know, never speaks truth, because it is always partial – but the Irish history, which must be the best, because it was written by an Irish poet of my own family, one Shemus Thurlough Shannaghan O'Brallaghan; and he says, in his chapter of genealogy, that the Scots are all Irishmen's bastards.

Quoted in Joep Leerssen, *Mere Irish and Fíor-Ghael. Studies in the Idea of Irish Nationality, Its Development and Literary Expression Prior to the Nineteenth Century*, 2nd ed. (Cork: Cork University Press, 1996), 338. Macpherson's initial expression of Scottish superiority may have been derived more from the general public perception of his compatriots than from a formal study of the question.

was not published with the *Fragments* but appeared as a footnote to "Croma," one of the shorter pieces accompanying *Fingal*.[6] We will have reason to discuss this poem again with reference to Thomas Gray and William Shenstone.

7. Macpherson notes in his letter of 24 March that Blair has promised to write the preface and that he will supply him with the relevant material and observations on each poem. In the event, Blair's preface was left unsigned and the earliest hitherto known reference to his authorship is found in his letter to Henry Mackenzie dated 20 December 1797.[7] Macpherson's letter of 24 March is both decisive and early corroborative evidence of Blair's authorship, but once again there is no reference made to an epic even though one third of the eventual preface was an actual summary of the epic Macpherson still had to recover. While the narrative element could only have been furnished by Macpherson, it is difficult to resist the conclusion that the idea of a Scottish epic can only have come from Blair himself.

8. Macpherson was convinced that the fragments he had latterly translated were much superior to the earlier ones which were "all of the mournful sort." These latter poems were noteworthy for their descriptions of nature which accord with "the beautiful wildness of our hills." "If there was ever any scenery it is here; but I am afraid much more natural and beautiful to me, who am brought up in the midst of wildness itself; than to a citizen."

9. Macpherson admits to having made some emendations on his former translations and to have kept the rough drafts of the later ones, "to prevent further trouble to you, or any other here after." This seems to indicate a greater commitment and a more professional approach to the scheme than in the initial stages.

10. In the final letter of the series, Macpherson expresses his gratitude to Adam Ferguson for his promise to correct his translations prior to publication. He regrets that he is not near enough to be able to show Ferguson the originals. If this were feasible, "the poems would be less spoiled in the translation."

Ferguson's involvement in the project manifests itself yet again, and though the idea of correcting a translation without consulting the original strikes one as bizarre, Macpherson may have felt that Ferguson's fluency in Gaelic and familiarity with Gaelic heroic verse

---

[6] *PO*, 189-92.

[7] Dafydd Moore (ed.), *Ossian and Ossianism*, 4 vols. (London and New York: Routledge, 2004), 3:371. Henceforth referred to as *OO*.

would have been sufficient to enable him to detect whether the translator was sufficiently faithful to the spirit of genuine Ossianic poetry.

11. Despite indications of a more organised and professional approach, the overall impression conveyed by Macpherson's letters to Lawrie, however, is his complete reluctance to be involved in the translation enterprise. This from the letter of 18 March:

> Tho I made a sort of a promise to Doctor Blair of sending more of our Highland Rhapsodies, I would rather chuse he would dispense with it on several accounts.
>
> I could not make out more among my northern correspondents, who, they say themselves, have been at pains to procure them. The truth is they think as little of them as I did myself and reckon me unreasonably curious. I have so little esteem for my own abilities that I have no desire my translations should appear in publick. Some may find beauty in these fragments, but the generality will not understand them; neither has one so much prospect of fame or proffit as to make it worthwhile either, to write notes or illustrations on them, were his abilities and leisure greater than mine. However I shall transmit a dozen in a few weeks to the Doctor, and let him and the rest of the genii do what seems fit. I am sure they will not readily expose me, if they are not worth the attention of the public, as it was with reluctance and out of no desire of applause I began to translate them at all.
>
> I shall be glad for the honour of my country if they are approven, and if otherwise, I have the comfort my expectations of them are not high. I am sorry I have no better subject to entertain you with, or to merit your acquaintance with something more than a flimsy bit of poetry.

Yet again in his letter of 24 March:

> You see what trouble there is in having public spirit; if you had allowed the translator of the poems lie concealed you would have none of these troubles; nor do I think the public would be much injured if you had. [...]

> If they be published you will have enough of them;
> but if they won't take their blood be upon your head.

And in the final letter:

> The publick is ungrateful to men of merit. What could a
> blockhead then expect from its hands? Few of my
> countrymen like to be laughed at, nor am I myself very
> fond to partake the risibility of many at my expense. I
> would with all my heart contribute to the mirth of the
> world on any other terms, than that of giving them the
> pleasure of censuring me.

Despite their undoubted value, Macpherson's letters to Lawrie only cover a short period of time from the end of February to nearly mid-April. Insights into the later pre-publication history of the *Fragments* are fortunately available, however, in the correspondence of Thomas Gray and his circle, and it is to these letters we next turn our attention. Hugh Blair was so impressed with the earliest specimens produced by Macpherson that he wished to put them into circulation as soon as possible. As David Dalrymple, Lord Hailes, had been educated at Eton, and was thus acquainted with many English *literati*, he became Blair's chief agent for transmitting the texts. In a letter dated 28 January 1760, but now missing, Dalrymple sent two samples, one of which was *Fragment XI*, to Horace Walpole.[8] Walpole sent copies to Thomas Gray from whom they made their way to Richard Stonehewer, William Mason and Dr Clerke. In an undated letter, Gray wrote back to Walpole looking for more poems but also raising the question of authenticity:

> I am so charmed with the two specimens of Erse poetry, that I
> cannot help giving you the trouble to enquire a little further
> about them, and should wish to see a few lines of the original,
> that I might form some slight idea of the language, the
> measures, and the rhythm.
>   Is there anything known of the author or authors, and of
> what antiquity they are supposed to be?

---

[8] Robert Hay Carnie, "Macpherson's *Fragments of Ancient Poetry* and Lord Hailes," *English Studies*, 9 (1960): 18-20.

> Is there any more to be had of equal beauty, or at all approaching it?[9]

Walpole wrote to Dalrymple on 4 April, enclosing Gray's letter requesting more samples. In the course of this letter, Walpole notes that William Mason, Lord Lyttleton and "one or two others whose taste the world allows are in love with your Erse elegies." On 24 April, Macpherson supplied Dalrymple with two more poems which were sent to Walpole and then to Gray. Macpherson's engagement with the process now seems to be much more committed and positive than during the period when he was writing to Lawrie:

> Inclosed, I send two short specimens of the Irish versification: I found no time to review critically pieces of great length; but, I hope the few lines sent will give an idea of the measure – One is not too bypass'd against the Harmony of the language for the many consonants in the present specimen, As I could not express the sound of the Erse otherwise in our characters. The Irish characters differ in pronunciation from the few alphabets I am acquainted with; and several of our Erse sounds are inexpressible in any other but our own.[10]

Gray's interest was so whetted by the four translations now in his possession that he apparently wrote to Macpherson himself in May and received yet another specimen from him, the poem sometimes known as "The Six Bards" referred to earlier. In a letter written to Thomas Wharton c. 20 June, Gray waxed eloquently on the Erse poems, though he was still preoccupied with the question of authenticity. He dealt with "The Six Bards" at length in a letter to Richard Stonehewer dated 29 June. Just a day earlier, Walpole wrote to Dalrymple lamenting the exclusion of "The Six Bards" from the printed version of the *Fragments*. It is quite possible, therefore, that Gray had received two copies of this poem, one from Walpole/Dalrymple, the other from Macpherson himself. With regard to this same poem, it is worth noting what Mason had to say in his *Memoirs of the Life and Writings of Mr Gray* (1775):

---

9 Paget Toynbee and Leonard Whitley (eds.), *The Correspondence of Thomas Gray* (London: Oxford University Press, 1935), 2:664-65 (No. 310).

10 *The Correspondence of Thomas Gray*, 2:665 (No. 310) n3.

[...] it is remarkable that the manuscript in the translator's own hand, which I have in my possession, varies considerably from the printed copy. Some images are omitted, and others added.[11]

It is also interesting that whereas the printed version was in prose, Macpherson's manuscript copy was in verse. Though quite a significant change in itself, it must be pointed out that it was achieved quite simply by changing the alignment of the phrases from short parallel lines to continuous prose.

Gray did not receive a copy of *Fragments of Ancient Poetry* until about the end of July, and in a letter to William Mason dated 7 August, he continued to profess his faith in the poems' authenticity despite the arguments to the contrary:

The Erse Fragments have been publish'd five weeks ago in Scotland, tho' I had them not (by a mistake) till last week.[...] I continue to think them genuine, tho' my reasons for believing the contrary are rather stronger than ever: but I will have them antique, for I never knew a Scotchman of my own time, that could read, much less write, poetry; & and such poetry too! I have one (from Mr Macpherson) which he has not printed: it is mere description, but excellent too in its kind. If you are good & will learn to admire, I will transcribe it.[12]

Overall Gray seems to have been caught in a dilemma between his genuine admiration for Macpherson's translations and the force of the arguments against their authenticity. If it was difficult for him to ignore these arguments, it was equally difficult for him to conclude that Macpherson had composed the poems.

Questions of authenticity aside, however, some very interesting features emerge from Gray's correspondence concerning the Ossianic poems. First of all, we have the circulation of texts in manuscript prior to publication, a circulation that was much wider than the Lawrie correspondence would indicate. Three of these texts we know: *Fragment VII*, "The Death of Oscur," *Fragment XI*, later to become part of "The Songs of Selma," and "The Six Bards." Then we have Macpherson's genuine concern as how best to convey the aesthetic qualities of Gaelic

---

[11] ibid., 2:668 n13.
[12] ibid., 2:690 (No. 317).

verse in English dress. This comes to the fore in his letter to Dalrymple quoted earlier. It also manifests itself in a lengthy account written by David Hume on the origins of the *Fragments*, an account written for the sole purpose of putting Gray's mind at ease:

> I am not surprised to find by your letter, that Mr Gray should have entertained suspicions with regard to the authenticity of the Fragments of our Highland poetry. The first time I was shewn the copies of some of them in manuscript, by our friend John Home, I was inclined to be a little incredulous on that head; but Mr Home removed my scruples, by informing me of the manner in which he procured them from Mr Macpherson, the Translator. These two gentlemen were drinking the waters together at Moffat last autumn; when their conversation fell upon Highland poetry, which Mr Macpherson extolled very highly. Our friend, who knew him to be a good scholar, and a man of taste, found his curiosity excited; and asked whether he had translated any of them. Mr Macpherson replied that he had never attempted any such thing; and doubted whether it would be possible to transfuse such beauties into our language; but for Mr Home's satisfaction, and in order to give him a general notion of the strain of that wild poetry, he would endeavour to turn one of them into English. He accordingly brought him one next day; which our friend was so much pleased with, that he never ceased soliciting Mr Macpherson till he insensibly produced that small volume which has been published.[13]

It is this same concern that led Macpherson to accept Ferguson's offer to correct his translations, mentioned earlier in the Lawrie correspondence. Macpherson's preoccupation is further indicated by the differences between the manuscript version and the published version of "The Six Bards," but as the Lawrie correspondence indicates, it was not until the second half of March that he thought it necessary to revise his texts. These revisions are not only verbal, but entail the very form itself. When and why was the decision taken to change from verse to prose and why was the poem excluded from the published version of the *Fragments*? A solution to these questions may be found in the correspondence of

---

[13] ibid., 3:1227 (Appendix L).

William Shenstone, the third channel through which Ossianic poems circulated prior to publication.

Shenstone, known among his contemporaries as 'the preeminent arbiter of taste,' received his copy of the *Fragments* in July 1760.[14] It was sent to him by John Macgowan, an Edinburgh solicitor with antiquarian interests who was connected with various Scottish intellectuals such as David Dalrymple. Shenstone made a number of manuscript additions to his copy, including an extract from a letter sent by Rev. James Bruce, a younger brother of Lord Elgin, to James Turton, a friend of the Shenstone family. In this letter, dated 15 May 1760 – a month before the publication of the *Fragments* – Bruce says that he is forwarding one of Macpherson's translations to Turton and asking him to send it to Shenstone in turn. The poem in question is another copy of "The Six Bards." Despite Macgowan's request "as a particular favour" for Shenstone's opinion of the *Fragments*, the latter did not reply until 24 September 1761, but made the telling point that there were considerable differences between his copy of "The Six Bards" and the one Macpherson had sent to Gray:

> It seems, indeed, from a former version of them by the same translator (which Mr Gray, the poet, received from him, and shewed my friend Percy), that he has taken considerable freedoms in adapting them to the present reader.[15]

Macpherson was to introduce still further changes before this poem was actually published in *Fingal*. In collating Shenstone's manuscript text with the thirteen lines quoted in Gray's letter of 29 June 1760, and with the version of the same thirteen lines published in 1761/2, Margaret Smith noted that there are seven variations between Shenstone's text and Gray's, five between Shenstone's text and that published in 1761/2, and nine between Gray's text and the published version.[16] Like Gray's version, Shenstone's is also in verse rather than in prose format.

The extract from Bruce's letter to Turton bears quoting in full:

[14] Margaret M. Smith, "Prepublication Circulation of Literary Texts: The Case of James Macpherson's Ossianic Verses," *Yale University Library Gazette*, 64 (1990): 135.

[15] Marjorie Williams (ed.), *The Letters of William Shenstone* (London: Oxford University Press, 1939), Letter 280.

[16] Smith, "Prepublication Circulation of Literary Texts," 147.

I know no way so good of making up for my long silence to you, as sending you the enclosed Poem, which if it gives you as much Pleasure as it did Me, you will give me no small Thanks for. It is translated from an old Highland Poem by one Mr M'Pherson, a Minister of ye Highlands. There are great numbers of these elegies all over ye Highlands which they sing to mournfull tunes in ye evening over their Fires. Mr M'Pherson has I hear translated some more of them which I fancy will soon be published. If they are not, I shall endeavour to get them & send them to you. It will be needless to say any thing in praise of ye Poem, as I think it can sufficiently recommend itself. The translation has a great deal of Merit. I think it is one of ye best I ever saw. I fancy Shenstone will be much pleased with ye Poem, which I shall be oblig'd to you if you will present to Him with my Compliments.[17]

Bruce was apparently unaware at the time of writing that it was only a matter of weeks before the *Fragments* appeared in print. He obviously did not think it would be difficult to gain access to Macpherson's manuscripts. He also knew that the Ossianic ballads were not only intended for public recitation but actually sung. This must be one of the earliest references to this facet of their performance, one that can only have come from Macpherson himself or from his inner circle, and one that would render the transposition of these ballads into English all the more difficult.

Macgowan's covering letter to Shenstone is very strong in its support for the "ingenious translator" and shows Macgowan to be very much *au fait* with the plan to recover the Scottish epic "which consists upwards of 9,000 lines."[18] Macgowan also alludes to Macpherson's willingness to undertake the task, "but the dependant situation of a Tutor, cannot afford him leisure to undertake so great a work."[19] It bears noting that on 23 June, exactly two days after Macgowan's letter was written, Hugh Blair wrote to Dalrymple proposing a subscription for Macpherson's search for the epic. This indicates that Macgowan was in close contact with Blair as well as Dalrymple, though how exactly Bruce came into contact with this circle is not at this moment clear.

---

[17] "Prepublication Circulation of Literary Texts," 134.
[18] ibid., 153.
[19] ibid., 154.

Like the channel involving Gray, the channel involving Shenstone contains evidence of Macpherson constantly revising his manuscript copies prior to publication and of wavering between prose and verse as to the best way to convey Gaelic verse in English. Bruce's reference to the Gaelic ballads being sung is a further dimension that Macpherson had to engage with, though it is significant that, in his preface to the *Fragments*, Blair categorically states the opposite: they are not set to music, nor sung.[20] Given that Macpherson supplied the information both to Blair and Bruce, Blair's decision to flout the evidence and ignore the musical dimension entailed in the recitation of the ballads is an important and early example of the influence he was wielding over Macpherson, an influence that would become stronger still in the production of *Fingal*, Scotland's national epic.

Both the Lawrie correspondence and Hume's account of the genesis of the Ossianic poems provide compelling evidence of Macpherson's reluctance to be involved in the project. This reluctance is confirmed by the submissions sent by Blair, Carlyle and Home to Henry Mackenzie for "The Highland Society of Scotland's Report into the Nature and Authenticity of the Poems of Ossian" (1805). Blair dated his submission 20 December 1797, Carlyle 9 March 1802, while Home's submission is undated. Even allowing for the lapse of time and the advanced ages of the testifiers, it is still none the less remarkable that forty years and more after the encounter at Moffat, Macpherson's unwillingness had embedded itself so strongly in the memory of the key protagonists. Though some commentators have taken this as evidence of *mauvaise foi*, Macpherson's own words in his dissertation to Fingal bear revisiting:

> The manner of those compositions is so different from other poems, and the ideas so confined to the most early state of society, that it was thought they had not enough of variety to please a polished age.
> This was long the opinion of the translator of the following collection; and though he admired the poems, in the original, very early, and gathered part of them from tradition, for his own amusement, yet he never had the smallest hope of seeing them in an English dress. He was sensible that the strength and manner of both languages were very different, and that it was next to impossible to translate the Galic poetry

---

[20] *PO*, 6.

into anything of tolerable English verse; a prose translation he could never think of, as it must necessarily fall short of the majesty of the original. It was a gentleman, who has himself made a figure in the poetical world, that gave him the first hint concerning a literal prose translation. He tried it at his desire, and the specimen was approved. Other gentlemen were earnest in exhorting him to bring more to the light, and it is to their uncommon zeal that the world owes the Galic poems, if they have any merit.[21]

Yet again it is the persuasive figure of Blair that comes to the fore in making the crucial decision. Once it was decided to opt for prose instead of verse, however, it was only logical to ignore the musical aspect, thus leaving Blair complete liberty in his preface to pronounce on the prosodic qualities of the verse recast in prose:

The versification in the original is simple; and to such as understand the language, very smooth and beautiful. Rhyme is seldom used: but cadence and the length of the line varied, so as to suit the sense. The translation is extremely literal. Even the arrangement of the words in the original has been imitated; to which must be imputed some inversions in the style, that otherwise would not have been chosen.[22]

Given the circulation of verse versions of "The Six Bards" as late as mid-May, it seems that the decision to opt for rhythmical prose was taken quite belatedly, within a month of actual publication. It might be germane to the discussion to mention that the Abbé Batteux's *Principles of Translation* was published in Edinburgh in 1760, part of his famous *Cours de Belles Lettres*. Batteux firmly believed that a literal prose rendering was the only way to translate poetry, and it is highly unlikely that Blair would have been unaware of Batteux's work.[23]

If "The Six Bards" was the poem that Macpherson wanted to get back from Dalrymple (letter to Lawrie, 24 March 1760), perhaps its exclusion from the *Fragments* was due to the fact that he retrieved it too late to 'reformat' it in time for publication. It is also possible that Macpherson was far from convinced of the wisdom of Blair's choice in

---

[21] *PO*, 50-51, 418-19.
[22] *PO*, 6.
[23] Robert R. Fitzgerald, "The Style of Ossian," *Studies in Romanticism*, 6 (1966): 33.

favour of prose versions, and continued circulating manuscript versions in verse. His eventual conversion to Blair's point of view, however unwilling, may well have been aided by the unsatisfactory nature of the only available precedent, Jerome Stone's verse translation of *Bás Fhraoich*, "The Death of Fraoch," in *The Scots Magazine*, January 1756.

It is hardly an exaggeration to say that Stone's faithfulness to the original is confined to the narrative content of the poem and little else. While the original contained thirty-three quatrains, Stone's version contains twenty stanzas of ten lines each, with an elaborate rhyming scheme of *ababcdcdee*. This expansion of the original enabled Stone to elaborate on what he claimed to be the qualities of Gaelic poetry, particularly "the softer passions of pity and humanity." Stone's elaboration, however, is in complete contrast with the laconic nature of Gaelic ballads both in form and content. His high linguistic register is also at variance with the simple diction of the ballads:[24]

> A purer azure sparkled in his eye,
> Than any icy shoal in fountain bound;
> Whene'er he spoke, his voice was melody,
> And sweeter far than instrumental sound.
> O he was lovely! Fair as purest snow,
> Whose wreaths the tops of highest mountains crown;
> His lips were radiant as the heav'nly bow;
> His skin was softer than the softest down,
> More sweet his breath, than fragrant bloom, or rose,
> Or gale that 'cross a flow'ry garden blows.[25]

However much Stone's translation appealed to English-speaking readers, Macpherson would have been more aware than most of just how far it deviated from the style of the Gaelic ballad tradition. I suggest that at least in the early stages, Macpherson was seriously trying to convey the aesthetic qualities of that tradition in English dress, and that this intention has been obscured as a result of Blair's decision to opt for prose instead of verse. Given that the decision in favour of prose seems to have been made quite late in the day, it is reasonable to surmise that Macpherson's first translations were made in verse. The standard unit of Gaelic prosody was the quatrain but as these were not separated in the

---

[24] *OO*, 1:xxx-xxxvii.
[25] *OO*, 1:110.

manuscript tradition, it is not surprising that Macpherson's verse going on the evidence of "The Six Bards" consists of continuous lines.

To test this hypothesis, I will select *Fragment VI*, a piece that is based on a genuine Gaelic ballad and adheres quite faithfully to the original. The oldest version, sometimes called *Eas Ruaidh*, is found in *The Book of the Dean of Lismore*, a sixteenth-century manuscript anthology that actually ended up in Macpherson's possession, but after he had published the *Fragments*.[26]

The outline of the story is as follows. The Fenian warriors see a boat coming to land. A beautiful woman disembarks and throws herself on the protection of the Fenians to save her from a fierce warrior who wishes to marry her. Fionn promises his protection and before long the pursuer lands. A fierce battle ensues and many of the Fenians are killed before the warrior himself is overcome.

There are interesting variations between the Dean's version and Macpherson's, some dealing with nomenclature, others more significant. In Macpherson's telling, the nameless heroine is killed by her lover, whereas the Daughter of the King of the Land under the Sea survives in the original. In the Dean's version, the pursuing lover is named Daighre Borb, son of the King of Sorcha, while he is called Ullin by Macpherson. The foe is vanquished by Goll mac Morna in the Gaelic text, whereas Oscar is the victor in the fragment.

In addition to the Dean's rendering, a number of other versions were collected in the eighteenth century. I refer in particular to the following collections: one made by Archibald Fletcher between 1750 and 1760, one made by Donald Mac Nicol, minister of Lismore, between 1755 and 1760 which actually contains two versions of this ballad (A and B), and one made by James Maclagan, minister of Blair-Atholl who died in 1805. Macpherson actually wrote to Maclagan on 27 October 1760 seeking the loan of his collection which he considered particularly "pure,"[27] though this was too late for the *Fragments*. Two further letters in January and February 1761 acknowledge Maclagan's cooperation.[28] Macpherson's rendering of the tale is much closer to those found in Fletcher, Mac Nicol (version B) and Maclagan than in the Dean's book.[29]

---

[26] Neil Ross (ed.), *Heroic Poetry from the Book of the Dean of Lismore*, Scottish Gaelic Texts Society, Vol. 3 (Edinburgh: Oliver & Boyd, 1939), 136-147 (No. 21).

[27] *OO*, 3:394.

[28] *OO*, 3:395-96.

[29] Derick S. Thomson, *The Gaelic Sources of Macpherson's 'Ossian'* (Edinburgh: Oliver & Boyd, 1952), 29-31.

It is worth noting that this flexibility, allowing for variation and expansion within fixed parameters, is considered an essential part of the creative process in the ballad tradition, though it is highly unlikely that Macpherson himself would have seen it as such, given his use of the word "pure" with regard to Maclagan's collection.

Fletcher's version begins with St Patrick asking Ossian the cause of his grief and the latter responds with the tale outlined above. In this version, the pursuing warrior's name is Iollunn, the heir of the king of Spain, and he kills one hundred of the Fenians as well as the unnamed maiden before his death at the hands of Oscar. The ballad concludes with Ossian pointing out the graves of the warrior and the maiden to St Patrick, son of Alpin, a Gaelicised corruption of the Latin name Calpurnius. Apart from one significant omission, *Fragment VI* accords quite closely with the sequence and details of events in this version as well as the nomenclature.[30] Those unfamiliar with the Gaelic tradition could not have known that the son of Alpin referred to St Patrick. By removing the specific reference to St Patrick and only retaining his father's name, Macpherson was able to disconnect the events his poems relate from the early Christian era and relocate them in a period anterior to the introduction of Christianity to Scotland. It is interesting that the first line of Maclagan's final quatrain has Ossian broken-hearted after the Fenians ("'s briste mo Chride mun Fheinn"), a more explicit assertion of grief than those found in the other versions, and thus in keeping with Macpherson's own penchant for melancholy.

As regards the prosody of the Gaelic text, the basic element of the metre entailed is a quatrain of heptasyllabic lines with monosyllabic endings. The final words of lines *b* and *d* should rhyme. The final word of line *a* should rhyme with any word in line *b* except the final word while the same holds for the final word of line *c* and an internal word in line *d*. Consonantal rhyme was an essential element of the prosody with the consonants divided into six classifications, the consonants in each group capable of rhyming with each other.[31]

---

[30] *The Gaelic Sources of Macpherson's 'Ossian,'* 30-31. Macpherson was to use this story again in *Fingal*, Book III, but Thomson suggests that he may only have been aware of the versions of the ballad found in Fletcher, Mac Nicol (version B), and Maclagan when he was composing *Fragment VI*.

[31] The groupings are as follows:
   1. b, g, d;
   2. c, p, t;
   3. ch, ph (f), th;
   4. bh, dh, gh, l, mh, n, r;

While this is an outline of the metrical rules that prevailed when the Gaelic culture was in its prime, it has to be taken into account that these rules were breaking down by the eighteenth century. Although this relaxation affected such essential elements as the fixed number of syllables per line, end rhyme and even the quatrain itself as the standard prosodic unit, this loosening never descended into total anarchy and the general pattern is nevertheless maintained from the Dean of Lismore's version down to Fletcher's.[32]

If *Fragment VI* is reformatted in verse, it can be cast into fourteen quatrains, five stanzas of six lines each and one stanza of three lines. Reproducing the heptasyllabic line in another language and still retaining the sense of the original is no mean challenge, yet an analysis of the syllabic count of Macpherson's eighty-nine lines yields interesting results:

4 lines are pentasyllabic;

14 are hexasyllabic;

34 are heptasyllabic;

18 are octosyllabic;

9 are nonosyllabic;

3 are decasyllabic;

7 are hendecasyllabic.

It is hardly coincidental that more than a third of the lines, thirty-four out of eighty-nine are heptasyllabic, while sixty-six vary between six and eight syllables, a flexibility that was not at all uncommon in the eighteenth century.[33]

---

5. ll, m(m), ng, nn, rr;

6. s.

For example *gad* rimes with *lag*, *cnoc* with *sop*, *sgeach* with *cleath*. The initial consonants of a word, however, need not belong to the same class. The best introduction to Gaelic prosody is Eleanor Knott, *Irish Syllabic Poetry 1200-1600* (Cork: Cork University Press, 1934; 2nd ed.: Dublin Institute for Advanced Studies, 1994).

32 J.F. Campbell's words on the similarities between the two versions of the "Ballad of the Maiden" found in Mac Nicol's collection bear quoting in full:

It is exceedingly curious to note the changes which have taken place in this ballad, written by the Dean of Lismore about 1512, and by the Minister of Lismore about 1755 to 1779. Every line has changed, but so as to preserve something like the sound, and something nearly equivalent to the meaning of each line, and each quatrain. A few verses have been forgotten; one verse in the second version is not in the first. The Story and Ballad continue the same in spite of the changes.

A better illustration of the power of tradition I never saw.

J.F. Campbell, *Leabhar na Féinne: Gaelic Ballads Collected in Scotland, chiefly from 1512-1871* (London: Spottiswoode & Co., 1872), 130.

33 Ruairí Ó hUiginn notes that this flexibility in the application of the metrical rules is a marked feature of the later ballad tradition, a flexibility that ensured its survival for

Even more interesting is an analysis of the end words. Sixty of the eighty-nine lines are monosyllabic, twenty-five are bisyllabic, three are trisyllabic and one is quatrosyllabic. As far as I am concerned, these figures clearly indicate that in *Fragment VI* Macpherson was not merely recounting a genuine Fenian story, but was making a very serious attempt to reproduce the essential features of Óglachas ar Rannaíocht Mhór, one of the most popular metres used in the composition of Fenian ballads. This is how a reformatted version of Macpherson's text would appear:

> Son of the noble Fingal,
> Oscian, Prince of men!
> What tears run down the cheeks of age?
> What shades thy mighty soul?

> Memory, son of Alpin,
> Memory wounds the aged.
> Of former times are my thoughts,
> My thoughts are of the noble Fingal.
> The race of the king return into my mind
> And wound me with remembrance.

> One day, returned from the sport of the mountains
> From pursuing the sons of the hill,
> We covered this heath with our youth.

> Fingal the mighty was here,
> And Oscar, my son, great in war.
> Fair on our sight from the sea,
> At once, a virgin came.

---

many centuries: "During the later stages of the lay tradition we find that even the basic requirement that lines follow a strict syllabic pattern is often dispensed with." Ruairí Ó hUiginn, "Cú Chulainn and Connla," in Hildegard L.C. Tristram (ed.), *(Re)Oralisierung*, ScriptOralia 84 (Tübingen: Günter Narr Verlag, 1996), 239 n55. In another article, he refers in particular to developments in the Scottish ballad tradition where the original heptasyllabic lines can be replaced by lines of five, six, eight or nine syllables. "Duanaire Finn," in Pádraig Ó Fiannachta (ed.), *An Fhiannaíocht Léachtaí Cholm Cille XXV* (Maigh Nuad: An Sagart, 1995), 62. Cf. Donald Meek, "Development and Degeneration in Gaelic Ballad Texts," *Béaloideas*, 54/55 (1986/87): 131-60. In this article, Meek also draws attention to changes in lexis as well as to metre after the collapse of the bardic schools.

Her breast was like the snow of one night.
Her cheek like the bud of the rose.
Mild was her blue rolling eye:
But sorrow was big in her heart.

Fingal renowned in war, she cries,
Sons of the king, preserve me!
Speak secure, replies the king,
Daughter of beauty, speak:
Our ear is open to all:
Our swords redress the injured.

I fly from Ullin, she cries,
From Ullin famous in war.
I fly from the embrace of him
Who would debase my blood,
Cremor, the friend of men, was my father.
Cremor, the Prince of Inverne.

Fingal's younger sons arose;
Carryl expert in the bow;
Fillan beloved of the fair;
And Fergus first in the race.—

Who from the farthest Lochlyn?
Who to the seas of Molochasquir?
Who dares hurt the maid
Whom the sons of Fingal guard?
Daughter of beauty, rest secure;
Rest in peace, thou fairest of women.

Far in the blue distance of the deep
Some spot appeared like the back of the ridge-wave
But soon the ship appeared on our sight.
The hand of Ullin drew her to land.

The mountains trembled as he moved.
The hills shook at his steps.
Death rattled his armour round him.
Death and destruction were in his eyes.
His stature like the oak of Morven.
He moved in the lightning of steel.

Our warriors fell before him,
Like the field before the reapers.
Fingal's three sons he bound.
He plunged his sword into the fair-one's breast.

She fell as a wreath of snow
Before the sun in spring.
Her bosom heaved in death;
Her soul came forth in blood.

Oscur my son came down;
The mighty in battle descended.
His armour rattled as thunder;
And the lightning of his eyes was terrible.

There, was the clashing of swords;
There, was the voice of steel.
They stuck and they thrust;
They digged for death with their swords.

But death was distant far,
And delayed to come.
The sun began to decline;
And the cow-herd thought of home.

Then Oscur's keen steel found the heart of Ullin.
He fell like a mountain oak
Covered over with glittering frost;
He shone like a rock on the plain.—

Here the daughter of beauty lieth;
And here the bravest of men.
Here one day ended the fair and the valiant.
Here rests the pursuer and the pursued.

Son of Alpin! The woes of the aged are many:
Their tears are for the past.
This raised my sorrow, warrior,
Memory awaked my grief.
Oscur my son was brave;
But Oscur is now no more.

Thou hast heard my grief, o son of Alpin;
Forgive the tears of the aged.[34]

In the light of the above it might be opportune to revisit
Macpherson's first ever effort at translating a Gaelic ballad, the piece
known as "The Death of Oscur," later published as *Fragment VII*.
Deviating so completely from the traditional accounts of the deaths of
Oscar and Diarmuid, this piece alone would have been sufficient to
attach the stigma of forger to the would-be translator. Macpherson must
have been as aware of this as his detractors. Given his strong reluctance
to translate in the first place as well as his repeated emphasis on the
difficulties entailed in translating Gaelic verse into English, it is not
impossible that Macpherson in this instance was so taken up with form
and prosody that content was of minimal interest to him. Once more a
statistical analysis yields interesting results. Of the one hundred and eight
lines:

   2 are quatrosyllabic;
   1 is pentasyllabic;
   17 are hexasyllabic;
   31 are heptasyllabic;
   31 are octosyllabic;
   15 are nonosyllabic;
   5 are decasyllabic.

One line each has eleven, fourteen, fifteen and sixteen syllables
respectively, with two lines having twelve syllables each. While this first
effort is understandably flawed, it is none the less remarkable that sixty
lines out of one hundred and eight, nearly two thirds of the text, contain
between seven and eight syllables and that ninety-four out of one
hundred and eight vary from six to nine syllables. As regards the end
words, seventy-nine are monosyllabic and twenty-six are disyllabic.
Macpherson's ear was remarkably good, and apart from a few hiccups,
the text reads quite well as an effort to capture something of the spirit of
a loose form of Rannaigheacht Mhór.

Although the decision to move from verse to prose may have been
an inspired one regarding the impact of the Ossianic poems on English-
speaking readers, one unfortunate consequence of this decision was to
obscure Macpherson's genuine attempt to grapple with the problem of
conveying the aesthetics of Gaelic prosody in English. If Derick

---

[34] *PO*, 14-15.

Thomson once described him as "wrestling with his sources,"[35] one can with equal validity describe him as wrestling with his form.

Another fateful decision was the removal of St Patrick from the Ossianic framework. He could easily have been retained without detriment to the search for an epic; but a Christian framework would have led commentators to postulate classical influences on Scotland's epic. With the elimination of St Patrick, however, the pristine epic could be located in a pre-Christian past untouched by any other literary influence, thus equalling if not surpassing the efforts of Homer and Virgil. In this effort to assert Scotland's claim to literary fame, as in the choice of rhythmical prose, one feels the heavy hand of Hugh Blair. Thomas Gray was quite right in calling Macpherson an admirable judge of poetry. He was equally judicious in adding the following rider: "if his learned friends do not pervert or over-rule his taste."[36]

---

[35] Thomson, *The Gaelic Sources of Macpherson's 'Ossian,'* 26.
[36] *The Correspondence of Thomas Gray*, 2:704 (No. 321).

NOTES ON CONTRIBUTORS

Aleida Assmann
studied English Literature and Egyptology in Heidelberg and Tübingen. She qualified as a professor in 1992 with a study on the cultural construction of time and identity. Since 1993 she has been Professor for Literature, with particular emphasis on English Literature, at the University of Constance. She was Fellow at the Kulturwissenschaftliches Institut in Essen (1992-93) and the Wissenschaftskolleg in Berlin (1998-99), and has taught at Rice University, Texas (2000), Princeton University (2001) and Yale (2002, 2003 and 2005). Her research interests include history of reading and historical anthropology of the media, in particular the theory and history of writing and cultural memory. Aleida Assmann's books include *Die Legitimität der Fiktion* (1980), *Arbeit am nationalen Gedächtnis. Eine kurze Geschichte der deutschen Bildungsidee* (1993), *Zeit und Tradition* (1999), *Erinnerungsräume. Formen und Wandlungen des kulturellen Gedächtnisses* (1999), *Geschichtsvergessenheit – Geschichtsversessenheit. Vom Umgang mit deutschen Vergangenheiten nach 1945* (with Ute Frevert, 1999) and *Das kulturelle Gedächtnis an der Milleniumsschwelle* (2004).

Jean Bessière
is a Professor in Comparative Literature at the Sorbonne Nouvelle (Paris). Educated at the Sorbonne and Ecole Normale Supérieure (Paris), he has taught at the Université Paris X, Indiana University, Stanford University, McGill University, the Université d'Amiens, and lectured in many universities in Europe, North and South America, Africa, and Asia. He is a former President of the International Comparative Literature Association. His publications include *Dire le littéraire* (1990), *Enigmaticité de la littérature* (1993), *La littérature et sa rhétorique* (1999), *Quel statut pour la littérature* (2001). Under the aegis of ICLA he co-edited *Théorie littéraire* (1989) and *Histoire des poétiques* (1987). He was responsible for a sub-project in the Cotepra network.

Anna Brzozowska-Krajka
is a Professor in the Polish Department, Maria Curie-Skłodowska University in Lublin, Poland. Her publications include three books and over one hundred articles. Her most recent book is *Polish Traditional Folklore: The Magic of Time* (Trans. Wiesław Krajka, Boulder: East European Monographs / Lublin: Maria Curie-Skłodowska University / New York: Columbia University Press, 1998). She has published widely in the areas of Polish magical folklore in the wider Slavic context, the theory of folklore, émigré folklore, and the links between folklore and literature – e.g. in *Folklore Forum* (USA), *SEEFA Journal (The Journal of the Slavic and East European Folklore Association,* USA), and *Literatura Ludowa* (Poland). She is the author of the entry "Polish Folklore" for the *Encyclopaedia of World Folklore* published by Greewood Press (USA). She has presented the

results of her research at numerous international conferences in Europe and North America. She is the chairperson of The International Commission on Science and Research of the International Organization of Folk Art (IOFA) affiliated to UNESCO.

Mara Cambiaghi

is affiliated with the University of Constance. She completed her BA and MA in English and German literature at the University of London (Birkbeck and University College London) and worked as a part-time language assistant in the Italian Department at Royal Holloway New College for three years. Subsequently she took up a full-time position as a cultural program specialist in Italy and also completed further studies in English literature there with a dissertation on *Possession*. Her research interests focus on the theory of cultural memory and contemporary fiction. She has contributed scholarly articles on the fiction of A.S. Byatt in both Italian and English, as well as reviews and interviews for the electronic publications *Iperstoria* and *Connotations* and the magazines *Diario, Linea d'ombra* and *Leggendaria*. She has written on Christine Brooke-Rose and the memory of Scott in Italian opera, and is currently engaged in a project on Mabel Dodge Luhan while continuing research on A.S. Byatt and cultural memory.

Riccardo Campi

is a lecturer in the Department of Philosophy, University of Bologna. He is the author of *Le conchiglie di Voltaire* (Florence, 2001) and *Citare la tradizione. Flaubert, Eliot, Beckett* (Florence, 2003). He is currently working on a book about the uses of allegory in twentieth-century literature (Kafka, Joyce and Beckett). His research interests include aesthetics, poetics and literary theory. He has edited works by Voltaire, Fontenelle and Alexander Pope. He is a translator of V. Larbaud, J. Paulhan, G. Genette, H. Meschonnic, and several essays by other literary critics.

Vita Fortunati

is Professor of English Literature at the University of Bologna. Her main areas of research are modernism, utopian literature, women's studies and interart studies. Since 2002 she has been the Co-ordinator of *ACUME – A European Thematic Network on Cultural Memory in European Countries*. Her main areas of interest in interart studies are the interaction between modernist fiction and avant-garde painting in Ford Madox Ford, J. Conrad, V. Woolf, D.H. Lawrence; verbal and visual representations of the body (*The Controversial Women's Body. Images and Representations in Literature and Art*, Bologna: Bononia University Press, 2003, with A. Lamarra and E. Federici); and female aging between culture and medicine. She is the author of *Ford Madox Ford: teoria e tecnica narrativa* (Bologna: Patron, 1975), the editor of *Scrittura e Sperimentazione in Ford Madox Ford* (with R. Baccolini, Florence: Alinea, 1994,), *Prove di un senso critico: saggi di Ford Madox Ford* (with E. Lamberti, Florence: Alinea, 2001) and *Ford Madox Ford and the Republic of Letters* (with E. Lamberti, Bologna: Clueb, 2002). She has also edited the *Dictionary of Literary Utopias* (with R. Trousson, Paris: Champion, 2000) and *Perfezione e Finitudine. La concezione della morte in utopia in età moderna e contemporanea* (with M. Sozzi and P. Spinozzi, Turin: Lindau, 2004).

Michael C. Frank

is Assistant Professor in the Department of English at the University of Constance, Germany. He studied English and German Literature in Constance and at Trinity College Dublin. In 2001-02 he was a member of the interdisciplinary Graduate College "Kulturhermeneutik im Zeichen von Differenz und Transdifferenz" (Cultural Hermeneutics in a World of Difference and Transdifference) at the University of Erlangen. His PhD thesis, *Kulturelle Einflussangst* (The Anxiety of Cultural Influence, 2005), deals with the construction and transgression of cultural boundaries in nineteenth-century travel writing. He co-edited *Vergessene Texte* (Forgotten Texts, 2004), and has published articles on Henry Rider Haggard, Robert Müller, Michel Foucault, and post-colonial theory.

Rainier Grutman

is Associate Professor of French and Comparative Literature at the University of Ottawa, Canada. He was trained in Romance literatures and linguistics at various European universities (Namur, Louvain and Madrid) before obtaining his PhD from the University of Montreal. His first book, *Des langues qui résonnent* (Montréal: Fides, 1997), was awarded the Gabrielle-Roy Prize for Canadian literary criticism. Since then, he has published a *Dictionnaire des termes littéraires* (co-authored, Paris: Champion, 2001), and a *Histoire de la littérature belge, 1830-2000* (co-edited, Paris: Fayard, 2001). He is currently guest editing two special issues of journals, one of which reflects his ongoing interest in multilingual writing, while the other focuses on nineteenth-century French literature, his main area of teaching – *Fictionalizing Language Contact: Translation and Multilingualism* (for *Linguistica Antverpiensia*, co-edited with D. Delabastita), and *Quel(s) XIXe siècle(s)? Considérations inactuelles* (for the newly created Canadian *Cahiers du XIXe siècle*).

Brigid Haines

is Senior Lecturer in the German Department at the University of Wales Swansea. Educated at King's College London and University College London, she is the author of a monograph on Adalbert Stifter and has also published widely on German women's writing, including articles on Lou Andreas-Salomé, Ilse Aichinger, Helga Königsdorf, Elfriede Jelinek and Christa Wolf. She has edited a volume of essays on Herta Müller in the Contemporary German Writers series, and a book she co-authored, *Contemporary German Women's Writing: Changing the Subject* (with Margaret Littler, University of Manchester) was published in 2004. Together with Lyn Marven, she has also edited *Libuše Moníková in memoriam* (Rodopi, 2005). She has just completed a research project entitled "Maritime Bohemias: Representations of 'Bohemia' in Libuše Moníková and other Contemporary German Writers." She is a founder member of the UK organization Women in German Studies and set up the discussion list wigsforum.

Ann Heilmann

is a Professor of English at the University of Hull, UK. Prior to that, she was the founding director of the Centre for Research into Gender in Culture and Society at Swansea University. The author of *New Woman Fiction: Women Writing First-Wave Feminism* (Macmillan Palgrave, 2000) and *New Woman Strategies: Sarah Grand, Olive Schreiner, Mona Caird* (Manchester University Press, 2004), she has edited two collections of essays, *Feminist Forerunners: New Womanism and Feminism in the Early Twentieth Century* (Pandora, 2003) and *New Woman Hybridities: Femininity, Feminism, and International Consumer Culture, 1880-1930* (with Margaret Beetham, Routledge, 2004). She is a member of the Arts and Humanities Research Council's Peer Review College (UK) and the general editor of Routledge's Major Works *History of Feminism* series. Other work includes four anthology sets: *The Late-Victorian Marriage Question* (Routledge Thoemmes, 1998), *Sex, Social Purity and Sarah Grand* (with Stephanie Forward, Routledge 2000), *Anti-Feminism in the Victorian Novel* (Thoemmes Continuum, 2003), and, most recently, *Anti-Feminism in Edwardian Literature* (with Lucy Delap, Thoemmes Continuum, 2005). She is now working on a critical edition of *The Complete Short Stories of George Moore* (with Mark Llewellyn, for Pickering and Chatto) and (also with Mark Llewellyn) on a monograph on gender, sexuality and turn-of-the century psychology in Moore's narrative work.

Shelley Hornstein

is Professor of Architectural History and Visual Culture at York University in Toronto and is widely published on the examination of place and spatial politics in architectural and urban sites. Her edited books include: *Capital Culture: A Reader on Modernist Legacies, State Institutions, and the Value(s) of Art* (McGill University Press, 2000); *Image and Remembrance: Representation and The Holocaust* (Indiana University Press, 2002), and *Impossible Images: Contemporary Art after the Holocaust* (NYU Press, 2003). She is currently completing a book entitled *Losing Site: Architecture Lost and Found* and is preparing another, *Romancing the Stone: Architectural Tourisms and our Fascination with Buildings and Places*. She is Executive Director and co-founder of www.mosaica.ca, the first online contemporary cultural space devoted to Jewish culture.

Martin Hurcombe

is a lecturer in French at the University of Bristol, England, who specializes in cultural representations of war in the early twentieth century. He is the author of

Novelists in Conflict: Ideology and the Absurd in the French Combat Novel of the Great War (Rodopi, 2004), the first English-language study of this popular genre, which includes novels such as Henri Barbusse's *Le Feu*, and has also published several articles and book chapters on political commitment and the French novel of the inter-war years. He is currently writing a book on French cultural representations of the Spanish Civil War, and is also working on the French author of crime fiction, Sébastien Japrisot. He is a senior member of the Group for War and Culture Studies, which is based at the University of Westminster.

Klára Kolinská

graduated in English at Charles University, Prague, and in Comparative Literature at the University of Western Ontario, London, Ontario, Canada. She completed her PhD in English and American Literature at Charles University, Prague in 2005. She is a lecturer at the Department of English and American Studies, Masaryk University, Brno, Czech Republic, and part-time lecturer at the Department of English and American Studies, Charles University, Prague. Her main areas of interest include Canadian Anglophone fiction, culture and literature of North American Native peoples, multiculturalism, ethnicity, and cultural translation.

Wojciech Kozak

works in the Centre for Conrad Studies at the Department of English at Maria Curie-Skłodowska University, Lublin, Poland. His main research interests include the methodology of literary study, with special emphasis on the mythological and archetypal approach, and the life and fiction of Joseph Conrad. His doctoral dissertation was written on the mythological structuring of the fictional world of Conrad's writing (2004). He has published on myth and Conrad in Polish and in international books and periodicals, including the international Conrad series *Conrad: Eastern and Western Perspectives* and *Interpreting/Translating European Modernism: A Comparative Approach.*

Wiesław Krajka

is professor of English and Comparative Literature at the English Departments of Maria Curie-Skłodowska University Lublin and University of Wrocław, Poland. He is the author of over one hundred and thirty articles and seven books published in the USA and Poland, including *Isolation and Ethos. A Study of Joseph Conrad* (Boulder: East European Monographs / New York: Columbia University Press, 1992), *Izolacja i etos. Studium o twórczości Josepha Conrada* (Wrocław: Zakład Narodowy im. Ossolińskich – Komitet Neofilologiczny Polskiej Akademii Nauk, 1988), *Joseph Conrad. Konteksty kulturowe* (Lublin: Uniwersytet Marii Curie-Skłodowskiej, 1995). He is the editor of the *Conrad: Eastern and Western Perspectives* series published by East European Monographs / Social Science Monographs, Boulder and Maria Curie-Skłodowska University Lublin. The series publishes a volume of Conrad studies per year; fourteen volumes have been published to date. Within this series, Professor Krajka has edited or co-edited seven volumes himself. He was Visiting Professor of English Literature and Polish Literature and Language at University of Rochester New York, University of Illinois at Chicago and University of Minnesota. He is a member of The Committee for Literary Research of the Polish Academy of Sciences, the Joseph Conrad Societies of America and Poland, and many other academic organizations.

Kirsten Mahlke

works as Junior Researcher in the Department of Literature at the University of Constance. She studied Romance and Slavic Languages and Literature and Ethnology in Frankfurt/Main. Her PhD thesis, *Offenbarung im Westen* (Revelation in the West, 2005), deals with Huguenot travel accounts to the Americas in the sixteenth century.

Mícheál Mac Craith

is a Franciscan priest and Professor of Modern Irish at National University of Ireland, Galway. He studied at Galway, Rome and Louvain. His books are *Lorg na hiasachta ar na Dánta Grá* (1989), a study of the external influences on Gaelic courtly poetry, and *Oileán rúin agus muir an dáin* (1993) a study of the poetry of Máirtín Ó Direáin. His research interests include the Renaissance, Jacobitism, Ossianism and twentieth-century Gaelic literature. He has published extensively in these areas. He has contributed a chapter on literature in Irish in the seventeenth century to the forthcoming Cambridge History of Irish Literature. In 1997 he was a Visiting Fellow at the Institute for the Advanced Studies in the Humanities at the University of Edinburgh. For the academic year 2003-4 he was a Visiting Fellow at St. Edmund's College, Cambridge and Honorary Research Associate in the Department of Anglo-Saxon, Norse and Celtic at the University of Cambridge. He is a regular contributor to the Irish Studies programme at Charles University, Prague.

Monica Matei-Chesnoiu

is Associate Professor of English at the University *Ovidius* Constanta, and is the author of *Shakespeare: Knowledge and Truth* (1997). She has published in international academic journals, and was awarded a Fulbright Scholar Fellowship (1999). Monica Matei-Chesnoiu is a member of the International Committee of Correspondents for the *World Shakespeare Bibliography*. Currently, she is contributing to the *Compendium of Renaissance Drama* on CD-ROM and is completing a book entitled *Shakespeare in the Romanian Cultural Memory*, (forthcoming, Fairleigh Dickinson University Press). She is a member of SHAKSPER, the international electronic conference for Shakespeareans, and research associate in Shakespeare studies for the *European Thematic Network Project ACUME – Cultural Memory in European Countries*, co-ordinated by the

University of Bologna under the Socrates programme and the European Commission.

Ondřej Pilný

lectures at the Department of English and American Studies, Charles University Prague where he is Director of the Centre for Irish Studies. His research interests include modern and contemporary Irish drama, Irish and European modernism, and critical theory. He is editor of Petr Škrabánek, *A Night Joyce of a Thousand Tiers* (with Louis Armand, Prague, 2002), and *From Brooke to Black Pastoral: Six Studies in Irish Literature and Culture* (*Litteraria Pragensia*, 2001). His translations include plays by J.M. Synge, Brian Friel, and Martin McDonagh, and Flann O'Brien's *The Third Policeman*. He is currently finishing a book on *Irony and Modern Irish Drama* and working on a critical edition of J.M. Synge's works in Czech translation (both forthcoming in 2006).

Martin Procházka

Professor of English, American and Comparative Literature, is the Head of the Department of English and American Studies at Charles University, Prague. He is the author of *Romantismus a osobnost* (Romanticism and Personality, 1996), a critical study of English Romantic aesthetics, Coleridge and Byron, and a co-author (with Zdeněk Hrbata) of *Romantismus a romantismy* (Romanticism and Romanticisms, 2005), a comparative study on the chief discourses in West European, American and Czech Romanticism. Together with Zdeněk Stříbrný he edited *Slovník spisovatelů: Anglie...* (An Encyclopaedia of Writers: England... 1996, 2003). He has written two textbooks: *Literary Theory* (1995, 1997) and *Lectures on American Literature* (2002), the latter jointly with Hana Ulmanová, Justin Quinn and Erik Roraback. Among his other publications are book chapters and articles on Shakespeare, Romanticism and poststructuralism, and translations of Byron's *Manfred* and M.H. Abrams's *The Mirror and the Lamp* into Czech (1991, 2001). He is the founding editor of the international academic journal *Litteraria Pragensia* and a member of the editorial boards of four international academic journals. He was Visiting Professor at the universities of Bristol and Bowling Green (Ohio), Visiting Lecturer at the University of Heidelberg (Germany), Distinguished Visiting Scholar at the University of Adelaide and Visiting Scholar at the University of California at Berkeley.

Erik Sherman Roraback

teaches US literature, James Joyce, intercultural studies, and critical theory at Charles University Prague and international cinema in Prague's film academy, FAMU; he also serves as an Adjunct Professor at Vermont College Union Institute and University. He first taught in the University of Oxford where in 1997 he earned his D.Phil. In 1995 he studied in the ENS and in the EHESS at Paris on a French government grant, and in 1993 studied in the University of Western Australia on a Rotary Ambassadorial Scholarship. In 2005 he held a short-term Visiting Professorship at the Université de Provence (Aix-Marseille I). Erik Roraback has articles published internationally on Michelangelo Antonioni and Spinoza, Orson Welles, architecture, intercultural studies, Maurice Blanchot, Henry James and Heidegger, Joyce's *Finnegans Wake*, Thomas Pynchon, US Literature, and Gilles Deleuze and Leibniz. His project *The Dialectics of Money and Power: James and Balzac* has been ongoing for more than a decade and for the last five years *Destroying the Cinema: Welles and Others* and *Ventures, Identities, Values: A Baroque Project from Spinoza to Nancy*.

Peter J. Schwartz
is Assistant Professor of German in the Department of Modern Foreign Languages and Literatures at Boston University. Born and raised in New York City, he holds a BA in European history from Harvard University and a PhD in German literature from Columbia University. His work centers on Goethe and his age (1749-1832). His professional interests also include Romantic historiography, European modernism, the critical theory of the Frankfurt School, the "science of culture" (*Kulturwissenschaft*) of the art historian Aby Warburg and his circle, and the historical sociology of Norbert Elias. He is currently writing a book on Goethe's novel *Elective Affinities* (*Die Wahlverwandtschaften*, 1809), and is conducting research on Aby Warburg's response to World War I.

Mariangela Tempera
is Professor of English Literature at the University of Ferrara and Director of the Ferrara "Shakespeare Centre." She is editor of the series *Shakespeare dal testo alla scena* and co-editor of the series *The Renaissance Revisited*. She has published widely on Renaissance drama and Shakespeare in performance and in popular culture. Her full-length studies include *The Lancashire Witches: lo stereotipo della strega fra scrittura giuridica e scrittura letteraria* (Imola: Galeati, 1981) and *Feasting with Centaurs: Titus Andronicus From Stage To Text* (Bologna: Clueb, 1999). Her most recent essays include "Rent-a-Past: Italian Responses to Shakespeare's Histories (1800-1950)," in Ton Hoenselaars (ed.), *Shakespeare's History Plays* (Cambridge: Cambridge University Press, 2004), "'Horror … is the sinews of the fable:' Giraldi Cinthio's Works and Elizabethan Tragedy," in Pierre Kapitaniak (ed.), *Shakespeare et l'Europe de la Renaissance* (Paris: Société Française Shakespeare, 2004), and "Political Caesar: *Julius Caesar* on the Italian Stage," in Horst Zander (ed.), Julius Caesar: *New Critical Essays* (New York: Routledge, 2005).

Stephanie Wodianka
works at the Collaborative Research Center "Memory Cultures" (Sonderforschungsbereich "Erinnerungskulturen"), Justus-Liebig-University, Giessen, Germany. Her research interests include myth and literature, and film, myth and collective memory, with an especial focus on Jeanne d'Arc and King Arthur, and also meditative literature of seventeenth-century France, Germany and England

in relation to individual memory and identity. She is co-editor (with Dietmar Rieger) of *Nationale Mythen – kollektive Symbole. Funktionen, Konstruktionen und Medien der Erinnerung* (Göttingen, 2005) and *Mythosaktualisierungen. Tradierungs- und Generierungspotentiale einer alten Erinnerungsform* (Berlin/New York, 2006). Recent publications include the monograph *Betrachtungen des Todes. Formen und Funktionen der meditatio mortis in der europäischen Literatur des 17. Jahrhunderts* (Tübingen, 2004) and a number of articles on memory and myth.

INDEX OF NAMES

Adorno, Theodor W., 29, 36, 37n, 47n
Aeschylus, 289-90
Afanasyev, A.N., 71n, 72n
Almansi, Guido, 317
Althusser, Louis, 123
Altieri, Ferdinando, 318
Ameen, Elin, 250
Anderson, Benedict, 1, 5, 9, 53n, 106-10, 114-15, 162, 164-66, 178
Ariosto, Ludovico, 294
Aristotle, 281
Armitt, Lucie, 242n
Armstrong, G.H., 182n, 185n, 189n
Asher, R.E., 229n
Assmann, Aleida, 7-8, 64n, 149n
Assmann, Jan, 4, 53n, 55, 59-60, 61n, 165-66
Atwood, Margaret, 239n, 285n
Auerbach, Erich, 109
Augustine, St, 77, 117
Avery, Gillian, 93n
Baccolini, Raffaella, 46n
Baedeker, Karl, 199
Bachmann, Ingeborg, 269-70
Baines, Jocelyn, 84n
Bakounine, Mikhail, 125
Baldus, Édouard-Denis, 200
Balibar, Étienne, 128, 131
Balzac, Honoré de, 286
Bardèche, Maurice, 259
Bartalotta, Gianfranco, 322
Barth, Fredrik, 163, 166
Barthes, Roland, 10, 54, 61n, 62n, 106, 123, 262-64, 267
Bassnett, Susan, 316, 319
Bataille, Georges, 2n, 6, 123-25, 127, 133
Batteux, Charles, 12, 356

Baudelaire, Charles, 200, 201n
Baym, Nina, 82n
Beaune, Colette, 54n
Beauvoir, Simone de, 123
Beer, Janet, 251n
Bell, Florence, 250, 251n
Bellocchio, Marco, 40, 48-49
Bene, Carmelo, 11, 316, 320-25
Beneš, Edvard, 278
Benjamin, Walter, 3, 33-37, 44-46, 109, 115, 196, 310
Bergdoll, Barry, 200
Bernanos, Georges, 256
Bèrot, Violaine, 56
Bessière, Jean, 1-2
Besson, Luc, 56-57, 58n, 64
Beyle, Henri, 294
Bhabha, Homi, 5, 110-11, 114n, 115, 164, 175
Billi, Mirella, 297n
Blackwell, Thomas, 214
Blair, Hugh, 12, 345, 347-49, 354-58, 365
Blanchot, Maurice, 121-23, 127, 131, 134-35
Bleeker, C.J., 77
Bloch, Ernst, 44, 47, 312
Bloch, Howard, 233n
Boehme, Jacob, 76
Böhm, Rudolf, 288-90
Boileau-Despréaux, Nicolas, 282n, 289
Boleyn, Anne, 325
Bond, D.G., 310n
Boorstin, Daniel, 180-81
Borges, Jorge Luis, 5
Borst, Arno, 211n, 212n, 213n, 217n, 224n
Bourdieu, Pierre, 123
Bourne, George, 86
Boyer, M. Christine, 201n

Boym, Svetlana, 40, 45n, 46-47
Brague, Rémi, 140n, 151n, 152n,
    155n, 161n
Branciaroli, Franco, 319-20
Brasillach, Robert, 257-60, 261n,
    265-66
Braun, Volker, 269-70
Braunbeck, Helga G., 273n, 275n,
    278
Brecht, Bertolt, 51n, 330, 332
Brentano, Bettina, 118
Bresc-Bautier, Geneviève, 198n
Bristol, Michael D., 107n, 337
Britain, Melisa, 253
Brooke, Emma Frances, 241, 244,
    252
Brooke-Rose, Christine, 299
Brough, Robert, 240
Brownlees, Nicholas, 297n
Bruce, James, 353-55
Brückner, A., 71n
Brückner, Martin, 179-80
Brzozowska-Krajka, Anna, 2, 80n
Bude, Heinz, 297n
Butler, E.M., 214n
Byatt, A.S., 296-301, 303-309, 312
Byron, George Gordon, 285, 289,
    292-93
Caird, Mona, 241, 247-49
Calderón de la Barca, Pedro, 285
Calenda, Antonio, 318-19
Cambiaghi, Mara, 10
Campbell, J.F., 360n
Campi, Riccardo, 2-3
Canel, Urbain, 286
Caratini, Roger, 56n
Carnie, Robert Hay, 349n
Cases, Cesare, 208n
Cassirer, Ernst, 53n
Caute, David, 297n, 307
Cavalcanti, Guido, 321-22
Cervantes Saavedra, Miguel de,
    267, 288, 294

Cessi, Donatella Montalto, 287,
    289n
Chamoiseau, Patrick, 22-23
Charbonnier, G., 70
Charles IV, 274
Charlevoix, Pierre de, 220
Chateaubriand, François-René-
    Auguste de, 292, 294-95
Chwalewik, Witold, 93n
Clifford, James, 170n
Clin, Marie-Véronique, 51n
Coetzee, J.M., 307
Coleridge, Samuel Taylor, 133
Conrad, Joseph, 81-92
Cook, James, 8, 167
Cooper, J.C., 75n
Corneille, Pierre, 238, 259-62, 264,
    267, 289
Corti, Lillian, 239
Corti, Maria, 299-304, 309, 312
Cox, C.B., 84n
Creyke, Jean, 251, 254
Cross, Victoria, 241, 252-53
Cunningham, Gail, 252n
Curtius, Ernst Robert, 146n
Dalrymple, Sir David, Lord Hailes,
    346, 349-50, 352-54, 356
Daniel, Malcolm R., 200
Dante, 142, 146n, 229, 284, 288-90,
    292, 300, 318
Davies, Norman, 271
De Filippo, Eduardo, 323
Debord, Guy, 123
Delabastita, Dirk, 331, 332n
Deleuze, Gilles, 2n, 5-6, 7n, 8, 12,
    107-10, 113, 123-24, 125n, 127-
    28, 131, 134, 193n, 202, 203n,
    298, 320, 321n, 322, 373
Derrida, Jacques, 108, 121n, 123,
    134, 334n
Diderot, Denis, 290
Diner, Dan, 156, 159
Donizetti, Gaetano, 324-25
Dörner, Andreas, 61n

Dorson, R.M., 73n
Dowling, Maria, 273n, 278, 279n
Drieu la Rochelle, Pierre, 257-58
Droixhe, Daniel, 212n
Du Bellay, Joachim, 229
Duban, Félix, 200
Ducange, Victor, 282n
Duguay, Christian, 55
Duval, Alexandre, 291
Eckhardt, Johann Georg von, 213
Eco, Umberto, 211n, 212n, 298
Eder, Jürgen, 275n, 276n
Egenolff, Johann Augustin, 212
Egerton, George, 240, 243-44
Ehlers, Joachim, 154n
Eliade, Mircea, 68n, 75, 76n, 77,
    87n, 88
Elias, Norbert, 210
Eliot, George, 240-42, 253, 287n,
    305
Eliot, Thomas Stearns, 26, 81-83,
    92, 146-49, 321-22
Elizabeth I, 177
Emerson, Ralph Waldo, 152n
Erll, Astrid, 4, 59-60, 63n
Escarpit, Robert, 93n
Esterházy, Péter, 158-59
Euripides, 238-39, 242, 247, 254-
    55, 289-90
Faber, Richard, 143n, 145n
Fabian, Johannes, 173-74
Fairchild, Hoxie Neale, 220n
Farrell, James J., 297n
Ferguson, Adam, 12, 344, 346-47,
    352
Ficino, Marsilio, 232n, 233n
Fiedler, Theodore, 269n
Fielding, Henry, 282n, 290
Fichte, Johann Gottlieb, 222-25
Filewood, Alan, 182
Filkins, Peter, 280
Fitzgerald, Robert R., 356n
Flaubert, Gustave, 241, 287-88
Fletcher, Archibald, 358-60

Flood, Christopher, 263
Forster, Georg, 8, 167-70, 172-73,
    175
Fortunati, Vita, 1, 3
Foucault, Michel, 29-30, 32, 37,
    123, 128n, 162-63, 170-71, 174,
    179, 298-99, 304
François I, 198
Frank, Michael C., 8, 170n
Frappier-Mazur, Lucienne, 286n
Fraser, Ronald, 297n, 312
Frazer, James, 81
Fréret, Nicolas, 213
Freud, Sigmund, 82
Frobisher, Martin, 177
Frye, Northrop, 11n, 287n
Fuentes, Carlos, 17
Fühmann, Franz, 269-70
Fuhrmann, Manfred, 220n
Fuqua, Antoine, 52n
Fynsk, Christopher, 123-24
Gadamer, Hans Georg, 3, 29-35,
    37, 149n
Ganong, William F., 9, 180
Gaskell, Elizabeth, 241
Gaskill, Howard, 344n
Geertz, Clifford, 106
Gehry, Frank, 194-98, 201
Genette, Gérard, 284, 286n, 287n,
    289n, 293n
Geoghegan, Vincent, 46n
Ghica, Scarlat Ioan, 329
Gillon, Adam, 84n
Gilman, Charlotte Perkins, 251
Glissant, Edouard, 22-23
Gluski, J.S., 78n
Goethe, Johann Wolfgang von, 34,
    208n, 217n, 218, 219n, 285,
    288, 290-93
Goldsmith, Oliver, 293n
Gonet, S., 79n
Grand, Sarah, 251
Gray, Thomas, 12, 345, 347, 349-
    53, 355, 365

Grèce, Michel de, 56
Green, R.L., 93n
Greenblatt, Stephen, 177, 318n, 334
Grigorescu, Dan, 331n
Grillparzer, Franz, 238
Grimm, Jacob, 219n
Grimm, Wilhelm, 219n
Grutman, Rainier, 11
Guasch, Anna M., 195
Guattari, Félix, 2n, 8n, 107, 108n, 123-24, 125n, 128, 131, 134, 193n, 202, 203n
Guriewicz, A., 74n
Gustawicz, B., 73n
Haecker, Theodor, 146, 149
Haines, Brigid, 10, 268n
Halbwachs, Maurice, 45
Hall, Edith, 238, 240n, 254n, 255n
Hall, Stuart, 167n
Hamilton, William B., 180n, 181, 185n
Hanka, Václav, 110
Hardt, Michael, 6, 7n, 122, 127-31, 133-35
Hardy, Thomas, 241
Harley, J.B., 177
Havel, Václav, 274, 279
Hawthorne, Christopher, 196, 197n
Hawthorne, Nathaniel, 242, 287n
Hegel, G.W.F., 33, 76, 110, 117, 125, 333
Heidegger, Martin, 121n, 126
Heilmann, Ann, 10, 247n, 249n, 251n, 252n, 253n
Heimpel, Hermann, 152n
Heise, Ursula K., 53n
Henri II, 198
Henry III, 226, 228n
Herder, Johann Gottfried, 208n, 216n, 220-22
Heuss, Alfred, 223n
Hewison, Robert, 297n
Hewitt, Nick, 259

Heydrich, Reinhard, 279
Highway, Tomson, 184
Hildebrandt, R., 93n
Himmel, Stephanie, 51n
Hitler, Adolf, 146, 158
Hobsbawm, Eric, 293, 297
Hoenselaars, Ton, 316n, 328n, 332n
Hofer, Johannes, 41
Hoffmann, Dustin, 57
Hofmannsthal, Hugo von, 143
Hohendahl, Peter Uwe, 284n, 292n
Holland, Lawrence B., 82n
Holy, Ladislav, 277n, 278-79
Home, John, 12, 344, 346, 352, 355
Homer, 91, 109, 141-42, 207, 214-16, 218, 220-22, 365
Horace, 281, 289-90
Horkheimer, Max, 125n, 126
Hornstein, Shelley, 8
Hugo, Victor, 286, 288-90, 292
Humboldt, Wilhelm von, 216-17, 222, 223n, 224-25
Hume, David, 352, 355
Hunt, John D., 120
Huppert, George, 213n
Hurcombe, Martin, 10
Hus, Jan, 278, 279n
Hutcheon, Linda, 40, 44
Huxley, Aldous, 48
Hyman, S.E., 70n
Ibsen, Henrik, 250
Ingrao, Chiara, 312n
Irigaray, Luce, 123
Jahnn, Hans Henny, 239
James I, 269
James, Henry, 287
Jameson, Fredric, 44
Jankélévitch, Vladimir, 43
Jaspers, Karl, 144
Jauß, Hans Robert, 217n, 221n
Javary, Geneviève, 234n, 236n
Jirásek, Alois, 276
Jobes, G., 74n

Johnson, Charles, 238
Johnson, Uwe, 300, 308-11
Joris, Pierre, 134, 135n
Jovovich, Milla, 57
Joyce, James, 82-83, 92, 142, 156n
Judt, Tony, 157-58
Kafka, Franz, 274-75
Kant, Immanuel, 43, 130, 209-10
Kastan, David Scott, 338, 339n
Kennelly, Brendan, 239, 244
Kermode, Frank, 82
Kipling, Rudyard, 93-105
Knight, Richard P., 120n
Kohl, Helmut, 153
Kohn, Hans, 211n
Kolberg, O., 71n, 72n, 74n, 78n
Kolinská, Klára 9
Komar, Michał, 84n
Komenský, Jan Amos, 278
Konrad, György, 149-51
Koselleck, Reinhart, 209
Koslowski, Peter, 140n, 151n,
    152n, 155n, 161n
Kosmas, 108
Kott, Jan, 11, 330, 331n, 332-33
Kowalska-Lewicka, A., 77n
Kozak, Wojciech, 2, 81n
Krajka, Wiesław, 2, 66n, 81n, 93n,
    97n, 98n, 99n, 100n, 103n
Krens, Thomas, 194
Kristeva, Julia, 123
Krumeich, Gerd, 51n
Kubišová, Marta, 278, 279n
Kundera, Milan, 111, 114-19, 148,
    272n
Lacan, Jacques, 123
Lacoue-Labarthe, Philippe, 123
Lafitau, Joseph François, 221n
Lamartine, Alphonse de, 286
Langguth, Gerd, 297n
Larra, Mariano José de, 281-84,
    286, 292, 295
Lasch, Christopher, 40
Latouche, Henri de, 285

Lawrence, D.H., 81, 83
Lawrie, George, 345-46, 348-52,
    355-56
Lăzărescu, Dan, 331n
Le Guin, Ursula, 40, 48
Le Pen, Jean-Marie, 257
Leach, M., 69n, 78n
Lee, Vernon, 240, 244-46, 249
Leerssen, Joep, 346n
Lefèvre de la Boderie, Guy, 10,
    227-36
Leibniz, Gottfried Wilhelm, 212
Lemaire des Belges, Jean 230
Lemon, Mark, 240
Lepenies, Wolf, 217n
Léry, Jean de, 220
Lescot, Pierre, 198
Lessing, Gotthold Ephraim, 214-
    15, 217
Levin, Harry, 11n, 292n, 294n
Lévinas, Emmanuel, 123
Lévi-Strauss, Claude, 55n, 69-70,
    107n, 108
Leviţchi, Leon, 331n
Levy, Amy, 240, 244-45
Lewis, Matthew "Monk," 287
Libeskind, Daniel, 196
Lilientalowa, R., 78n
Lombardo, Agostino, 316-17
Lorenz, Konrad, 306
Lotman, Iouri, 24n, 69n
Louis XIII, 198, 213
Louis XIV, 198, 213, 219
Ludolf, Hiob, 212
Lumley, Robert, 297n, 298n, 302
Luther, Martin, 117, 211n
Lyotard, Jean-François, 123, 274n
Mac Craith, Mícheál, 12
Mac Nicol, Donald, 358, 359n,
    360n
MacCannell, Dean, 191-92
MacCulloch, J.A., 70n
Macgowan, John, 353-54
Macintosh, Fiona, 240n, 247n

Mackenzie, Henry, 347, 355
Maclagan, James, 358-59
Macpherson, James, 12, 221, 344-65
Mahlke, Kirsten, 10
Maier, Charles, 44
Maillard, Jean-François, 230n
Mair, Charles, 182, 183n, 184
Malkovich, John, 57
Mallarmé, Stéphane, 26, 125, 288
Malraux, André, 256
Manea, Aureliu, 331n
Mánes, Josef, 109
Mann, Thomas, 210
Manolescu, Ion, 333
Marcuse, Herbert, 47n, 107n
Marchand, Suzanne L., 214n
Marie de France, 288
Marwick, Arthur, 297n, 308n
Marx, Karl, 125, 210
Masaryk, Tomáš Garrigue, 272n, 273-74, 279
Mason, William, 12, 349-51
Massis, Henri, 257, 260, 261n, 265, 266n
Massumi, Brian, 197-98, 202
Matei-Chesnoiu, Monica, 11
Mathieu, Adolphe, 285-86
Maturin, Charles, 287, 290
Mátyás, K., 71n
Maurras, Charles, 257-58, 261-62
Mazzini, Giuseppe, 42
McClellan, Andrew, 198, 199n
McDonagh, Josephine, 240n, 242, 253-55
McDonald, Marianne, 239n
McFarlane, I.D., 290n
McFarlane, James, 82, 83n, 85
McGrane, Bernard, 174n
Meek, Donald, 361n
Meier, Christian, 152n
Meigs, Cornelia, 93n
M[i]eletinski, Eleazar, 67n, 83, 87
Meyer, Simone, 239

Michałowska, T., 78n
Mikšíček, Petr, 160n
Millon-Delsol, Chantal, 312n
Mimoso-Ruiz, Duarte, 239
Moinot, Pierre, 54n
Molière, 282, 288
Moníková, Libuše, 10-11, 268-80
Montreath, Peter, 263
Moore, Dafydd, 347n
Morgan, Evelyn de, 239
Moritz, Karl Philipp, 218
Morrison, Toni, 239
Moses, Daniel David, 183
Moszyński, K., 73n
Mourousy, Paul, 54n, 56n
Moylan, Tom, 46n, 47
Mukařovský, Jan, 283
Murray, Gilbert, 255
Muschamp, Herbert, 194
Musset, Alfred de, 286, 288
Najder, Zdzisław, 84n, 92
Nancy, Jean-Luc, 2n, 6, 121-35
Napoleon I, 198, 208, 211, 222, 294
Napoleon III, 198, 200
Negri, Antonio, 6, 7n, 122, 127-31, 133-35
Niebuhr, Barthold Georg, 222-23, 224n
Nietzsche, Friedrich, 30, 44, 251, 327-28, 335
Niewiadomska, M., 72n
Nicholas of Cusa, 233
Nodier, Charles, 290
Nora, Pierre, 154, 155n
Novalis, 111-14, 118
Noverre, Jean-Georges, 239
Nünning, Vera, 155
Ó hUiginn, Ruairí, 360n, 361n
Ockman, Joan, 194-96
Offenbach, Jacques, 15
Olender, Maurice, 211n, 212n
Orwell, George, 48
Osterhammel, Jürgen, 169

Oświecimski, S., 78n
Oudard, Georges, 261
Ovid, 238
Palacký, František, 277-78, 280
Palach, Jan, 270, 279
Panfilov, Gleb, 51n, 56
Parandowski, J., 74n
Pasolini, Pier-Paolo, 239, 308
Pasquier, Etienne, 230
Passerini, Luisa, 297n, 302, 303n, 307, 308n
Patočka, Jan, 277
Payot, Daniel, 37n
Pei, I.M., 198
Pennacchia, Maddalena, 316n
Pernoud, Régine, 51n
Petrarch, 229, 246, 288-90, 292
Petrow, A., 71n
Philippe-Auguste, 198
Piaget, Jean, 98n
Pietkiewicz, C., 73n
Pizan, Christine de, 239
Planché, James Robinson, 240
Plantin, Christoph, 230
Plato, 232n, 233n, 246
Podbielski, H., 68n
Poli, Magda, 320n
Postel, Guillaume, 10, 227-28, 230-31, 234-36
Potkowski, E., 77n
Preminger, Otto, 56
Preston, Paul, 261n
Prete, Antonio, 42n, 43
Price, Uvedale, 120n
Probst, Ingmar, 177, 178n
Probyn, Elspeth, 49n
Prodi, Romano, 153
Procházka, Martin, 1, 162, 203n
Proust, Marcel, 5, 143, 287n
Pugliatti, Paola, 335
Pujante, A. Luis, 328n
Purkyně, Jan Evangelista, 276
Pynsent, Robert, 277n, 278n
Quinby, Lee, 40

Racine, Jean, 289
Radcliffe, Ann, 287
Radice, Laura Lombardo, 312n
Raimond, C.E. [Elizabeth Robins], 249
Ranke, Leopold, 30
Rayburn, Alan, 182, 189
Réal del Sarte, Maxime, 257-58, 262
Renan, Ernest, 163-66, 173
Rettigová, Magdalena Dobromila, 276
Ricoeur, Paul, 2, 18, 123
Rieger, Dietmar, 51n, 59n, 61n
Richardson, Angelique, 251, 252n
Rio, Michel, 55n
Ritter, Henning, 149n
Rivette, Jacques, 56
Robins, Elizabeth, 241, 249-51, 254
Rogers, Shelagh, 307n
Rogoff, Irit, 191
Romani, Felice, 325
Romoli, Giorgio, 195
Roraback, Erik S., 2, 6
Rosa, George M., 293n
Rossetti, Christina, 290
Rossi, Ernesto, 315
Rossi, Paolo, 304
Roudaut, François, 227n, 228n, 232n, 233n
Rousseau, Jean-Jacques, 42, 125, 219-20, 282n, 294
Rudbeck, Olof, 212-13, 217
Rumsfeld, Donald, 153
Rytkönen, Seppo, 223n
Rzepińska, M., 73n
Said, Edward W., 8, 92n, 163, 170-72, 174-75
Salvini, Tommaso, 315
Sand, George, 288
Sandys, Anthony Frederick, 239
Sanford, Ellis, 57
Sapio Garbero, Maria del, 331
Sartre, Jean-Paul, 123, 145

Sassoon, Donald, 297, 307n
Saunders, Thomas Bailey, 344n
Sayer, Derek, 271n, 273-76, 278,
    279n, 280
Scott, Walter, 285-87, 289, 292, 294
Secret, François, 227n, 231n, 234n
Sekula, Allan, 195
Seltzer, Leon F., 84n
Seneca, 238
Serlio, Sebastian, 198
Shakespeare, William, 11, 107, 268-
    70, 284, 289, 315-43
Shanley, Mary Lyndon, 240n
Shelley, Mary, 245
Shenstone, William, 12, 345, 347,
    353-55
Sherman, Daniel J., 191
Showalter, Elaine, 249n
Schelling, F.W.J. von, 133
Schiller, Friedrich, 51n, 119, 285,
    288-90, 292
Schlegel, August Wilhelm, 215n,
    216n
Schlegel, Friedrich, 125, 215, 217
Schmitz, Robert Morell, 344n
Schoeps, Joachim, 224n
Schöne, W., 73n
Schubert, Franz, 50
Schwartz, Joan M., 201n
Schwartz, Peter J., 9, 219n, 223n
Simmel, Georg, 163, 171-72
Simonsuuri, Kirsti, 215n
Sivan, Gabriel, 228n
Smetana, Bedřich, 276
Smith, Anthony D., 110
Smith, Margaret M., 353
Smólski, G., 77n
Soja, Edward W., 178, 179n
Sontag, Susan, 150, 151n, 161
Sophocles, 21
Sorel, Georges, 265-66
Southey, Robert, 292
Spengler, Oswald, 143-44
Spitzer, Leo, 45

Stafford, Fiona, 344n
Starobinski, Jean, 41, 43
Stead, W.T., 252
Steinbach, Peter, 160
Stendhal, 290, 293-94
Sterne, Laurence, 290
Sternhell, Zeev, 266
Stieler, Caspar, 212
Stoicescu, Bogdan, 332
Stomma, L., 67n, 70n
Stone, Jerome, 357
Stonehewer, Richard, 349-50
Stratan, Ion, 11, 331-40
Strehler, Giorgio, 315, 316n
Sullivan, Scott, 298n
Surridge, Lisa, 247n
Swift, Jonathan, 339n
Szondi, Peter, 217n
Tacitus, 211n, 220-21
Taegert, Werner, 214n, 215n, 216n
Tarantino, Quentin, 40
Tasso, Torquato, 288-92, 295, 318
Taylor, Drew Hayden, 176, 186,
    187n, 188-89
Tempera, Mariangela, 11, 316n,
    331
Tharaud, Jérôme and Jules, 261
Thomas, Nicholas, 174n
Thomson, Derick S., 358n, 359n,
    365
Thorndike, Sibyl, 255n
Thou, Auguste du, 228n
Tomicki, Ryszard, 66n, 68n, 69n,
    72n, 75, 96n
Toporov, V.N., 68n, 71n
Trystram, Florence, 54n, 56-57
Turner, Frederick J., 152n
Turner, Victor, 76n, 77, 79n
Turton, James, 353
Tye, J.R., 287n
Tylor, E.B., 73n, 74n, 75n
Ujejski, Józef, 84n
Urbańczyk, S., 71n
Valduga, Patrizia, 11, 316-20,

Valois, Marguerite de, 228n
van der Leeuw, Gerardus, 66
Vega, Lope de, 285
Verdi, Giuseppe, 317, 324
Vico, Giovanni Battista, 171
Vigny, Alfred de, 286
Villiers de l'Isle-Adam, J. de, 287n, 288
Virgil, 142, 146-47, 207, 213-16, 218-19, 289-90, 294, 365
Voss, J.G., 215
Vrtel-Wierczyński, S., 78n
Wagner, Richard, 125
Waugh, Patricia, 297n
Weber, Alfred, 144, 145n
Weber, Eugen, 258n
Webster, Augusta, 240, 244
Webster, Noah, 179
Weinrich, Harald, 52n
Weischedel, Wilhelm, 224n
Whedbee, J. William, 121n
White, Hayden, 4, 11n, 275n
Wiley, Catherine, 251n
Williams, Marjorie, 353n

Williams, Raymond, 44
Winckelmann, Johann Joachim, 207, 214, 217-18, 220-21
Winichakul, Thongchai, 178
Wodianka, Stephanie, 3-4, 51n, 61n
Wohlleben, Joachim, 214n, 225n
Wolf, Christa, 239
Wolin, Sheldon, 299n
Wood, Robert, 214, 218
Woodward, David, 177
Worthen, W.B., 332
Yates, Frances, 304
Yeats, William Butler, 81, 83
Young, Edward, 214
Zadra, D., 76n
Zgorzelski, Andrzej, 93n, 97n, 100n, 103n
Zhang Yimou, 40
Zink, Michel, 55n
Zola, Émile, 287-88
Zorn, Christa, 246, 247n
Zulaika, Joseba, 195
Zweig, Stefan, 143